The House of Seleucus

Edwyn Robert Bevan

Nabu Public Domain Reprints:

You are holding a reproduction of an original work published before 1923 that is in the public domain in the United States of America, and possibly other countries. You may freely copy and distribute this work as no entity (individual or corporate) has a copyright on the body of the work. This book may contain prior copyright references, and library stamps (as most of these works were scanned from library copies). These have been scanned and retained as part of the historical artifact.

This book may have occasional imperfections such as missing or blurred pages, poor pictures, errant marks, etc. that were either part of the original artifact, or were introduced by the scanning process. We believe this work is culturally important, and despite the imperfections, have elected to bring it back into print as part of our continuing commitment to the preservation of printed works worldwide. We appreciate your understanding of the imperfections in the preservation process, and hope you enjoy this valuable book.

THE HOUSE OF SELEUCUS

VOL. I

ANTIOCHUS III, THE GREAT KING

(From a Bust in the Louvre)

HOUS

THE
HOUSE OF SELEUCUS

BY

EDWYN ROBERT BEVAN, M.A.

VOL. I

WITH PLATES AND MAPS

LONDON
EDWARD ARNOLD
Publisher to the India Office
1902

All rights reserved

PREFACE

THERE is much to discourage an attempt to write a history of the Seleucid dynasty. It will be only too apparent how often the narrative must halt for deficiency of materials, how the picture must be disfigured by blanks just where they are most vexatious. I hope, however, that if the reading of this book makes these disabilities felt, the question prompted at the conclusion will be, not "Why has such an attempt been made?" but "How comes it that such a subject has been neglected so long?" If the book itself fails to make clear how closely the subject touches us, as students of the world, as Christians and as Englishmen, it would be absurd to think that a preface could do so. It is indeed surprising, defective though the materials are, that the Seleucid dynasty has not been made as a whole the subject of a special study since the Jesuit Frölich wrote his *Annales compendiarii regum et rerum Syriae* in the middle of the eighteenth century (1744). In recent times it has only been treated in works dealing with the "Hellenistic" epoch generally, or in catalogues of the Seleucid coinage, such as Mr. Percy Gardner's *Coins of the Seleucid Kings of Syria in the British Museum* (1878) and M. Ernest Babelon's *Rois de Syrie, d'Arménie et de Commagène* (*Catalogue des monnaies grecques de la Bibliothèque National*), Paris, 1890. Of works dealing with the history of the Greek world between the death of Alexander and the establishment of the Roman Empire an English reader has but few at his disposal. When one has named the latter part of Thirlwall's *History of Greece*, some of Professor Mahaffy's books, *The Story of Alexander's Empire, Greek Life and Thought*, and the translation of the last volume of A. Holm's *Greek History*, one has, I think, named all that are of account. But Bishop Thirlwall's *History*, however excellent for its day, was written more than fifty years ago, and the works of Mr. Mahaffy and A. Holm, full as they are of suggestion and of the breath of life, are obliged by their plans to be sketchy. In German we have the standard work of J. G. Droysen, the *Geschichte des Hellenismus*, brought up to date in the French translation of M. A. Bouché-Leclercq (1883-85). This treats the history of the Seleucids to the accession of Antiochus III. We have also in progress B. Niese's *Geschichte der griechischen und makedonischen Staaten*, the second volume of which (1899) carries the history to the end of the reign of Antiochus III, and J. Kaerst's *Geschichte des hellenistischen Zeitalters*, of which vol. i. appeared last year (1901); this, however, only covers the life of Alexander. Besides these regular histories, there are numerous articles and monographs on particular parts of Seleucid history, references to some of which will be found in the footnotes of this book at the appropriate places. One may only name here, as the most important, the articles in Pauly's *Real-Encyclopädie der classischen Altertumswissenschaft*, re-edited by G. Wissowa (in progress since 1894). One's obligations to Droysen and Niese are, of course, so constant and extensive, that they must in the majority of cases be taken for granted; it is where one's own conclusions do not altogether tally on some point that they are in many cases referred to—a circumstance which may give the work of a younger writer an appearance of presumption, which is far from the truth. M. Haussoullier's book on the history of Miletus under Seleucid rule, which has come out within the last few days, I have not yet been able to read.

I must acknowledge the friendly help given me by Mr. D. G. Hogarth, who was good enough to struggle with some of my MS. when it was in a desperately amorphous stage, and by Mr. G. F. Hill of the British Museum, by whose advice I have been guided in choosing the coins for the plates; I owe to Mr. Hill also my knowledge of the superb bust which has furnished the frontispieces. I have had the advantage of discussing some numismatic questions with Mr. G. Macdonald of Glasgow, who will shortly publish important work on the Seleucid coinage (in vol. iii. of the *Catalogue of Greek Coins in the Hunterian Collection*). My brother, Professor Ashley Bevan, has given me the benefit of his special knowledge in an attempt to write the Semitic and Persian names on an approximately uniform system.

It is tiresome that at this date it is still necessary to explain one's transcription of Greek. On the principle of not giving forms which no one could pronounce in ordinary conversation without pedantry—Seleuk*os*, etc.—I have in proper names followed the usage, consecrated by the English literary tradition, of writing the Latin form. In the case of words not proper names I have transliterated the Greek. Surnames of kings and gods are in a sort of intermediate category, and here I have been inconsistent. But it is inevitable that where two distinct systems are in use joins should appear.

E. R. B.

November 1902.

CONTENTS

CHAPTER I
Hellenism in the East 1

CHAPTER II
The Physical Environment 21

CHAPTER III
Perdiccas 28

CHAPTER IV
Events in the East, 321–316 40

CHAPTER V
Seleucus conquers the East 50

CHAPTER VI
From Ipsus to the Death of Seleucus . . . 61

CHAPTER VII
The Problems of Asia Minor 74

CHAPTER VIII
Antiochus I (Soter) 127

CHAPTER IX

	PAGE
Antiochus II (Theos)	171

CHAPTER X

Seleucus II (Kallinikos) and Seleucus III (Soter) . 181

CHAPTER XI

Syria 206

CHAPTER XII

Babylonia 238

CHAPTER XIII

Irán 258

CHAPTER XIV

India 292

CHAPTER XV

The First Years of Antiochus III (223–216) . . 300

APPENDICES 321

Antiochus III, the Great King (*from a bust in the Louvre*) Frontispiece
Plate I . . . . . . *To face page* 154
Map of the Area of the Macedonian Conquests
    in Asia . . . . . „ 21
Map of the West of the Seleucid Empire . „ 75

NOTE ON ABBREVIATIONS
USED IN THE FOOTNOTES

Polyb.—I cite Polybius according to the arrangement in the edition of F. Hultsch (Berlin).

Joseph.—The sections in citations from Josephus are those which appear in the editions of Niese (Berlin) and of Naber (Teubner, Leipzig).

Plin.—The *Naturalis Historia* of Pliny the Elder is cited by the sections in the edition of D. Detlefsen (Berlin).

Eus.—Eusebi *Chronicorum* Libri Duo, A. Schoene (Berlin). Vol. i. contains a Latin version of the Armenian translation of the lost work of Eusebius.

Isidor.—The Σταθμοὶ Παρθικοί of Isidore of Charax (Müller's *Geographi Graeci Minores*, vol. i. p. 244 f.).

Malalas, Syncell.—The *Chronographia* of John Malalas and that of George Syncellus are cited by the pages in the *Corpus Scriptorum Historiae Byzantinae* (Bonn).

F.H.G.—Müller's *Fragmenta Historicorum Graecorum* (Didot, Paris).

C.I.G.—Boeckh's *Corpus Inscriptionum Graecarum*.

C.I.Att.—The *Corpus Inscriptionum Atticarum*.

J.H.S.—*Journal of Hellenic Studies*.

Bull. corr. hell.—*Bulletin de correspondance héllénique*.

Ath. Mitth.—*Mittheilungen des kaiserlichen deutschen archäologischen Instituts zu Athen*.

Droysen.—J. G. Droysen, *Histoire de l'Héllénisme*, traduite de l'allemand sous la direction de A. Bouché-Leclercq. [I quote from the French translation, because it represents this work in its completest form.]

Niese.—Benedictus Niese, *Geschichte der griechischen und makedonischen Staaten seit der Schlacht bei Chäronea*.

Schürer.—Emil Schürer, *Geschichte des jüdischen Volkes im Zeitalter Jesu Christi*. The pages in vols. ii. and iii. are those of the last edition (the third) of 1898, in vol. i. of the edition of 1901.

MICHEL.—Charles Michel, *Recueil d'Inscriptions Grecques* (Paris, 1900). I cite from this collection, wherever possible, as containing the largest number of important inscriptions. It gives the number of every inscription in other well-known previous collections. The edition of Dittenberger's *Sylloge*, which has appeared subsequently, has itself a register which enables any one using it to identify an inscription by its number in Michel.

BABELON.—Ernest Babelon, *Les Rois de Syrie, d'Arménie et de Commagène.*

PAULY-WISSOWA.—Pauly's *Real-Encyclopädie der classischen Altertumswissenschaft*, Neue Bearbeitung herausgegeben von Georg Wissowa.

Sitzungsb. Berl.—*Sitzungsberichte der königl. kaiserl. Akademie der Wissenschaften zu Berlin.*

CHAPTER I

HELLENISM IN THE EAST

It is a common phrase we hear—"the unchangeable East." And yet nothing strikes the thoughtful traveller in the East more than the contrast between the present and a much greater past whose traces meet him at every turn. He seems to walk through an enormous cemetery. Everywhere there are graves —graves in the lonely hills, where there are no more living, graves not of persons only, but of cities; or again, there are cities not buried, whose relics protrude forlornly above ground like deserted bones. Beside the squalid towns, the nomads' huts, the neglected fields of to-day are the vestiges of imperial splendour, of palaces and temples, theatres and colonnades, the feet of innumerable people. So utterly gone and extinct is that old world, so alien is the sordid present, that the traveller might almost ask himself whether that is not a world out of all connexion with this, whether that other race is not severed from the men he sees by some effacing deluge. And yet there is this very peculiarity in the sensations that a European traveller must experience at the sight of these things, that he becomes aware of a closer kinship between himself and some of these fragments of antiquity than exists between himself and the living people of the land. The ruins in question do not show him the character of some strange and enigmatic mind, like those of Egypt or Mexico, but the familiar classical forms, to which his eye has grown used in his own country, associated in his thought with the civilization from which his own is sprung. What do these things here, among people to whom the spirit that reared and shaped them is utterly unknown? The European traveller might divine in the history which lies behind them something of peculiar interest to himself. It is a part of that history which this book sets out to illuminate—the work accomplished by the dynasty of Seleucus in its stormy transit of the world's stage two thousand years ago.

It is not so much the character of the kings which gives the house of Seleucus its peculiar interest. It is the circumstances in which it was placed. The kings were (to all intents and purposes) Greek kings; the sphere of their empire was in Asia. They were called to preside over the process by which Hellenism penetrated an alien world, coming into contact with other traditions, modifying them and being modified. Upon them that process depended. Hellenism, it is true, contained in itself an expansive force, but the expansion could hardly have gone far unless the political power had been in congenial hands. As a matter of fact, it languished in countries which passed under barbarian rule. It was thus that the Seleucid dynasty in maintaining itself was safeguarding the progress of Hellenism. The interest with which we follow its struggles for aggrandizement and finally for existence does not arise from any peculiar nobility in the motives which actuate them or any exceptional features in their course, but from our knowing what much larger issues are involved. At the break-up of the dynasty we see peoples of non-Hellenic culture, Persians, Armenians, Arabs, Jews, pressing in everywhere to reclaim what Alexander and Seleucus had won. They are only checked by Hellenism finding a new defender in Rome. The house of Seleucus, however feeble and disorganized in its latter days, stood at any rate in the breach till Rome was ready to enter on the heritage of Alexander.

But what does one mean by Hellenism?

That characteristic which the Greeks themselves chiefly pointed to as distinguishing them from "barbarians" was *freedom*. The barbarians, they said, or at any rate the Asiatics, were by nature slaves. It was a proud declaration. It was based upon a real fact. But it was not absolutely true. Freedom had existed before the Greeks, just as civilization had existed before them. But these two had existed only in separation. *The achievement of the Greeks is that they brought freedom and civilization into union.*

We, like the Greeks, are apt to speak in our loose way of the Asiatic or the "Oriental," reflecting on his servility, his patience, his reserve. But in so doing we lose sight of that other element in the East which presents in many ways the exact opposite of these characteristics. Before men had formed those larger groups which are essential to civilization they lived in smaller groups or tribes, and after the larger groups had been formed the tribal system in mountain and desert went on as before. We can still see in the East to-day many peoples who have not emerged from this stage.

The men of these primitive tribes are free. And the reason is plain. In proportion to the smallness of the group the individual has greater influence. Where the whole community can meet for discussion, the general sense is articulate and compulsive. The chronic wars between clan and clan make all the men fighters from their youth up. On the other hand civilization is promoted by every widening of intercourse, everything which fuses the isolated tribal groups, which resolves them in a larger body. The loss of freedom was the price which had to be paid for civilization.

It was in the great alluvial plains, where there are few natural barriers and a kind soil made life easy, along the Nile and the Euphrates, that men first coalesced in larger combinations, exchanging their old turbulent freedom for a life of peace and labour under the laws of a common master. The Egyptians and Babylonians had already reached the stage of civilization and despotism at the first dawn of history. But in the case of others a record of the transition remains. The example of the great kings who ruled on the Nile and the Euphrates set up a mark for the ambition of strong men among the neighbouring tribes. The military power which resulted from the gathering of much people under one hand showed the tribes the uses of combination. Lesser kingdoms grew up in other lands with courts which copied those of Memphis and Babylon on a smaller scale.

The moment of transition is depicted for us in the case of

Israel. Here we see the advantages of the tribal and the monarchical system deliberately weighed in the assembly of the people. On the one hand there is the great gain in order and military efficiency promised by a concentration of power: "We will have a king over us; that we also may be like all the nations; and that our king may judge us, and go out before us, and fight our battles." On the other hand there is the sacrifice entailed upon the people by the compulsion to maintain a court, the tribute of body-service and property, the loss, in fact, of liberty.[1]

By the time that Hellenism had reached its full development the East, as far as the Greeks knew it, was united under an Irânian Great King. The Irânian Empire had swallowed up the preceding Semitic and Egyptian Empires, and in the vast reach of the territory which the Persian king ruled in the fifth century before Christ he exceeded any potentate that the world had yet seen. He seemed to the Greeks to have touched the pinnacle of human greatness. And yet monarchy was a comparatively new thing among the Irânians. The time when they were still in the tribal stage was within memory. Even now the old tribal organization in Irân was not done away; it was simply overshadowed by the pre-eminent power attained by the house of Achaemenes, whose conquests beyond the limits of Irân had given it the absolute disposal of vast populations. Tradition, reproduced for us by Herodotus, still spoke of the beginnings of kingship in Irân. The main features of that story are probably true: the ambition excited in Deïoces the Mede after his people had freed themselves from the yoke of Assyria; the weariness of their intestine feuds, which made the Medes acquiesce in common subjection to one great man; the strangeness of the innovation when a Mede surrounded himself with the pomp and circumstance which imitated the court of Nineveh. After the False Smerdis was overthrown it was even seriously debated, Herodotus assures us,[2] by the heads of the Persian clans, whether it would not be a good thing to abolish the kingship and choose some form of association more consonant with ancestral customs,

---

[1] 1 Sam. 8, 5 f.
[2] Spiegel takes the story to have a historical foundation.

in which the tribal chiefs or the tribal assemblies should be the ruling authority.

As an alternative, then, to the rude freedom of primitive tribes, the world, up to the appearance of Hellenism, seemed to present only unprogressive despotism. Some of the nations, like the Egyptians and Babylonians, had been subject to kings for thousands of years. And during all that time there had been no advance. Movement there had been, dynastic revolutions, foreign conquests, changes of fashion in dress, in art, in religion, but no *progress*. If anything there had been decline. Between the king and his subjects the relation was that of master and slave. The royal officials were the king's creatures, responsible to him, not to the people. He had at his command an army which gave him transcendent material power. Upon the people he made two main demands, and they on their part expected two main things from him. He took firstly their persons, when he chose, for his service, and secondly as much of their property as he thought good. And what they asked of him in return was firstly external peace, since he alone by his army could repel the foreign invader or the wild tribes of hill and desert, and secondly internal peace, which he secured by being, himself or through his deputies, the judge of their disputes.

It was under these circumstances that the character we now describe as "Oriental" was developed. To the husbandman or merchant it never occurred that the work of government was any concern of his; he was merely a unit in a great aggregate, whose sole bond of union was its subjection to one external authority; for him, while kings went to war, it was enough to make provision for himself and his children in this life, or make sure of good things in the next, and let the world take its way. It was not to be wondered at that he came to find the world uninteresting outside his own concerns—his bodily wants and his religion. He had to submit perforce to whatever violences or exactions the king or his ministers chose to put upon him; he had no defence but concealment; and he developed the bravery, not of action, but of endurance, and an extraordinary secretiveness. He became the Oriental whom we know.

Then with the appearance of Hellenism twenty-five centuries ago there was a new thing in the earth. The Greeks did not find themselves shut up to the alternative of tribal rudeness or cultured despotism. They passed from the tribal stage to a form of association which was neither the one nor the other —the city-state. They were not absolutely the first to develop the city-state; they had been preceded by the Semites of Syria. Before Athens and Sparta were heard of, Tyre and Sidon had spread their name over the Mediterranean. But it was not till the city-state entered into combination with the peculiar endowments of the Hellenes that it produced a new and wonderful form of culture.

The race among whom the city-state bore this fruit was not spread over rich plains, like those in which the older civilizations had their seat. It was broken into a hundred fragments and distributed among mountain valleys and islands. These natural divisions tended to withhold its groups from fusion, whilst the sea, which ran in upon it everywhere in long creeks and bays, invited it to intercourse and enterprise. Under these circumstances the original tribal villages grouped themselves upon centres which constituted cities. For so large a number of men to enter upon so close co-operation as the city-state implied had not been possible under the old tribal system. But their doing so was a pre-requisite for that elaboration of life which we call civilized. At the same time the city was not too large for the general voice of its members to find collective expression. It was a true instinct which led the Greek republics to be above all things jealous of their independence to fret at any restraint by which their separate sovereignty was sacrificed in some larger combination.

Hellenism, as that culture may most conveniently be called, was the product of the Greek city-state. How far it was due to the natural aptitudes of the Greeks, and how far to the form of political association under which they lived, need not now be discussed. It will be enough to indicate the real connexion between the form of the Greek state and the characteristics which made Hellenism different from any civilization which before had been.

We may discern in Hellenism a moral and an intellectual

side; it implied *a certain type of character*, and it implied *a certain cast of ideas*. It was of the former that the Greek was thinking when he distinguished himself as a free man from the barbarian. The authority he obeyed was not an external one. He had grown up with the consciousness of being the member of a free state, a state in which he had an individual value, a share in the sovereignty. This gave him a self-respect strange to those Orientals whom he smiled to see crawling prostrate before the thrones of their kings. It gave him an energy of will, a power of initiative impossible to a unit of those driven multitudes. It gave his speech a directness and simplicity which disdained courtly circumlocutions and exaggerations. It gave his manners a striking naturalness and absence of constraint.

But he was the member of a *state*. Freedom meant for him nothing which approached the exemption of the individual from his obligations to, and control by, the community. The life of the Greek citizen was dominated by his duty to the state. The state claimed him, body and spirit, and enforced its claims, not so much by external rewards and penalties, as by implanting its ideals in his soul, by fostering a sense of honour and a sense of obligation. Corruption and venality have always been the rule in governments of the Oriental pattern. The idea of the state as an object of devotion, operating on the main body of citizens and in the secret passages of their lives—this was a new thing in the Greek republics. It was this which gave force to the laws and savour to the public debates. It was this as much as his personal courage which made the citizen-soldier obey cheerfully and die collectedly in his place. It is easy to point to lapses from this ideal in the public men of ancient Greece; even Miltiades, Themistocles, and Demosthenes had not always clean hands. But no one would contend that the moral qualities which the free state tended to produce were universal among the Greeks or wholly absent among the barbarians. It is a question of *degree*. Without a higher standard of public honesty, a more cogent sense of public duty than an Oriental state can show, the free institutions of Greece could not have worked for a month.

The Hellenic character no sooner attained distinct being than the Greek attracted the attention of the older peoples as a force to be reckoned with. Kings became aware that a unique race of soldiers, upon which they could draw, had appeared. In fact, the first obvious consequence of the union of independence and discipline in the Greek, as it affected the rest of the world, was to make him the military superior of the men of other nations. At the very dawn of Greek history, in the seventh century B.C., Pharaoh-Necho employed Greek mercenaries, and in recognition of their services (perhaps on that field where King Josiah of Judah fell) dedicated his corslet at a Greek shrine.[1] The brother of the poet Alcaeus[2] won distinction in the army of the king of Babylon. Under the later Egyptian kings the corps of Greek mercenaries counted for much more than the native levies. The Persian conquest, which overspread Western Asia in the latter part of the sixth century and the beginning of the fifth, was checked on Greek soil, and the armies of the Great King rolled back with appalling disaster. By the end of the century the Persians had come, like the Egyptians, to place their main reliance on Greek mercenaries. The superiority of the Greeks was displayed openly by the Ten Thousand and the campaigns of Agesilaus. From this time it was clear that if the Hellenic race could concentrate its forces in any political union it might rule the world.[3]

Besides a certain type of character, a new *intellectual* type was presented by the Greeks. The imagination of the Greeks was perhaps not richer, their feeling not more intense than that of other peoples—in the religious sentiment, for instance, we might even say the Greek stood behind the Oriental; but the imagination and feeling of the Greeks were more strictly regulated. The Greek made a notable advance in seeing the world about him as it really was. He wanted to understand it as a rational whole. The distinguishing characteristic which marks all the manifestations of his mind, in politics, in philosophy, in art, is his critical faculty, his rationalism, or, to put the same thing in another way, his bent of referring

---

[1] Hdt. ii. 159. [2] Strabo xiii. 617.
[3] δυνάμενον ἄρχειν πάντων, μιᾶς τυγχάνον πολιτείας, Aristot. *Polit.* vii. 7.

things to the standard of reason and reality. He was far more circumspect than the Oriental in verifying his impressions. He could not always take a traditional opinion or custom for granted and rest satisfied with the declaration, "So it was from the beginning," or "Such was the manner of our fathers." His mind was the more emancipated from the tyranny of custom that it might be the more subjected to the guidance of truth.

And here again we may see the influence of his political environment. There is nothing in a despotism to quicken thought; the obedience demanded is unreasoning; the principles of government are locked in the king's breast. In a Greek city it was far otherwise. In the democracies especially the citizens were all their lives accustomed to have alternative policies laid before them in the Assembly, to listen to the pleadings in the law-courts, to follow opposed arguments. What one moment appeared true was presently probed and convicted of fallacy. Institutions were justified or impugned by reference to the large principles of the Beautiful or the Profitable. The Greek lived in an atmosphere of debate; the market-place was a school of gymnastic for the critical faculty. Plato could only conceive of the reasoning process as a dialogue.

Under these circumstances, in spite of the natural reverence for accepted custom and belief, in spite of the opposition of the more conservative tempers — an opposition which we still hear grumbling throughout Greek literature — the critical faculty came increasingly into play. It came into all spheres of activity as an abiding principle of progress. Of progress, as opposed to stagnation, because it held the established on its trial; of progress, as opposed to random movement, because it regulated the course of innovation. The state, in which this faculty operates, shows the characteristic of a living organism, continuous modification according to environment.

The critical faculty, the reason—in one light it appears as the *sense of proportion;* the sense of proportion in politics, "common sense," balance of judgment; the sense of proportion in behaviour, which distinguishes what is seemly for the occasion and the person concerned; the sense of proportion in art, which eliminates the redundant and keeps each detail in its due subordination to the whole. How prominent this aspect of the critical faculty was with the Greeks their language itself shows; *reason* and *proportion* are expressed by a common word. "The Hellenes," Polybius says, "differ mainly in this respect from other men, that they keep to *what is due* in each case."[1] Μηδὲν ἄγαν, "Nothing in excess," is the most characteristic piece of Hellenic wisdom.

We have arrived at this, that the distinctive quality of the Hellenic mind is a rationalism, which on one side of it is a grasp of the real world, and on another side a sense of proportion. How true this is in the sphere of art, literary or plastic, no one acquainted with either needs to be told. We can measure the bound forward made in human history by the Greeks between twenty and twenty-five centuries ago if we compare an Attic tragedy with the dreary verbiage of the Avesta or the relics of Egyptian literature recovered from temple and tomb. Or contrast the Parthenon, a single thought in stone, a living unity exquisitely adjusted in all its parts, with the unintelligent piles of the Egyptians, mechanically uniform, impressive from bulk, from superficial ornament, and the indescribable charm of the Nile landscape.

But notable as were the achievements of the Greeks in the sphere of art, still more momentous for mankind was the impulse they gave to science. With them a broader daylight began to play upon all the relations of human life and the appearances of nature. They submitted man and the world to a more systematic investigation, they thought more methodically, more sanely, about things than any people had done before them. In process of doing so they brought into currency a large number of new ideas, of new canons of judgment, embodied in systems of philosophy, in floating theories, in the ordinary language of the street. The systems of philosophy were, of course, as systems, provisional, inadequate, and full of crudities; each of them had ultimately to be discarded by mankind; but many of the ideas which made up their fabric, much of the material, so to speak, used in their

[1] Τὸ κατ' ἀξίαν ἑκάστοις τηρεῖν, Polyb. v. 90, 8.

construction, survived as of permanent value, and was available for sounder combinations hereafter. And secondly, besides a body of permanently valid ideas which represented the finished product of the Greek method of inquiry, the Greeks transmitted that method itself to the world. We can see to-day that the method, in the form to which the Greeks brought it, was as imperfect as the results it yielded. But it was nevertheless an advance on anything which had gone before. The Greek stood far behind the modern scientific inquirer in his comprehension of the means to extort her secrets from Nature, but he arrived at a juster conception of reasoning, he dealt more soberly with evidence, than it had been within the power of mankind up till his time to do. And, imperfect as the method was, it contained within itself the means for its own improvement. Men once set thinking on the right lines would carry the process farther and farther. Hellenism was great in its potency; in its promise it was far greater.

We have attempted to explain what we mean by Hellenism, to place in a clear light what distinguished the civilization developed in the city-republics of the Greeks between the tenth and fourth centuries before Christ from all that the world had yet known. It remains to consider what the fortunes of that civilization, once introduced into the world, had been. It had been developed by the city-state in virtue of certain qualities which this form of association possessed, but which were not possessed by the Oriental despotisms—comparative restriction of size, internal liberty, and the habit of free discussion. But by the fourth century before Christ it had become apparent that these very qualities carried with them grave defects. The bitterness of faction in these free cities reached often appalling lengths and led to terrible atrocities. Almost everywhere the energies of the race were frittered in perpetual discord. The critical faculty itself began to work destructively upon the institutions which had generated it. The imperfections of the small state were increasingly exposed, and yet the smallness appeared necessary to freedom. Also the Greeks now suffered for their backwardness in the matter of religion. The Jews were left at the fall of their state still in presence of a living God, who claimed their allegiance; the Greek religion was so damaged by the play of criticism that at the decay of *civic* morality the Greeks had no adequate religious tradition to fall back upon.

Again, the separation of the race into a number of small states, while it had produced an incomparable soldiery, prevented the formation of a great military power. It was in vain that idealists preached an allied attack of all the Greeks upon the great barbarian empire which neighboured them on the east. The Persian king had nothing serious to fear from the Greek states; each of them was ready enough to take his gold in order to use it against its rivals, and the dreaded soldiery he enrolled by masses in his own armies.

It was in the union of a great force under a single control that Oriental monarchy was strong. Could Hellenism remedy the defects of disunion by entering into some alliance with the monarchic principle? Would it be untrue to itself in doing so? What price would it have to pay for worldly supremacy? These problems confronted Greek politicians in a concrete form when, in the fourth century before Christ, MACEDONIA entered as a new power upon the scene.

Macedonia was a monarchic state, but not one of the same class as the Persian Empire, or the empires which had preceded the Persian. It belonged rather to those which have but half emerged from the tribal stage. There had been an "heroic" monarchy of a like kind in Greece itself, as we see it in the Homeric poems. It resembled still more closely perhaps the *old* Persian kingdom, as it had been when Cyrus went forth conquering and to conquer. The bulk of the people was formed of a vigorous peasantry who still retained the rude virtues engendered by tribal freedom, and showed towards the King himself an outspoken independence of carriage. The King was but the chief of one of the great families, of one which had been raised by earlier chiefs to a position of power and dignity above the rest. The other houses, whose heads had once been themselves little kings, each in his own mountain region, now formed a hereditary nobility which surrounded, and to some extent controlled, the throne. But this comparative independence did not impair the advantage, from the military point of view, which came from the concentration of power in one hand. When the King resolved to go to war he could call out the whole ban of the kingdom, and his people were bound to obey his summons. The nobles came to the field on horse, his "Companions" they were called (ἑταῖροι); the peasantry on foot, his "Foot-companions" (πεζέταιροι).[1] The stout pikemen of Macedonia saw in their King not their hereditary chief only, but a good comrade; and the sense of this made them follow him, we may believe, with a prouder and more cheerful loyalty in those continual marchings to and fro across the Illyrian and Thracian hills.

Philip the Second of Macedonia, having made his kingdom the strongest power of the Balkan peninsula, presented himself to the Hellenes as their captain-general against barbarism. There were many considerations to make this offer one which the Hellenes could with dignity accept. In the first place, the Macedonians, though not actually Hellenes, were probably close of kin, a more backward branch of the same stock. In the second place, Hellenism itself had penetrated largely into Macedonia. Although it had required a certain set of political conditions to produce Hellenism, a great part of Hellenism, once developed—the body of ideas, of literary and artistic tastes—was *communicable to men who had not themselves lived under those conditions.* We find, therefore, that by the fourth century B.C. Hellenism was already exerting influence outside its own borders. The Phœnicians of Cyprus, for example, the Lycians and Carians were partially Hellenized. But in no country was the Hellenic culture more predominant than in the neighbouring Macedonia. The ruling house claimed to be of good Greek descent and traced its pedigree to the old kings of Argos. The court was a gathering-place of Greek *literati*, philosophers, artists, and adventurers. Euripides, we remember, had ended his days there under King Archelaus. Philip, who had spent a part of his youth as a hostage in Thebes, was well conversant with Greek language and literature. The man in whom Greek wisdom reached its climax was engaged to form

---

[1] The formation of the Macedonian infantry was certainly subsequent to that of the Companion cavalry, and perhaps the work of Philip. Kaerst, *Geschichte des hellenist. Zeitalters*, i. (1901), p. 136.

the mind of his son. Alexander's own ideals were drawn from the heroic poetry of Greece. The nobility as a whole took its colour from the court; we may suppose that Greek was generally understood among them. Their names are, with a few exceptions, pure Greek.

Should the Hellenes accept Philip's terms—confederation under Macedonian suzerainty against the barbaric world? In most of the Greek states this question, the crucial question of the day, was answered Yes and No with great fierceness and partizan eloquence. The No has found immortal expression in Demosthenes. But history decided for the affirmative. Philip, who offered, had the power to compel.

So Hellenism enters on quite a new chapter of its history. On the one hand that separate independence of the states which had conditioned its growth was doomed; on the other hand a gigantic military power arose, inspired by Hellenic ideas. The break-up of the Macedonian Empire at Alexander's death, it is true, gave a breathing space to Greek independence in its home, and imperilled the ascendancy of Greek culture in the newly conquered fields. But for a long time the ruling powers in the Balkan peninsula, in Asia Minor, Egypt, Babylon, Irân, the lands of the Indus—of all those countries which had been the seats of Aryan and Semitic civilization—continued to be monarchic courts, *Greek in speech and mind.*

Then when the Greek dynasties dwindle, when the sceptre seems about to return to barbarian hands, Rome, the real successor of Alexander, having itself taken all the mental and artistic culture it possesses from the Greeks, steps in to lend the strength of its arm to maintain the supremacy of Greek civilization in the East. India certainly is lost, Irân is lost, to Hellenism, but on this side of the Euphrates its domain is triumphantly restored. Hellenism, however, had still to pay the price. The law of ancient history was inexorable: a large state must be a monarchic state. Rome in becoming a world-power became a monarchy.

This, then, is the second chapter of the history of Hellenism: it is propagated and maintained by despotic kings, first Macedonian, and then Roman. The result is as might have been expected. Firstly, Hellenism is carried far beyond its original borders: the vessel is broken and the long-secreted elixir poured out for the nations. On the other hand the internal development of Hellenism is arrested. Death did not come all at once. It was not till the Mediterranean countries were united under the single rule of Rome that the Greek states lost all independence of action. Scientific research under the patronage of kings made considerable progress for some centuries after Alexander, now that new fields were thrown open by Macedonian and Roman conquests to the spirit of inquiry which had been developed among the Hellenes before their subjection. But philosophy reached no higher point after Aristotle; the work of the later schools was mainly to popularize ideas already reached by the few. Literature and art declined from the beginning of the Macedonian empire, both being thenceforth concerned only with the industrious study and reproduction of the works of a freer age, except for some late blooms (like the artistic schools of Rhodes and Pergamos) into which the old sap ran before it dried. Learning, laborious, mechanical, unprogressive, took the place of creation. As for the *moral* side of Hellenism, we find a considerable amount of civic patriotism subsisting for a long time both in the old Greek cities and in the new ones which sprang up over the East. When patriotism could no longer take the form of directing and defending the city as a sovereign state it could still spend money and pains in works of benevolence for the body of citizens or in making the city beautiful to see. The ruins of Greek building scattered over Nearer Asia belong by an enormous majority to Roman times. Athens itself was more splendid in appearance under Hadrian than under Pericles. But even this latter-day patriotism gradually died away.

It was not only that the monarchic principle was in itself unfavourable to the development of Greek culture. The monarchy became more and more like those despotisms of the older world which it had replaced. We know how quickly Alexander assumed the robe and character of the Persian king. The earlier Roman Emperors were restrained by the traditions of the Republic, but these became obsolete, and the court of Diocletian or of Constantine differed nothing from the type shown by the East.

It is an early phase of this second chapter of Hellenic history that we watch in the career of the Seleucid dynasty. By far the largest part of Alexander's empire was for some time under the sway of Seleucus and his descendants, and *that* the part containing the seats of all the older civilizations, except the Egyptian. It was under the aegis of the house of Seleucus that Hellenism struck roots during the third century before Christ in all lands from the Mediterranean to the Pamir. We see Hellenic civilization everywhere, still embodied in city-states, but subject city-states, at issue with the two antagonistic principles of monarchy and of barbarism, but compelled to make a compromise with the first of these to save itself from the second. We see the dynasty that stands for Hellenism grow weaker and more futile, till the Romans, when they roll back the Armenian invasion from Syria, find only a shadow of it surviving. Lastly, we can see in the organization and institutions of the Roman Empire much that was taken over from the Hellenistic kingdoms which went before.

We have tried to define the significance of the Seleucid epoch by showing the place it holds in ancient history. But we should have gained little, if we stopped short there, if we failed to inquire in what relation the development of ancient history in its sum stands to the modern world of which we form part. The Hellenism of which ancient history makes everything, developed in the city-republics of Greece, propagated by Alexander, sustained by the Seleucids and Rome, and involved in the fall of the Roman Empire—what has become of it in the many centuries since then?

No antithesis is more frequent in the popular mouth to-day than that between East and West, between the European spirit and the Oriental. We are familiar with the superiority, the material supremacy, of European civilization. When, however, we analyze this difference of the European, when we state what exactly the qualities are in which the Western presents such a contrast to the Oriental, they turn out to be just those which distinguished the ancient Hellene from the Oriental of his day. On the moral side the citizen of the modern European state, like the citizen of the old Greek city, is conscious of a share in the government, is distinguished from the Oriental by a higher political morality (higher, for all its lapses), a more manly self-reliance, and a greater power of initiative. On the intellectual side it is the critical spirit which lies at the basis of his political sense, of his conquests in the sphere of science, of his sober and mighty literature, of his body of well-tested ideas, of his power of consequent thought. And whence did the modern European derive these qualities? The moral part of them springs in large measure from the same source as in the case of the Greeks—political freedom; the intellectual part of them is a direct legacy from the Greeks. *What we call the Western spirit in our own day is really Hellenism reincarnate.*

Our habit of talking about "East" and "West" as if these were two species of men whose distinctive qualities were derived from their geographical position, tends to obscure the real facts from us. The West has by no means been always "Western." Before the Hellenic culture came into existence the tribal system went on for unknown ages in Europe, with no essential difference from the tribal system as it went on, and still goes on, in Asia. Then, in the East, the tendencies which promoted larger combinations led to monarchy, as the only principle on which such combinations could be formed. Asia showed its free tribes and its despotic kingdoms as the only two types of association. The peoples of South Europe seemed for a time to have escaped this dilemma, to have established a third type. The third type, indeed, subsisted for a while, and generated the Hellenic spirit; but the city-state proved after all too small. These peoples had in the end to accept monarchy. *And the result was the same in Europe as it had been in Asia.* If before the rise of Hellenism, Europe had resembled the Asia of the free tribes, under the later Roman Empire it resembled the Asia which popular thought connects with the term "Oriental," the Asia of the despotic monarchies. The type of character produced by monarchy was in both continents the same. In Greece and Italy under Constantine there was the same lack of spirit, of originality, of political interest; men's interests were absorbed by the daily business and theological controversy.

The result was the same in the West, one important

respect left out of count. Sterile, fixed, incased in an old literature, the intellectual products of Hellenic thought remained—remained as the dry seed of a dead plant, which may yet break into life again in a congenial soil. By the irruption of the Northern races, which began the Middle Ages, Europe went back again to times like those before Hellenism was; again there was the rude freedom of fighting tribes, and from this kingdoms emerged, near enough to the tribal state to retain its virtues—kingdoms resembling the Macedonian. And all through the chaos the seeds of the old culture were carefully nursed: yes, even to some small extent bore fruit in a few ruling minds. Then comes the process we call the Renaissance, the springing of the seed to life again, the seed which could only grow and thrive in the soil of freedom. The problem which had been insoluble to the ancient world—how to have a state, free and civilized, larger than a city—has been solved by the representative system, by the invention of printing which enormously facilitated the communication of thought, and still more completely in recent times by the new forces of steam and electricity that have been called into play.

Men at the Renaissance took up the thoughts of the Greeks again where they had dropped them. The old literature was no longer simply a thing for parrot-learning; it was the seed from which other literatures, other philosophies and sciences, wider and more mature than the ancient, but identical in germ, sprang into being. "We are all Greeks," Shelley truly said. The Renaissance was four or five centuries ago; it is only so long that the "Western" spirit has been at work in its new incarnation, and it has achieved some notable results. We do not yet see whereto this thing will grow.

There is one particular part of the activity of Western civilization since the Renaissance which lends its principal interest to the history of the Macedonian kings in the East—the extension of European rule in the East of to-day. It was a consequence of the smallness of the ancient free state that it could not compete with the great monarchies of the world in military power. But this limitation has been done away, and as a result the states of Western culture have risen to a position of immeasurable military superiority. This is one of the capital features of modern history. Instead, therefore, of the internal development and outward expansion of rational culture being processes which are mutually exclusive, they have in these centuries gone on side by side. Free states have been able, without prejudice to their freedom, to bring under their rule the more backward races of the earth. To-day an enormous part of the East is under the direct government of Europeans; all of it is probably destined (unless it can assimilate the dominant civilization, as the Japanese appear to have done) to be so at no distant date.

We may say then with perfect truth that the work being done by European nations, and especially by England, in the East is the same work which was begun by Macedonia and Rome, and undone by the barbarian floods of the Middle Ages. The civilization which perished from India with the extinction of the Greek kings has come back again in the British official. What will the effect be? An experiment of enthralling interest is being tried before our eyes. Those who predict its issue by some easy commonplace about the eternal distinction of "East" and "West" have given inadequate consideration to the history of East and West. Hellenism has as yet had very little time to show what it can do.

Whatever the issue be, a peculiar interest must be felt by Englishmen in those Western kings who ruled in Asia twenty centuries ago. And it is not only the continuity of Hellenic culture which links their days to ours. Hellenism lives again, we have said, in the civilization of modern Europe, but Hellenism is not the only animating principle of that civilization. Our religion came to us from Zion. Israel holds as unique a position in the world's history as Greece. It was under the Macedonian kings in the East twenty centuries ago that Hellenism and Israel first came into contact, under the Ptolemies into more or less friendly contact, under the Seleucids into contact very far from friendly, resulting in wild explosion, which shook the fabric of Seleucid power. It is a meeting of very momentous significance in the history of man, the first meeting of two principles destined to achieve so much in combination. The lands over which the house of Seleucus bore rule, the lands which it overspread with Greek speech and culture, were the lands which the faith of Christ first leavened; in its royal city the word "Christian" was first uttered. Antioch was the cradle of the first Gentile church.

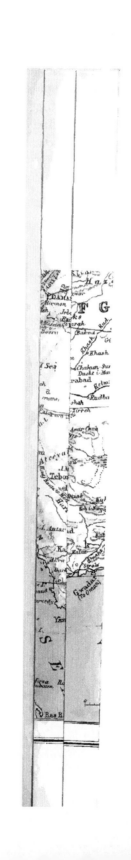

2(

la
w
la
ci
th

CHAPTER II

THE PHYSICAL ENVIRONMENT

WESTERN ASIA—all that group of countries which by the last turn of destiny in 323 B.C. had fallen to the Macedonian chiefs to be dealt with at their pleasure—had been the soil of many histories, wonderful and momentous enough for the human race, before the Macedonians had ever known it, and was to be the soil of histories more wonderful and more momentous still. It is marked out by certain general features as a different world from Europe, by features which shape and qualify to a considerable extent the histories enacted in it, and of these the most fundamental, uninteresting as it may sound, is a generally low rainfall. The atmosphere is peculiarly dry.

The consequences of this one peculiarity reach far. In the first place large tracts are either absolutely barren, mere sun-baked stone and sand, or able only to support men who roam with their herds over a large area. But it happens to be traversed by mountain ranges whose summits reach up and, catching the fugitive vapour from the sea, roll it down their sides in the form of rivers. It is only in the neighbourhood of the mountains and along the sea-board that a settled population can sow and reap, or where the rivers generated in the mountains are strong enough to carry their waters far out into the desert, so that men living on their banks can make up for the defect of rain by irrigation. In this contest with the desert many of the rivers of Western Asia are ultimately worsted, and perish before they find the sea.

Take a map of Europe, and the different departments we

see marked out represent tracts available throughout, but in a map of Alexander's Empire only part of each province *counts*. The rest is waste land—the desolation of the level desert, the desolation of the mountains. The mountains, although they catch and store the rain, are necessarily barren themselves in their higher parts, and only on their lower slopes and foot-hills can furnish the means of life to a civilized population—a population with more requirements than rude and ill-housed mountain tribes. The belts between mountain and desert, the banks of the great rivers, the lower hills near the sea, these are the lines of civilization (actual or potential) in Western Asia. The consequence of these conditions is that through all the history of Western Asia there runs the eternal distinction between the civilized cultivators of the plains and lower hills and the wild peoples of mountain and desert. The great monarchies which have arisen here have rarely been effective beyond the limits of cultivation; mountain and desert are another world in which they can get, at best, only precarious footing. And to the monarchical settled peoples the near neighbourhood of this unsubjugated world has been a continual menace. It is a chaotic region out of which may pour upon them at any weakening of the dam hordes of devastators. At the best of times it hampers the government by offering a refuge and recruiting-ground to all the enemies of order. Between the royal governments and the free tribes the feud is secular. The ordinary policy of the Asiatic monarchies has been simply to safeguard the great highways of communication. It obviously follows from the restriction of civilized habitation to the narrow belts of territory just described that the main roads are fixed by nature to certain definite lines. The task set before itself by these governments has been, not that of holding an immense continuous area, but the comparatively simpler one of holding these lines. It is important to remember this in connexion with rapid conquests like that of Alexander. To conquer the Achaemenian Empire did not mean the effective occupation of all the area within its extreme frontiers—that would have been a task exceeding one man's lifetime—but the conquest of its cultivated districts and the holding of the roads which connected them.

THE PHYSICAL ENVIRONMENT

In this eternal contest between civilized government and the free children of mountain and desert the frontiers which divide the two are necessarily shifting. Sometimes a region able, if proper pains be spent on it, to support civilization has been so overrun by the nomads as to fall altogether to their domain. This has been the case with most of the country along the lower Euphrates, once populous and lined with flourishing cities, and now, under the wretched Turkish administration, only the pasture ground of the Bedawin. On the other hand, sometimes civilized government has been able to push its way farther into the desert, higher up the mountain, either by conquest, or, more often, by the strong men of the tribes founding monarchies in imitation of the monarchies of the plain. This was the case with the Persians, highland clans at the dawn of history, but inhabiting valleys which were not unfruitful.

A thorough subjugation, however, of mountain and desert has been beyond the power of any Asiatic monarchy. If the great roads can be protected from marauders, enough seems accomplished. And even this was very imperfectly achieved by the Achaemenian government which preceded Alexander. With the entrance of Alexander upon the scene a new spirit, more vigorous, more alert, and, above all, more consequent than that of Asiatic monarchy, comes into action. It is not Alexander's intention to acquiesce in the defiance to his government offered by the free tribes. The Macedonians knew, by their old experience of Illyrian and Thracian, the habits of such folk. For the hill-tribes of Asia were not very different from the hill-tribes of Europe; they were both peoples who had remained at the same stage of barbarism when the lowlanders had gone on to civilization. It is significant that Alexander, at his first entry into Asia, goes out of his way to chastise the Pisidians and the tribes of Antibanus.[1] When the Hûzha (Uxii) a little later on ask for the immemorial blackmail they have to learn by a sharp stroke that the ways of Alexander are not the ways of a Persian king.[2] The tribes of the wilderness also feel his hand.

[1] Plutarch, *Alex.* 24.
[2] Arr. *Anab.* iii. 17; cf. Antigonus and the Cossaeans, Diod. xix. 19, 3.

On the Scythians of the Central-Asiatic steppe he did actually inflict some salutary blows; he was preparing in 323 to deal with the Bedawin. His policy perhaps envisaged the ultimate subjection of mountain and desert; but little more than a beginning of such a work had been made at his death, and its accomplishment would have taken centuries.

When the day comes for European government to be re-established in Western Asia it will be seen whether its operation, immensely more powerful than that of any Asiatic monarchy, does not bring the old license of mountain and desert to an end. Already weapons of scientific precision are working a transformation in the Nearer East. We hear so much of the decay of the Ottoman and Persian monarchies, and their power in relation to other states is in truth so fallen, that we hardly realize that there has never been a time when they have been so consolidated internally, when the central government has made its authority so effective throughout the realm. Already some of the extreme provinces of Alexander's Empire are once more under European rule; British and Russian administrators are grappling with the problem of the mountain and desert tribes, with the Afridi of the frontier hills and the Kirghiz of the steppe. But instead of the *sarissa* and bow with which Alexander had to work, his modern successors have the rifle and the mountain battery, and who knows but progressive science may put into their hands before long means of mastery more certain still?

From considering the general characteristics of Western Asia we must pass to some review of its arrangement. The enormous plateau of Central Asia is adjoined on the west by a separate smaller plateau, that of Irân, and this again on the west by a third, still smaller plateau, the Anatolian (Asia Minor). The two last of these fall within the political system of Western Asia. All the three plateaus have some features in common. The centre of each is desert, or at best steppe, and they are each surrounded by mountain ramparts. Between the Central-Asiatic plateau and the Irânian intervenes the mountain mass whose nucleus is the Pamir, and whose offshoots, from the Hindû-Kush to the Sulaimân range, spread like a fan over Eastern Irân, the country which corresponds roughly to the modern principality of Afghanistan. The Irânian plateau again is separated from Asia Minor by the mountain mass of Armenia. There is yet a fourth plateau in Western Asia, the Arabian peninsula; but this, although it did not lie outside the bounds of Alexander's Empire, as he projected it in idea, did lie outside the actual possession of Alexander and his successors, and therefore outside our field of vision in this book. All the sides of the Anatolian plateau slope down to the sea except that towards Armenia. The Irânian plateau, contrariwise, is only bordered by water on its southern side, and along part of its northern, where its rim overlooks the Caspian. Its north-west corner mingles with the "Alpine" country of Armenia, which links it to Anatolia; along most of its eastern side it is bordered by the Alpine country of East Irân (Afghanistan), which links it to Central Asia. At all other points it slopes down to the level desert; at its north-eastern extremity to the deserts of the Caspian and Azov basins (Russian Turkestan); along its south-western face to the desert, which is variously called in its different parts Syrian, Mesopotamian, and North Arabian, but which, since it is altogether the domain of the Bedawin Arabs, we will call simply the Arabian desert; and lastly, at its south-eastern extremity to the sand-drifts of Beluchistan. Between the deserts which take up so much of the interior of the plateaus and the deserts or seas which stretch outside of them intervene the belts of mountain country which constitute the plateaus' rim. The Anatolian plateau, being comparatively small, has no part beyond the reach of rains—it is not want of water in this case which makes the central region sterile—but farther east the border ranges and the two intermediate mountain groups (Armenia and the Pamir), together with that long line of mountain shot out from Armenia between the Arabian desert and the eastern end of the Mediterranean (making Syria) — these various mountains and hills catch all the moisture which avails to redeem from the desert on either side some productive tracts. Some of this moisture drains down into the interior of the plateaus, making a sort of verdure along the inward faces and the crevices of the border ranges, but since the faces turned towards the sea naturally get most of it, the great rivers of Nearer Asia flow, not into the interior, but outwards to the sea.

Of the rivers west of Irân the mightiest are those two which take their rise in the Armenian uplands and flow through the Arabian desert to the Persian Gulf. Were it not for the Euphrates and Tigris all the space between Syria and Irân would be an area of immense dearth. But these rivers are to the Arabian desert what the Nile is to the Libyan, carrying with them a green line of fertility, and capable of nursing a succession of cities. The Tigris takes the straighter course south-east, parallel with, and not very far from, the ranges which border Irân, swelled as it goes by the waters which these send down their sides. Both the head streams of the Euphrates flow west; then, as a single river, it sweeps round, enters the Arabian desert, and crosses it diagonally. At one point, about 350 miles from its mouth, it seems about to mingle with its brother river on the east. From Baghdad on the Tigris the Euphrates is only 25 miles distant. But thence it again diverges to enter the sea—in ancient times—by a separate mouth; now the two rivers do really join at Kurna. This narrow waist of land between the rivers in the region of Baghdad marks a change in the character of the country. North of it the land between the two rivers is desert—part of the great Arabian desert which sweeps from Syria to the confines of Irân—only the immediate neighbourhood of the rivers being habitable. South of it the rivers were connected in ancient times by a network of canals, quickening the soil, dark alluvium, into exuberant fertility. This was Babylonia, a level fat land, like the Egyptian delta, a land of corn-fields and gardens, of osiers and palms. It was the richest country of Nearer Asia, the seat of its oldest civilization, the natural focus of its life.

The Asiatic part, therefore, of Alexander's Empire, with which the Empire of Seleucus at its greatest extent nearly coincided, falls into certain clearly marked divisions :—

(1) The "country beyond the Taurus," *i.e.* the Anatolian peninsula (Asia Minor) without Cilicia.[1]

---

[1] Our authorities living in the West call it the country on *this* side of the Taurus, ἐπὶ τάδε τοῦ Ταύρου. I write "beyond" from the point of view of some one at the geographical centre of the empire.

THE PHYSICAL ENVIRONMENT

(2) Syria, and, closely connected with it, Cilicia on the west and Mesopotamia on the east, *i.e.* the Aramaean country.

(3) The lowlands about the Euphrates and Tigris, the seats of the old Assyrio-Babylonian civilisation, together with Susiana (Elam).

(4) Irân.

(5) The Indian provinces, covering a great part of the Panjab.

After narrating the series of events which led up to the virtual conquest of the whole heritage of Alexander by Seleucus, I propose in the first instance to follow the history of his successors up to the death of Seleucus III only in so far as it is concerned with the first of the divisions above mentioned—Asia Minor; then to take each of the other divisions in turn and see what can be gleaned of its life under these Hellenistic kings.

An important contribution has lately been made to the literature bearing on the geography of the Nearer East by Mr. D. G. Hogarth's telling book (*The Nearer East.* Heinemann. 1902)—a book which no one interested in the past or present history of these countries can afford to leave unread. My own chapter naturally purports to do no more than call attention to a single characteristic of this part of the world, which has been of great moment for its history.

CHAPTER III

PERDICCAS

It would not be easy to name any other period of ten years in the history of the world beside the reign of Alexander in which as momentous a change passed over as large a part of the earth—a change which made such difference in the face of things. Suddenly the pageant of the greatest empire ever known had been swept away. And the power that took its place was ruled by ideas which were quite new to the most part of mankind, which had hitherto only been current in the petty republics of the Hellenes. In the spring of 323 before Christ the whole order of things from the Adriatic away to the mountains of Central Asia and the dusty plains of the Panjab rested upon a single will, a single brain, nurtured in Hellenic thought. Then the hand of God, as if trying some fantastic experiment, plucked this man away. Who could predict for a moment what the result would be? (May or June 323 B.C.)

The master was removed, but the instrument with which he had wrought, the new force he had wielded, was still unimpaired—the Macedonian army. It was still only necessary to get command of that in order to rule the world. The Macedonian chiefs took council together near the dead King's body in Babylon. To all of them the prospects opened out by the sudden turn things had taken must have been at that time confused and strange, lightened only by adventurous hopes and shadowy ambitions. The question which required instantly to be met was what head was to be given to the Empire. He must be of the royal house; so far every one was agreed.

But the royal house did not offer a brilliant choice—Philip Arrhidaeus, a half-witted son of the great Philip by a Thessalian wife, the son still unborn of Alexander and the Irânian princess Roxane (if it proved to be a son), and Heracles, the son of Alexander and the Persian Barsine, a boy of about three years. The last was not yet seriously put forward, being apparently considered illegitimate.[1] None of the vast populations over whom the new king would reign had any voice in choosing him; the Macedonians encamped in the plains of Babylon, men who, eleven years before, knew nothing outside the narrow borders of their own land, now chose a king for half the world as absolutely as if he were to be only king of the Macedonians as of old. Discords immediately appeared. The cavalry, our books say, determined to wait for the son to whom it was hoped Roxane would give birth; the infantry were bent on having Philip Arrhidaeus. This distinction of cavalry and infantry was not military only, but social. Just as the mediaeval knight was of a higher grade in society than the foot-soldier, so it was the *petite noblesse* of Macedonia who followed the king as troopers, his " Companions " (ἑταῖροι); the rank and file of the foot were drawn from the peasantry. There are indications that it was especially the narrow-minded, free-spoken Macedonian pikemen, less open than the class above them to liberal influences and large ideas, who had been alienated by the restless marchings of Alexander and the Oriental trappings he had put on. King Philip was still to them the pattern king; they would not endure to see their old master's son passed over in favour of the half-barbarian, still prospective issue of Alexander. They had, moreover, nothing to gain, as many of the nobles had, by a break-up of the Empire, and they suspected that the proposal to wait for the delivery of Roxane veiled a design to deprive the Empire of a head altogether. Not till it had come near bloodshed was the dispute settled by a compromise. Philip Arrhidaeus and the son of Roxane were both to reign conjointly. Perdiccas, a member of the old ruling house in the Orestis region of Macedonia, the foremost of all the chiefs gathered in Babylon, was to be Regent.

---

[1] ἀλλ' Ἀλέξανδρος . . . οὔτε ἄλλην ἔγνω γυναῖκα πρὸ γάμου πλὴν Βαρσίνης. Plutarch, *Alex.* 21.

There were many other great lords and generals in the realm, in Babylon, in Macedonia, in the provinces, to whom the death of Alexander brought new thoughts. Would the Empire hold together, and, if so, what would their position in it be? Would it fall to pieces, and, if so, what could each lay hands on for himself? The agreement between cavalry and infantry was followed by a redistribution of the satrapies. To say nothing of the possibilities of aggrandizement, no one of mark would be safe in such times as those which were coming on, unless he could dispose of some power of his own. And no power could be well grounded unless it had a territorial support —a basis for warlike operations and a source of revenue. It was such considerations which now made several of the great chiefs, whose commands had hitherto been purely military, desire the government of a province. The first to see clearly what was required by the new conditions, our authors tell us, was Ptolemy the son of Lagus, the most cool-headed and judicious of Alexander's generals. It was he, they say, who first proposed a resettlement of the satrapies and brought the Regent over by representing it as his interest to remove possible rivals to a distance from himself. As a defensible base, at any rate, and a source of revenue, no satrapy could have been more sagaciously chosen than the one he marked out for himself, Egypt, fenced as it was with waterless deserts and almost harbourless coasts, and at the same time rich exceedingly, opening on the Mediterranean, and suited to become one of the world's great highways. But for the most part the new settlement was a confirmation of the *status quo*; nearly all the existing satraps were left in possession, the only new appointments which we need remark here being that of Eumenes, Alexander's Greek secretary, to Cappadocia, that of Pithon the son of Crateuas to Media, and that of Lysimachus to Thrace.

Among the notable figures of the great assemblage in Babylon that summer of 323 was one which commands our special attention in this book—a robust young officer of good Macedonian birth, of about an age with the dead King, who had come to win honour under Alexander, as his father Antiochus before him had won honour under Philip. This young man's name was Seleucus. He had accompanied the King at his first setting out into Asia in 334. In the Indian campaign of 326 he had been advanced to a high command. Services for us unrecorded among the hills of Afghanistan and Bokhara had doubtless disclosed to the quick eye of Alexander a substantial ability in this lieutenant of his. He was commander of the *Royal Hypaspistai*, and attached to the King's staff. At the crossing of the Hydaspes one boat carried Alexander, Ptolemy, Perdiccas, Lysimachus and Seleucus—a suggestive moment, if the later history of these five men is considered—and in the battle with the Paurava king, which followed, Seleucus fought at the head of his command.[1]

He is next heard of two years later (324) at the great marriage festival in Susa, when Alexander, on his return from India, took to wife the daughter of Darius, and caused his generals to marry each an Irânian princess.[2] And the bride allotted to Seleucus shows how high a place the young commander of *hypaspistai* held in the circle about the King. Among the most strenuous opponents of the advance of Alexander had been two great lords of Further Irân, Spitamenes and Oxyartes. When Alexander captured the rock-castle of Oxyartes the family of this chief had fallen into his hands. Oxyartes had then made his peace. His confederate, Spitamenes, had already been killed. The daughter of Oxyartes, Roxane, was Alexander's chief queen; the daughter of Spitamenes, Apama, was given at Susa to Seleucus.

It has been remarked as curious that of the eight or nine Persian princesses mentioned in this connexion only two reappear later on.[3] One of these exceptions, however, is Apama. There can be no question that her marriage with Seleucus was a real thing. She is the mother of his successor, and her husband founded three cities, according to Appian, bearing her name.[4] The Seleucid dynasty, while one of its

---

[1] See Appendix A.   [2] Arr. *Anab.* vii. 4.

[3] Professor J. P. Mahaffy, *Empire of the Ptolemies*, p. 34. He suggests that "the whole affair was considered as a huge joke as soon as Alexander was dead." But it is fair to remember that of the eight bridegrooms five disappear very soon from the scenes.

[4] App. *Syr.* 57. It does not contradict this statement that there were many more than three Apameas. For of some of them tradition expressly

roots is in Macedonia, has the other in the ancient families of Eastern Irân.

Seleucus was not one of the principal actors in the events of the next ten years. But among the secondary figures he plays a part which now and again arrests our attention. Even did he not, it would be necessary to review in a general way the course of these events in order to understand the situation when the time comes for Seleucus to step forward as protagonist. The first thing that strikes us when we take up a historian of this epoch is that the history of the world seems to have reduced itself to a history of the Macedonian army and its chiefs. But already in 323 two episodes give a sign that the predominance of the Macedonian army is to suffer reduction, that the elements of the old world it has supplanted will perhaps succeed in reasserting themselves. The Empire of Alexander suppressed the old barbarian East, and it suppressed the old free Hellas. At his death the former does not as yet stir; there are no immediate attempts on the part of the Oriental peoples to shake off the Macedonian yoke. But both in East and West the Hellenes think they have their freedom back again. In Greece itself Athens calls the states to arms, and we have the Lamian war, or, as the Greeks themselves called it, the *Hellenic* war. In the far East the Hellenes whom Alexander transported *en masse* to Bactria determine to renew the enterprise of Xenophon and march home across Asia. A great body of them, over 20,000 foot and 3000 horse, breaks away. Both these movements the Macedonian chiefs are still able to repress. Athens and her allies are crushed next year (322) by Antipater and Craterus. The Bactrian Greeks are met by Pithon, the new satrap of Media, and, by the Regent's orders, annihilated.[1] One revolt the Macedonians fail to suppress, that of Rhodes, which, on the news of Alexander's death, expels the Macedonian garrison[2]

asserts that they were founded by Antiochus I, the son of Apama. There are, it is noteworthy, exactly three Apameas of which it is definitely stated that they were founded by Seleucus—(1) Apamea in Syria on the Axius (Orontes): (2) Apamea, "condita a Seleuco rege inter Ciliciam, Cappadociam, Cataoniam, Armeniam" (Plin. *Nat. Hist.* v. § 127); and (3) Apamea on the Euphrates *zeugma*, mod. Bîrejik (Plin. *Nat. Hist.* v. § 86).

[1] Diod. xviii. 7.   [2] *Ibid.* 8.

and begins to stand out as a free Greek state able to deal on equal terms with the Macedonian world-rulers.

The compromise arrived at by the cavalry and infantry took effect. Roxane was duly delivered of a son — King Alexander from the womb. But it was not long before troubles began. It soon became apparent that the predominant position of Perdiccas was more than the other Macedonian chiefs would endure. Before eighteen months from the death of Alexander were out, two antagonistic parties had defined themselves in the realm. On the one hand Perdiccas represented the central authority; the simpleton and the baby, who were called Kings, were in his keeping. Olympias, the mother of Alexander, supported him with the whole strength of her influence. The cause of the royal house was in fact bound up with that of Perdiccas. Leagued against him were most of the other Macedonian chiefs. The soul of the opposition was Antigonus, the satrap of Phrygia, but the party included Antipater, Philip's old general, who had commanded in Macedonia since Alexander left it, and had just suppressed the rising of the Greek states; it also included Craterus, one of the chiefs most popular with the Macedonian soldiery, and Ptolemy, the satrap of Egypt. These chiefs did not professedly oppose the royal authority, but Perdiccas only; their action was none the less bent in effect against any central authority whatever. Even among those who remained at the side of the Regent there were many whose hearts, as the event showed, were with the opposition. Of the great men of the realm only one beside Perdiccas was earnest in the royal cause, Eumenes of Cardia, Alexander's chief secretary, who had been given the satrapy of Cappadocia. His invidious position as a Greek among the Macedonian nobles made his chances in a general scramble poor; for him all depended on the authority of the Kings being maintained.

In 321 the antagonism came to open war. The *casus belli*, as far as Antigonus was concerned, was his refusal to obey the Regent's summons, followed by his flight to Macedonia, where Antipater and Craterus openly espoused his quarrel. With Ptolemy the *casus belli* was his seizure of the body of Alexander, a fetich which gave immense prestige to its possessor. Antigonus, Antipater and Craterus took the offensive by crossing from Macedonia into Asia Minor; Ptolemy remained on the defensive in Egypt. To crush this double rebellion the Regent divided his forces. Eumenes was left in Asia Minor to drive back the invaders. Perdiccas himself, with the Kings, marched upon Egypt. Those of the Macedonian chiefs who still obeyed him, but were too powerful to be safe, he kept by his side under observation. He had tried the policy of removing possible rivals to a distance!

And Seleucus, whom we last saw as a young man of brilliant prospects in Babylon—what line was he taking during these first years of anarchy that followed Alexander's death? In the settlement which had given so many of his fellow-chiefs a portion of the conquered lands he had received no province. He had been given instead a high command in the imperial army[1] under the Regent. It can hardly be that, had he wished it, he could not have secured a province like the rest. Lysimachus, who had got Thrace, was perhaps younger than he. Many of the satraps in possession were not persons of sufficient importance to help giving place, should a young man like Seleucus press his claims. It must be that the high command which he took seemed to him more advantageous than a provincial governorship. It was certainly a more splendid office, if the authority of the Kings, of the Regent, held. Yes, there we have it; he had laid his plans for the continuance of the Empire, he had thrown in his lot with the Regent, he had missed his chance in the settlement of 323.

But that was two years ago, and if he had not then shown the same intelligent anticipation of events as Ptolemy he had been learning since then. He accompanied the Regent in the expedition against Egypt. Perhaps he was among those whom Perdiccas considered dangerous. Pithon, the satrap of Media, went too, and Antigenes, who commanded the Silver Shields, the Macedonian foot-guards. The campaign was to prove an object-lesson of another sort than any the Regent intended. The contrast was to be driven home to Seleucus between his own position, bound as he was by his

[1] See Appendix B.

office to perpetual subordination to the central power, and that of Ptolemy, who demonstrated his ability on a wisely-chosen and wisely-prepared ground to hold his independence against all attacks. Three times Perdiccas made an attempt to cross the arm of the Nile which separated Egypt from the desert, each time with enormous loss. His army was soon completely demoralized; numbers went over to Ptolemy; those who did not looked askance at their leader. In this predicament the temper of the unhappy man passed beyond his control. His relations with the Macedonian chiefs whom he had gathered about him became embittered. It was the last straw. Seeing that his cause was a lost one, and repelled by his demeanour, the Macedonian chiefs quickly agreed to put an end to an impossible situation. Pithon, the satrap of Media, and about a hundred more officers openly mutinied. Seleucus took his stand with the winning side. And he followed up his choice with remorselessly energetic action. He himself led the body of cavalry officers who broke into the Regent's tent. The men of the body-guard joined them,[1] and Antigenes, their commander, himself dealt Perdiccas the first blow.[2] Then the mass of his assailants flung themselves upon him and ended the work.[3] The army at once made its peace with Ptolemy, and returned with the Kings to join the forces of Antipater and Antigonus which were advancing from the North. Pithon and another chief called Arrhidaeus assumed the command of the army and the guardianship of the Kings.

Craterus, the popular general, who had left Macedonia with Antipater, was now no more. His division had been signally defeated by Eumenes, and he himself had fallen (May 321). But this victory of Eumenes did not make him strong enough to arrest Antipater, who traversed Asia Minor by land, or Antigonus, who moved along its coasts by sea. Antipater found the army, which had been that of Perdiccas, encamped at Triparadisus in Northern Syria.[4]

[1] ὑπὸ τῶν σωματοφυλάκων, Paus. i. 6, 3; cf. Just. xiv. 4, 11.
[2] Diod. xviii. 39, 6; Arr. Τὰ μετ' Ἀλέξ. 35.
[3] Diod. xviii. 36; Arr. Τὰ μετ' Ἀλέξ. 28; Strabo xvii. 794; Seleucus is mentioned with Antigenes, Nepos, *Eum.* 5, 1.
[4] Diod. xviii. 39, 1. The site of Triparadisus, the "Three Parks," is uncertain. It has been supposed to be the same as the Paradisus of Strabo xvi.

The Macedonian infantry was still in a chafed and suspicious mood. In the murder of Perdiccas its part seems to have been mainly passive; it was the nobles and the cavalry who had acted over its head. And although it had acquiesced in the change of command, it could not help feeling it was somehow being got the better of by its leaders. It responded readily to Eurydice, the ambitious wife of Philip Arrhidaeus, when she began to complain that Pithon was encroaching upon the rights of its idol, the poor half-witted King. It was pacified somehow by Pithon and Arrhidaeus resigning the regency; they continued only to exercise their powers till Antipater should come, whom the army forthwith elected Regent in their place. Antipater, the great representative of the old days of Philip, would put everything right.

But now that Antipater was come, the result was that he too fell foul of the Macedonian soldiery. It was a question of money, which Alexander had promised, and which Antipater either would or could not immediately pay. Eurydice and the adherents of Perdiccas worked them up into a fury. The army was encamped on the banks of a river. On the other side lay the forces which Antipater had brought from Macedonia. The allegiance of these new recruits was safe enough, but the grand army, which included the veterans who had conquered the world, which had chosen the Kings and considered itself the sovereign disposer of the Empire, was in open mutiny. When Antipater crossed over to reason with them he was received with stones. Two men confronted the angry mob and saved him. One was, like himself, a general of Philip's time, Antigonus, the satrap of Phrygia, the other belonged to the new generation, and stood in the brilliance of youth and military prestige, Seleucus, the

---

756; Plin. *N.H.* v. 19; Ptolemy v. 15, 20, and Stephen of Byzantium, near the sources of the Orontes. P. Perdrizet (*Revue archéol.* 3me série, xxxii. (1898), p. 34 f.) identifies it with Riblah (mod. Rableh), which figures in the Old Testament as the gateway into Southern Syria from the north. This identification is disputed by R. Dussaud (*Revue archéol.* 3me série, xxxiii. (1898), p. 113 f.), who places it at Jûsiya. The difference of view is not very important since the distance between Jûsiya and Riblah is said to be "une demi-heure de cheval au pas."

commander of the horse. These two had influence enough to hold the attention of the angry multitude whilst Antipater fled over the bridge to his own camp. There the officers of the cavalry joined him, and before the united will of their hereditary leaders the infantry shrank grumbling into submission.[1] The accession of Antipater to the regency brought with it, as the accession of Perdiccas had done, a resettlement of the dignities of the Empire. The functions which had been united in Perdiccas were divided between Antipater, who became guardian of the Kings, and Antigonus, who was made commander-in-chief of all the Macedonian forces in Asia, with the task of crushing Eumenes and the rest of the old royalist party. Antigonus continued, of course, to hold his original satrapy of Phrygia, to which this new general authority was superadded. Various changes were at the same time made in the other satrapies. The value of a territorial base had become far more evident than it had been three years before. Pithon went back to Media; Arrhidaeus got Hellespontine Phrygia. To Seleucus the settlement of Triparadisus brought back the chance which he had missed at the settlement of Babylon. The part he had lately taken in saving Antipater's life put him in a strong position. There were probably few satrapies he might not now have had for the asking. His choice shows to what purpose he had studied the example of Ptolemy. Resigning his command of the "Companion" cavalry to Cassander, the son of Antipater, he set out to govern the province which, of all parts of the Empire, had most features in common with Egypt, the province of Babylonia.

In view of the immense importance of Babylonia among the provinces, it is at first surprising to find it assigned in the settlement after Alexander's death to any but one of the greatest chiefs. It had been given to a certain Archon of Pella.[2] The explanation is surely that Babylon was to be the seat of the Regent's government, and Perdiccas did not want

---

[1] Diod. xviii. 39; Arrian, Τὰ μετ' Ἀλέξ. 30 f.; Polyaen. iv. 6, 4.

[2] Diod. xviii. 3, 3; Just. xiii. 4, 23; Arr. *Ind.* 18, 3. Mazaeus died in 328, and Alexander had appointed Stamenes to succeed him. Whether Stamenes was also dead in 323 or simply superseded by Archon we do not know.

any too powerful chief in his immediate neighbourhood. The satrap of Babylonia must be a mere subordinate even in his own capital. Archon did not relish his circumstances if we may judge by the fact that he had ranged himself two years later with the opposition to Perdiccas, or Perdiccas, at any rate, believed that he had done so. The Regent — then in Cilicia on his way from Asia Minor to Egypt—sent one of the officers on whom he could depend, Docimus, to supersede him; the ex-satrap was to become merely collector of the provincial revenue. Archon tried to hold his province by force of arms. The Regent's emissary, however, was joined by a portion of the native population, and in an engagement which took place Archon fell mortally wounded. After this Babylon received Docimus with open arms, who held it for Perdiccas, till a few months later the situation was suddenly transformed. The Regent lay, struck through with many wounds, on the banks of the Nile, and the opposition had triumphed. It could not be expected that Docimus would be left in possession. Babylonia was transferred by the chiefs at Triparadisus to Seleucus.[1]

What ensued at this juncture between Docimus and Seleucus we do not know.[2] Next year Seleucus was in possession of Babylon, and Docimus, with others of the late Regent's partisans, had taken to the Pisidian hills.[3] The position of the satrap of Babylonia had gained in importance by the new arrangements. He was no longer overshadowed by the imperial court. The two chiefs who had succeeded to the power of Perdiccas had one his seat in Macedonia and the other in Celaenae (Phrygia). Seleucus was now master in the house of Nebuchadnezzar. On the same terraces where Nebuchadnezzar had walked three centuries before and said, "Is not this great Babylon which I have built for the royal dwelling-place by the might of my power and for the glory of my majesty?" the young Macedonian now walked as lord, and

---

[1] For Docimus and Babylonia see Arrian, Τὰ μετ' Ἀλέξ. *frag.* Reitzenstein (*Breslauer Philologische Abhandlungen*, vol. iii.).

[2] "Principio Babylona *cepit*" (Justin xv. 4, 11), which Baumstark refers to in this connexion (*Pauly-Wissowa*, art. "Babylon"), describes the capture of Babylon in 312.

[3] Diod. xviii. 44.

looked over the same Babylon spreading away to the south, as over his own domain.

SOURCES.—Diodorus xviii. is the main authority for this period. It is supplemented by Arrian, Τὰ μετὰ Ἀλέξανδρον (of which we have the abstract of Photius, given in the Didot edition of Arrian, Paris, 1846, and the Reitzenstein fragment); Justin xiii.; Plutarch, *Eum.;* Nepos, *Eum.;* Curtius x. 5, 7 f.; Dexippus (*F.H.G.* iii. p. 666 f.), and incidental notices elsewhere, which will be found in the works of Droysen and Niese. Nearly all our information is probably derived in the last resort from the contemporary historian, Hieronymus of Cardia.

CHAPTER IV

EVENTS IN THE EAST, 321-316

BABYLONIA, possessing so many features in common with Egypt, differed in one respect, both to its advantage and its disadvantage—in its central position. By the Euphrates and Northern Syria it was in touch with the Mediterranean and the West, while a few days' journey across the plain separated the Tigris on the east from the mountain-wall behind which rose the plateau of Irân—Irân, where the face of the world and the ways of men were far other than by the waters of Babylon. If one had it in one's heart to rule the whole Empire of Alexander, Babylon was a better seat of government than Egypt; if, on the other hand, the ruler of Babylonia was not strong enough to aspire to more than independence, he was certain to be more entangled in the affairs of his neighbours than the ruler of Egypt. Seleucus would watch with anxiety the course of events both in the lands about the Mediterranean, where the star of Antigonus seemed in the ascendant, and in Irân, where Macedonian chiefs, Macedonian and Greek armies, were still a problematic element.

The eastern satraps included two chiefs of the first rank, Pithon and Peucestas. Both had belonged to that inner circle of eight, the *somatophylakes*, who stood closest to the late King. These two men were the cardinal personalities at this moment in Irân.

Pithon the son of Crateuas, of Alcomenae in Eordaea,[1] had obtained the satrapy of Media at the partition made in Babylon after Alexander's death. None of those who went to their

---

[1] Arr. *Ind.* 18, 6; *Anab.* vi. 28, 4.

several provinces seems to have carried with him a heart more full of magnificent projects; none realized more quickly the openings to individual ambition in the new state of things. His province was the most important in Irân. In Ecbatana the first Irânian kingdom had had its seat. Under the Achaemenians it still continued to be one of the great capitals of the Empire, the summer residence of the Persian kings. Media was reckoned the richest of all the Irânian provinces, as is shown by the figure at which Darius assessed it.[1] Its upland plains were excellent pasture; they nourished innumerable herds of horses, the best in the world. Its hills were tenanted by hardy tribes, the ancestors of the modern Kurds, from whom the ruler of Media could draw immense material of fighting men.[2] To an ambitious man the possession of Media opened wide possibilities.

The governor who sat in the golden palace of Ecbatana already held a sort of primacy among the satraps of Irân. To change that to an absolute lordship of Irân, and from that again step—to what? to the throne of Alexander? Thoughts such as these seem to have danced before the mind of Pithon. His first opportunity had come soon after the death of Alexander in the insurrection of the Greeks planted in the Far East. Not only had Pithon been charged by the Regent Perdiccas with the quelling of the revolt, but large accessions had been sent to his troops, and he had been empowered to call upon the other satraps of Irân for contingents. It was then that Pithon had formed the design of winning the revolted Greeks to his own standard—a design which was only frustrated by the astuteness of the Regent in giving up the mutineers as a prey to the Macedonians.[3]

Thenceforward the Regent seems to have thought it prudent to keep Pithon in his own *entourage*—a change in Pithon's position which accounts for his deserting to Ptolemy in 321.[4] After the murder of Perdiccas, Pithon becomes joint-regent of the Empire with Arrhidaeus. Then after the Partition of Triparadisus, while Seleucus goes to take possession of Babylonia, Pithon returns with increased prestige to Media.

[1] Hdt. iii. 92.   [2] Polyb. v. 44; Strabo xi. 525.
[3] Diod. xviii. 7.   [4] Diod. xviii. 36.

The other great satrap in the East was Peucestas of Mieza in Macedonia. Before he had been added as eighth to the seven *somatophylakes* he had carried before Alexander the sacred shield taken from the temple of Athena at Troy,[1] and had warded Alexander's body with his own in the taking of the Mallian city (mod. Multān). It was from Alexander himself that he had received his satrapy, Persis, the country of the ruling tribe among the Irânians, with Pasargadae, the cradle of the Achaemenian house, and Persepolis, the royal city. Peucestas had thrown himself heartily into that scheme so dear to Alexander's heart of fusing the Macedonian and Persian aristocracies. He had, in dress, in language, in deportment, done all he could to show himself to the people of his province as one of themselves.[2] The death of Alexander found him with a well-rooted power.

The ambition of Pithon was of the kind that cannot wait for the fruit to ripen. The news suddenly flew through Irân that he had seized the adjoining province of Parthia. Philip, the satrap appointed at Triparadisus, he had made away with and replaced by his own brother Eudamus. The other satraps all felt their own seats threatened, and came quickly to an understanding among themselves, with a view to resisting Pithon's aggression. This movement against Pithon gave Peucestas his opportunity to rise to a pre-eminent position in Irân by a less invidious method than his rival. He had but to join the confederate satraps to secure the leadership, for amongst them there was no one of equal standing. He did so, and was voluntarily recognized as chief. The armies of Irân invaded Parthia under his command, and drove Pithon out of the province.[3]

Pithon retired at first upon Media, but he soon felt himself insecure even there. It was now that he appeared with some following in Babylon, and called upon Seleucus to make common cause with him and share gains. Here was an entanglement in prospect. What the interests of Seleucus required was that he should hold aloof from the turmoil till he had consolidated his power. But this was hard to do in

---

[1] Arr. *Anab.* vi. 9, 3 ; 28, 4.
[2] *Ibid.* 30.　　　[3] Diod. xix. 14.

Babylon. He might refuse Pithon's suggestion, but fresh complications already loomed in sight. The disturbances in the West were about to become intermingled with those of Irân.

The death of Perdiccas had left his party, the royalist party, who were for holding the Empire together under the central authority of the royal house, apparently doomed. Eumenes, its one remaining champion of any account, was left isolated in Asia Minor. And in the year following the settlement of Triparadisus, Antigonus had conducted the war against Eumenes with great success, and shut him up in the Cappadocian fortress of Nora (320). Then unexpectedly the prospects of the royalist party improved. In 319 Antipater, the Regent, died. He bequeathed his great office to a chief called Polyperchon. It was this transference of the supreme authority which brought about a revival of the royalist cause; for, in the first place, Antigonus now began to take so masterful and independent a line in Asia Minor that many who had supported him from fear of Perdiccas came to fear Antigonus no less. Arrhidaeus, for instance, the satrap of Hellespontine Phrygia, and Clitus, the satrap of Lydia, were soon his enemies, and thereby allies of Eumenes and the royalists. In the second place, the son of Antipater, Cassander, had expected to succeed to his father's office, and threw himself into violent opposition to the new Regent. Antigonus and he made common cause. As a consequence, Polyperchon was driven to ally himself with the queen-mother Olympias, whose authority the royalists maintained. The royalists, instead of being hunted outlaws, now had the Regent of the Empire himself on their side.

The effect of these changes was rapidly seen in Asia Minor. The siege of Nora was raised; Eumenes was again recognized by the supreme authority in Macedonia as commander-in-chief of Asia, and the picked corps of Macedonian veterans, the Silver Shields, commanded by Antigenes and Teutamus, put themselves under his orders. He also seized by royal warrant the treasures which had been transferred from Susa to Cyïnda in Cilicia. In 318 he was in Phœnicia preparing a fleet to drive the party of Antigonus from the sea.

But the new hopes of the royalists were dashed by an untoward event—the annihilation by Antigonus of the fleet of Clitus in the Bosphorus. This entirely upset the plans of Eumenes, and even made his position in Phœnicia, between Antigonus and Ptolemy, insecure. That wonderful man, however, whom no reverse found at the end of his resources, turned his eyes to another field, in which he could strike a telling blow. He saw that the situation in Irân, which had been created by the confederation against Pithon, might be turned to account. The confederate satraps had in effect identified their interests with those of the royalist party. The smaller chiefs knew that they would lose far less by being to some extent subject to a central authority than if they were severally swallowed up by Antigonus or Pithon. Accordingly, about the time of the battle in Parthia, Eumenes had moved eastwards, and crossed the Euphrates apparently without opposition. Amphimachus, the satrap of Mesopotamia, was an ally.[1] His winter-quarters (318-317) Eumenes took up within the satrapy of Seleucus, in some villages which went by the name of the Villages of the Carians (Καρῶν κῶμαι).[2] So much for any hopes Seleucus may have nursed of keeping the broils from his door!

There were no forces in Babylon whom Seleucus dared to oppose to the Silver Shields, with Eumenes to command them. Eumenes wintered in the villages undisturbed, and summoned Seleucus and Pithon by messengers to come to the help of the Kings. These chiefs still felt a coalition with Eumenes, the detested Greek, to be impossible, and refused to see in him the Kings' representative. But the despatches he sent to the confederate satraps met with a favourable reception. His post found the united army which had defeated Pithon not yet disbanded. Eumenes appointed the neighbourhood of Susa as the place where it should meet his own forces in the spring.

The agents of Seleucus and Pithon vainly endeavoured during the winter to detach the Silver Shields from their allegiance, and with the spring (317) the army of Eumenes was on the move. Seleucus soon learnt that he was encamped

---

[1] Diod. xix. 27, 4.   [2] *Ibid.* 12, 1.

on the bank of the Tigris, only 34 miles from Babylon. Eumenes had, in fact, approached nearer to Babylon than was safe; for he had now exhausted the country between the rivers, and could find no more supplies except by crossing to the eastern side of the Tigris. And so near to the capital, Seleucus had it in his power to make the passage of the river next to impossible. But Seleucus, for his part, was by no means desirous to have a hostile army, and that including the Silver Shields, penned up at his doors. To block the march of the army was almost as perilous for him as to allow it to go on to Susiana. All would be well could he only induce the Silver Shields to desert, and in his extremity he desperately clung to this forlorn hope. He sent an embassy on the ships which Alexander had built in Babylon just before his death to make a last attempt; but the Silver Shields still held by Eumenes. The agents of Seleucus then tried a more forcible method of persuasion. They opened an ancient canal, which had silted up, and the camp of Eumenes was flooded. Eumenes was in an ugly position. The next day his force, which was greatly superior to the troops sent by Seleucus, seized the punts in which the latter had come, and the best part of the army succeeded in crossing. Next day a native showed him how the water could be drained off, and when the officers of Seleucus saw him set about doing it, they withdrew all opposition to his passage.

Seleucus had never (if the view just given is correct) been really anxious to detain him, but the alternative had been to allow Eumenes and the satraps to unite. The combined force could certainly crush him. To meet this peril Seleucus was obliged to call in Antigonus.

Antigonus was already in Mesopotamia on the track of Eumenes when the messengers of Seleucus found him. He had, in fact, wintered there, hoping that when spring allowed military operations to continue he would be able to come up with Eumenes before a junction with the satraps was effected. Being too late for this, he was reduced to remain a while stationary in Mesopotamia, raising new levies for the approaching campaign. In the summer of 317 he came at length to Babylon, and concerted a plan of operations with Seleucus and

Pithon. Each furnished contingents. Then the whole force, with the three generals, crossed the Tigris, and the new phase in the great war of the Successors began.

It is no part of our purpose to follow its movements. The satrap of Babylonia ceased at an early stage to act with the main body. The first objective of Antigonus was Susa, and this he reached unopposed. A garrison, however, had been left by the confederate satraps to hold the fortress and guard the treasure. Antigonus, assuming already supreme powers, authorized Seleucus to join the Susian satrapy to his own, and left him with a detachment to reduce the fortress whilst he himself moved to Media. Xenophilus, the commander of the garrison, was perhaps only half-hearted in his resistance. At any rate we find him a year later still occupying his post as guardian of the treasure, but now as the lieutenant of Seleucus.

Within a year from the day that Antigonus crossed the Tigris, the mutual jealousies of the satraps and the treachery of the Silver Shields had delivered Eumenes into the hand of his enemies. Antigonus put him to death. The royalist cause in Asia was thereby extinguished. Antigonus was now the dominant person in all the country from the Mediterranean to Central Asia. Then the Macedonian grandees, who had followed Eumenes so grudgingly, found that with his disappearance the main prop of their defence was gone.

Eudamus, not the brother of Pithon, but the murderer of King Porus, the man whose 120 elephants had given him weight among the confederate satraps, was among the first to perish by the word of Antigonus. Antigenes, one of the commanders of the Silver Shields, who had been made satrap of Susiana at Triparadisus, was burnt alive. But it was not his late adversaries only whom the new lord of Asia could not tolerate. With them, if they were unlikely to give trouble in the future, there might be reconcilement. It was not the having fought in the royalist cause which was the damning thing. It was the possession of any power or prestige which might menace the new monarchy.

There was not, for instance, room in the world for both Antigonus and Pithon. Antigonus quartered his troops for the winter (317-316) in Media, and Pithon quickly set to work in secret upon them. Antigonus did not dare to risk an open attack upon his supposed ally. He therefore enticed him to a friendly conference, and then ordered him to instant execution. Lest the possession of Media should lead any one else to harbour the same designs as Pithon, Antigonus established a double authority there (according to Alexander's system), making a native satrap and appointing a Macedonian to command the troops.

After seizing the bullion in the treasuries of Ecbatana and stripping the silver tiles from the palace,[1] Antigonus moved to Persis. Here in the home of the Achaemenian kings he purposed to make a fresh settlement of the Eastern satrapies. He did not, while a son of Alexander lived, assume the title of King, but in fact he was King of Asia, and the natives received him with royal honours. It would indeed have been dangerous to strain his authority in the farther provinces, which his arms had never approached, and whose satraps, Macedonian and native, were strong in the affection of their subjects. The satrap of Aria was replaced by a nominee of Antigonus. Amphimachus, the satrap of Mesopotamia, who had joined Eumenes, was replaced by a certain Blitor.[2] Those more remote were allowed to retain their government.

Peucestas, who, now that Pithon was gone, was the most formidable rival of Antigonus in the East, remained to be dealt with. A residence in Persis seems to have brought home to Antigonus how great the popularity of Peucestas with his native subjects was, and how alarming his power. He declared him deposed. This at once raised a storm. A Persian notable had the boldness to tell Antigonus to his face that the Persians would obey no one else. Antigonus put the man to death, but he thought it prudent to use no violence against Peucestas. He rather designed to allure him out of the country by splendid promises. Perhaps Peucestas believed him; perhaps he only thought that his best chance lay in falling in with whatever Antigonus proposed. At any rate, from this time he disappears without a trace from history. A nominee of Antigonus ruled Persis with a strong hand in his stead.

[1] Polyb. x. 27, 11.   [2] App. *Syr.* 53.

The time was now come for Antigonus to turn his face again to the West. He set out by way of Susiana. On crossing the Pasitigris he was met by Xenophilus, the warden of the city of Susa. Xenophilus explained that Seleucus, the governor of the country, had ordered him to place the royal treasures at Antigonus' disposal. And now Antigonus laid his hands upon the fabulous riches of "Shushan the palace." The climbing vine of gold, which had been in the imagination of the Greeks what the Peacock Throne of the Moguls was to our fathers, became his. When he left Susa the 5000 talents he brought from Ecbatana had swelled to 25,000.

Seleucus was the last man left east of the Euphrates whom Antigonus could regard as a rival. The lessons of the fate of Pithon and Peucestas had not been lost upon the satrap of Babylonia. He must have felt bitterly the difference between his position and that of Ptolemy in Egypt. He had done all in his power to keep his province unembroiled, and now he must ask himself whether he was to keep it at all. To hold it by force against Antigonus was out of the question. His one chance lay in conciliating the conqueror; and if he failed—well, there was nothing for it but to throw up the game and save his life at least for more fortunate times.

The army of Antigonus, with its immense train of waggons and camels bearing the spoils of the East, moved from Susa to Babylon. But an ominous indication of the mood of Antigonus preceded his departure. The province of Susiana, which in the stress of the war he had assigned to Seleucus, he now took away again and put under a native. At Babylon, Seleucus received him and his forces with every form of observance and sumptuous entertainment which might allay his suspicions. But he was on the alert for the least sign of hostility on the part of Antigonus in order to escape the fate of Pithon. He had not long to wait. Antigonus, alleging that some act of his was a breach of order, called for an account of his administration. Seleucus could not, without surrendering all claim to independence, comply. He allowed a discussion to run on for several days, and then, whilst Antigonus was no doubt expecting something which might be a colourable pretext for arrest, he was suddenly gone. He was riding for his life with fifty horsemen to Egypt—the one secure place; Ptolemy had a reputation for generosity. Perhaps he reflected that the very man he was now flying from had himself fled in like manner from Perdiccas.

Sources.—Diod. xix.; Plutarch, *Eum.*; Nepos, *Eum.*; App. *Syr.*

CHAPTER V

SELEUCUS CONQUERS THE EAST

SEVEN years had passed since the death of Alexander, and Seleucus found himself at the end of them a landless fugitive. As a whole, these years had served to reduce the situation to a much simpler form. The old royal house of Macedonia was become a practically negligible quantity, although the boy Alexander still lived with the name of King. For in the West also, the years 317 and 316 had sealed the fate of the royalist cause. First, as a consequence of the distastrous battle in the Bosphorus, Greece had been for the most part in 317 wrested from the Regent Polyperchon by Cassander. Then came a split in the royalist party itself, a natural result of the double kingship. The Kings, the child and the simpleton, were cyphers, but Olympias, the grandmother of the little Alexander, and Eurydice, the wife of Philip, stood in fierce opposition. The Regent had lent himself to the designs of Olympias, and in 317 Philip and Eurydice were both made away with. The nominal kingship was now vested in Alexander alone. Before 317 was out Cassander attacked Macedonia itself. The murder of Philip and Eurydice had made the country hostile to Olympias and Polyperchon. When the winter fell, the Regent was pinned by Cassander's forces in Azorus, and Cassander was besieging the royal family in Pydna. In the spring of 316 Pydna fell. Cassander held the King in his hands. He soon made himself master of Macedonia. Olympias was put to death.

It was not only through the suppression of the royal house that the situation was simplified. Out of the struggle of the

Macedonian chiefs four now emerged as the fittest or the most fortunate. The rest had either disappeared, like Perdiccas and Eumenes, Pithon and Peucestas, or had acquiesced in subordination to one of the four, as the new satraps in the East to Antigonus, and Seleucus to Ptolemy. And of these four, Antigonus held a position which overshadowed all the rest. His power extended over all Asia from the Mediterranean to Khorassan, whilst of the other three Ptolemy held only Egypt and Southern Syria, Cassander had a newly-grounded and precarious power in Macedonia, and Lysimachus maintained his independence in the semi-barbarous country of Thrace.

It was a curious revolution in the position of Antigonus that he now found himself practically the successor of Perdiccas. So long as the principle of one central government for the Empire had meant an authority over his head, his ambition had set him among its opponents; his ambition, mounting higher, now made him the champion of that principle, but with the difference that the central government should be his own. Accordingly he found himself before long at war with his old allies, and allied with many of his old enemies, the wreck of the royalist party. The history of the next fourteen years (315-301) is the long fight of Antigonus for Macedonia.

Before Antigonus returned to the West in 315 common action had been determined on by Ptolemy, Cassander and Lysimachus. Our authority assigns a great part to Seleucus in prompting this alliance, but the other three chiefs probably needed little instruction to be on their guard against Antigonus.[1] Their ambassadors met Antigonus in the spring of 315 in Northern Syria, and laid before him the demands which they made as his allies in the late war against the royalists. These included a partition of the conquered territory in Asia, Seleucus being restored to Babylonia, and of the captured treasure. Antigonus repulsed these demands with scorn. Then either side got ready for the battle. The peoples of Asia saw the evidence of their monarch's resolution along all their highways, the posts fixed at intervals for rapid communication, the heights crowned with beacons.[2]

[1] Diod. xix. 56. [2] *Ibid.* 57, 5.

The war with Antigonus, as far as Seleucus was concerned, falls into two phases. In the first, 315-312, Seleucus was merely a subordinate, "one of the captains" of Ptolemy, as the book of Daniel describes him.[1] We hear of him in command of the Ptolemaïc fleet, which in 315 menaces the coast of Ionia, when Antigonus is set on gaining mastery of the sea as a preliminary to an attack on Macedonia.[2] Shortly afterwards Seleucus is in Cyprus with Ptolemy's brother Menelaus, combating the partizans of Antigonus in the island.[3] He is again in the Aegean the following year (314).[4] These operations, which form part of a plan of campaign, in which Seleucus is not a principal, do not concern us farther.

Then comes the year 312, the great year of Seleucus, the starting-point of the era, which was established by the kings of his line in the East, and was still used as the "year of the Greeks" long after his line had passed away. The spring of that year found Antigonus in Asia Minor, believing that the way to Europe was at last open. To secure himself against a flank attack from Egypt, his son Demetrius, the brilliant, dissolute man to whose career the rather hackneyed metaphor of a meteor can be applied with peculiar appropriateness, had been left with an army to hold Cilicia and Syria. Southern Syria (Palestine), as well as Northern, was occupied at this moment by the forces of Antigonus, the troops of Ptolemy having been expelled in 315 at the outbreak of the war. It was determined in the council of Ptolemy that the time was ripe for a forward movement. Seleucus, according to our account, was the main advocate of this step.[5] A large army, led by Ptolemy and Seleucus, moved across the desert upon Palestine. They were met at the threshold of the country, near Gaza, by Demetrius. A decisive battle—one of the great battles of the time—took place. Demetrius was completely beaten. Syria was lost for the time to Antigonus. His movement upon Macedonia was arrested; his whole scheme of operations had to be modified. It was the severest

---

[1] Ch. 11, 5. "The king of the south (Ptolemy) shall be strong; but as for one of his captains, he shall become stronger than he."
[2] Diod. xix. 58, 5; 60, 4.   [3] *Ibid.* 62, 4 f.
[4] *Ibid.* 68, 3 f.   [5] *Ibid.* 80, 3.

blow that had been dealt him since the beginning of the war.

But its ultimate consequences were to prove more momentous than its immediate effect. The opportunity of Seleucus was now come, and he sprang swiftly. Immediately after the battle he had received from Ptolemy, who favoured his enterprise, a body of 800 foot and 200 horse, and with these he set out to recover his old province of Babylonia. The little company moved along the road which struck the Euphrates in Northern Syria. Even for the recovery of one province the force seemed ridiculously small. We are told of the companions of Seleucus that on the way their hearts misgave them. They contrasted themselves with the great power against which they were going. But Seleucus was not to be discouraged. The history of those eventful days, as it stood in the author followed by Diodorus, narrated by those who looked back upon them in the light of subsequent triumphs, is transfigured by a prophetic halo. Seleucus was sure of his destiny. He reminded his followers of the fall of the Persian power before the superior science of Alexander; and indeed he was right if he saw upon how insecure foundations these monarchies maintained by military force alone, without the cement of nationality, of which the East has seen so many, do really rest. The narrator makes him further sustain his followers' courage by an oracle of the Didymaean Apollo, which had hailed him *King*, and by a vision of Alexander. "He also set before them how all that is held in honour and admiration among men is achieved by labours and hazards."[1] It is an occasion when some idealizing touches are justified. In this form, indeed, did those days actually live in the minds of men.

The party of Seleucus crossed the Euphrates into Mesopotamia and appeared at Carrhae, an old town on the high road between Syria and Babylon where a colony of Macedonian soldiers was settled. Some of these were ready at once to join a commander of the reputation of Seleucus, and the rest were not numerous enough to offer resistance. With these reinforcements Seleucus traversed the length of Mesopotamia and

[1] Diod. xix. 90.

entered Babylonia. The hopes he had cherished, that the work of his previous four years there still stood in the disposition of the people, were not found vain. The satrap appointed by Antigonus, Pithon the son of Agenor, had been with Demetrius at Gaza and fallen on the field.[1] The natives flocked to the standards of their old governor. One of the Macedonian officials came over to him with more than 1000 men. The partizans of Antigonus were overborne by the popular movement, and shut themselves up under a commander called Diphilus in one of the palace-citadels of Babylon. Here they still held as hostages those who had formed the adherents and retinue of Seleucus in his governorship.[2] But Seleucus carried the place by assault and rescued all who belonged to him.

This was the moment which the Seleucid kings regarded as the birthday of their Empire.

Seleucus ruled once more in Babylon. But he must expect ere long to have his possession challenged; and he set earnestly to work to form a force of both arms and to confirm his influence with the natives and resident Macedonians. Antigonus personally was busy in the West, but he left the command of all the eastern provinces in the hands of the satrap of Media, Nicanor, who had succeeded the Mede Orontobates.[3] Nicanor was soon on his way to Babylon with an imposing force, drawn from different regions of Irân, of more than 10,000 foot and 7000 horse. To set against him Seleucus had no more than 3000 foot and 400 horse. But making up for this by mobility, he crossed the Tigris before Nicanor had reached it, took him completely by surprise, and routed him. Euager, the satrap of Persis, was among those who fell in the affray. The army of Nicanor came over in a body to Seleucus. Nicanor himself barely made good his escape into the deserts with a handful of his staff, and thence reached his satrapy.

The effect of the battle was immediately to open the East to Seleucus. It was seen how insubstantial the hold

---

[1] Diod. xix. 85, 2.

[2] τὰ φυλαττόμενα σώματα τῶν παίδων καὶ τῶν φίλων, Diod. xix. 91, 4. The παῖδες of the governor probably correspond to the παῖδες βασιλικοί of the king. Cf. τῶν Εὐμένους παίδων ἴλας δύο, Diod. xix. 28, 3; 90, 1.

[3] Nicanor is called στρατηγὸς τῆς τε Μηδίας καὶ τῶν ἄνω σατραπειῶν, Diod. xix. 100, 3.

of Antigonus upon the East really was. The Greek and Macedonian garrisons by which his nominees had held Media, Persis, Susiana, and Babylon were quite ready, if it appeared profitable, to exchange his service for that of Seleucus. The natives, no doubt, remembered the old governors he had taken from them with regret. The satraps of the further provinces he had never really subdued.[1] Seleucus seems to have annexed Susiana almost immediately, and perhaps Persis, whose satrap had fallen. Then he advanced upon Media itself, to attack Nicanor in his own province.

Meanwhile in the West, Antigonus, warned by the battle of Gaza, had determined to leave Ptolemy unassailed no longer. He had reoccupied Palestine, and, as a preliminary to the invasion of Egypt, had attempted to reduce the Nabataean Arabs, who controlled the road through the desert (311). He had met in this with indifferent success, and had just come to terms when a dispatch from Nicanor, explaining the desperate position of affairs in the East, reached him. Antigonus, even with the risk of losing the East, could ill spare troops for any long time in view of the complications in the West. But he determined to try the effect of one sudden blow at the seat of Seleucus' power. He gave 15,000 foot and 4000 horse to Demetrius, ordered him to make a flying excursion into Babylonia, recover the province, and return as soon as possible. Demetrius assembled this force at Damascus, and moved rapidly upon Babylonia by way of Mesopotamia.[2]

Seleucus had left in Babylon, to hold command during his absence, an officer called Patrocles, no doubt the same person of whom we hear later on as his foremost counsellor and the explorer of Central Asia. Patrocles learnt that Demetrius was coming down on him from Mesopotamia. He knew that his forces were too small to risk a battle. But at any rate he meant to save them from defeat or seduction, and ordering a considerable part of them to take refuge in the deserts to the west of the Euphrates or the swamps of the Susian coast,

[1] Niese, i. p. 299, supposes that Seleucus had already an understanding with these satraps before coming to Babylon.

[2] The route across the desert by way of Palmyra is not mentioned, I believe, till 41 B.C. (App. *B.C.* v. 9). Even Seleucus on his way from Gaza to Babylon goes as far north as Carrhae.

he himself moved with a small body about the province to observe the enemy. At the same time he kept Seleucus in Media continually informed of what took place.

Demetrius found the city of Babylon evacuated, except the two royal palaces which confronted each other across the river. Of these he took and looted one, but the other held out for some days, and the time allowed him was at an end. He was obliged to return with this incomplete result, but he left one of his friends with a quarter of his force to go on with the siege and hold the province. Before leaving he pillaged the country, an act which only served to injure his own cause, so that, as Plutarch says, he "left the power of Seleucus firmer than ever."[1]

The incursion of Demetrius was a mere momentary interruption in Seleucus' conquest of the East. Nicanor was unable to make head against him in Media. Appian says that Seleucus "killed the satrap Nicator (*sic*) in the battle."[2] It may be that Appian had the battle on the Tigris in his mind when Nicanor was defeated and fled; or, of course, Nicanor may have given battle again in Media with his remaining troops and fallen.

The ancient authors have allowed us to follow up to this point with tolerable completeness the progress of Seleucus, the son of Antiochus, towards empire. If the material were before us, we should now have to narrate the actual formation of the Empire in the East with a fulness proportionate to its importance. The observance of such proportions in his narrative is, however, impossible to a historian of the Seleucid house. He has to take his information as he can get it, and it is not always the passages he would most like to know about which are lit up for him by the capricious chances of the records. On an incident which, according to its relative importance, should be disposed of in a sentence he is obliged, in order to make his work complete, to spend a page; about a development, to which he would wish to give a chapter, he can only get enough information to fill a sentence. We have at the point to which we are now come an example of this disability. After the return of Demetrius from Babylon in

---

[1] Plutarch, *Dem.* 7. [2] App. *Syr.* 55.

311 Seleucus once more repossessed himself of the province, and during the following nine years (311-302) made his authority supreme in Irân as well as in the Euphrates valley, or, in other words, over all the eastern part of the Empire to the Jaxartes and the Indus. *This bare fact is almost all that can be elicited from the documents.*

It is the war with Antigonus in the West which once more draws Seleucus, as king of the East, into the field of vision. There the situation was still very much in 302 as Seleucus had left it in 312. The most important modification was the total extinction of the old royal family of Macedonia in the male line. The child Alexander had been murdered by Cassander in 311, and Heracles, the illegitimate son of the great Alexander, by Polyperchon in 309. Cassander might claim to inherit its rights by his wife, Thessalonice, who was the sister of Alexander the Great. In 306 Antigonus assumed the title of King.[1] In the following year the other dynasts, Ptolemy, Cassander, Lysimachus and Seleucus, followed suit. Seleucus had already been "King" to his native subjects. Now the Macedonians and Greeks admitted to his presence saw him wearing the linen band, the *diadem*, which had been with the old Persian kings the symbol of royalty, and the official Greek documents ran in the name of *King* Seleucus.[2]

We may pause to note that the name of king had no *territorial* reference. These kings are never officially styled kings *of Egypt* or kings *of Asia*. If they are called so by historians, it is merely for the purpose of convenient distinction. It connoted rather a personal relation to the Macedonian people. *Ideally* there was one Macedonian Empire as in the Middle Ages there was one Roman Empire.[3] But the dignity of Macedonian King was borne conjointly or concurrently by several chieftains, just as the dignity of Roman Emperor was

---

[1] He had already been so called by the Athenians in 307, *C. I. Att.* ii. No. 238.
[2] Plutarch, *Dem.* 18.
[3] "Das Reich Alexanders ist trotz den Teilungen immer noch als ein Ganzes anzusehen . . . Die Teilungen waren so rasch aufeinander gefolgt, dass sie feste Territorien mit sicheren Grenzen und ausgeprägten Eigenheiten nicht bilden konnten . . . Jeder der neuen Könige hielt sich berechtigt, nach Vermögen und Gelegenheit seinen Teil zu vergrössern, *ja selbst das Ganze in Anspruch zu nehmen.*" Niese ii. p. 123.

borne concurrently by the Western and the Byzantine prince.[1] *In practice*, of course, each of the rivals had to acquiesce in the others being kings within a certain territorial sphere. But their connexion with that sphere was never as close and essential as that of the king of England or the king of France with his territory. Ptolemy and Seleucid were to the end Macedonian kings who happened to reign in Egypt and in Asia.

Materially, however, the situation in the West had changed little since 312. Antigonus still held Asia Minor and Syria securely. But his attempts to enlarge his dominion further had met with poor success. He had never succeeded in reaching Macedonia, and his attack on Egypt in 306 had broken down disastrously. He had wrested Cyprus from Ptolemy, and he had established a fluctuating influence in Greece, but that was the utmost he could do. And during the siege of Rhodes by Demetrius, 305-304, the war between Antigonus and the other dynasts seems to have languished.

But it was in itself a momentous change in the general situation that the rule of Antigonus beyond the Euphrates had been superseded by the rule of Seleucus. It was so much lost to Antigonus in resources, and a fourth independent power had arisen in his rear. If against his three enemies he had been unable to make advance, against four he could not even hold his own ground.

After the failure of his attempt on Rhodes he turned once more in 304 to assail Cassander in Greece. During the distractions of the last three years his hold on Greece had been almost lost. Cassander and his ally, the old Regent Polyperchon, who was now fallen to be a sort of *condottiere*, had restored their influence almost everywhere, except in Athens; and Athens was hard pressed. Demetrius now returned to Greece, and next year (303), in a victorious campaign, swept the hostile forces from the field. The states of Greece were federated under the presidency of Antigonus and Demetrius against Cassander.

Such victories were useless. Their immediate effect was

---

[1] Cf. Plutarch, *Dem.* 25. Demetrius does not recognize the royalty of the rival dynasts.

SELEUCUS CONQUERS THE EAST

to revive into activity the alliance of Cassander, Lysimachus and Ptolemy, to which Seleucus now added his strength. While Demetrius had been conquering Greece, Antigonus had remained on the defensive in Northern Syria. In this central region the roads which led to Asia Minor from Egypt and from Babylonia converged, so that his position gave Antigonus equal opportunities for observing Ptolemy and Seleucus. But in the spring of 302 the alliance against him came into play. Lysimachus crossed over from Thrace, and, in combination with a force sent by Cassander, overran the Western part of Asia Minor. When Antigonus marched against him he simply retired into a strong position on the coast near Heraclea and stood at bay. And in the meantime Antigonus had been obliged to leave the roads from Irân and Egypt inadequately defended behind him. In such a predicament it was of no avail that Demetrius was pressing Cassander hard in Thessaly. Antigonus was obliged to call him back to Asia and let Greece go.

During these events in the summer of 302 Seleucus was making his way from the Panjab, marching ever westward over the immense distances which separate India from the Mediterranean lands. When the winter 302-301 closed in he had reached Cappadocia, and there turned his troops into winter-quarters.[1] His force amounted to 20,000 foot, 12,000 cavalry and mounted archers, the latter no doubt from Central Asia, 480 elephants, brought straight from the Panjab, and over 100 scythed chariots. He had with him his son Antiochus, then twenty-two or twenty-three years old.

In the spring of 301 he advanced again along the central highway of Asia Minor. Antigonus failed to prevent his junction with Lysimachus, and at Ipsus, which lay on the highway,[2] he had to meet the united armies of the two kings. Plutarch gives an account of the battle with various picturesque details. It was preceded, he tells us, by omens which portended disaster to Antigonus. In the course of the fight Demetrius, who commanded the flower of his father's cavalry, came into collision with the young prince Antiochus, and, after

---

[1] Diod. xx. 113, 4.
[2] Ramsay, *Historical Geography of Asia Minor*, p. 35.

a brilliant passage of arms, routed his opponents. But he pressed the pursuit too far. This spoilt the victory. The elephants of Seleucus thrust in between him and the phalanx of Antigonus. The forces of Seleucus and Lysimachus circled round that powerful but unwieldy mass, threatening attack, but trying in reality to frighten the troops of Antigonus into desertion. And in fact a large section voluntarily went over to the winning side. The rest fled. Then a body of javelin-men bore down upon the place where Antigonus himself was stationed. Some one drew his attention to them: "These men are levelling at you, O king." The old man was unmoved "Let them; Demetrius will come to my support." To the end he believed his son was at hand, and kept scanning the horizon. Then the javelins struck him and he fell, pierced with many wounds. Only Thorax of Larissa remained beside the body.[1]

[1] Plutarch, *Dem.* 29.

SOURCES.—Diod. xix., xx.; App. *Syr.*; Plutarch, *Dem.*; Justin xv.

CHAPTER VI

FROM IPSUS TO THE DEATH OF SELEUCUS

THE battle of Ipsus is one of the landmarks of the period after Alexander. The Asiatic empire of Antigonus, which had been the great factor in the history of the last fifteen years, was annihilated for ever. The house of Antigonus still survived in the person of Demetrius, who fled from the disastrous battle to Ephesus. His power was unbroken on the seas, and many places in the Levant were still held by his garrisons—Cyprus, Caunus, Tyre and Sidon. But for the moment the other four houses had almost driven the house of Antigonus from the field. "The victorious kings proceeded to cut up the empire of Antigonus like a great carcase, taking slices for themselves and adding its provinces to those they already ruled."[1] It was Seleucus and Lysimachus who gained the most in territory. Seleucus now annexed Syria, and Lysimachus a great part of the territory ruled by Antigonus in Asia Minor; where exactly the new frontier was drawn we cannot say.[2] Cilicia was ceded to Plistarchus, the brother of Cassander.

There was one territorial controversy which the partition after Ipsus bequeathed to later generations—the question between the house of Seleucus and the house of Ptolemy as to the possession of Coele-Syria, the country we call Palestine. Ptolemy had long been concerned to possess Syria south of the Lebanon; during the war with Antigonus he had on several occasions seized this country and again lost it. When the alliance of the four kings had been renewed in 302,

[1] Plutarch, *Dem.* 30. [2] See page 98 and Appendix D.

Ptolemy had stipulated for it as his share in the gains, and to this the others had agreed. At the same time that Lysimachus attacked Antigonus in Asia Minor, Ptolemy invaded and occupied Palestine. Then on some false report that Lysimachus had been crushed, Ptolemy made haste to evacuate it. This was the action on which the controversy turned. Seleucus, and apparently the other two kings whose forces had fought at Ipsus, contended that this withdrawal of Ptolemy's was a desertion of the common cause, and that his claim to Palestine in virtue of the original agreement was forfeit. Ptolemy on the other hand maintained that it still held good. When Seleucus crossed the Taurus again after Ipsus to take possession of his new Syrian provinces, he found that Ptolemy had once more occupied Palestine. Seleucus could only obtain the country by superior force. But he felt himself restrained by decency from applying force to Ptolemy, not only an ally of old standing, but the man to whom he owed his own rise. He contented himself with an indignant protest. He declared to Ptolemy that "he would for the present take no active measures for friendship's sake," but that "he should consider later how to deal with a friend who seized more than his share."

As a matter of fact, Seleucus, in consequence of the battle of Ipsus, had stepped, one might almost say, into the place of Antigonus, just as Antigonus had stepped into the place of Perdiccas. Seleucus now held a position which overshadowed that of all the other chieftains. And accordingly, just as Antigonus found himself in 315 in opposition to his old allies and allied with his old enemies, so it also happened with Seleucus. His neighbours Lysimachus and Ptolemy drew together. Lysimachus took Arsinoë, the daughter of Ptolemy, to wife. On his part Seleucus made overtures to the roving Demetrius. He asked the hand of Stratonice, his daughter by Phila the daughter of Antipater. Demetrius himself was invited to Syria.

This offer came to Demetrius as an "unexpected piece of fortune." He at once set sail for Syria with Stratonice. On the way he raided Cilicia, the province of Plistarchus, and carried off 1200 talents from Cyinda, a residue of the

Achaemenian hoards. Demetrius, Phila and Stratonice were received by Seleucus at the coast town of Rhossus. "The intercourse of the two kings was marked from the first by frankness, confidence and royal splendour. They took their pastimes, conversed and lived together with no setting of guards or wearing of arms, until Seleucus took Stratonice with imposing ceremony and went up to Antioch."[1] The new alliance was notified to the Greek cities in the occupation of Demetrius by envoys sent out in the name of both kings.[2]

With his position thus improved, Demetrius began to meditate new aggressions. He occupied Cilicia, Plistarchus withdrawing apparently to complain to his brother, King Cassander. Seleucus would seem to have countenanced this proceeding, for we find him soon after using his good offices with Ptolemy, with whom his relations, in spite of the matter of Cœle-Syria, were still friendly, to obtain the betrothal to Demetrius of one of Ptolemy's daughters. But the fresh ambitions of Demetrius showed that the house of Antigonus was not yet eliminated, and this to some extent restored the common antagonism of the four kings to their old enemy. A rupture between Seleucus and Demetrius took place. Its immediate cause was the demand of Seleucus that Demetrius should sell him Cilicia. When Demetrius refused, Seleucus in more menacing terms asked for Tyre and Sidon, which garrisons of Demetrius still retained. He received the proud answer that not even if Demetrius had to live through ten thousand other battles of Ipsus would he wish for Seleucus as a son-in-law on mercenary conditions, and the garrisons in the two cities were strengthened. Soon after this he left the East to restore his fortunes on the other side of the Aegean.

The years following Ipsus were, no doubt, fruitful in the internal development of the Empire of Seleucus. Seated now in Antioch, the new city he had built on the Orontes to replace Antigonia, Seleucus could survey both East and West and consolidate his power throughout the vast regions he had come to rule. But here again all record has perished. One administrative measure only finds mention in our traditions,

---

[1] Plutarch, *Dem.* 32.
[2] The embassy of Nicagoras the Rhodian to Ephesus, Michel No. 492.

the division of the Empire into an eastern and western part, the former with its capital in Babylonia, in the new city of Seleucia-on-the-Tigris. Here the son of Seleucus and the Bactrian Apama is installed as viceroy of the dominion beyond the Euphrates.[1]

This measure, however, owes its mention, not to its historical importance, but to its being connected with a story of that sentimental flavour, tinged with incest, which so pleased the taste of the later Greeks. Appian elaborates the story in greater detail than any other part of the history of Seleucus and his successors. Briefly, the prince Antiochus conceived a passion for his young step-mother Stratonice, and pined in silence. When, however, the court physician Erasistratus discovered the nature of his malady and revealed it to the King, Seleucus, with a paternal devotion considered exemplary, resolved to pass on his wife to his son. He further determined to make over to him at the same time the eastern half of the Empire. An assembly of all ranks of the Macedonian troops at Antioch was convoked, and the King proclaimed to them the betrothal of Antiochus and Stratonice, and their appointment to be King and Queen of the East. To remove any scruples as to a union abhorrent to Greek morality, Seleucus adopted the maxim of statecraft which Herodotus attributes to the royal judges of Cambyses, that the King is above law: "The King's decree makes every action right" (about 293).[2]

Its association with a story of this kind has served to rescue a great political measure from oblivion. Otherwise the history of Seleucus after Ipsus is lit up for us only by the meteoric personality of Demetrius. In 297-296 Cassander died, leaving no strong successor. His eldest son, Philip, died a year after his father; and then came a divided kingship in Macedonia, two other sons, Antipater and Alexander, reigning conjointly, held in leading strings by their mother, Thessalonice, the great Philip's daughter. Such a state of things gave Demetrius his chance. He began once more to make himself master of the cities of Greece. The children of Cassander were not in a

---

[1] App. *Syr.* 62.

[2] App. *Syr.* 59 f.; Plutarch, *Dem.* 38; Lucian, *De Syria dea*, 17 f.; cf. Hdt. iii. 31.

position to hinder his progress. Soon there were open feuds in the house of Cassander. Antipater murdered his mother, the last representative of the old royal line, and the two brothers fell to fighting. Demetrius dashed into this chaos and seized the Macedonian throne (293).

It is certainly one of the ironies of history that the object which Antigonus the One-eyed, with all his resources as lord of Asia, had vainly pursued so long should have been attained by his son after that Asiatic empire had perished. But the throne of Demetrius was anything but secure. The other three kings, alarmed at this resurrection of the house of Antigonus, united once more against it. Lysimachus had already driven the forces of Demetrius from a number of the coast cities of Asia Minor, where they had held on after Ipsus; Ptolemy had reconquered Cyprus. The three kings found an instrument in Pyrrhus of Epirus. He and Lysimachus simultaneously invaded Macedonia, whilst Ptolemy's vessels appeared off the coast of Greece. It was perhaps at the same time that Seleucus occupied Cilicia.

Demetrius was driven by the desertion of his troops to quit Macedonia, and the country was divided between Lysimachus and Pyrrhus (287). For a while after this Demetrius mixed in the confused politics of Central Greece, where there were still troops afoot which paid him allegiance, and he had soon collected a sufficient power to annoy Athens. But it was too narrow a world for his ambitions and he was outmatched by Pyrrhus. Then once more he turned his eyes to the East. With an army of 11,000 foot and a body of cavalry he landed in Asia Minor. He met with some success. Even Sardis fell. The tide of desertion in Caria and Lydia began to set in his favour. But Agathocles, the son of Lysimachus, drew near with a force to redress the balance. Demetrius plunged into the interior. He conceived the daring plan of invading Irân. Perhaps he counted on the favour of his daughter, who reigned as queen of that land. The great difficulty in his plan was to reach Irân at all. It was difficult for two reasons: the mercenaries of those days had a profound objection to expeditions into out-of-the-way regions, whence it was difficult to bring back loot and where there was no opportunity of changing their service; and secondly, Agathocles pressed the pursuit so closely that Demetrius was unable to procure supplies. There was soon famine in his camp. Then he lost a number of men in the passage of the river Lycus.[1] Then disease broke out. His army was, from all causes, reduced by 8000 men.

It was in this predicament that he determined to enter the realm of Seleucus and throw himself upon the compassion of his late ally. He crossed the Taurus into Cilicia and entered Tarsus. But he was careful to show that he did not come as an enemy. The fields through which he passed were left unharmed, and from Tarsus he wrote a letter of appeal to Seleucus in Syria. Seleucus seems to have been a good-natured man, and even apart from that, the age was favourable to acts of showy magnanimity. He at once wrote orders to his generals in Cilicia to furnish Demetrius with all that befitted royalty and to victual his starving troops.

But here another voice was raised, that of Patrocles, the King's chief counsellor. He represented strongly to Seleucus the danger of allowing a man of Demetrius' ambition and abilities to take up his residence in the kingdom. His arguments worked so upon Seleucus, that the King completely reversed his first intentions. He marched in person into Cilicia at the head of a large force to complete Demetrius' ruin.

To Demetrius this sudden change of policy was disconcerting. He took refuge among the defiles of the Taurus, and thence dispatched fresh appeals. Might he be allowed to establish himself as the petty chief of some of the free mountain folk? He promised to be content with such a kingdom. At any rate he implored Seleucus to suffer him to maintain his force where it was during the winter (286-285), and not force him back into the clutch of his implacable foe, Lysimachus.

But Seleucus was still under the influence of Patrocles. He gave Demetrius leave to take up quarters for two of the winter months, if he liked, in Cataonia, the highland country adjoining Cappadocia, on condition that he sent his principal friends as hostages. He then proceeded to barricade the passes

[1] Cf. Polyaen. iv. 7, 12.

of the Amanus, just as Agathocles had those of the Taurus, so that Demetrius was penned up in Cilicia with no outlet either into Asia Minor or Syria. But now Demetrius turned fiercely like a beast at bay. He began to waste the fields that he had hitherto spared. He defeated detachments of the troops of Seleucus, including the scythed chariots. He secured the passes, beating the people of Seleucus from the barricades.

With these strokes the spirit of his followers rose. Their tidings caused anxiety at the courts of the other kings. In those days, when power was so swiftly lost and won, it was unwise to underrate the importance of any successes, and the prestige of Demetrius the Besieger was enormous. Lysimachus sent an offer of help to Seleucus. But Seleucus was in doubt which to fear most, Demetrius or Lysimachus. He declined the offer. At the same time he was not over-eager to join battle with the desperate man.

At this critical moment Demetrius fell ill. Thenceforward his cause was lost. When after forty days he was himself again, his army had melted away. Many of his soldiers were now in the ranks of Seleucus. With the few who remained a guerilla war could still for a while be carried on. Even in this extremity his genius secured him flashes of triumph. When the generals of Seleucus believed him about to raid the Cilician lowlands, he suddenly dashed across the Amanus and was in the rich plains of Syria, spreading havoc as far as Cyrrhestice, where Seleucus had been carefully planting the new civilization. Seleucus himself brought up a force to run him to ground. His camp narrowly escaped a surprise by night, and the next day Demetrius gained a partial success on one of his wings. But if Demetrius was bold, so too could Seleucus be. He understood where the weakness of Demetrius lay. With courage worthy of an old companion of Alexander, he took off his helmet, and with nothing but a light shield to defend his head, rode straight up to the enemy's lines and himself, in a loud voice, invited them to desert. The effect was electrical. With a shout of acclaim the little band of Demetrius hailed Seleucus king. Demetrius made off with a handful of followers. His one idea was to reach the Aegean. His friends, he hoped, were still in possession of the harbour of Caunus. Till nightfall he took refuge in the neighbouring woods, so that he might recross the Amanus in the dark. When, however, his party crept close to the passes they saw them lit up by the fires of Seleucus' pickets. They were too late. The checkmate was achieved. The little party grew still less. All that night Demetrius wandered aimlessly in the woods. Next day he was at last persuaded to surrender himself to Seleucus.

Once more the first impulse of Seleucus was to show himself generous. When he received Demetrius' emissary he exclaimed that it was to *him* that fortune had been kind in preserving Demetrius alive to this hour, in affording him an opportunity to add to his other glories a signal exhibition of humanity and goodness. His chamberlains were ordered to erect a royal pavilion for the reception of the fallen king. He chose as his envoy to carry his answer to Demetrius a person of his *entourage*, Apollonides, with whom Demetrius had once been intimate. The King's mood set the tune for the court. The courtiers, by twos and threes at first, then *en masse*, sped to Demetrius, almost tumbling over each other in their eagerness to be beforehand. For the favour of Demetrius, they reckoned, would be particularly worth having at the court of Seleucus in the days to come.

This rush had not been expected by Seleucus. It alarmed him. The enemies of Demetrius got his ear. He began actually to dread that in his own house this magnetic personality might supplant him. Once more, therefore, his generous impulse was revoked by second thoughts. Apollonides had hardly reached Demetrius and charmed away his bitterness by the picture of what Seleucus intended towards him, an assurance confirmed by the courtiers who came pouring in, when the party found itself surrounded by a thousand men, foot and horse. Demetrius was a prisoner indeed.

He never saw the face of Seleucus. He was carried to the "Syrian Chersonese," the steamy, luxuriant plains about the middle Orontes where the new city of Apamea was rising, and there were royal parks full of all sorts of game. Here, under a strong guard, he was given liberty to hunt and drink.

No material provision for his comfort and dignity was omitted. Any friends who chose were allowed to keep him company. Sometimes people from the court joined him. They brought gracious messages from Seleucus. Antiochus and Stratonice were expected at Antioch, and when they came—it was always when they came—Demetrius would be set free. As a matter of fact, Seleucus may well have wished to keep Demetrius in reserve as a bolt he might, if need were, launch upon the world.

In 285 Lysimachus succeeded in ousting Pyrrhus from his share of Macedonia and in annexing Thessaly. The Empire of Alexander was now become three kingdoms, under the three survivors of that great generation, Seleucus, Lysimachus, Ptolemy. Of these three Seleucus held the most commanding position. It was he whom the popular story represented to have put on the diadem of Alexander. "Seleucus," Arrian says, "became the greatest of those kings who inherited the Empire of Alexander, the most kingly in his designs, the ruler of more land than any save Alexander himself."[1] And now his prestige had been raised yet higher by his capture of Demetrius, by his holding the sometime king of Macedonia, the representative of the great house of Antigonus, in a cage.

But the position of Lysimachus at this time was hardly less imposing. He was King in Macedonia, in the original seats of the ruling race. His dominion stretched from the Cilician Gates westward over the tableland of Asia Minor, the Greek cities of the coast, Bithynia, Thrace, Macedonia, Thessaly, to the pass of Thermopylae. Would the three kings acquiesce in the existing tripartite division?

It is probable that Seleucus at any rate nursed the hope of making the whole Empire his. He held in Demetrius an instrument by which the actual king in Macedonia could be assailed with some show of legitimacy. Lysimachus was not insensible to this danger. He sent to Seleucus an offer of 2000 talents if he would put Demetrius to death. Seleucus repelled the suggestion with demonstrative indignation. "Not only to break faith, but to commit such foulness towards one

[1] *Anab.* vii. 22, 5.

connected with his own house!" He now wrote to Antiochus in Media announcing his intention to restore Demetrius to the Macedonian throne. Antiochus was to plead for his release, as Seleucus wished that his act of generosity should go to the credit of his son.

Whatever the real intentions of Seleucus with regard to his prisoner may have been, his opportunity to execute them was soon gone. Demetrius sought to drown the bitterness and tedium of his captivity in wild indulgence. In two years he drank himself to death (283).

Seleucus, even with what he had already attained, must still have seemed far from possessing the whole Empire. The houses of Lysimachus and Ptolemy were well provided with heirs. Agathocles, the son of Lysimachus, had won distinction as a commander and had hunted Demetrius himself across the Taurus. Ptolemy, besides his eldest son Ptolemy, nicknamed Keraunos, had several other sons already grown to manhood.

And now Fate seemed to work miracles on Seleucus' behalf and set his rivals to destroy their own defences. A chain of events took place which began with the old Ptolemy abdicating in favour, not of his eldest son Keraunos, but of his son by Berenice, the Ptolemy whom later generations called Philadelphus (end of 285).[1] Keraunos at once fled, and found reception at the court of Lysimachus. But Lysimachus was taking a serpent into his bosom. His court was soon riddled with subterranean intrigue, and Ptolemy Keraunos contrived to awake the suspicions of Lysimachus against his son. Agathocles was assassinated by his father's orders and a massacre of his adherents began. This criminal outbreak had two consequences. In the first place, as soon as the truth came to light and Agathocles was cleared, Ptolemy Keraunos had once more to flee, and this time betook himself to Seleucus. *Fate without any effort of his had brought into Seleucus' hand the claimant by right of birth to the Egyptian throne.* In the second place the murder of Agathocles raised about Lysimachus a swarm of domestic enemies. The father's yoke had never been easy, but the son

[1] This surname during the life of Ptolemy II belonged, not to himself, but to his sister-wife Arsinoë.

was universally popular, and now all the hopes which had been fixed upon him had failed. The city-states within the dominions of Lysimachus began to fall away from allegiance. The remnant of the party of Agathocles, his wife and children, had taken refuge with Seleucus. The army was thoroughly disaffected and officers continually made their way to Syria. Even a son of Lysimachus, Alexander, followed the current. Hundreds of voices called on Seleucus to take up arms against the tyrant. *Fate had made his way open into the realm of Lysimachus.*

Seleucus felt indeed that his moment had come. The world, weary of the long conflict, saw once more, forty years after the great conqueror's death, his two remaining companions, now old men,[1] address themselves to the crowning fight for his inheritance. In view of the danger from Asia, Lysimachus looked, as of old, to an alliance with Egypt. His daughter Arsinoë was given in marriage to the young king Ptolemy. But Egypt seems to have remained true to its reputation as a broken reed. We do not hear of any help sent to Lysimachus from that quarter.

Asia Minor was the theatre of the campaign. We are nowhere told its movements. Whether the capture of Sardis by Seleucus[2] and of Cotyaïum in Phrygia by Alexander, the son of Lysimachus,[3] preceded the decisive battle or followed it we do not know. The site of that battle is uncertain; it is convenient to call it, after Eusebius,[4] the battle of Corū-pedion, the plain of Corus, but where that was we cannot say.[5] The result, however, of the battle we know. Lysimachus fell. A refugee from Heraclea in the service of Seleucus gave the mortal blow with his lance. The widow of Agathocles would have had the victor leave the body unburied, but was mollified by Alexander, who got leave to take it away (Spring 281). The tomb of Lysimachus was visible for many centuries between the little towns of Pactyë and Cardia in the Chersonese.

---

[1] Their ages are variously given. See Niese i. p. 404, note 3.
[2] Polyaen. iv. 9, 4.   [3] *Id.* vi. 12.   [4] *Chron.* i. 233 f.
[5] Niese i. p. 404 suggests that it is equivalent to the Κύρου πέδιον in Lydia mentioned by Strabo (xiii. 626, 629), where Κόρου πέδιον is one reading. This entails a correction of Appian (*Syr.* 62), who says the battle was in Hellespontine Phrygia. [The site in Lydia is proved by a new document. See Appendix C.]

Seleucus had seen his last rival disappear. No doubt, to assume actual possession of the realm of Lysimachus would take some time. The garrisons distributed throughout it, the governments in the various cities may not have instantly accepted the conqueror. But there was no heir of Lysimachus able to offer serious resistance. And in many places the mere news of Corū-pedion was enough to overthrow the existing *régime*. The case of Ephesus probably shows the sort of thing that took place in a number of cities. Here Arsinoë, the queen of Lysimachus, was residing when the news of the battle arrived. The whole city was instantly in an uproar, the adherents of Seleucus (οἱ σελευκίζοντες) seized the direction of things, and Arsinoë narrowly escaped in disguise.[1] Already, by the overthrow of the Western king, Seleucus considered the West his. So the dream which had been the motive in all the wars of the last forty years—the dream which Perdiccas, Eumenes and Antigonus had perished in pursuing—had come true at last! The whole realm of Alexander from Greece to Central Asia and India was fallen to Seleucus, with the one exception of Egypt, and the claimant to the Egyptian throne by natural right was a pensioner of his bounty. As to Egypt then he could make the claims of Ptolemy Keraunos a specious ground for intervention, and indeed we are told that he intended to round off his work by so doing.

And now that Seleucus had touched the summit of his ambition, his heart turned to the land of his birth. Perhaps it was because his greatness as the last of his peers was so lonely that he was driven to the associations of the past; there might still be about his old home faces he would recognize. He intended, we are told, to resign all his Asiatic realm into the hands of Antiochus, and be content for the remainder of his days with the narrow kingdom of his race.

He "pressed eagerly" (ἠπείγετο), Pausanias says, towards Macedonia. But Fate, which had given him so much, denied his last desire. His position left no room for any minor independent power. This was a reflection naturally disagreeable to one with the hopes of Ptolemy Keraunos. Keraunos was a man in whom no trace can be discovered of humanity or

[1] Polyaen. viii. 57.

gratitude. He saw that the immense agglomeration of power rested as yet on one slight support—the person of Seleucus himself. Were he removed, the fabric must collapse, and smaller people would again have the chances of a scramble. The conclusion was obvious. Keraunos was soon at his old trick of intrigue; his plots ramified through the army of the King.

Seleucus crossed the Hellespont into Europe (Summer 281). The main part of the army accompanied him and was quartered at Lysimachia. At a spot not far from the city, a little way off the road, was a rude pile of stones. Tradition called it Argos, and asserted it to be an altar raised long ago by the Argonauts or the host of Agamemnon. The interest of the old king as he passed that way was excited by the story. He turned his horse aside to look at it. Only a few attendants followed him. Of these Ptolemy was one. It was while Seleucus was examining the monument and listening to the legend of remote heroic days which clung to it that Ptolemy came behind and cut him to the ground. Then the murderer leapt upon a horse and galloped to the camp at Lysimachia.

SOURCES.—Plutarch, *Dem.*; Polyaen. iv. 9, 2 f.; Justin xv. 4, 23; xvii. 2, 5; App. *Syr.* 56 f.; Paus. i. 10; 16; Memnon, 8 f. (*F.H.G.* iii. p. 532).

CHAPTER VII

THE PROBLEMS OF ASIA MINOR

§ 1. *The Accession of Antiochus I*

THE murder of Seleucus fulfilled the hopes of Ptolemy Keraunos and brought back chaos. Once more the Empire, on the point of regaining its unity, found itself headless. Seleucus indeed, unlike Alexander, left a grown-up heir, but by the time that the couriers, flying post across Asia, had told the tidings in Babylon, other hands had already clutched the inheritance. The army was lost. When Ptolemy suddenly appeared in the camp at Lysimachia wearing the diadem and attended by a royal guard, the mass of the army was taken completely by surprise. Ptolemy had prepared his ground well. He had already tampered with many of the officers. The army, bewildered and without direction, acquiesced in the *fait accompli*. It put itself at the disposal of the murderer.

Antiochus, the son of Seleucus, found that, instead of succeeding quietly to the great heritage, it was only by a stiff fight he might hope to piece together a kingdom from the fragments. The prince upon whom this task fell had some things in his favour. In the first place, his hold upon the eastern provinces was firm. His mother, it must be remembered, was of Irânian race, and those peoples might naturally cleave to a king who, by half his blood, was one of themselves. Through his mother many perhaps of the grandees of Irân were his kindred. He had actually resided, as joint-king, for the last twelve years (293-281) in the East; and this must not only have confirmed the influence which he owed to his birth, but have made him specially acquainted with the

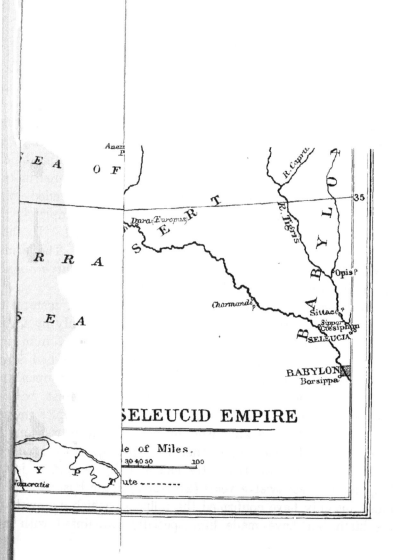

local conditions. It had also trained him in the practice of government. Again, he was not without experience of war. In the battle of Ipsus he, a youth of little over twenty, had measured himself with Demetrius the Besieger; nor can he have been for twelve years ruler of Irân without having to do with the unruly tribes who made the mountain and desert dangerous for travellers. Then he held Babylonia, the richest province of the Empire. He would probably take into the conflict a longer purse than that of any prince, save perhaps the Egyptian Ptolemy.

These were his advantages in the East, but he had some in the West as well. To the Greek states of the coast Seleucus had come as a deliverer from the tyranny of Lysimachus; their hearts were given to his house. At any rate they might be inclined to look more favourably on a rule which was still prospective than on those whose burden they had learned to know. We shall soon examine, so far as can be known, how at this juncture they acted.

All these circumstances would tell on the side of Antiochus in the long run, but they did not counterbalance the immediate inconveniences of his position. In the first place, he was surprised far from the scene of action, embarrassed at the start; in the second place, the defection of a great part of the imperial army left him for the time being terribly short of men. However, he strikes in rapidly, hurrying westward, and the first of all those wars for the restoration of the Empire of Seleucus begins.

For us a great cloud comes down upon the contest. History has mainly forgotten it. We can only see dim glints of armies that sweep over Western Asia, and are conscious of an imbroglio of involved wars. But we can understand the stupendous nature of that task which the house of Seleucus set itself to do—to hold together under one sceptre, against all the forces which battered it from without, forces stronger than any by which the Achaemenian Empire had ever been assailed till the coming of Alexander, against all the elements of disruption which sapped it within, the huge fabric built up by Seleucus Nicator. It was a labour of Sisyphus. The Empire, a magnificent *tour de force*, had no natural vitality. Its history from the moment it misses the founder's hand is one of decline. It was a "sick man" from its birth. Its construction occupied the few glorious years of Seleucus Nicator, its dissolution the succeeding two and a quarter centuries. Partially restored again and again, it lapses almost immediately into new ruin. The restorations become less and less complete. But it does a great work in propagating and defending Hellenism in the East till the advent of Rome.

The natural clefts of the Empire, the fissures which were so apt at any weakening of the central authority to gape, followed geographical barriers. From Northern Syria the western provinces were cut off by the line of the Taurus; on the east the desert separated it from the seats of Assyrio-Babylonian civilization, and beyond that again the mountain-wall of Zagrus fenced Irân. To hold these geographically detached members from a single base is the standing problem. The long struggle for each one has a more or less separate history. In the following chapters it is proposed to follow that of the struggle for Asia Minor—the Trans-Tauric Question, if one may use the modern phrase—till the accession of the third Antiochus, the king under whom it was finally settled (281-223).

§ 2. *Asia Minor*

It is convenient to speak of the region in question as Asia Minor, although that term for it did not come into use till long after the Seleucids had passed away.[1] To them it was always "the country beyond the Taurus," or "on this side of the Taurus," according to the speaker's standpoint.[2] An oblong peninsula, washed by the Black Sea, the Aegean, and the Sea of Cyprus, it formed one of the main divisions of the ancient world, with a physical character, an ethnology, and a history of its own. In feature it is a sort of miniature Irân. Both are plateaus connected on the east and west respectively with

---

[1] First found in Orosius i. 2 (about 410 A.D.).

[2] ἡ ἐπὶ τάδε τοῦ Ταύρου. Polyb. iv. 2, 6, etc. Our "Asia Minor" does not in all points coincide with the "country beyond the Taurus"; it includes Cilicia, for example, which was regarded as being on the *Syrian* side of the Taurus.

the mountain complex of Armenia. In both a central desert is surrounded by a hill country, the nurse of rivers. But there is one great difference. At its opposite extremity to Armenia the Irânian plateau is shut in by the inhospitable world of Central Asia, whilst Asia Minor, at its western end, sinks in a series of warm, moist valleys and rich alluvial plains to the friendly Aegean. In size it bore no proportion to Irân; but, insignificant as on the map it appears by the side of its huge neighbour, this corner of their Empire called out the interest of Hellenic kings in ways in which Irân could not. In the first place, it formed the bridge between Asia and their motherland; their hearts always turned westward. In the second place, it was to a Greek full of historical associations; it was the *Asia* which his fathers had known when Irân was an undiscovered world; its names were familiar to him since his childhood; Ilion, Sardis, Gordium, such places figured large in his traditions as the seats of old-world barbaric princedoms, the theatre of heroic wars. Lastly, Hellenism had already taken firm root there; Greek influence had reached its more civilized races, Carians and Lycians; its western coast was as Greek as the Peloponnesus, occupied by a line of Greek cities which stood little behind Athens in riches, in culture, and in old renown.

During the long history of which it had been an important part, Asia Minor had never had either national or political unity. There was no *people* of Asia Minor. Since dim antiquity wandering races from every quarter had streamed into it, making the confusion of its motley tribe worse confounded. It has furnished ethnologists, ancient and modern, with a puzzle which has the charm of never being able to be found out. Its predominant languages seem to have belonged to the Aryan family; and there is good ground for believing that the races in its north-western region, Phrygians, Mysians, and Bithynians, were of one stock with the Thracians on the European shore. There had never been a kingdom or empire of Asia, as there had been an Egyptian, an Assyrian, and an Irânian. Perhaps if the Mermnad dynasty in Lydia had had time it might have created such an empire. But it came into collision prematurely with the rising power of Persia and was shattered (547-546 B.C.). Thenceforward over the whole of Asia Minor, with its farrago of peoples, languages, and religions, was drawn the prevalence of one alien race, of an Irânian Great King.

§ 3. *Persian Rule*

(a) *The Native Races*

Persian rule in Asia Minor, however, had ado to maintain itself. It was beset by three great difficulties. One of these was presented by the native races. As a matter of fact, the Persian subjugation of Asia Minor was very incomplete, according to our standard in such things. As in the rest of the Empire, the arm of the central government never reached far from the great highroads. The mountain people went on with their old life and obeyed their hereditary chiefs with the occasional necessity of supplying men or tribute to the Great King. Their independence fluctuated according to the circumstances of the moment, the energy of a neighbouring satrap, their own power of resistance. Sometimes the government could save its face and its pocket by recognizing the native chief as imperial satrap in return for a due payment of tribute. But such a state of things has been the normal one, as was said before, in Asiatic empires.

The eastern and northern part of the country beyond the Taurus was known to the Persians as *Katpatuka*, a name which the Greeks transformed into Cappadocia (Kappadokia). The region designated embraced the eastern tract of the bare central uplands and the belt of mountain country, forest-clad, seamed with rivers, which comes between those uplands and the Black Sea. Its native inhabitants belonged to all sorts of different breeds. In old Assyrian days the two great races here had been the Meshech and Tubal of our Bibles, and the remains of them still held on in the land among later comers, and were known as Moschi and Tibareni to the Greeks. Under Persian rule a foreign Irânian aristocracy, priestly and lay, had settled down upon the nearer part, at any rate, of Cappadocia, great barons and prelates, living in castles and burgs, among the subject peoples, like the Normans in England.¹ To these incomers the old inhabitants stood as serfs, tilling their estates, hewing their wood and drawing their water generation after generation.² We never hear of any revolt among the Cappadocian peasants. In fact, all communication of the court with the Aegean sea-board by way of the Cilician Gates must go through the Cappadocian plateau, and one or other of the roads that ran through it was always one of the main arteries of the Empire.³ But in the more outlying parts of the province, among the mountains and along the northern coast, a very different state of things prevailed. Here the King's government was a mere shadow, or less. Even in that part of the Taurus which overlooked Cilicia, in the Cataonian highlands, there were clans which knew no law except their own.⁴ Along the Black Sea coast, again, Greek writers give us a catalogue of independent tribes.⁵ When Xenophon went that way in 400 he found himself quite outside the sphere of Persian rule. Towards the mouth of the Halys the coast population became more predominantly Paphlagonian, and west of the Halys the Paphlagonian country proper extended to the Parthenius.⁶

The Paphlagonians were barbarians of the same stamp as their neighbours, but they had made a step in the direction of national unity. East of the Halys there was in 400 only a chaos of petty tribes, following each its own will, but strong men had arisen among the Paphlagonians who had hammered them together into some consistency. As a military power even, the Paphlagonian principality was not to be despised; they furnished a fine type of barbaric cavalry.⁷ Their chief, Corylas, openly flouted the Great King's ban.⁸ Officially, he was by the usual device styled the King's satrap;⁹ it was explained at court that the Paphlagonians had no *Persian* satrap over them by the

---

¹ Nepos, *Dat.* 4; cf. Polyb. xxxi. 17, 1 (τοὺς ἡγεμόνας); Strabo xii. 535 f.
² Isidorus of Pelusium, *Ep.* i. 487.   ³ Reinach, *Mithridates*, p. 24.
⁴ Nepos, *Dat.* 4; Plutarch, *Dem.* 47.
⁵ Καρδοῦχοι δὲ καὶ Χάλυβες καὶ Χαλδαῖοι καὶ Μάκρωνες καὶ Κόλχοι καὶ Μοσσύνοικοι καὶ Κοῖται καὶ Τιβαρηνοὶ αὐτόνομοι. Pseudo-Xen. *Anab.* vii. 8, 25; cf. Reinach, *Mith.* p. 14, and the references there given.
⁶ Reinach, *Mith.* p. 13.   ⁷ Xen. *Anab.* i. 8, 5; v. 6, 8.
⁸ *Ibid.* v. 6, 8.   ⁹ Pseudo-Xen. *Anab.* vii. 8, 26.

King's favour, because they had joined Cyrus of their own accord.¹

Otys, the successor of Corylas, was equally contumacious (393).² Some fifteen years later (about 378)³ the Paphlagonian prince, Thuÿs, was captured by the unusually able satrap of Cappadocia, Datames, and for a spell the King's word was of force in Paphlagonia.⁴ The importance of this country to the Persian government was derived largely from the trade-route which found its outlet to the Black Sea in the Greek city of Sinope, the great mart of the northern coast. An independent Paphlagonia cut off the government from this gate of the kingdom. And after the capture of Thuÿs the country seems to have remained to some extent at any rate in the hand of Persian satraps. Datames laid siege to Sinope itself about 369⁵ and got possession of Amisus.⁶ Coins are found of the Sinopean type which bear his name in Greek.⁷ Others, of the same type, but apparently somewhat later, bear in the official Aramaïc script a name which seems to be 'Abd-susin (עבדסס). These, it is thought, were struck by a successor of Datames, perhaps by his son, whom Nepos calls Sysinas.⁸ Others, still Sinopean, have the name Ariōrath (Ariarathes).⁹ This last is, no doubt, the same Ariarathes who, at the coming of Alexander, was established in the northern and mountainous part of the Cappadocian province farther east. His castle seems to have been at Gaziūra in the valley of the Iris,¹⁰ and he strikes money with the figure and name of the local Baal (Baʻal-Gazir).¹¹ In what degree of dependence Ariarathes stood to the central government may be questionable; he was at any rate an Irânian lord, and his presence in Paphlagonia and Northern Cappadocia shows that these regions had been penetrated in the last days of the Achaemenian Empire, if not by the

---

¹ Xen. *Cyrop.* viii. 6, 8.   ² Xen. *Hell.* iv. 1, 3.
³ Judeich, *Kleinasiatische Studien*, p. 192, note 1.
⁴ Nepos, *Dat.* 2 f.   ⁵ Polyaen. vii. 21, 1 ; 5.
⁶ Arist. *Oec.* ii. 2, 24 ; cf. Judeich, p. 193 f.
⁷ Babelon, *Perses Achém.* p. xl.
⁸ Six, *Num. Chron.* 1894, p. 302 f. ; Marquart, *Philol.* liv. (1895), p. 493 f.
⁹ Babelon, *Perses Achém.* p. lxxxiii. It does not seem to me necessarily to follow from the coins being of Sinopean type that they were struck *at* Sinope, as Babelon says.
¹⁰ Strabo xii. 547.   ¹¹ Babelon, *Perses Achém.* p. lxxxiii.

authority of the Great King, at any rate by Persian influence. The Paphlagonians do not appear to have been politically under Ariarathes in 336. They had again ceased to pay tribute,[1] and they send, as an independent nation, ambassadors to Alexander.[2]

Beyond Paphlagonia, at the north-western corner of the peninsula, the dark pine forests and mountain pastures which lay above the entrance of the Black Sea were tenanted by two kindred tribes whom the Greeks knew as Thynians and Bithynians. Sometimes they spoke of them by the latter name as a single people. They were Thracian immigrants from the opposite shore, and had the same characteristics as their European cousins, savage hardihood, wild abandonment to the frenzy of religion and of war. The terror of them kept the Greeks from making any settlement along their coast, from Calchedon to Heraclea, and woe betide the mariner driven to land there![3] The Greeks on their side took, when they could, fearful reprisals. In 416 the Calchedonians procured the help of Byzantium, enrolled Thracian mercenaries to meet the Bithynians at their own game, and made a raid into their country which was long remembered for the atrocities which marked it.[4]

The Bithynians, like the Paphlagonians, found leaders able to draw together under one head the elemental forces which exist in rude and unbroken races. During the latter part of the fifth century a chief called Dœdalsus appears to hold in Bithynia the same sort of position as Corylas in Paphlagonia. In 435 the town of Astacus in the Propontis was refounded as an Athenian colony.[5] It was well fitted by its situation to take a leading part in the coast traffic, but up to this time its advantages had been neutralized by the chronic warfare it had to maintain with the neighbouring Bithynians. It had sunk lower and lower. From its new foundation, however, it rapidly rose to new prosperity. And this was in large part due, we are given to understand, to the rational policy of Dœdalsus, who about that time got his wild countrymen into hand, and

---

[1] Curt. iii. 1, 23. [2] Arr. ii. 4, 1.
[3] Xen. *Anab.* vi. 4, 1. [4] Diod. xii. 82.
[5] *Ibid.* xii. 34. Read Ἀστακόν for Λέτανον, Niese.

saw his profit in protecting the Greek cities of the coast. Bithynia was beginning to become conscious as a new-born state and learn the uses of the world.[1] How far the success of Dœdalsus in bringing the Bithynians under his single sway went we do not know; in 409 there is an indication of disunion among the tribes.[2] But Dœdalsus established a dynasty which served at all events as the *nucleus* of a national kingdom. And his house had better fortune than the neighbouring Paphlagonian. The power of *that* the Persian overlord succeeded in breaking, but Dœdalsus and his successors were too much for him. The Bithynians were a thorn in the side of the satrap of Hellespontine Phrygia, to whose government they nominally belonged. Although Pharnabazus might combine with them in opposition to a common foe, like Xenophon's Ten Thousand,[3] he normally regarded their domain as hostile territory, which he was glad enough to see ravaged.[4] The dynasty of Dœdalsus survived all the onsets of the Achaemenian Empire; it outlasted that Empire itself, and in the closing century before Christ, when all the face of the world was changed, and powers that Dœdalsus never knew possessed it, his line still reigned, the relic of an older day, beside the Bosphorus.

We have seen that all the mountain country along the north of Asia Minor, from the Phasis to the Bosphorus, was a region from which the authority of the Great King was excluded. It was only now and then that, thanks to the exertions of a Datames, Persian rule could break through this wall at some point to the Black Sea. But the case was just as bad in the south of the peninsula. Here, too, Persian rule was shut off from the sea by a long stretch of mountains which it could never subdue, the mountains lying on the left hand of the road which ran from the Cilician Gates westward. They were inhabited by hardy marauding tribes, whose

---

[1] Memnon 20 = *F. H. G.* iii. p. 536. The statement of Strabo xii. 563, that Dœdalsus refounded Astacus as a Bithynian city after the Athenian refoundation, seems to be questionable, Töpffer, *Hermes* xxxi. (1896) p. 124 f.

[2] Seven years after their savage raid the Calchedonians, when threatened by an Athenian fleet, entrust their money to some *friendly* Bithynians, Xen. *Hell.* i. 3.

[3] Xen. *Anab.* vi. 4, 24.   [4] *Ibid. Hell.* iii. 2, 2.

ethnology indeed may be obscure, but whose general character and manner of life were like that of the other highlanders of Asia Minor. They not only held their country against the imperial armies, but made the King's highroad insecure.[1] The Lycaonians, who lived in that part of the mountains nearest the Cilician Gates, had even descended into the central plain in 401 and made something like a regular occupation of the country.[2] The names which Greek writers apply to these mountain tribes and their several territories are as shifting and uncertain as the relations of the tribes themselves and their frontiers. In the fourth century a name, unknown to Herodotus, embracing all the mountaineers between the coast peoples and the inner plateau, comes into use, that of *Pisidians* (Xenophon, Ephorus, Theopompus). The name by which Herodotus had indicated the inhabitants of this region, Milyes, was now restricted to those of the most westerly part of it, the *Hinterland* of Lycia, the region Milyas, regarded sometimes as identical with, sometimes as including, another familiar to Herodotus, that of Cabalis.[3] The people again in the country along the coast between Rough Cilicia and Lycia, where the mountains leave only a strip of level land a few miles broad between themselves and the sea, a people whom the Greeks had always known as Pamphylians, were in reality simply Pisidians somewhat civilized by contact with the outside world and the Hellenes.[4]

West of the Pamphylians the mountains gather into a mass, which bulges in a semicircular projection, 180 miles across, into the sea. The uplands of this promontory—the region, that is, which the Greeks called Milyas—are shrouded from our knowledge in the times before Alexander by barbarian darkness. Their contours merged in the Pisidian hills, and the hard-faring mountaineers who ranged over them, the Solymi, lived and died, no doubt, in the same sort of way as their Pisidian and Pamphylian neighbours. But along the sea-board of the promontory, and in the three river valleys, those of the Xanthus, the Myrus, and the Limyrus, which run

---

[1] Xen. *Anab.* ii. 5, 13 ; iii. 2, 23.   [2] *Ibid.* iii. 2, 23.
[3] Forbiger, *Handbuch der alten Geographie*, ii. p. 323.
[4] Hdt. vii. 91.

up from the coast, dwelt the ancient people of the Lycians.¹ In them we have a very different type from the rude highlanders with whom we have hitherto had to deal. The Lycians, from whatever dim origins they sprang, stood in character near to the Hellenes. It would be straying from our path to discuss the part they play in the heroic age of Greek legend—those mysterious people who seemed to the simple fathers of the Hellenes a race of wizards, able to make enormous stones dance together into magic palaces, whom yet the light of the historic age shows so primitive, that they still reckoned descent by the mother. In the time of the Persian Empire the Lycians did not yet form the developed federal republic which we find described in Strabo. They were distributed under the rule of a number of petty princes, whose names we still read on their coins. Such a state of things must have meant a good deal of internal friction. And we find, in fact, essays on the part of a single dynast to oust the others and make himself chief of the whole nation. Such an attempt was made by the son of Harpagus (his name is obliterated), who put up the *stele* in Xanthus; he "took many citadels by the help of Athene, the sacker of cities, and gave a portion of his kingdom to his kin."²

King Pericles, who captured Telmessus (about 370?), seems to have almost succeeded for a time.³ But these efforts failed in the end before internal resistance or foreign attack. At the same time, in spite of the divisions, there appears to have existed among the Lycians some rudimentary recognition of national unity.⁴ The symbol which is thought to be connected with the Apollo of Xanthus occurs on all sorts of Lycian coins, and is held to show some kind of sacred Amphictyony⁵ formed about a central shrine of the Sun-god.

¹ Their original settlement seems to have been in the Xanthus valley, their extension eastwards to have proceeded during the Persian period.

² πο]λλὰs δὲ ἀκροπόλεις σὺν Ἀθηναίᾳ πτολιπόρθωι
π]έρσας συγγενέσιν δῶκε μέρος βασιλέας.

The text is given in the new Corpus of the Greek inscriptions of Asia, No. 44, and in the new edition of Hicks (Hicks and Hill), No. 56.

³ Theopompus, frag. 111 = *F.H.G.* i. p. 296; Polyaen. v. 42.

⁴ They pay tribute to Athens as a single people, Λύκιοι καὶ συν[τελεῖς], *C. I. Att.* i. No. 234.

⁵ Treuber, p. 112; Babelon, *Perses Achém.* p. xc.

Two main external influences were at work upon the inner life of Lycia during the Persian period, the Irânian and the Hellenic. It is, of course, impossible to gauge either from the few traces we can now discover. The Irânian influence is shown in the dress of the Lycian princes, as they appear on the monuments and in the names (Harpagus, Artembases, Mithrapatas) which some of them bear. The Hellenic influence, on the other hand, is shown by the name of King Pericles and by the witness of the monuments, some, like the Nereïd monument, the very work of Attic masters, and others exhibiting a style in which native elements and Greek are combined.

Between the conquest of Asia Minor by the Persians and the coming of Alexander we can make out four phases in Lycian history. The *first* is one of subjection to the Achaemenian power. Their resistance at the beginning had been forlornly heroic—one desperate battle against overwhelming numbers, and then the self-immolation of the whole people of Xanthus, except eighty households, who happened at the time to be away.[1] After that they had to pay tribute into the Great King's treasury and give their youth for his armies. The *second* phase is introduced by the operations of Cimon in Asia Minor (466 ?), whereby the Persian power in these regions is crippled. Lycia now throws off the Persian yoke to enter the League over which Athens presides.[2] How long this phase lasted is uncertain. In 446 the Lycians are still paying tribute to Athens;[3] in 430 a *third* phase has begun, the Lycians are raided as an unfriendly nation by the Athenian admiral Melesander.[4] How far the Lycians in this third phase fell again under Persian influence, how far they attained an independence both of Persia and Athens, is impossible to determine. In 380 the orator Isocrates declares with some inaccuracy that Lycia has *never* had a Persian master.[5] It is during this period that we have the attempts of the son of Harpagus and of King Pericles to consolidate Lycia under their own rule. This third phase is closed by

[1] Hdt. i. 176.   [2] Diod. xi. 60.
[3] *C. I. Att.* i. No. 234.   [4] Thuc. ii. 69.
[5] Λυκίας δ' οὐδεὶς πώποτε Περσῶν ἐκράτησεν, Isocr. *Paneg.* 161.

the Lycians (under Pericles, perhaps) taking part with the satraps in the great revolt against the house of Achaemenes. Maussollus, the Carian dynast who betrayed the confederation, is authorized by the Persian King to add Lycia to his dominions. This he succeeds in doing, and the *fourth* phase is one of annexation to Caria.[1]

The Carians in the fourth century are in a state of semi-dependence upon the Persian King. They are governed by a dynasty of native princes, who are, however, recognized as satraps of the Empire. The loyalty of these princes to the Achaemenian King fluctuates; Maussollus first joins in the rebellion of the satraps and then deserts it in 362. But the Carians are now no longer the race of barbarian fighting men who might be distinguished by their large crests alongside of the Greek mercenaries two or three centuries before. It is on their coasts that some of the illustrious Greek cities stand—Miletus and Halicarnassus,—and the old Carian towns inland have more or less taken on the character of Greek cities themselves. They formed, not improbably, a federation, with the temple of Zeus Chrysaoreus for its religious centre. And these Carian cities seem to have cherished all the Hellenic aspirations after autonomy; the yoke of their princes they found very grievous, and Maussollus lived in a web of conspiracies.[2] But prince and people alike were open to the influences of Hellenism. The decrees of the city of Mylasa are in Greek; Maussollus, who had extended his power over the Greek cities of the coast and made Halicarnassus his

[1] Whether the Carian rule in Lycia continued till the advent of Alexander is not certain. Treuber supposes the Carian yoke to have been shaken off when Idrieus lost the King's good-will. But of this there is no evidence at all. See Judeich, *Kleinasiatische Studien*, p. 253.

Authorities for Lycia: Sir C. Fellows, *Travels and Researches in Asia Minor* (1852). *The Inscribed Monument at Xanthos* (1842). W. Moritz Schmidt, *The Lycian Inscriptions*, Jena (1868). J. P. Six, *Monnaies lyciennes*. O. Treuber, *Geschichte der Lykier* (1887). O. Benndorf and G. Niemann, *Reisen in Lykien und Karien* (1884-1889). Babelon, *Perses Achéménides* (1893), p. lxxxix. f. [The theories of J. Imbert (*Babylonian and Oriental Record*, vol. iv. (1890), p. 153 f.; vol. v. (1891), p. 105 f.; vol. vi. p. 185 f.; vol. vii. (1894), p. 87 f.) appear to me too fanciful to have any scientific value.] To these must now be added vol. i. of the Vienna Corpus, by Kalinka, *Tituli Asiae Minoris*.

[2] Michel, Nos. 460, 471. See Judeich, *Kleinasiatische Studien*, p. 236 f.

capital, was buried in the "Mausoleum," designed and decorated by Scopas and others of the greatest Greek sculptors.[1]

Cut off thus by barbarian peoples from both the northern and the southern coast of Asia Minor, the King's government was confined to a strip of country running through the interior. The Cappadocian plateau, the two Phrygian provinces and Lydia, it was only here that mandates from Babylon ran, and even here there were districts, like the Mysian hills, which their authority could not penetrate.[2] Besides the Cappadocian serfs, it was only the Lydians and Phrygians, now a race of patient husbandmen dispersed in poor villages,[3] though their name had once been greatest among the peoples of the land— it was only these who were beaten flat by the Achaemenian conquest. But though the King's arm reached over Lydia, his hold on the western coast also was vexatiously restricted. His rule here encountered, not barbarian races, but an obstacle in some ways more formidable still.

(b) *The Asiatic Greeks*

The second difficulty which beset Persian rule in Asia Minor consisted in the occupation of a great part of the coasts by Greek cities. Here was something which in itself created a problem for any power aspiring to rule Asia. Under any circumstances these Hellenes, with their inbred abhorrence of everything which restricted the sovereign autonomy of each city-state, with their inveterate assumption of a higher culture, were bound to form an indigestible element in an Asiatic monarchy. But, left to themselves, they might be held down by an arm as long and as mighty as the King's. Here, however, came in the circumstance which so dangerously complicated the problem. On the other side of the sea and in the intermediate islands, the free Greeks were established in their sea-faring republics. So that, while on the one hand the Asiatic Greeks had kinsmen at their back whom they might call in, on the other hand the free Greeks found the door held

---

[1] Large remains of the Mausoleum, it is hardly necessary to say, are in the British Museum—including the statue of Maussollus himself.
[2] Xen. *Anab.* ii. 5, 13; iii. 2, 23.   [3] Curt. iii. 1, 11; vi. 11, 4.

open for them whenever they might attack. To hold the coast against a combination of the Greeks who inhabited it and the Greeks who came in from beyond—fighting men better than any the Asiatic monarch could command—was obviously impossible. There was some method in the madness of Xerxes when he set out to trample down European Greece; it was a measure of self-defence. This was shown by what followed the great failure. During the days of Athenian power in the fifth century the Persian king had even to acquiesce in the humiliation of not being allowed to send any troops within a prescribed distance of his own coast, or ships of war west of the Bosphorus or the Chelidonian promontory.[1]

Then the wars of Athens and Sparta suggested to him a better way of isolating the Asiatic Greeks—the policy of playing off one Greek state against another. And this design the brutal egoism of Sparta made at last successful. By the Peace of Antalcidas (387-386) the Persians regained possession of the western coast of Asia Minor, and held it unchallenged by the states of Greece till the coming of Alexander.

We are very imperfectly informed as to the condition of the Greek states under Achaemenian rule, how far the normal functioning of each body politic was interfered with by the paramount power. Generally speaking, the cities were probably no worse off under Persian than under Spartan, or even Athenian, supremacy. In all these cases the two chief burdens were the same—the necessity of paying tribute and the occupation by a foreign garrison. The weight with which the King's hand pressed must have differed greatly from city to city, or even in the same city at different moments. Some, like Cyzicus, seem to have maintained their independence unimpaired by the Peace of Antalcidas. Others from time to time threw off the yoke for longer or shorter periods.[2] Where a city was held by a military force, the garrison was composed probably in most cases, not of Orientals, but of Greek mercenaries.[3] Here and there we have indications of the King's authority reaching the internal administration. Iasus in conferring *ateleia* has to

---

[1] Whether there was an actual treaty to this effect is, of course, doubtful.
[2] Judeich, *Kleinasiatische Studien*, p. 260 f.
[3] Arr. *Anab.* i. 17, 9; 18, 4 f.; 24, 4.

limit its grant to those dues over which the city has control.¹ At Mylasa it looks as if the right of inflicting the punishment of death was reserved to the King.² But both Mylasa and Iasus were under the Carian dynast who acted as the King's satrap. Often, no doubt, the Persian government thought it enough to maintain in power tyrants and oligarchies, leaving them a free hand in internal administration so long as they sent in the tribute.³ When we ask whether the cities were generally prosperous or not in the days before Alexander, we have conflicting evidence. Isocrates paints their condition in the blackest colours. "It is not enough that they should be subjected to tribute, that they should see their citadels in the occupation of their foes, but besides these public miseries they must yield their persons to worse usage than the bondmen which we buy and sell meet with among us. No one of us puts injuries upon his slaves so bad as the punishments they (*i.e.* the Persians) mete out to free men."⁴ Such a description, coming from Isocrates, is not to be taken too literally; but so much we may gather from it, that the Persian rule provoked a certain amount of discontent. On the other side we have testimonies to the increasing wealth and fulness of life in the Greek cities of Asia given us by their coins, their literary and artistic activity, and the great works whose beginning goes back to this period.⁵

(c) *The Provincial Nobility*

The mountain tribes and the Greek cities circumscribed Persian rule in Asia Minor; there was a third element there which threatened, not the supremacy of the Irânian race, but the supremacy of the house of Achaemenes. This element was the disaffection of the Irânian nobility in Asia Minor towards their overlord. It had been hard from the early days of Persian rule for the court in Babylon to keep a perfect control over its own satraps in Asia Minor. The satraps had almost

---

¹ ἀτέλειαν πάντων ὧν ἡ πόλις κυρία ἐστιν, *C.I.G.* No. 2673.
² *C.I.G.* No. 2691 c.
³ *E.g.* Syrphax in Ephesus, Arr. *Anab.* i. 17; Suidas, *s.v.*   ⁴ *Paneg.* 123.
⁵ *E.g.* the temples of Ephesus and Priene, Judeich, p. 262 f.

the station of petty kings. To remove a powerful governor was a matter in which the government had to proceed delicately, as the story of Orœtes shows.[1] Tissaphernes had to be surprised and assassinated.[2] They raised mercenary troops and made war on their own account, sometimes against each other; they issued coins in their own name.

Beside the provincial satraps there were a number of Irânian families settled down on estates, not only in Cappadocia but in the western sea-board. We hear, for instance, in Xenophon of the Persian Asidates, who has a castle in the neighbourhood of Pergamos,[3] and the Itabelius who comes to his assistance is probably another Persian lord established hard by. The family of Pharnabazus stands in close connexion with Hellespontine Phrygia; to this house all the satraps of the country belong,[4] and the son of Ariobarzanes (satrap from 387 to 362), Mithridates, who does not himself ever become satrap, appears to have ruled a small principality which included the Greek city of Cius.[5] How dangerous to the King this provincial aristocracy might be the repeated revolts are enough to show.

§ 4. *The Macedonian Conquest*

These, then—the native races, the Greek cities and the Irânian nobility—were the three elements making up the problem of Asia Minor when the house of Achaemenes was in the ascendant. But by the time that Asia Minor fell to the house of Seleucus to be dealt with, the conditions had been in one circumstance significantly modified. Fifty years before that date Irânian had given place to Greek overlords. By this change the relation of the different elements to the supreme government had been variously affected. One immediate result was that the resident Irânian nobility, as a class distinct at once from the imperial house and the native tribes, disappeared. Some of them joined the train of one or other of the Macedonian chiefs, as Mithridates, the dynast of

---

[1] Hdt. iii. 128.   [2] Diod. xiv. 80, 8.
[3] *Anab.* vii. 8, 9 f.   [4] Nöldeke, *Gött. gelehr. Anz.* 1884, p. 294 f.
[5] Marquart, *Philologus* liv. (1895), p. 490.

Cius, did that of Antigonus;[1] others, like the son of this Mithridates, sought to evade the foreign yoke by taking to the hill countries and forming principalities among the native tribes, of the same category as the principalities we have seen in Bithynia and Paphlagonia, only with this feature, that at their courts in remote valleys a distinctly Irânian tradition lived on. When, therefore, one speaks of the problem of the *native* races under Greek overlords, there are included in the term the dynasties of Irânian as well as those of more strictly native origin.

There were still, however, three elements constituting the Trans-Tauric problem, for the difficulty felt by the Achaemenian court in maintaining a due control over its Irânian subordinates was no greater than the difficulty of a Greco-Macedonian court in controlling from a distant centre its Greek subordinates. We have now to consider how up to the time when the house of Seleucus entered into possession these three elements had been dealt with by the new rulers of the world.

(a) *The Native Races*

The native races, as we have seen, had some of them been completely subjugated by the Persians, others imperfectly, and others not at all. In what measure the first of these, the Lydians, Phrygians, and Southern Cappadocians, were affected by the change of masters we have hardly any means of determining. The Phrygians of the north-west were ordered by Alexander to "pay the same tribute as they had paid to Darius."[2] Under Antigonus they seem to have found themselves exceptionally well off, or perhaps it was only that they looked back to his days as a reign of gold from the troublous times which ensued.[3] The Carians were left under their

---

[1] We find an Aribazus as governor of Cilicia in 246-245 (see p. 185), and another Aribazus as governor of Sardis under Antiochus III, Polyb. vii. 17, 9. These may have been representatives of the Irânian families settled in Asia Minor.

[2] Arr. *Anab.* i. 17, 1.

[3] Plutarch, *Phoc.* 39. Arr. says of Alexander (*Anab.* i. 17, 4), Σαρδιανοὺς δὲ καὶ τοὺς ἄλλους Λυδοὺς τοῖς νόμοις τε τοῖς πάλαι Λυδῶν χρῆσθαι ἔδωκε καὶ ἐλευθέρους εἶναι ἀφῆκεν. It is very difficult to say what this implies. The Persian government is not likely to have interfered with the customs of the

native dynasty, represented by the Princess Ada—perhaps only temporarily, as the dynasty has disappeared by Alexander's death. The unsubjugated races, on the other hand, had cause to feel that a different hand held the reins. A Greek ruler could not tolerate the old slipshod methods, the indolent compromises, which mark the monarchies of Asia. Alexander seems to have made up his mind at once to put an end to the turbulent independence of the highlanders which rendered the King's highway insecure. In his passage through Asia Minor he found time, although intent on greater things, to make a winter expedition into the hills behind Lycia, the Milyas region,[1] to destroy a fort of the Pisidians which vexed Phaselis,[2] and push his way through the heart of the Pisidian country, storming Sagalassus. A year later he had crossed the Taurus never to return. But the subjugation of Asia Minor was to be methodically pursued by his generals. They do not seem to have been particularly successful. Calas, the satrap of Hellespontine Phrygia, marched an elaborately equipped force into the Bithynian country, but was overpowered by Bas, the grandson of Dœdalsus.[3] Balacrus, the satrap of Cilicia, perished in the attempt to reduce the Pisidian strongholds, Laranda and Isaura.[4]

At the death of Alexander in 323 a good part of Asia Minor had still to be registered as unsubdued. The northern regions had been hardly touched by the Macedonian arms.[5] Alexander in 333, hastening on to meet Darius, had been forced to be content with the formal expressions of homage brought him at Gordium by a deputation from the Paphlagonian chiefs. How far from complete their submission had been was shown by the fact that they expressly stipulated that none of the imperial troops should cross their borders.[6]

Lydian villages beyond making its demand for tribute and men, and Alexander is not likely to have remitted these demands. We may conjecture that it applies rather to the Lydian *cities*, which, while retaining undoubtedly a reverence for many ancestral customs, had become more or less Hellenized, and received accordingly the favoured treatment accorded to Greek cities.

[1] Arr. *Anab.* i. 24, 5.   [2] *Ibid.* 24, 6.
[3] Memnon 20 = *F.H.G.* iii. p. 537.   [4] Diod. xviii. 22, 1.
[5] *Ibid.* 3, 1.
[6] Arr. *Anab.* ii. 4, 1. Curtius (iii. 1, 23) says that they even stipulated that they should pay no tribute.

Farther east, in the valley of the Iris, the Irânian prince, Ariarathes, continued unmolested to form a great power out of the materials supplied him by the hardy mountain races. He had by 323 at his disposal an army of 30,000 foot and 15,000 horse.[1]

To the south the tribes of the Taurus were as independent as ever, unless some permanent occupation of the route opened by Alexander by way of Sagalassus had been maintained. Termessus, the great fortress of Western Pisidia, commanding the road between Perga and the interior, remained, as Alexander had left it, unhumbled.[2] Selge, the rival Pisidian town, had made indeed a treaty with Alexander, but with the express declaration that it was as a *friend*, not as a subject, that it was prepared to comply with the rescripts.[3] Still farther west, the hills behind Lycia, the regions called Milyas and Cabalis, lay, as far as we can tell, beyond the reach of Macedonian arms. Cibyra, with a population of mixed origins, Lydian and Pisidian, was probably already a strong mountain state under native chiefs. A century and a half later its villages stretched from the Rhodian Peraea and the Lycian valleys to the confines of Termessus, and it could put an army of 30,000 foot and 2000 horse in the field.[4]

East of Selge, the hills as far as the Cilician Gates were, as far as we know, untouched ground. In fact it is impossible to trace any progress in the subjugation of Asia Minor from the date of Alexander's passage to the date of his death. Occupied in distant expeditions, he had hardly time to begin the work of consolidating. The abandonment of schemes of further conquest after his death gave the Regent Perdiccas scope for dealing with the omissions in Alexander's rapid work. In the year after Alexander died, Perdiccas was with the Kings in Asia Minor to support Eumenes, on whom, as satrap of Cappadocia and Paphlagonia, the task of subduing Ariarathes and any other native dynasties had been laid. Together Perdiccas and Eumenes, with the imperial army, advanced into northern Cappadocia. Ariarathes threw his native levies

---

[1] Diod. xviii. 16; cf. App. *Mith.* 8.
[2] Arr. *Anab.* i. 28, 2; Diod. xviii. 45.
[3] Arr. *Anab.* i. 28, 1; Strabo xii. 571.
[4] Strabo xiii. 631.

before them in vain. He lost two battles, and found himself and his house in the Macedonians' hands. Perdiccas treated him with the same cruel rigour which Asiatic kings had made the rule in the case of rebels. The old prince, now eighty-two, was crucified and his family destroyed. Eumenes immediately took measures to organize the province.[1]

From dealing with the northern part of Asia Minor, the Regent immediately went on to deal with the highlanders of the south. Laranda was stormed and its population exterminated. Siege was next laid to Isaura. Then the fierce tribesmen who held it acted with the same spirit which was displayed on other occasions by the peoples of the Taurus; they themselves set fire to the town and perished with their old men, their women and children, in one conflagration.[2]

At this point the new rulers seemed to be really in a fair way to carry their empire in Asia Minor to a logical completion, satisfactory to a Greek mind. That this would have been done had the Greek Empire remained a unity can hardly be doubted, just as it was done later on by Rome. But with the death of Perdiccas there ceased to be a single Greco-Macedonian power. The energies of the conquering aristocracy were almost entirely taken up with fighting each other. Asia Minor, it is true, fell, as a whole, under the dominion of a single chief, Antigonus; it was there even that the seat of his government was established; after the reconquest of Babylon and Irân by Seleucus it looked as if a separate kingdom of Asia Minor, under the house of Antigonus, might emerge from the confusion, like the kingdom of Egypt under the house of Ptolemy. But even though Asia Minor formed the peculiar possession of Antigonus, he was too much occupied with his Macedonian rivals to extend, or even to maintain, Greek rule internally.

In the south the conquest of the Pisidian country appears to have been suspended with the death of Perdiccas. Antigonus was drawn thither in 319-318, but it was not to subjugate the

---

[1] Diod. xviii. 16; xxxi. 19, 4; Plut. *Eum.* 3; Arr. Τὰ μετ' Ἀλέξανδρον, 11.

[2] Diod. xviii. 22; cf. the case of the Marmareis (Diod. xvii. 28) of Xanthus in the sixth century (Hdt. i. 176) and of Xanthus in 43 B.C. (App. *Bell. Civ.* iv. 81).

Pisidians that he came. It has been remarked that the inconvenience to Asiatic monarchies of unsubdued tracts within their confines arises not only from the depredations of the free tribes, but from the fact that any one opposed to the central government has these standing enemies of the central government to fall back upon for shelter and support. The partizans of Perdiccas, finding themselves after his death a weak minority, had made common cause with the disruptive elements within the realm of Antigonus. Alcetas, the Regent's brother, had long set himself, in view of contingencies, to gain popularity among the Pisidians. The young men who had been drawn from the hills to join the Macedonian armies[1] returned home to report how good a friend they had found in this great chief. And now in the day of his adversity the Pisidians received Alcetas and his companions with open arms. It was to track down his Macedonian rivals that Antigonus pushed with a great force into the Pisidian hills. When Alcetas had been delivered up to him by the old men of Termessus behind the back of the young men, who stood by their friend to the last, Antigonus withdrew satisfied. He did not attempt to reduce Termessus itself or effect anything like a permanent settlement of the country. All his energies were required for the great war.[2]

In the north his measures with regard to the native tribes were equally inconclusive. The heritage of Dœdalsus was still in strong hands; Ziboetes,[3] the son and successor of that Bas who had beaten back Alexander's general,[4] himself profited by the troubled times to descend from the Bithynian hills upon the Greek cities. In 315 he was besieging Astacus and Calchedon. Polemaeus, the general of Antigonus, passing that way, compelled him indeed to give up the attempt. But it was no time for reducing Bithynia. Polemaeus was obliged to

---

[1] It will be remembered how at the present time in India numberless men are attracted to the British standards from hill tribes which are still unsubjugated.

[2] Diod. xviii. 44 f.

[3] The accession of Ziboetes falls between 328 and 325, because he reigned forty-eight years (Memnon 20), and his death falls after the accession of Antiochus I (281-280), but before the coming of the Gauls to Asia (277).

[4] Memnon 20.

make some bargain with the Bithynian chieftain, which was embodied in an alliance.[1] The policy of compromise with regard to the non-Hellenic elements in Asia which marks the rule of Antigonus is seen in another instance—that of Mithridates. This Persian nobleman, whom the Achaemenian government had rewarded for betraying his father in 362-361 by making him dynast of Cius, had been dispossessed by Alexander. Mithridates became, after Alexander's death, a hanger-on of any Macedonian chief whose star seemed to be in the ascendant. At one time he fought under Eumenes.[2] Antigonus, rewarding probably his infidelity to Eumenes, reinstates him in his old lordship of Cius in 309-308; *he actually replaces a Greek city under a barbarian despot.* The son of the old intriguer, a younger Mithridates, became a bosom friend of Demetrius. Antigonus was nourishing a breed destined to play a chief part in reclaiming Asia Minor for the Irânian from the European, in sustaining the last fight which the barbarian fought in Asia Minor against Rome for seven hundred years.

As soon as the cause of Antigonus began to look bad Mithridates was at his old game of treason. Antigonus caught him making overtures to Cassander. He determined then to crush the serpent's brood, to make away with father and son together. The old Mithridates was put to death on his own domain, but the younger got a hint from Demetrius and fled.[3] He plunged into the mountains of Paphlagonia, and established himself at Cimiata under the Olgassys (mod. Ulgaz Dagh).[4] Thence he began fighting his way eastwards along the valley of the Amnias (mod. Gyuk Irmak), across the Halys, along the valley of the Iris (mod. Yeshil Irmak), drawing the hill peoples under him.

About the same time Macedonian rule was driven back at another point. Ariarathes, the son or nephew[5] of the old

---

[1] Diod. xix. 60.   [2] *Ibid.* 40.

[3] *Ibid.* xx. 111, 4; Plutarch, *Dem.* 4; App. *Mith.* 9. See Marquart, *Philologus*, liv. (1895) p. 490.

[4] Strabo xii. 562.

[5] He is called *son* of Ariarathes I in Diod. xxxi. 19, 5, but this, according to § 3, means son by adoption. He is there stated to have been the son of Holophernes, the brother of Ariarathes I, and to have been adopted by his uncle

prince whom Perdiccas had crucified in 322, had taken refuge with Ardoates, a petty king in Armenia. He now (302 or 301) appeared upon the scene with a band of Armenians and attacked Amyntas, the general of Antigonus in Cappadocia. Ariarathes was possibly acting in concert with Seleucus and other allied kings, who were drawing their forces together around Antigonus. Amyntas was killed and the Macedonian garrisons expelled.[1] The northern part of Cappadocia, the valley of the Iris, where the old Ariarathes had been strong, the younger either did not occupy or soon abandoned, since it passed within a few years, as we have seen, under the dominion of Mithridates. The principality which Ariarathes II carved out for himself lay more to the south, within the province indeed that the old Ariarathes, according to Diodorus, claimed as his, but covering how much of the later Cappadocian kingdom we do not know.

All this country, which now fell to the two Persians, had been organized twenty years before by Eumenes as a Macedonian province. But after the rapid Macedonian conquest of the East *the tide had already turned; in the reconquest of this territory by barbarians the long ebb of two and a half centuries had already begun.*

With the partition after Ipsus (301) Asia Minor ceases to form part of a single kingdom. Now for the first time Seleucus is brought into contact with the problem of its native races. The Bithynians indeed of the north-west, in so far more redoubtable than the two newly-founded principalities in Cappadocia that they had already sustained the shock of Macedonian arms, fell to the share of Lysimachus between the battles of Ipsus (301) and Coru-pedion (281). Lysimachus was to have his turn in tackling them before they engaged

---

because Ariarathes had himself no legitimate issue. Holophernes, however, seems to belong to the mythical persons of the genealogy. Marquart (*loc. cit.*) denies that the younger Ariarathes can have been the son of Ariarathes I in a literal sense, because in Diod. xviii. 22, 6, it is said all the *relatives* (συγγενεῖς) of the old Ariarathes perished with him. But this argument would go to prove that the younger Ariarathes was no relation at all of the elder, which is improbable. The expression in Diod. may describe a general massacre of the princely house, ordered by Perdiccas, without meaning strictly that *no individual* escaped.

[1] Diod. xxxi. 19, 5.

the attention of Seleucus or his house. He was not blind to the importance of reducing this turbulent corner to submission; he took in hand the task with earnestness of purpose. Bithynia was still destined to be the grave of reputations; Zibœtes led the tribesmen as ably as his grandfather Bas. Only the outline of events is given us in the few words extracted from Memnon.[1] Lysimachus sends a body of troops; it is defeated and the commander killed. He sends another force; this Zibœtes "chases far away from his own territory." Then Lysimachus leads an army against him in person; he is worsted.[2] That is all we know. Whether Lysimachus after his repulse acquiesced in the independence of the Bithynians, or whether he was preparing to renew the attack when his reign ended, we do not know. In 297 it appears that Zibœtes assumed the title of king.[3] He had certainly won the right to do so. The dynasty which had proved its ability to hold its own against Persian and Macedonian for a hundred years seems entitled to assume the marks of sovereignty.

Whether the country to the north now being conquered by Mithridates fell within the sphere of Lysimachus or of Seleucus, as the kings drew the map after Ipsus, there is nothing to show.[4] Perhaps it matters little how the official map in this case was drawn, since neither king had apparently

---

[1] Memnon 20 = *F.H.G.* iii. p. 537.

[2] It *seems* to be implied in the account reproduced by Photius from Memnon that Lysimachus was defeated in person: Ζιποίτης, λαμπρὸς ἐν πολέμοις γεγονώς, καὶ τοὺς Λυσιμάχου στρατηγοὺς τὸν μὲν ἀνελών, τὸν δὲ ἐπὶ μήκιστον τῆς οἰκείας ἀπελάσας ἀρχῆς, ἀλλὰ καὶ αὐτοῦ Λυσιμάχου, εἶτα καὶ Ἀντιόχου τοῦ παιδὸς Σελεύκου ἐπικρατέστερος γεγονώς. Lysimachus seems specially distinguished from his generals. It may, however, be that this construction is wrong, or that possibly Photius misrepresents Memnon, since Antiochus, who is coupled with Lysimachus, was only defeated in the person of his general. When Antiochus himself came into Asia Minor, Zibœtes had been succeeded by Nicomedes. In that case Memnon's meaning would have been that in defeating the generals sent against him by Lysimachus and Antiochus successively, Zibœtes had shown himself more than a match for two kings of such great power.

[3] Reinach, *Trois Royaumes*, p. 131 f.

[4] The argument of Niese (i. p. 352, n. 1), that it fell to Lysimachus because the Pontic kings dated the beginning of their monarchy from the year of his death, appears weak in view of the fact that the year of Lysimachus' death was also the year in which Seleucus died. If indeed one could rely on the phraseology of Memnon 11, it would show that Mithridates was already king before the death of Seleucus, but in any case τὸν Πόντου βασιλέα is an anachronism. See Appendix D.

any leisure to send troops into those outlying parts or interfere with Mithridates in his work. It was in Southern Cappadocia that Seleucus found himself by the partition with unsubjugated tracts on his hands. Two scanty notices point to his activity in this direction. One is a passage of Pliny, in which he quotes Isidorus as saying that King Seleucus exterminated the fierce tribes (*ferocissimas gentes*) of Arienei and Capreatae, in the region " between Cilicia, Cappadocia, Cataonia, and Armenia," where he founded in memory of their quelling the city of Apamea Damea.[1] This region geographers have not yet been able to identify. The other passage[2] speaks of some forces of Seleucus under Diodorus being lost, apparently after Coru-pedion, in Cappadocia. Whether the victorious enemy was Ariarathes, or indeed what the relations of Seleucus and Ariarathes were, we are not told. Only the fact stands out that the house of Ariarathes was left in secure possession of part of Cappadocia, and that the part which Seleucus was able to occupy was now distinctly described as Cappadocia *Seleucis*, to mark it out from the regions held by the two Persian princes.[3]

After the destruction of Lysimachus the whole of Asia Minor is once more brought (by the theory at least of the Macedonian courts) under a single sovereignty. Seleucus has now to determine his relations to the most western of the three native principalities, the Bithynian. He has to recognize King Ziboetes or declare him an enemy of the realm and take measures accordingly. He chooses the latter alternative, as indeed any one aspiring to complete the Macedonian conquest of Asia was bound to do.[4] Of the hostilities which ensued, the historian of Heraclea mentions only a raid made by Ziboetes upon that city as an ally of Seleucus—a raid in which the historian boasts that he got as good as he gave. With Mithridates too Seleucus would have had soon to deal had his life been longer. At the moment when he dies, Mithridates has already begun to be recognized by the world as a power antagonistic to the Greek king of Asia. The Heracleots open negotiations with him after their rupture with Seleucus.[5] On

---

[1] Plin. *N.H.* v. § 127. [2] Trogus, *Prol.* xvii. [3] App. *Syr.* 55.
[4] Memnon 10. [5] Memnon 11 = *F.H.G.* iii. p. 533.

neither Zibœtes nor Mithridates has Seleucus the Conqueror brought his power to bear when all his designs are cut short by the hand of the assassin.

The result, then, of fifty years of Macedonian rule in Asia Minor had not been, as one might have expected, to bring it all under a single strong and systematic government. *No noticeable advance in this direction had been made on the state of things prevailing under the Persian Empire.* The Greek kings had, indeed, brought with them better ideals; Alexander and Perdiccas had begun to level old barriers, but since the break-up of the Empire those ideals had been unrealized and the work of Alexander had been suspended in consequence of the long intestine struggle of the Macedonian princes. So that now in 281 B.C. the Bithynians and Pisidians still defied external control, the old unsubdued tracts on either side of the great high-roads were unsubdued still, and the northern races of the Black Sea regions were not only still free, but were growing into formidable powers under Irânian leaders. Greek rule had never yet had a chance; first it had been checked by Alexander's premature death, then by the long fight between the rivals, then, when at last the Empire seemed to have become a unity again under Seleucus, once more the fabric had collapsed, and the problem of the barbarian peoples of Asia Minor confronted in its old shape any one who now aspired to take up the burden of Empire.

(b) *The Greek Cities*

We go on now to examine how the change of *régime* from Persian to Macedonian affected the Greek cities. *They obviously were in the highest degree interested in a turn of things which substituted a Hellenic for a barbarian King.* The rosiest dreams of Panhellenic enthusiasts, like Isocrates, seemed to have become fact. In truth, however, there was something radically false and incongruous from the start in the position in which the new rulers now found themselves. They claimed to be the champions of Hellenism; they were determined to be paramount kings. The two characters were absolutely irreconcilable. The great crucial question of

Hellenic politics—the independence of the several cities—could not be honestly met. The *"autonomy of the Hellenes"*—it had become already a cant phrase of the market-place; as an absolute principle, no Greek could impeach it with a good conscience; even those who violated it in practice were ready to invoke it, as something sacrosanct, against their opponents—Spartans against Athenians, and Athenians against Spartans; the Persians themselves had been induced to promulgate it in the Peace of Antalcidas. The autonomy of the Asiatic Greeks, understood in the sense of their being freed from the barbarian yoke, had been the ostensible cause in which Alexander drew his sword against Darius. But once lord of Asia, a Hellenic no less than a Persian king wanted to be master in his own house.

We must remember, in order to realize the difficulty of the situation, how genuine and earnest the desire of Alexander and his successors was to secure the good word of the Greeks. Many considerations would move them. There were firstly those of material advantage. The city-states, although none singly could cope in the long run with such powers as were wielded by the great Macedonian chiefs, had by no means become cyphers. There were still civic forces, land and naval, which they could put in action. There were still moneys in the city treasuries which could procure mercenaries. It was of real importance into what scale Cyzicus or Rhodes threw its weight. Cities like these were capable, even singly, of making a good fight. And their importance was, of course, immensely increased by the division of the Macedonian Empire. Even a small accession of power to one or other of the rival chiefs now told. A good name among the Hellenes, which should make the cities willing allies, was worth striving for.

And it was not the cities only, as political bodies, which it was necessary to win. Princes who no longer had authority in the Macedonian fatherland, and could no longer call up fresh levies of Macedonian countrymen to make good the wear and tear of war, rulers like Antigonus and Ptolemy and Seleucus, came to depend far more upon attracting to their standards the floating class of adventurers who swarmed over the Greek world and sold their swords to whom they would.

It was of immense consequence to be well spoken of among the Greeks.[1]

But besides these considerations of material gain, a good reputation among the Greeks seemed to the Macedonian rulers a thing to be prized for its own sake. They really cared for Greek public opinion. Yes, practical, ambitious, and hard as they appear, they were still not inaccessible to some sentimental motions. They desired fame. And fame meant—to be spoken of at Athens![2] The only letters with which they had been imbued were Greek. The great men of the past, the classical examples of human glory, were the men about whom they had learnt when boys in their Greek lesson-books. The achievements of the Macedonian sword seemed to lose half their halo unless they were canonized by the Greek pen. And so the strange spectacle was seen, of the Greeks, after the power of their republics had shrunk and their ancient spirit had departed, mesmerizing the new rulers of the world, as later on they mesmerized the Romans, by virtue of the literature, the culture, and the names which they inherited from their incomparable past. The adulation which the Greeks of those days yielded with such facile prodigality still had a value for their conquerors. The wielders of material power rendered indirect homage to the finer activities of brain.

The interest and the pride of a Macedonian dynast lay no less in his being a champion of Hellenism than in his being a great king. But to be both together—there was the crux! A king could do a great deal for Hellenism; he could shield the Greeks from barbarian oppression; he could make splendid presents to Greek cities and Greek temples; he could maintain eminent men, philosophers, captains, *literati*, at his court; he could patronize science and poetry and art, but really to allow Greek cities within his dominions to be separate bodies

---

[1] See Diod. xviii. 28, 5; xix. 62, 2.

[2] Ὦ Ἀθηναῖοι, ἆρά γε πιστεύσαιτε ἂν, ἡλίκους ὑπομένω κινδύνους ἕνεκα τῆς παρ' ὑμῖν εὐδοξίας; Plutarch, *Alex.* 60, the words of Alexander in a perilous moment of the war in the Panjab. That Alexander was not peculiar in his feeling we may infer from the great honour paid to Greek men of letters in the courts of the Successors, and the large gifts bestowed upon the illustrious Greek cities, especially Athens. Demetrius the Besieger and Antiochus Epiphanes were especially distinguished for their passionate worship of Athens.

with a will independent of the central power was, of course, impossible. Frankly to acknowledge this impossibility would not have been in accordance with the practice of politicians at any period of history. To cheat the world—to cheat themselves perhaps—with half-measures and imposing professions was the easy course. They could go on talking about the autonomy of the Hellenes, and interpret the phrase in the way prescribed by the example of Athens and Sparta. It was an uncomfortable thing for a man of Greek education to feel himself the "enslaver" of Greek cities. What the Macedonian rulers would have liked would have been the voluntary acceptance of their dictation as permanent allies by the Greek cities. That was the ideal. And because it was not capable of being realized in fact, the natural course of politicians was, not to discard it boldly, but to pretend that what they desired was true, to preserve the outward forms, to be magnanimous in phrases. Philip and Alexander always veiled the brutal fact of their conquest of European Greece by representing themselves as captains-general elected by the federated Hellenic states. The relation of Hellenic states (European and Asiatic) to the Macedonian king was always, in the official view, one of *alliance*,[1] not of subjection.

The opening campaign of 334 puts Alexander in the place of the Great King in the regions tenanted by the Asiatic Greeks. It is now to be seen how their autonomy takes substance. There is, at any rate, one measure of interference in the internal affairs of the cities which seems to be demanded in the interests of autonomy itself. The control of foreign powers, Hellenic and barbarian, had not in the past, as we have seen, taken the shape of external pressure only. It had worked by placing the party within the city favourable to itself in the saddle. The destruction of the foreign power did not therefore immediately and *ipso facto* liberate the

[1] There are actual στῆλαι mentioned in the case of Mitylene (τὰς πρὸς Ἀλέξανδρον σφισι γενομένας στήλας, Arr. *Anab.* ii. 1, 4), and in the case of Tenedos (*id.* ii. 2, 2): Kaerst, *Geschichte des hellenist. Zeitalt.* i. p. 261, discusses the question whether the Asiatic Greeks were attached to the *Corinthian* Confederation, or formed smaller confederations (the Ilian, the Ionian) of their own. He decides that the latter is probable in the case of the mainland cities, whilst the islands were incorporated in the Corinthian Confederation.

oppressed faction. The tyrants and oligarchies established in the cities by the Persian government were left standing when the hand of the Great King was withdrawn. It is therefore the first business of the liberator to overthrow the existing government in the several cities and establish democracies in their place. In doing this he might justly argue that he was acting for, not against, the sacred principle of autonomy. At the same time, in view of actual instances of this change of constitution wrought by an outside power which are furnished us by the history of the times before and after Alexander, one can see how the practice lent itself to hypocrisy—how easily a ruler could use the very measure by which he pretended to assure the autonomy of a city in order to attach it more securely to himself. Every Greek city was divided against itself; "not one but two states, that of the poor and that of the rich, living on the same spot and always conspiring against one another."[1] The autonomy might, indeed, be held to consist in the supremacy of the *demos* rather than of the oligarchs; but in practice it was merely one faction against another, a clique of men whose influence was derived from their ability to catch the popular vote, another of men whose influence was derived from family or riches. Inevitably if one of these parties lent on the aid of an outside power, the opposite party sided with that power's enemies. It was open to any foreign power to represent the party favourable to itself as the true soul of the city. It is no wonder, with so useful an application, that the autonomy of the Hellenes was a phrase often in the mouths, not only of the city politicians, but of foreign potentates.[2]

The Greek cities of Asia Minor, as Alexander finds them, are held by tyrants and oligarchs in the interests of Persia. His first step, therefore, is to establish democracies everywhere.[3] He is careful to keep his hand upon the new constitutions. In a letter to Chios he ordains that the city is to choose *nomographoi* to draw up the amended code, *but their*

---

[1] Plato, *Republic*, viii. 552.   [2] Diod. xviii. 55.

[3] Ephesus, Arr. *Anab.* i. 17, 10; Aeolian and Ionian cities, Arr. *Anab.* i. 18, 2; Amisos, App. *Mith.* 8; Chios, Michel, No. 33. At Heraclea the revolution is threatened, but averted by the diplomacy of the tyrant Dionysius. Memnon 4 = *F.H.G.* iii. p. 529.

work is to be submitted to the King for his sanction.[1] And now in what relation does the renovated city stand to the ruler of Asia? There were three main ways, according to Greek ideas, in which the autonomy of a city could be violated—by the exaction of tribute, by the imposition of a garrison and by the commands of a superior power meddling with the constitution or administration.[2] How far in each of these respects does the autonomy of the Greek cities of Asia hold good under Alexander and his first successors?

First as to the payment of tribute. Alexander is specially said to have remitted in a number of cases the tribute which the city had been paying to the Persian King.[3] To do this he considered apparently an essential part of the work of liberation. At Ephesus he directs that the tribute which had been paid to the barbarians should be paid thenceforth into the treasury of the local Artemis.[4] Aspendus, on the other hand, is ordered to pay tribute to the Macedonians.[5] But the case of Aspendus was exceptional; it was to be specially punished. And even here it is said that the imposition of tribute was not to be permanent, but for a certain number of years only.[6] It is clearly an exception proving a rule.

But we should be too simple if we inferred from the remission of tribute that no money was demanded of the cities. A showy act of magnanimity has not seldom in history covered the old grievance under a new form. A city no longer obliged to pay tribute as a subject might be called upon to make a handsome contribution as an ally. How far this was actually the case under Alexander and his successors eludes our observation. It was, in the case of Aspendus, apparently a requisition of this sort, a demand for fifty talents and the horses maintained by the city for the Persian court, which provoked the quarrel with Alexander. The liberated Chios is commanded to furnish at the expense of the city a

---

[1] Michel, No. 33. Cf. the διαγραφή sent by Alexander to Eresus prescribing the form of trial for the ex-tyrants, Michel, No. 358.

[2] Polyb. xxi. 43, 2.

[3] Aeolian and Ionian cities, Arr. *Anab.* i. 18, 2. Cf. for Erythrae, Michel, No. 37; Ilion, Strabo xiii. 593.

[4] Arr. *Anab.* i. 17, 10.   [5] *Ibid.* 27, 4.

[6] φόρους ἀποφέρειν ὅσα ἔτη Μακεδόσι.

contingent of twenty triremes ready manned to the imperial fleet and to provide for the maintenance of the temporary garrison.[1] A rescript of Alexander dealing with Priene specially remits the "contribution" ($\sigma\acute{u}\nu\tau\alpha\xi\iota\varsigma$).[2] The money contributed by Mitylene is returned by Alexander as an extraordinary mark of favour.[3] So, too, after the death of Alexander we find Antipater requiring the cities to contribute to the war,[4] and the order is felt by the cities as an unwelcome burden. Antigonus speaks of the heavy expenses of his allies in his war against Cassander and Ptolemy.[5]

The second of the three modes mentioned in which a city's autonomy might be violated was the imposition of a garrison. That indeed reduced at once the forms of a free state to a comedy. It was the most odious embodiment of brute force. We may well believe that Alexander was unwilling to stultify his own action as liberator in so open a manner. It is only as a temporary measure, or where his hold on an important point is threatened by external enemies, or there has been some mark of hostility on the part of the population, that Alexander permits himself to introduce a Macedonian garrison into a Hellenic city. At Mitylene, for instance, while the Persian fleet still holds the Aegean in 333, we find a contingent of mercenaries sent from Alexander "in fulfilment of the alliance."[6] At Chios the new democratic *régime*, including the return of exiles, is carried out under the eyes of a garrison. Till the settlement is complete the garrison is to remain in the city.[7] And we may suppose that the case of Chios was typical, and that the revolutions carried through by Alexander in the Greek states involved in other places also such a temporary occupation by imperial troops. At Priene, for instance, an incidental notice shows a garrison.[8] Rhodes is saddled with a garrison at Alexander's death.[9]

But even if a city enjoyed immunity from tribute and was unburdened by a garrison, it was impossible that its affairs

---

[1] Michel, No. 33.
[2] *Inscr. in the Brit. Mus.* No. 400.
[3] Curtius, iv. 8, 13.
[4] χρήματα εἰς τὸμ πόλεμον εἰσφέρην, Michel, No. 363.
[5] *J.H.S.* xix. (1899), p. 334.
[6] Arr. *Anab.* ii. 1, 4.
[7] Michel, No. 33.
[8] *Inscr. in the Brit. Mus.* No. 400.
[9] Diod. xviii. 8, 1.

should not attract the attention of the rulers of the land, or that, attracting it, they should go uncontrolled. Under Alexander, indeed, the representatives of the royal authority in the provinces of the realm, the satraps, do not seem to have been given any regular authority over the Greek cities except in such cases as that of Aspendus.[1] But the King himself was constantly called to interfere; the "royal rescripts"[2] had to break in, as rude realities, upon the dream of independence. Even at the very institution of liberty and democracy in Ephesus (334), Alexander had directed how the money formerly raised as tribute to the court was to be applied, and he had been compelled to restrain by his intervention the furious excesses of the restored democrats,[3] showing at the outset to any who had eyes to see how hollow a pretence under the circumstances of the time autonomy must be. Before the end of his reign he had published the celebrated edict at the Olympic games, commanding the cities of the Greek world everywhere to receive back their exiles.[4] This was to push his interference into the vitals of every state, to override the competence of the city government in a most intimate particular, to set at naught in the eyes of the whole world the principle of autonomy. The real fact of the Macedonian sovereignty, which had been cloaked in so many decent political fictions, is here brutally unveiled.

In spite, however, of these discrepancies with the perfect ideal of autonomy, the Greek cities of Asia spring, with the removal of the Persian yoke, into a richer and more vigorous life. The King himself was a zealous patron in all ways that did not compromise his authority, and public works began to be set on foot, of a larger scale than the resources of the individual cities could have compassed. At Clazomenae, the island to which the citizens had transferred their town, out of fear of the Persians, Alexander connects with the mainland by a causeway[5] a quarter of a mile long.[6] The neighbouring

---

[1] See Niese i. p. 162.   [2] βασιλικὰ προστάγματα or διαγράμματα.
[3] Arr. *Anab.* i. 17, 12.
[4] Diod. xviii. 8. This order seems to have been given to some cities individually, *e.g.* Chios (Michel, No. 33), at an earlier date. Cf. the dealings of Alexander with Eresos (Michel, No. 358).
[5] Paus. vii. 3, 5.   [6] Chandler, *Travels in Asia Minor*.

promontory, Mimas, on the other hand, with the city of Erythrae, he designs to make an island—an operation which would have put Erythrae in a better position for the coast traffic; unfortunately, the work, after being begun, proved impracticable.[1] The temper of Alexander was such as to make him peculiarly sensitive to historic or legendary associations, and turn his special interest to places glorified by a great past. In Asia Minor he does not stud barbarian regions with new Greek cities, as he does in the farther East,[2] but he pays great attention to the old cities of the Greek sea-board. Above all, his imagination is fired with the project of making the Homeric Ilion once more great and splendid. He found already upon a mound near the coast (mod. Hissarlik) an old temple of Athena, with a little town or village of Greek speech clustering round it. This village asserted its claim to be the very Troy of story.[3] There the ingenuous traveller could inspect the altar of Zeus Herkeios, at whose foot Priam was slain, and shields battered in the Trojan war which were hanging on the temple walls. With such a legend the temple had long been of high prestige among the Greeks. Xerxes, when he passed that way, had sacrificed there with great circumstance.[4] Greek generals had followed his example.[5] The temple, according to Strabo, was small and mean[6] in outward aspect; a statue of the phil-hellenic Ariobarzanes lay prostrate before it.[7] Alexander could not fail to visit this historic spot and offer sacrifices there the moment that he set foot in Asia.[8] After Granicus he visits it again, and enriches the shrine with some new dedications. He pronounces that Ilion is now a village no longer, but a Hellenic city of full rights; and in order to make fact conform to this fiat, he instructs the royal officials to create the shell of a city by throwing up buildings

---

[1] Paus. ii. 1, 5; Plin. *N.H.* v. § 116.

[2] Droysen can find only one Greek city in the barbarian part of Asia Minor north of the Taurus distinctly claiming Alexander as founder, Apollonia in Phrygia (ii. p. 661), and this claim does not appear till the time of the Roman Empire.

[3] Modern excavation has established the fact that it did actually stand on the site of the prehistoric city.

[4] Hdt. vii. 43.   [5] Xen. *Hell.* 1, 4.

[6] μικρὸν καὶ εὐτελές, Strabo xiii. 593.   [7] Diod. xvii. 17, 6.

[8] Arr. *Anab.* i. 11; Diod. xvii. 17, 6; Plutarch, *Alex.* 15.

of a suitable scale. Again, after the destruction of the Persian power, Alexander writes to Ilion fresh promises of what he means to do for city and temple.[1] His sudden death leaves him time for little more than magnificent intentions. Among the official documents made public at his death is the project of making the temple of Athena at Ilion outdo the wonders of Egypt and Babylon.[2]

To extend the privileges of the Greek temples, to make contributions to their enlargement, their adornment, and maintenance, to fill their treasuries with costly vessels, all this not only showed piety, but was the easiest way in which a king, who had more resources than any private person, could demonstrate his usefulness to the Greek cities without prejudice to his crown. It was not the pride only, but the pocket of the citizens which was touched by the honour of the city shrine. The prestige and splendour of the city shrine were the things which brought worshippers and visitors, which made the festivals well thronged, quickened trade, and brought money into the city.[3] Every motive would impel Alexander to devote himself to the glorification of the Hellenic temples and to press his action upon the attention of the Greeks. According to the story in Strabo (from Artemidorus) Alexander offered the Ephesians to bear the whole expenses of the restoration of the temple, past and current (it had been burnt down on the day of Alexander's birth),[4] if he might inscribe his name as the dedicator of the new edifice—a condition which the Ephesians would none of.[5] An inscription found at Priene is evidence both of Alexander's liberality to the temple of Athena Polias in that city, and of a greater complaisance on the part of the citizens than had been shown at Ephesus, for Alexander appears as sole dedicator.[6]

Under the sun of the favour of the new Great King, with the increase of commerce following the Macedonian conquest, the Hellenic cities of Asia expand into new bloom. The

---

[1] Strabo xiii. 593. [2] Diod. xviii. 4, 5.
[3] See the view of Demetrius the silversmith, Acts 19, 24 f.
[4] Plutarch, *Alex.* 3.
[5] Strabo xiv. 640.
[6] Michel, No. 1209. (The actual inscription is to be seen in the vestibule of the British Museum.)

festivals, which formed so important a part in the life of a Greek citizen, and reflected his material well-being, are celebrated with new zest. The great religious union of the twelve Ionian cities had, in the days of Persian rule, shrunk to a union of only nine cities, and had been obliged to transfer its assembly and festival from the Panionion on the headland of Mycale to the safer resort of Ephesus.[1] Under Alexander the old order is restored. The famous shrine of the Didymaean Apollo at Branchidae in the domain of Miletus, silent and neglected under the Persian domination, is restored to its former honour, and once more utters oracles to glorify the Hellenic King.[2] The light in which Alexander was regarded is shown in the worship of him maintained by the Ionian Body till Roman times.[3]

The break-up of the Empire is not an unmixed good to the cities. If, on the one hand, it opens the way to liberty, if Rhodes can now expel its garrison[4] and Cyzicus defy the satrap of Hellespontine Phrygia,[5] on the other hand it entangles the Greek states in chronic war, and renders them liable to be seized by one or other of the rival chiefs. They are no longer in face of the irresistible might of a united empire, but the inferior powers, in the exigencies of the struggle, are far less able to study their sensibilities than an omnipotent and paternal sovereign. The signal in Asia Minor of a new state of things is the attempt made in 319 by Arrhidaeus, the satrap of Hellespontine Phrygia, to force a garrison upon Cyzicus. It is now for the first time[6] that a Macedonian chief makes it a part of his policy to introduce garrisons into Greek cities without any preceding quarrel. But the menace

---

[1] Diod. xv. 49, 1; Dionys. Hal. iv. 25. See Judeich, *Kleinasiatische Studien*, p. 241, note 1.

[2] Strabo xvii. 814; cf. Haussoullier, *Rev. de Philol.* xxiv. (1900), p. 244.

[3] In an inscription of the earlier part of the third century (Michel, No. 486), the birthday of Alexander is kept as a holiday by the Ionian Body; his festival, the Alexandreia, is not fixed to any particular one of the twelve cities. In Strabo there is a special precinct of Alexander on the Isthmus near Teos (Strabo xiv. p. 644), and it is there that the Ionian Body holds his festival. This must represent a later stage than the inscription.

[4] Diod. xviii. 8, 1.

[5] *Ibid.* 51.   [6] *Ibid.* 52, 3.

from Antigonus seems to Arrhidaeus to leave him no choice. About the same time Clitus follows suit in Lydia, and *the Greek cities, from which the Persian garrisons had been driven fifteen years before by the Macedonian liberator, now find Macedonian garrisons taking their place.*[1]

This step on the part of the two satraps, even if dictated by strategic reasons, gives a great political advantage to the satrap of Phrygia. He had indeed determined to be supreme lord in Asia Minor, and he is now able to pursue his ambition as the champion of Hellenic autonomy. Antigonus immediately adopts this rôle before the world, and is careful from this time forward to distinguish his policy by this luminous mark from that of his opponents. Clitus has hardly seized the Ionian cities before Antigonus appears as the deliverer, ejects the garrisons, and wrests the great city of Ephesus from those who hold it. The satrap of Lydia had already abandoned his province and withdrawn to Macedonia. Antigonus acts in like manner with regard to Arrhidaeus. He had immediately on the siege of Cyzicus sent an embassy to read him a lecture on the rights of Hellenic cities, and he soon brings force to bear.[2] By the following year (318) he has himself invaded the satrapy and pinned Arrhidaeus to the town of Cius.[3] The Greek cities of the Propontis—Byzantium, Calchedon, Cyzicus—see in him a friend, and are ready with their help. His naval victory over Clitus in the Bosphorus secures him in possession of the Hellespontine province. What became of Arrhidaeus we do not hear.

The Greek cities over whom Antigonus now throws his shield, as lord of Asia, are, however, exposed to attack by his enemies from the sea. Asander, the satrap of Caria, with whom Antigonus had not yet had time to reckon, has by 315, when Antigonus returns from the East, thrown troops into Northern Cappadocia and laid siege to Amisus.[4] Then when the great war between Antigonus and the other chiefs begins, the Greek cities all along the coast of Asia Minor have to bear the brunt of the hostile forces. That the sympathies of the Hellenes of Asia are generally with Antigonus at this moment is shown in

[1] Diod. xviii. 52, 6.   [2] *Ibid.* 52.
[3] *Ibid.* 72, 2.   [4] *Ibid.* xix. 57, 4.

the permission given him by Rhodes to build ships in its harbours.¹ But they are in a perilous case. The forces of Antigonus have to move rapidly about the coasts and islands to drive off the enemies who sweep down upon them. Amisus and Erythrae are relieved in 315,² Lemnos in 314.³ Even the Greek cities of the European coast of the Black Sea are embraced in the purview of Antigonus. In 313 he attempts to send a force to the help of Callatis, which has expelled the garrison of Lysimachus and "laid hold of autonomy."⁴ In the same year Antigonus presses home his attack on the satrap of Caria. Asander, like Arrhidaeus and Clitus, has occupied the Greek cities of his province with garrisons. Their deliverance is written large in the manifestoes of Antigonus. His generals appear before Miletus, call the citizens to liberty, and drive the garrison out of the citadel. Tralles, whether garrisoned or simply ruled by the partizans of Asander, is taken. Caunus is taken, although the garrison hold out in one of the two citadels. Iasus is compelled to give its adherence to the cause of Antigonus.⁵ Cnidus appears soon after as a friendly state.⁶

Rhodes is at this time rapidly rising to the position of a first-class power, marked out by its character as Hellenic republic to be a champion of Greek liberty, and Rhodes now formally recognizes Antigonus as the paladin of the sacred cause, and makes an alliance, under which it furnishes him with ten ships "*for the liberation of the Hellenes.*"⁷ When the great war comes to a temporary pause in 311, a special clause in the terms of the Peace provides that the Hellenes shall be autonomous. To the principle indeed all the Macedonian dynasts now formally declare their adherence; it was still possible to interpret the principle in a way which would not hamper, but would further, their egoistic designs.⁸

The letter, or a great part of it, has been recently discovered,⁹ in which Antigonus announces to the city of Scepsis,

---

¹ Diod. xix. 58, 5.   ² *Ibid.* 60.
³ *Ibid.* 68, 4.   ⁴ *Ibid.* 73, 1.
⁵ *Ibid.* 75, 5.   ⁶ *Ibid.* xx. 95, 4.
⁷ *Ibid.* xix. 77, 2.   ⁸ *Ibid.* 105, 1.
⁹ "A letter from Antigonus to Scepsis," J. A. R. Munro, *J.H.S.* xix. (1899), p. 330.

as one of his allies, the conclusion of the Peace. It is his chief concern to show how all through the negotiations he had made the freedom of the Greeks his first consideration. To secure the adhesion of Cassander and Ptolemy to the principle, he had waived important interests of his own. He wished nothing to stand in the way of a settlement which would put the liberty of the Greeks upon a lasting foundation. The Greeks, we observe, are carefully treated *as allies*; each state is expected to take for itself the oath in which the Macedonian chiefs, as heads of each federation, have sworn to the principle of Hellenic autonomy and the other terms of the Peace. The comment which history writes to state documents is often an ironic one. Before ten years were out, the people of Scepsis were being driven from their homes by the decree of Antigonus to be merged in the new city he created for his own glory.

Antigonus himself is not able to avoid garrisoning some of the cities.[1] At Caunus, for instance, after he has succeeded in reducing the hostile garrison, he feels it necessary to place in both the citadels garrisons of his own.[2] The consequence, of course, is to give his enemies just the same sort of handle as had been given him by Arrhidaeus and Clitus. Ptolemy now (309) appears on the coast of Asia Minor in the guise of liberator. Phaselis and Caunus are wrested from Antigonus.[3] Siege is laid to Halicarnassus, but this city Demetrius comes up in time to secure.[4] Next year (308) Myndus and Cos appear in Ptolemy's possession, and, passing through the islands, he drives a garrison of Antigonus out of Andros.[5]

A growing coolness between Antigonus and Rhodes is marked by the refusal of Rhodes in 306 to compromise its neutrality by supporting Demetrius in his attack on Ptolemy.[6] Next year (305) comes the attack on Rhodes itself, in which Antigonus openly throws to the winds all the professions he has been making for years. The magnificent defence of Rhodes

---

[1] Diod. xx. 19, 3.   [2] *Ibid.* 27, 2.
[3] *Ibid.* 27, 1 f.   [4] Plutarch, *Dem.* 7.
[5] Diod. xx. 37. Cf. the language of the Nesiotai: ἐπειδὴ ὁ βασιλεὺς καὶ σωτὴρ Πτολεμαῖος πολλῶν καὶ μεγάλων ἀγαθῶν αἴτιος ἐγένετο τοῖς [τ]ε Νησιώταις καὶ τοῖς ἄλλοις Ἕλλησιν, τάς τε πόλεις ἐλευθερώσας καὶ τοὺς νόμους ἀποδοὺς [κ]αὶ τὴμ πάτριομ πολίτειαμ πᾶσιγ καταστήσα[ς κ]αὶ τῶν εἰσφορῶγ κουφίσας, Michel, No. 373.
[6] Diod. xx. 46, 6.

secures a peace in which it is expressly stipulated that the city shall be autonomous, free from a garrison, and sovereign over its own revenues.[1]

The correspondence of Antigonus with Teos towards the year 304-303,[2] preserved for us in stone,[3] throws an interesting light upon his action with regard to the Greek cities. The matter in hand is the *synoikismos* of Lebedus and Teos. The times were against a large number of small cities, and the lesser ones tended to coalesce or be absorbed by the greater. This process, which might take place spontaneously, as in the case of Rhodes, Antigonus began deliberately to further, as we shall see in the Troad. Lebedus was a case where a migration of the inhabitants might seem appropriate. Lying between Ephesus and Teos, the little town had failed to hold its own.[4] A transference of the population to Teos might appear an advantage both to them and to the city which received the accession. Such a step, however, involved a number of practical difficulties. Should the new-comers build new houses adjacent to the existing city of Teos, or now that the population as a whole was grown greater, should the city be rebuilt more towards the peninsula?[5] How in the meantime should the people of Lebedus be housed? What would become of the public obligations contracted by Lebedus? How should the outstanding suits between the two cities be settled? Each city having hitherto had its own laws, under what code should the combined peoples now live? On these and similar questions Antigonus pronounces a decision. But there is little in the document to show whether the *synoikismos* is taking place at his command, whether, that is to say, he gives his verdict *as the sovereign*, or whether he is merely deciding as arbitrator on questions voluntarily submitted to himself by the cities. It was quite in accordance with the practice of the time for the Greek states to refer their disputes to the arbitration of a neutral power. They might naturally choose the Greek king, on whose confines they dwelt, without

---

[1] αὐτόνομον καὶ ἀφρούρητον εἶναι τὴν πόλιν καὶ ἔχειν τὰς ἰδίας προσόδους, Diod. xx. 99, 3.

[2] He is already "King." [3] Michel, No. 34.

[4] Ad. Wilhelm conjectures that it had been injured by earthquake, *Ath. Mitth.* xxii. (1897), p. 212. [5] Cf. l. 70.

implying his possession of any sovereign rights over them. His interference with their internal affairs, as voluntarily chosen arbitrator, would be of an utterly different character from the interference of a high-handed over-lord. Antigonus, in the document before us, says little to imply sovereignty. Only once the ugly fact looks through. Alexander had ordered the Chians to submit their new constitution to him for ratification (p. 106). Antigonus thinks it well to exercise the same sort of control. "You are further to send to us," he writes, "the laws upon which you have agreed, and indicate those which were introduced by the *nomothetai* and those which were framed by other citizens, in order that, if any persons are shown to be bringing in laws which are not desirable but the reverse, *we may visit them with our censure and punishment.*"[1] It is no mere arbitrator that speaks there!

Such were the relations, as far as we can now trace them, between Antigonus and the old Greek cities of Asia Minor. But by the side of the old cities there begin under Antigonus to rise the new Greek cities which were called into being by Hellenistic kings. We have no proof of any foundation of a new Greek city in the country north of the Taurus before the time when Antigonus brought it under his sovereignty. Two cities, illustrious in a later age, called Antigonus their founder. One of these rose in the fertile plain at the eastern extremity of the Ascanian Lake, on the high-road between Phrygia, the seat of government, and the Bosphorus. It declared itself, by its very form, a city of the new age, an exact square, each face of the boundary wall four stades long with a gate in the middle, the thoroughfares intersecting at nice angles, and so strictly ruled that from a stone in the central gymnasium every one of the four gates was visible.[2] The other city was designed to become the seaport of the Troad. It was a case of *synoikismos*. The population of the small towns of the neighbourhood were dragged into the new foundation; Larissa, Colonae, Chrysa, Hamaxitus, Cebrene, Neandria, and Scepsis

---

[1] l. 53 f.

[2] Strabo xii. 565. It is curious that the new American and Australian cities present the same contrast of mechanical regularity to the cities of Europe.

were absorbed.[1] These were the two cities which owed their existence to Antigonus the One-eyed. To both he gave, with unimaginative egoism, the same name of Antigonia; but it was under another name that each was destined to become famous.

A third city laid out by Antigonus purported rather to be a revival than a new creation. The name of Smyrna had ceased four hundred years before to denote a living city; only a group of villages marked the site of what had once been the seaport of that coast.[2] Its importance had drawn upon it early the attack of the Lydian kings.[3] When the Persians came, all that was left of Smyrna were some old temples, like that of the Nemeses,[4] and the straggling villages. But the fame of the old Smyrna lived on in the songs of the Greeks, and now under Antigonus a new Smyrna began to rise two miles from the old site on the southern side of the bay,[5] built after the admired pattern, with regular streets intersecting each other at exact right angles. Thus Smyrna began a second existence, destined to be a long one. By the irony of fate that city, which seemed earliest to have perished, has survived all its rivals and, still bearing its old name, dominates a coast where Ephesus and Miletus are forgotten.

Two years after the raising of the siege of Rhodes the dominion of Antigonus in Asia Minor begins to break up (302). Over the Greek cities is thrown the shadow of a new personality. Lysimachus, satrap of Thrace since 323, now, like the other dynasts, styling himself King, crosses into Asia. His reception differs in the case of different cities. Of those that hold by Antigonus, it is impossible to say in each instance whether the city's action is determined by a garrison, or by fear, or by real loyalty. Lysimachus, indeed, himself does not spend much time over the Greek cities; his object is to strike at the seat of his adversary's power in Phrygia; he presses on into the interior, leaving it to his lieutenant Prepelaus to deal with the cities. In person he only summons those which lie

---

[1] Strabo xiii. 593, 604. [2] Hdt. i. 149, 150; Strabo xiv. 634.
[3] Hdt. i. 15; Paus. iv. 21, 5; ix. 29, 4. [4] Paus. vii. 5, 1.
[5] Strabo xiv. 646. The tradition which ascribes the foundation of the new Smyrna to Alexander (Paus. vii. 5, 1) is discredited by Droysen in view of Strabo's statement.

on his road, Lampsacus and Parium, which voluntarily join him, Sigeum, which he has to reduce by force, and Abydos, the siege of which he begins but does not prosecute. Into Sigeum he introduces a garrison. Of the Greek cities approached by Prepelaus, Adramyttium is overpowered in passing, Ephesus is intimidated into submission, Teos and Colophon give in their adherence, apparently from a sense of weakness, Erythrae and Clazomenae, into which the generals of Antigonus throw forces by sea, hold out.[1] In Ephesus, at any rate, Prepelaus puts a garrison. This garrison is expelled within a few months by Demetrius, who introduces one of his own. When Demetrius goes on to the Hellespont, Lampsacus and Parium again change sides.[2] Meantime Lysimachus has retired northwards and attaches Heraclea to his person by marrying Amestris, who is ruling the city as widow of the late tyrant.[3] Heraclea has all these years constituted a singular case among the Greek cities of Asia. Here the old dynasty of tyrants, a relic of Achaemenian days, still survived. This was due to the tyrant Dionysius, who had the good sense to fortify himself with the goodwill of his subjects, and contrived by admirable diplomacy to keep on friendly terms with successive Macedonian rulers. His alliance with Antigonus had been peculiarly close, cemented by a marriage between their two families. At his death, which took place while Antigonus was still ruling Asia, that chief continued to protect his widow, who now ruled Heraclea as regent for his infant sons.

Amestris was a remarkable woman, whose person still connected the present with a vanished past. She was the niece of the last Persian Great King, and had spent her early life in a royal harem. After the Persian Empire had been swept away by Alexander, she became the wife of the Macedonian chief Craterus. Craterus, after Alexander's death, passed her on to Dionysius. Now, after ruling for some time over a Greek city, she gets a third husband in Lysimachus.[4]

The partition after Ipsus confirms Lysimachus in possession of Western Asia Minor. Some of the Greek cities indeed

[1] Diod. xx. 107. [2] *Ibid.* 111, 3. [3] *Ibid.* 109.
[4] Memnon 4 = *F.H.G.* iii. p. 529 f.

remain for a time in the hands of Demetrius, notably Ephesus, the most important of all. An inscription [1] records the arrival in that city of an ambassador sent by Demetrius and Seleucus jointly, to notify their reconciliation (about 299). Ephesus appears, of course, in this official document as a sovereign state receiving the envoy of external powers. Not a word to show that a garrison, composed largely of pirates, was all this while determining the city's policy, as appears to have been the case. By 294, however, all or most of these cities have been acquired by Lysimachus; [2] at Ephesus his general Lycus bought over the pirate captain Andron.[3] Demetrius in 287-286 is received at Miletus by Eurydice, the repudiated queen of Ptolemy. It is not clear by whose forces, those of Demetrius or Ptolemy, Miletus is at this time held. Other cities perhaps passed after Ipsus into the hand of Ptolemy.[4]

The appearance of Demetrius in Asia Minor in 287-286 leads to his regaining possession of a number of cities, "some joining him voluntarily, and some yielding to force." [5] Which cities these were is not said, but next year Caunus is still held by his forces,[6] and had therefore either never been lost or was recaptured now. This is, of course, a merely temporary disturbance in the domination of Lysimachus, the cities being soon compelled to return to their former "alliance." [7]

There are indications that the hand of Lysimachus weighed more heavily upon the Greeks than that of Antigonus. It is perhaps not mere chance that an inscription [8] shows us now for the first time *a governor set by a Macedonian king over the cities of Ionia.* In a letter to Priene, Lysimachus speaks of having "sent an order to the city that it should obey his *strategos.*" [9] At Lemnos we are told that the Athenian colonists found Lysimachus play the master in a particularly disagreeable way.[10] We have instances of his autocratic dealing. The

---

[1] Michel, No. 492.   [2] Plutarch, *Dem.* 35.   [3] Polyaen. v. 19.

[4] Niese (ii. 101) supposes that Ptolemy regained after Ipsus his conquests of 309-308 on the coasts of Asia Minor.

[5] Plutarch, *Dem.* 46.   [6] *Ibid.* 49.   [7] Trog. *Prol.* xvi.

[8] Michel, No. 485; *Ath. Mitth.* xxv. (1900), 100.

[9] *Inscr. in the Brit. Mus.* No. 402; Lenschau, *De rebus Prienensium* [*Leipziger Studien*, xii. 1890, p. 201].

[10] Athen. vi. 255 a.

city of Astacus he wiped out of existence.[1] Ephesus he determined to replace by a new city, Arsinoëa,[2] called after his latest wife, Ptolemy's daughter, on a somewhat more convenient site nearer the sea. When the citizens objected to being haled from their old homes at his pleasure, Lysimachus blocked the drains on a stormy day and flooded the city. This induced the citizens to move. To swell the new city, Lebedus[3] and Colophon were emptied of their population and reduced to villages. The Colophonians, with pathetic audacity, gave battle to the forces of the King, and their feelings found lasting voice in the lament of the native poet Phœnix. The new city of Lysimachus prospered, but it was still Ephesus, never really Arsinoëa.[4] The Scepsians, on the other hand, who had been swept by Antigonus into the new city of the Troad, Lysimachus allowed to return to their former seat.[5]

At Heraclea his action was conspicuously capricious. Amestris, after living with him happily for some time, when she found him contemplating the new marriage with Arsinoë, chose to leave him at Sardis and go back to govern Heraclea. When her sons Clearchus and Oxathres reached an age to assume the reins, her adventurous life came to a tragical end by her putting to sea in a boat which they had specially prepared in order to drown her. Being not only wicked but stupid, they alienated the citizens by tyrannic behaviour, and thus lost the advantage of Dionysius in regard to the Macedonian rulers. Lysimachus now intervened amid popular plaudits, put the two wretched criminals to death, and restored the long-desired democracy. The city congratulated itself on having won at this late date its freedom. But it rejoiced too soon, for Lysimachus, the liberator, soon followed the custom of old Persian days in making it over as an appanage to the queen Arsinoë. So the Heracleots now found the former tyrants simply replaced by the queen's agent, Heraclides —a change hardly for the better.[6]

---

[1] Strabo xii. 563.

[2] The form of the name was Ἀρσινόεια not Ἀρσινόη, *Ath. Mitth. loc. cit.*

[3] Its *synoikismos* with Teos seems therefore to have become abortive by the fall of Antigonus.

[4] Strabo xiv. 640; Paus. i. 9, 7; vii. 3, 4.

[5] Strabo xiii. 597, 607.   [6] Memnon 4-7 = *F.H.G.* iii. 530 f.

The activity of Lysimachus as a builder of cities left a durable mark upon the country of the Asiatic Greeks. The case of Ephesus has been already described. For foundations, indeed, which were altogether new, Lysimachus did not find room, but where others had begun Lysimachus carried to completion. There were the three new cities of Antigonus, the two Antigonias and Smyrna. To all of these Lysimachus set his hand. The name of the two first, designed to perpetuate the glory of Antigonus, was altered. Lysimachus, having already created a Lysimachia in the Chersonese, did not happily think it necessary to go on giving the same name with dull monotony to all his cities. The Antigonia on the Ascanian lake received the name of his earlier wife, Nicaea the daughter of Antipater;[1] it was the Nicaea or Nice which was to give its title to the *Nicene* creed. The other Antigonia was renamed Alexandria in honour of his old master and known as Alexandria Troas (or Troas simply) to distinguish it from all the other Alexandrias.[2] The old name of Smyrna was left unchanged.[3] In the case of Ilion also, Lysimachus was at pains to realize some of the good intentions of Alexander. It was now that the city received a temple worthier of its fame, if not quite what Alexander had contemplated, and a wall of forty stades (about $4\frac{2}{3}$ miles). Its population was increased by a *synoikismos* of the surrounding villages.[4] The new Ilion became in the third century before Christ a place of considerable importance, not indeed as a political power, but as the centre of a religious union.[5]

The murder of Agathocles brings the disaffection of the Greek cities towards Lysimachus to a head; they begin openly to invoke the intervention of Seleucus.[6] There is thus an immense advantage secured to the house of Seleucus, in that its first appearance to the Greek cities[7] is in the guise of liberator. It starts with the flowing tide. As the great power of the East, it had indeed already shown its sympathy

---

[1] Strabo xii. 565.
[2] *Ibid.* xiii. 593.
[3] *Ibid.* xiv. 646.
[4] *Ibid.* xiii. 593.
[5] See Haubold, *Re rebus Iliensium* (Leipzig, 1888).
[6] Memnon 8 = *F.H.G.* iii. 532.
[7] One does not, of course, count the action of Seleucus on the Asiatic coast in 315, when he merely commands on behalf of Ptolemy.

with the interests of the Hellenic world, especially with the cult of Apollo, from whom it professed to descend.[1] The temple of Apollo at Branchidae was among the great shrines of Pan-Hellenic regard, such as Delphi or Delos. The work of restoration after the Persian tyranny was now going forward.[2] A good Hellene, king or private man, might feel it claim his contributions and offerings. Seleucus, long before he had any political connexion with Miletus, had shown himself a zealous benefactor both of the city and the temple connected with it. On becoming master of Irân he had sent back to Branchidae from Ecbatana the bronze image of Apollo by Canachus, which had been carried off by the Persians.[3] A Milesian inscription[4] represents Antiochus, during his father's lifetime, as promising to build a *stoa* in the city, from the lease of which a permanent revenue may be drawn to be devoted to the expenses of the temple.[5] Miletus, we saw, was still outside Lysimachus' sphere of power in 287-286, and may never have been acquired by him.

The Delian Apollo was also honoured by the house of Seleucus. Stratonice especially seems to have shown herself a

---

[1] That the claim to descend from Apollo goes back to the beginning of the dynasty is shown by the Ilian inscription (*C.I.G.* No. 3595), where Apollo is called ἀρχηγὸς τοῦ γένους of Antiochus I in the early days of his reign. The claim must therefore go back to the first Seleucus. It remains in that case a mystery why Apollo and his emblems should figure so rarely upon the coins of Seleucus. To suppose it an innovation of the new King Antiochus I in the first stormy days of his reign seems impossible. It may, however, have been an innovation of Seleucus at the end of his reign, when he came into closer contact with the Didymaean temple, and was perhaps saluted by the oracle as son of Apollo, in the same way in which Alexander had been saluted by the Ammonian oracle as son of Zeus.

[2] Haussoullier, *Rev. de Philol.* xxiv. (1900), p. 243 f.

[3] Paus. viii. 46, 3.

[4] Published by Haussoullier, *Rev. de Philol.* xxiv. (1900), p. 245.

[5] The date of the inscription is between 306, when Seleucus began to be called king, and 293, when the title was shared by Antiochus. When, however, Haussoullier argues that it must be after Antiochus' marriage with Stratonice because the privileges are decreed to him, "and also to his issue," he seems to me to go too far, since (1) we know that Antiochus had another wife besides Stratonice by whom he had children (Polyaen. viii. 50), and (2) even if we suppose him unmarried, the clause, a common one in such decrees, might surely be used in the case of a man who was expected at some future time to have issue.

munificent votaress of this god. The temple registers show presents from both herself and Seleucus.[1]

To Seleucus himself only seven months are allowed, from the battle of Coru-pedion to his death, in which to deal with all the questions involved in the relations between the Greek cities of the Asiatic sea-board and the power ruling the interior. In seven months he has time to do little but inform himself of the situation, and of even that little almost all record has perished. He seems at any rate to have addressed himself promptly to the question of the Greek cities, and to have sent out "regulators" (διοικηταί) to the various districts to report. Such at least is what the historian of Heraclea represents him as doing in the case of the northern cities.[2] It is only by what he tells us that light is flashed upon a single spot in the darkness of these seven months. The commissioner appointed to visit the cities of Hellespontine Phrygia and the northern coast is a certain Aphrodisius. He comes in due course to Heraclea. In this city, as we may suppose in most others, the fall of Lysimachus has previously aroused a ferment favourable to the cause of Seleucus. As soon as the news of Coru-pedion reached Heraclea, the people rose to shake off the hated yoke of the queen. A deputation waited on the agent Heraclides, informed him that the people were bent on recovering their freedom, and offered to treat him handsomely if he would quietly leave. Heraclides, misreading the situation, flew into a passion, and began ordering people off to execution. There was still a garrison to hold the people down. But the garrison unfortunately had been stinted of pay, and saw their profit in coming to an agreement with the townspeople, by which they were to acquire the franchise of the city and the arrears due to them. Heraclides accordingly found himself lodged under guard. The walls of the fortress by which the city had been coerced so long were levelled with the ground. A leader of the people was chosen and an embassy sent to Seleucus. This embassy has already left when Aphrodisius appears in

---

[1] *Bull. corr. hell.* vi. (1882), p. 29; Michel, No. 833, l. 16, 78. Her statue stood prominently in one of the chambers, Michel, No. 594, l. 92.

[2] Fränkel, *Inschr. von Pergamon*, No. 245 C, makes it seem probable that the settlement of frontiers was a main part of their business, a διανομή.

the city. All seems to promise excellent relations between Heraclea and the King, especially since they are already fighting the battle of the central government against Ziboetes the Bithynian. For some unexplained reason, Aphrodisius falls out with the Heracleots. He returns to Seleucus with a report unfavourable to Heraclea alone of all the cities he has visited. The Heracleot envoys are still with the King, and as a result of the commissioner's report an interview takes place in which an unhappy breach is made between the city and the house of Seleucus. The King begins with high words. Provoked by these, a sturdy citizen breaks out with the retort: "Heracles is the stronger, Seleucus."[1] His Doric is so broad that the King does not understand, stares angrily, and then turns away his face.

The news of the King's averted countenance, carried to Heraclea, brings about a reversal of policy. A league now comes into being, antagonistic to the ruling house. It includes Heraclea, its sister-states, Byzantium and Calchedon, and, more ominously, the Persian prince Mithridates. The enmity between Greek and barbarian was one of the circumstances most to the advantage of a Greek house, desiring to hold these coast regions where the two elements came into contact. Maladdress in handling the Greek cities might, it is seen, convert the enmity into alliance. The cities of this League form, however, in the present case an exception. With the other northern ones Aphrodisius, as we saw, had no fault to find, and the Greeks of Asia Minor generally seem to regard the house of Seleucus at this moment with feelings of gratitude and hope.

Looking, then, at the history of the Greek cities of Asia Minor, as a whole, from the fall of the Persian Empire to the time when Antiochus is called to take up his inheritance, we must admit that the result of the Irânian, giving place to a Hellenic, power has hardly come up to the forecast of Isocrates. Those whose memories went back to the visions and assurances of an earlier period, whose youth had been fed by the *Panegyricus* and *Letter to Philip*, must have felt a certain disillusionment now that nearly half a century had gone by since the morning of Granicus. After all, then, Hellenic civilization

---

[1] Ἡρακλῆς κάρρων, Σέλευκε, Memnon 11 = *F.H.G.* iii. p. 533.

was to end in monarchy? The autonomy of the cities seemed as little secure from princes like Lysimachus as from an Artaxerxes or Darius. To "obey the King's governor" was still a hard word that the cities were compelled to hear. That the cities had to do with kings whose brute strength exceeded their own, that the course of the world was governed, not by the legalities of theorists, but by *force majeure*, that what the city counted its rights were only held on sufferance, that the sovereignty of the kings over the cities not being recognized in political theory, the action of the kings was not restrained by any constitutional forms but solely by their own discretion—all these were facts which must have been present to any one who looked below the surface.

On the other hand, it would be untrue to deny that the Greeks had profited enormously by the Macedonian conquest. If the rule under which they had passed was not less autocratic than the Persian, it was far more sympathetic. If the chains were not taken off, they were at any rate charmingly gilded, and to a sensitive people like the Greeks the sparing of their *amour propre* removed half the injury. If some facts were unpleasant to contemplate, the King's government would help every one to cloak them over; it would call the cities its "allies" and the money it exacted a "contribution." The moral and sentimental grievance which the old barbarian rule had entailed was thus mitigated; in the material sphere the cities had gained more unquestionably. We may perhaps distinguish three main ways in which the rule of the Macedonian chiefs was a benefit. Firstly, they had shown themselves, as has been seen, ready enough to use their riches for the good of the cities, for embellishing the shrines and furthering public works. In the second place, they were the natural protectors of the cities against the barbarians, and the barbarians, as we have seen, were still a danger in many parts of Asia Minor. Lastly, if the quarrels of the different Macedonian houses drew in the cities to some extent as allies of one or the other, the establishment of a dominion prevented within its sphere the desolating feuds between city and city. There was one overshadowing authority by whose judgment the relations between the cities were regulated. In compensation then for hurt done to the self-respect and the ambitions of the cities by their subjection, they were given a measure of peace and enlarged resources.[1]

With such advantages balanced against such drawbacks the rule of the Macedonian houses must have given rise to very mixed feelings among the Greeks; the constitution of the individual citizen, the circumstances of the moment, must have made it appear in different colours, according as light was thrown upon its useful or its unpleasant side. There were numbers of well-to-do people whose material interests prospered, who were little troubled by ideal grievances, and whose main concern was the maintenance of an established order. There were others whose heads were heated by the phrases of orators, and whom nothing could console for the curtailment of their city's sovereignty. One must take account of this vein of feeling as always there, ready, as soon as it is reinforced by any tangible grievance or any general discontent, to break out in the old blind struggle for liberty. As a rule, however, the question before the cities was not between Macedonian rule in the abstract and unqualified independence, but between one Macedonian ruler and another. A diplomatic prince might reap all the profit of another's odium, and to escape from a yoke that bruised them, the Greek cities might willingly accept one more considerately adjusted. They were, at any rate, effusive enough in their professions of loyalty to many of their masters. How much sincerity lay in these professions we can only divine by weighing the circumstances of each case.

It is in this period that a practice begins to become general in the Greek world which forms a prominent feature in the last stage of classical heathenism—the rendering of distinctively divine honours to eminent men even during their lifetime.

[1] Les deux siècles qui s'écoulèrent entre la conquête d'Alexandre et la mort d'Attale Philométor sont l'époque de la plus grande prospérité de toutes les villes d'Asie Mineure. Les guerres des Attales, des Seleucides et des Ptolémées n'étaient ni très meurtrières ni très ruineuses pour le pays, et l'autorité du vainqueur du jour était toujours trop menacée pour pouvoir devenir oppressive. Au milieu de ces interminables compétitions, les cités populeuses et riches parvenaient aisément à se faire ménager, à obtenir des privilèges et à mettre à haut prix leur fidélité." Rayet, *Milet et le golfe Latmique*, i. p. 66, quoted with approval by Haussoullier, *Revue de Philol.* xxiv. (1900), p. 258.

Alexander had already before his death received from many of the Greek states honours which marked him as divine,[1] and the cities were ready to act in like manner toward his successors. The usual externals of worship—*temenos* and altar, image, sacrifice, and games—were decreed by Scepsis to Antigonus in 310,[2] and honours no less elaborate were tendered Antigonus and Demetrius by Athens in 307.[3] Lysimachus was worshipped during his lifetime by the cities within his sphere of power.[4] Ptolemy and Seleucus were worshipped both before and after their death.[5]

(c) *The Provincial Authorities*

We have now considered how two of the difficulties which the old Persian rule had encountered in Asia Minor, the difficulty of the native races and the difficulty of the Greek cities, presented themselves in 281 to Antiochus when he found himself called to assert the authority of his house in the country north of the Taurus. A third difficulty which the house of Achaemenes had experienced, that of controlling its own officers, the house of Seleucus also, should it aspire to rule Asia Minor from a seat of government outside it, was likely to experience in its turn. Alexander, had his life been longer—his house, had he left issue under whom the Empire held together—would doubtless have encountered this difficulty in course of time; we may indeed say that the break-up of the Empire after Alexander's death was nothing else but this difficulty destroying the central government altogether. In 281 Antiochus, the grandson of a Macedonian captain and an Irânian grandee, put his hand to the task which had proved too hard for the King of kings.

---

[1] Arr. *Anab.* vii. 23, 2. [2] *J.H.S.* xix. (1899), p. 335.
[3] Diod. xx. 46; Plutarch, *Dem.* 10 f.; Athen. vi. 253 *a*; xv. 697 *a*.
[4] Cassandrea, Michel, No. 323; Priene, *Inscr. in the Brit. Mus.* No. 401; Samothrace, Michel, No. 350.
[5] For Ptolemy, Diod. xx. 100, 3 f.; Paus. i. 8, 6; Michel, Nos. 595, 1198; Delamarre, *Revue de Philologie*, xx. (1896), p. 103 f. For Seleucus, Haussoullier, *Revue de Philologie*, xxiv. (1900), p. 319; Phylarch. ap. Athen. vi. 254 *f*. For the whole subject of the worship of the kings see Beurlier, *De divinis honoribus Alexandro et successoribus eius redditis*, Paris, 1890; Kornemann, *Beiträge zur alten Geschichte*, i. Leipzig, 1901. An article of mine on the subject appeared in the *English Historical Review*, October 1901.

CHAPTER VIII

ANTIOCHUS I (SOTER)

§ 1. *The Early Days*

THE course of events in Asia Minor which followed the death of Seleucus is mainly hidden from us. We must not imagine that by the crime of Ptolemy Keraunos and the desertion of the army at Lysimachia the power of the house of Seleucus in the West was instantly annihilated. As the news of the catastrophe travelled from city to city, it would find in many places a population who still saw their best course at this juncture in holding by the King of the East, or a garrison which resolved to abide faithful to their old master's son. Even in Europe, during the short time since Coru-pedion, the house of Seleucus had begun to make its supremacy effective. Silver coins are found bearing the name of King Seleucus, and stamped with the symbols of the city of Callatis (mod. Mangalia in Roumania).[1] And after the death of Seleucus coins are struck for a time in parts of Europe with the name of King Antiochus, some of them showing the anchor in the centre of the Macedonian shield, a declaration that to the house of Seleucus the throne of Philip and Alexander now belongs.[2] The news

---

[1] Babelon, p. xxxviii. There are also coins with the name of Seleucus which seem by the monogram to belong to Mesembria (Misirri in Bulgaria) and to Coele on the Thracian Chersonese. For Cassandrea, see Polyaen. vi. 7, 2.

[2] Babelon, p. xlviii. Some of these coins have as symbol a boar's jaw-bone, the Aetolian mark. In view of the fact that Seleucus died on the threshold of Europe, and Antiochus, so far as we know, never crossed thither, the house of Seleucus can never have exercised any sovereignty in Aetolia. Either then these coins were struck by royal authority in a city connected in some way with the Aetolian League, as indeed Cius, Lysimachia and Calchedon were at a later

indeed of what had occurred must have left it quite uncertain in many places in whose hands the government of the world would now rest. It must have depended upon the way in which the authorities in each city, each *condottiere* who had a fortress in charge, each mountain chief, read the signs of the times, who of the various claimants was recognized in those confused days as master.[1]

Ptolemy Keraunos, with the army and fleet gathered at Lysimachia, held indeed a point of vantage for striking at Macedonia. But he had leapt into a dangerous seat. His crime had raised all the moral feelings of the Greek world against him. Antiochus was bound by filial piety, as well as interest, to open war on him. His pretensions to Macedonia made both Antigonus Gonatas and Pyrrhus of Epirus his enemies. His brother of Egypt might now be alarmed for his own security and join his enemies. The last danger Keraunos succeeded in conjuring; he let the Court of Alexandria know that he definitely renounced all claims to Egypt and procured his brother's neutrality.[2] But the attack of Antigonus and Antiochus he had to sustain. These two kings seem soon to have come to a mutual understanding. There were other things besides the common enmity to Keraunos to draw Antigonid and Seleucid together. The House of Antigonus had been lifted from its abasement after Ipsus by Seleucus;

---

time, or, if they were struck in Aetolia, it must have been on the authority of the Aetolian magistrates, to whom at some moment Antiochus seemed a profitable ally. [Since writing the above note I have learnt from Mr. Macdonald that he considers the European origin of all these coins as not yet proved.]

[1] All the five Macedonian houses who had fought for supremacy since 315 still had representatives. The *House of Seleucus* is represented by Antiochus, whose supremacy is acknowledged in Irân and Babylon; the *House of Antigonus* by Antigonus Gonatas, the son of Demetrius, who is still master in a large part of Central and Southern Greece; through his mother, Phila, Antigonus derives blood from Antipater, but the *House of Antipater* still has one representative at any rate in the male line, Antipater, the son of Cassander's brother Philip; the *House of Ptolemy* is doubly represented, in Europe by Ptolemy Keraunos (whose mother, Eurydice, is, like Phila, a daughter of Antipater) and his half-brother Meleager, in Egypt by the younger Ptolemy and other brothers; lastly, the *House of Lysimachus* is represented by the three sons of Arsinoë, Ptolemy, Lysimachus and Philip. (Of Alexander, the son of Lysimachus, nothing is heard after the death of Seleucus.)

[2] Just. xvii. 2, 9.

Demetrius in his captivity had found at any rate princely treatment and security for his life; Stratonice, the queen of Antiochus, was the sister of Antigonus Gonatas.

Antigonus was nearer the scene of action than his brother-in-law and could strike first. The tidings of events at Lysimachia brought him hurrying north with a land and naval force to occupy Macedonia before Keraunos. The fleet constituted by Lysimachus, and including a contingent from Heraclea,[1] had passed to Keraunos with the army, and this he now opposed to the ships of Antigonus. The encounter was a victory for Keraunos—a result which the historian of Heraclea attributes mainly to the bravery of the Heracleots.[2] After this reverse Antigonus withdrew again to Central Greece, and Macedonia was left exposed.

Any outposts of Seleucid power in Europe had been cut off from succour by the defection of the forces at Lysimachia. Ptolemy Keraunos succeeded in occupying Macedonia, although, if those numismatists are right who assign coins with the name of King Antiochus to a European origin, the process must have been a gradual one, and adherents of the house of Seleucus must have held out for a time here and there. What measures the Seleucid court took in the early days of Antiochus to safeguard its interests north of the Taurus, what form its hostilities against the new Macedonian king assumed, is unknown to us. Antiochus had, as has been said, hurried westward on the news of his father's murder, and a war of some sort between Ptolemy Keraunos and Antiochus came to pass.[3] Antiochus himself did not yet cross the Taurus; he was delayed by the necessity of suppressing the revolt in Syria.[4]

What took place in Asia Minor, in those cities which a few months before had hailed Seleucus as liberator, is unrecorded. From the few things told us we can conjecture that many declared themselves at that crisis adherents of the house of Seleucus, that its popularity stood it in good stead. The

---

[1] Either, then, the Heracleot squadron had not been withdrawn from the imperial fleet after the rupture of that city with Seleucus, or a contingent had been sent after the death of Seleucus to Ptolemy Keraunos, Heraclea being now a declared enemy of the house of Seleucus.

[2] Memnon 13 = *F.H.G.* iii. p. 534.

[3] Just. xvii. 2, 10; xxiv. 1, 8; Trog. *Prol.* xvii.

[4] Michel, No. 525.

Athenian colonists in Lemnos erected temples to Antiochus as well as to his father.¹ If the account of the Ilians a few years later can be trusted, they had immediately begun on the news of Antiochus' accession to offer sacrifices and prayers on his behalf.² But the best evidence that the chances of the house of Seleucus seemed good in those days in Asia Minor is that Philetaerus of Pergamos now saw his profit in earning its good-will.

This man was a native of the little Greek town of Tios or Tieum.³ One account (possibly later court scandal) asserts that his mother was a Paphlagonian flute-girl.⁴ At some crowded funeral, to which he was carried as a baby, he had been crushed in his nurse's arms and rendered impotent.⁵ In spite of his condition his abilities secured him advancement. He had first mixed in the political game as a friend of that Docimus who had been prominent in the second rank of Macedonian chiefs, the lieutenant first of Perdiccas, then of Antigonus, and lastly of Lysimachus.⁶ Philetaerus had accompanied his friend in his passages from one camp to another. Lysimachus marked him out as a useful instrument. He was made warden of the treasure which Lysimachus had stored on the strong hill of Pergamos. In the dissensions of the family of Lysimachus, Philetaerus had sided with Agathocles, and after Agathocles' murder he no longer felt himself safe from the vindictive hatred of the queen, Arsinoë. He was among those who invoked Seleucus; the assurance was conveyed to Antioch that the warden and the treasure of Pergamos were at the King's disposal.⁷ And now when a great blow had been dealt to the house of Seleucus in the moment of its triumph, Philetaerus, with a judicious eye for the winning side, still showed himself its friend. He begged

---

¹ Phylarch. ap. Athen. vi. 254 *f*. ² Michel, No. 525.
³ Strabo xii. 543. ⁴ Carystius ap. Athen. xiii. 577 *b*.
⁵ Of course the story of his low barbarian origin may be the true one, and he may have been just what Pausanias bluntly calls him, a Paphlagonian eunuch (Paus. i. 8, 1). In that case the story of the funeral may have been invented later, to reconcile by the supposition of an accident his pretended Greek nationality with the fact of his condition. [An inscription just published (*J.H.S.* xxii. p. 195) gives the name of his father Attalus. The name at any rate is Macedonian.]
⁶ Paus. i. 8, 1. ⁷ Strabo xiii. 623; Paus. i. 10, 4.

the body of Seleucus from the murderer. Ptolemy put his price high, but Philetaerus knew when it was profitable to dip his hand into the treasure of Pergamos. He acquired the body, himself saw to its cremation, and sent the ashes to Antiochus.[1] We may be sure that any party in which Philetaerus is found has many other adherents in Asia Minor.

We may indeed divine that the Seleucid cause in Asia Minor had at that moment to trust rather to the willing loyalty or the far-sighted fears of princes and peoples than to a display of force. Antiochus was probably obliged to gather all his strength to fight for existence in Syria. It was only "by many wars," Memnon says, that he recovered "hardly and in a diminished form his father's Empire."[2] As soon, however, as it could be spared, a body of troops was sent to enforce the authority of the Seleucid king in the country beyond the Taurus. How near an interest is felt in this country is shown by the man who now appears there as the King's representative—Patrocles. Only for a moment does this distinguished figure appear in Asia Minor to vanish again in the darkness which wraps the period. The shifting light falls once more upon the Bithynian coast. A lieutenant of Patrocles, one Hermogenes of Aspendus, is here in command of a force with which he endeavours to bring again the revolted Greek cities into allegiance to the Seleucid house. Heraclea, since its rupture with Seleucus, had strengthened itself by allowing its exiles to make peace with the ruling faction and return home, but now, in presence of this instrument of compulsion, it thought best to temporize. By coming quickly to terms the city saved its fields. A more formidable foe of the Greek king was close at hand, the Bithynian chieftain, and against him Hermogenes now turned his arms. A fight between the King's forces and its ancient Bithynian enemy was an event which Heraclea was only too willing to bring about by promising Hermogenes its friendship.[3]

The sight of Macedonian armies fleeing down the valleys before the tribesmen was almost familiar in Bithynia. It was

---

[1] App. *Syr.* 63.   [2] Memnon 15 = *F.H.G.* iii. p. 534.   [3] Memnon *loc. cit.*

seen once more ere Zibœtes, now an old man of over seventy, left the sphere of his triumphs. The Bithynians were upon Hermogenes when he least expected them; he saw that his reputation had gone the way of his predecessors. Disdaining to survive, he chose at least the death of a brave man.[1] Zibœtes aspired to a greatness which went beyond mere victories of the spear. He had a comprehension of the value of the life which demanded a richer environment than the hill-side village: he wished to rival the Greek kings as a builder of cities. Before he died he had founded a Zibœtium under Mount Lypedrum.[2]

The hostilities between the forces of Antiochus and Ptolemy Keraunos did not last long. Either king was too much threatened at home not to desire a *modus vivendi*. And one was found which must have marked some frontier between the sphere to be dominated from Macedonia and the sphere of Seleucid authority.[3]

Perhaps there were fair hopes at that moment of a period of tranquillity opening for Seleucid Asia. The dangers which had compassed Antiochus at his accession seemed melting away. If the house of Seleucus could confine its ambitions to Asia, there was no reason why it should fear molestation from its rivals. Ptolemy Keraunos, to whom Macedonia had been abandoned, had his hands full in that country, crushing what remained of the house of Lysimachus, and defending himself against his barbarian neighbours; his brother in Egypt was not aggressive; Antigonus, although checked in Central Greece, served to right the balance of power against

---

[1] Memnon *loc. cit.*; cf. ch. 20, p. 537. I follow Niese (ii. p. 75) in taking Hermogenes, not Patrocles himself, to be the commander in Bithynia. Droysen understood Patrocles; Neumann (*Hermes* xix. pp. 165-185), who follows him, admits that "the subject of the sentence can grammatically only be Hermogenes," but contends that Patrocles is meant because otherwise we should hear of him in the further course of the war. That argument would be all very well if Memnon had been writing a history of the war in Asia Minor as a whole, and not simply in so far as it touched Heraclea.

[2] Steph. Byz.; Memnon 20 = *F.H.G.* iii. p. 537; cf. Fränkel, *Inschr. von Perg.* No. 65. Neither the mountain nor site have yet been identified.

[3] Trog. *Prol.* xvii.; Just. xxiv. 1; Droysen ii. p. 621, supposes that Antiochus abandoned by the peace all claims to dominion in Europe, but there is no documentary evidence as to its terms.

the house of Ptolemy; and lastly, Pyrrhus of Epirus had fortunately turned his thoughts westward and quitted the scene to plunge into adventures across the Adriatic. His brother kings, to get rid of him, were forward to give him help—ships, men, elephants; Antiochus,[1] who required all the troops he had been able to raise since the defection of the grand army to hold his outspread provinces, sent money.

And now, at peace without, the house of Seleucus might address itself to the task, for which the Greek kings had never yet had leisure, the task of bringing into subjection the stubborn elements within. Now the strength of a great empire might be turned upon self-styled kings like Ziboetes and Mithridates, and restive cities taught the true meaning of autonomy.

Whether it was before or after the peace that Patrocles took over Asia Minor and the disaster to Hermogenes occurred we do not know. It was probably after it that Antiochus himself, accompanied by his queen, crossed the Taurus.[2]

The presence of the King probably went far towards bringing to an end the anarchic state of things which had prevailed in Asia Minor since the death of Seleucus, and give his partizans in most places assured supremacy. To bring peace to the Hellenic cities and restore authority to his house was the double object which Antiochus gave the country to understand he set before him. To achieve it, he had to make sure of the allegiance of those troops who, in scattered garrisons, held the points of vantage, but whom maladroit treatment might easily cause to sell their swords to another master. Antiochus, if the expressions used by the Ilians in an honorific inscription have any truth, dealt ably and successfully with the situation.[3] But his success did not extend to the most troublesome corner of his realm, Bithynia.

[1] Opibus quam militibus instructior, Just. xvii. 2, 13.   [2] See Appendix E.
[3] νῦν τε παραγενόμενος ἐπὶ τοὺς τόπους τοὺς ἐπὶ τάδε τοῦ Ταύρου μετὰ πάσης σπουδῆς καὶ φιλοτιμίας ἅμα καὶ ταῖς πόλεσιν τὴν εἰρήνην κατεσκεύασεν, καὶ τὰ πράγματα καὶ τὴμ βασιλείαν εἰς μεῖζω καὶ λαμπροτέραν διαθέσιν ἀγήγοχε, μάλιστα μὲν διὰ τὴν ἰδίαν ἀρετὴν, εἶτα καὶ διὰ τὴν τῶμ φίλων καὶ τῶν δυνάμεων εὔνοιαν. Michel, No. 525.

Antiochus had come into Asia Minor determined to avenge Hermogenes and make a supreme effort to vindicate the supremacy of Macedonian arms. Ziboetes, the redoubtable chieftain, had died full of years, and his house was shaken by discords. Nicomedes, his eldest son, had marked himself out as the "executioner" of his brothers.[1] One of these brothers, however, called, like his father, Ziboetes, had contrived to escape massacre and make himself master of the Thynian part of his father's dominion. It seemed a favourable opportunity for the Macedonian government to intervene. But Nicomedes, however barbarous, had inherited his father's strength of will and understanding. In his predicament he boldly reversed the policy of his house and proposed an alliance to Heraclea against the Seleucid king. Heraclea, who had already negotiated with one barbarian dynast (see p. 123), was not unwilling to listen to the overtures of the Bithynian. Nicomedes is now admitted to membership in the anti-Seleucid League, and even becomes its head.

To secure this end, Nicomedes had astutely ceded to Heraclea that region which was in his brother's possession. This, of course, at once brought the Heracleots into collision with Ziboetes, and a sanguinary battle was fought. The city gained all it wanted, Memnon says, but Ziboetes continues to appear in possession of a part of Bithynia.

Heraclea was using this moment,[2] in which the Macedonian government was embarrassed and its Bithynian neighbours divided, to extend its power. It set about buying back the places which had once been annexed to it but were now alienated, Tios, Cierus, Amastris. Into whose hands these had fallen is not stated except in the case of the last, where a certain Eumenes appears as master. This man is generally taken to be the brother or nephew of Philetaerus of Pergamos, whose native place Tios was one of the cities which had been drawn into the *synoikismos* of Amastris. Tios had rapidly broken away again and renewed its separate existence.[3] In whose possession Tios and Cierus now were, whether in those

---

[1] τοῖς ἀδελφοῖς οὐκ ἀδελφὸς ἀλλὰ δήμιος γεγονώς, Memnon 20 = *F.H.G.* iii. p. 537.

[2] Memnon 17 = *F.H.G.* iii. 535.   [3] Strabo xii. 544.

of tyrants of their own or of Nicomedes, we are not told—the latter is generally assumed. These towns at any rate Heraclea now succeeds in redeeming, but Eumenes, who seems to have had some special animus against Heraclea (perhaps he was an adherent like Philetaerus of the Seleucid house), refused to sell Amastris on any terms. When Heraclea tried force, he preferred to make the place over to Ariobarzanes, the son of King Mithridates.[1]

Antiochus lost no time in opening war on the Northern League. The Seleucid fleet appeared in the neighbourhood of the Bosphorus, but the Heracleot squadron manœuvred against it, and no decisive result was obtained. Now, however, fresh complications arose. An estrangement between Antiochus and Antigonus, his late ally against Ptolemy, came to open war. Antigonus at once joined forces with the Northern League. There was a good deal of fighting of which we have no account in North-Western Asia.[2]

But this phase was not a long one. Antigonus presently made peace with his brother-in-law, and left the League to maintain the struggle by its own strength.[3]

§ 2. *The Gauls*

But already in Europe the game of politicians and kings had been confounded by a cataclysm, which swept across old landmarks and submerged old feuds and ambitions in a universal terror. Ancient Mediterranean civilization lived all its life on the edge of a great peril, which it forgot perhaps between the moments of visitation, but by which it ultimately perished. From time to time the forests and fens of Central Europe spilt upon it some of their chaotic, seething peoples. They passed—wild-eyed, jabbering strangers—over a land not

---

[1] Memnon 16 = *F.H.G.* iii. 535.

[2] Memnon 18 = *F.H.G.* iii. 535; Trogus, *Prol.* xxiv. Antiochus begins the war with the League *before his* (Antiochus') *rupture with Antigonus* (οὔπω συρραγεὶς Ἀντιγόνῳ: cf. Dio Cass. xlviii. 28, συνερρωγότων . . . αὐτῶν εἰς τὸν πόλεμον). There is a curious mistranslation in Droysen iii. 185, "Antiochos attaqua Nicomède *avant qu'il* (i.e. Nicomède) *eut fait sa jonction avec Antigone.*"

[3] Just. xxv. 1, 1. See Appendix F.

theirs, which they saw only as a place to devour and destroy. Such a visitation the Greeks knew four centuries before, when Cimmerians and Treres had burst upon Asia Minor and left a memorial in the elegies of Callinus. Such a visitation again had come a century before to Italy, when the Gauls had almost stamped the infant city rising on the Tiber out of existence. They were hordes of Gauls, or, as the Greeks called them, Galatians, who now poured southward over the Balkans. Ptolemy Keraunos reaped his reward for seizing the Macedonian throne in having first to meet the shock of the invasion. Less than a year from the time of his deed of blood his head was waving on the point of a Gaulish spear[1] (spring 280). That summer all the country-side of Macedonia was overrun. With winter the wave ebbed, leaving a tract of desolation behind it. The Greek world waited breathlessly for next year. Although not immediately threatened, the Seleucid king shared the general anxiety. Apart even from selfish motives the deliverance of Hellas was a cause in which it flattered the vanity of any Greek king to shine. Antiochus sent a contingent to take part in the defence.[2] The invasion came with terrific force (279). The Greeks massed at Thermopylae. It was the road over Mount Oeta which the five hundred men of Antiochus were posted to hold. There in fact the Gauls at one moment directed their assault, and the contingent distinguished itself in repelling them, with the loss, however, of its commander, Telesarchus. Then the barbarians succeeded in turning the Greek position by the pass which Xerxes had traversed, and Central Greece was overwhelmed. But now the defence prevailed. At Delphi a Greek force inflicted a crushing defeat upon the horde, and the shattered remnants withdrew. Greece was delivered.[3]

The Seleucid court had, no doubt, been following the struggle with anxiety. So far no Gauls had crossed the sea. But they were coming perilously near. A body under Leonnorius and Lutarius had broken off from the rest before

[1] Just. xxiv. 5, 7.
[2] Niese (ii. p. 22, note 6) supposes, against the statement of Pausanias, that this contingent was one of the Seleucid garrisons in Europe. I do not see why Antiochus should be held incapable of sending 500 men across the Aegean.
[3] Paus. x. 20 f.

ANTIOCHUS I (SOTER)

the invasion of Greece and turned eastward. They traversed Thrace, levying blackmail as they went. They pushed on to the Bosphorus and harried the territory of Byzantium. Heraclea and the other allies of Byzantium sent help in vain. But the narrow strip of sea seemed to oppose an impassable barrier. They had no boats or skill to make them, and Byzantium refused to give them any assistance. The Gauls next tried the straits at the other end of the Propontis, the Hellespont. They seized Lysimachia by a ruse and overran the Chersonese. But here the Seleucid governor, Antipater, was watching them from the Asiatic shore, and would not give them unconditional passage. Then a great part of the horde returned to the Bosphorus under Leonnorius; a part remained with Lutarius opposite Antipater.[1]

It was the moment when the Northern League was left by Antigonus still in grapple with Antiochus. To either side perhaps the thought occurred of hiring these terrible wild men against the other. Antipater had entered into some sort of negotiation with them, but had not been able to make a secure bargain. Nicomedes, when Leonnorius returned to the Bosphorus, was more successful. A treaty was agreed to by the Gaulish chief, in which he placed himself absolutely under Nicomedes' orders and made himself an instrument of the League.[2] His bands were at once conveyed across the Bosphorus. Meanwhile, Lutarius also had seized some boats in which the agents of Antipater had come over. With these in a few days he got his following over the Hellespont, whether Antipater would or not, and turning northwards rejoined Leonnorius. The terrified inhabitants of Asia Minor soon learnt that the Galatians were in the land (278-277).[3]

The League, with its redoubtable auxiliaries, first turned upon Ziboetes, who had probably an understanding with the Seleucid court. The Thynian country was given up to ravage and massacre. All that could be moved was carried off by the Galatians.[4] But they had soon passed beyond Nicomedes'

---

[1] Memnon 19 = *F.H.G.* iii. p. 535; Livy xxxviii. 16.

[2] The cities of the League are enumerated—Byzantium, Tios, Heraclea, Calchedon, and Cierus, the towns which Heraclea had just reannexed still figuring as autonomous communities.

[3] Paus. x. 23, 14; Trog. *Prol.* xxv.   [4] Memnon 19 = *F.H.G.* iii. p. 535.

control and left the gutted Bithynian valleys far behind them. They knew neither master nor law outside their own horde, and turned to right or left wherever the sight of smiling lands and villages provoked their appetite. No men felt themselves secure or knew whether they might not any day see the frightful apparition of these strong men from the north in their familiar fields.

The figure of the Galatian, as the Greeks of Asia saw him, is given us in the descriptions and in the remains of their art. We are shown the great strapping bodies, sometimes naked, sometimes cased in a strange garb, shirts and trousers of many colours, plaids brooched on the shoulder, the necklets and bracelets of gold, the straw-coloured hair stiffened with grease till it stood up on the head like the bristles of a Satyr, the huge shields which covered a man's whole body, the swords as long as a Greek javelin, the pikes whose broad iron heads were longer than a Greek sword. We are told of their full-chested voices, their loud boastings and extravagant gestures, the unreasoning frenzy with which they flung themselves into battle, and which seemed to make them insensible of wounds, their unbridled love of wine, the nameless abominations of their camps.[1]

In such guise did the children of the North introduce themselves twenty-two centuries ago to the civilized, that is to say the Hellenic, world. To the men of the Mediterranean they seemed the embodiment of brute and brainless force, which could by its bulk for a while overbear the higher qualities, but which the "firm, deliberate valour" and disciplined intelligence of the Hellenic character[2] must in the end subdue or use as an instrument for its own ends. On the one side seemed mere volume of force, on the other the mind, by which alone force could be efficiently directed. But what if those Northern races of abounding physical vitality learnt some day of the Southern to think? That question it probably occurred to no one to ask twenty-two centuries ago.

The body of Galatians which had entered Asia numbered,

---

[1] Paus. x. 19 f.; Diod. v. 26 f.; cf. Brunn, *Geschichte der griechischen Künstler* (ed. 2) vol. i. p. 311 f.   [2] Cf. Paus. x. 21, 2.

we are told, only 20,000 men, and of these only half were combatants.¹ But the terror of their name caused the heart of the people of the land to melt. Their mobility, their elusiveness, and the extent of their depredations made them seem like a swarm of hornets that filled the land.² Of what the native peasantry suffered there is no record. Only a trace here and there—some words on a worn stone or a tale gathered long after from the lips of the people by writers curious of those things—preserves some memorial of the agonies of the Greek cities. An inscription³ shows us Erythrae paying blackmail to Leonnorius. At Miletus they had a legend of how the Galatians had caught the women of the city outside the walls on the feast of the Thesmophoria and carried off all who could not pay the required ransom,⁴ and how seven Milesian maidens had destroyed themselves to escape shame.⁵ Some lines of the poetess Anyta of Tegea are preserved⁶ which purport to be an epitaph on three Milesian maidens who had won glory by this act. At Ephesus they told the same story of an Ephesian girl which was told of Tarpeia at Rome.⁷ At Celaenae they told a story of how, when the Galatians had beset the city, its river-god Marsyas had risen in flood against them, while the air was filled with a mysterious sound of flutes, and the barbarians had been driven backward.⁸ At Themisonium the local story clung to a neighbouring cavern. Heracles, Apollo and Hermes had appeared in a dream to the magistrates, and revealed this cavern to them as a hiding-place for the whole population from the Galatian terror.⁹ However much fiction may go to make up such legends, they show at least how the memory of those days of fear was burnt into the popular imagination.

The whole question of the Trans-Tauric country, as it lay before the house of Seleucus, was materially affected by the introduction of this new element. The entrance of the Galatians marks the beginning of a new phase. Hitherto

---

[1] Liv. xxxviii. 16, 9.
[2] Just. xxv. 2, 8.
[3] Michel, No. 503.
[4] Parthenius, περὶ ἐρωτ. παθημ. viii. i. (Sakolowski) cited by Haussoullier *Revue de Phil.* xxiv. (1900), p. 321.
[5] Jerome, *Adv. Jov.* i. 41.
[6] *Anth. Palat.* vii. 492.
[7] Plutarch, *Parall. Min.* 15.
[8] Paus. x. 30, 9.
[9] *Ibid.* 32, 4.

we have seen Greek rule, as represented successively by Alexander, Antigonus, Lysimachus and the house of Seleucus, always promising to bring the country under effectual government, but defeated over and over again by some apparently accidental occurrence—the early death of Alexander, war after war between the Successors, changes of dynasty. There seemed no absolute impossibility that a Greek house should succeed in the task if it could only have a period of freedom from external complications. But now the task had become infinitely more difficult. For its achievement it was an indispensable condition that the Galatians should be not only defeated but exterminated or subdued. It was not so much that they hampered the paramount authority as an independent power; they formed indeed no state with a consistent policy of its own. They hampered it—as governments in the East are chiefly hampered by such unassimilated elements—by being always there to furnish material to any antagonist of the paramount power. All the opponents with whom the house of Seleucus had hitherto to deal, all future rebels, had now an unfailing source of strength on which to draw. It was not as a new state but as a great mass of mercenary soldiers encamped in the land that the Galatians—selling themselves now to one employer, now to another, one part of them to the Seleucid king, another to the King's enemies—kept all the conflicting powers in Asia Minor in unstable balance and prevented the establishment of a single supreme lord.

To the Greek cities the result was twofold. On the one hand they had to suffer from the incursions of the barbarians or pay blackmail; on the other the power of the kings to curtail their autonomy was restricted. According as they looked at the matter from this side or that, they saw in the barbarians a danger and in the kings the saviours of Hellenism, or in the kings a danger and in the barbarians a safeguard.[1] It would seem that at first it was the former aspect which presented itself; the early days of the Gallic invasion were probably the worst, before repeated blows had pushed the Galatians towards the interior; and the cities at that time

[1] Memnon 19 = *F.H.G.* iii. p. 536.

may have sincerely regarded the kings as fighting in their cause against the barbarian. Then as the strokes told and the kings gained a certain advantage, the cities began to forget their sufferings and to look with pleasure on the Galatian adversary who made the King's victory incomplete.

For Asia Minor did not contrive, like Greece, to throw off again the strange element which had entered its system. The Galatians came into Asia to stay. Probably from the first moment of their appearance Antiochus set what forces he could dispose of (for he was short of men)[1] in action against them. There was also a certain power of resistance in the Greek cities. Meeting with these rebuffs, the Galatians were gradually obliged to put a limit to their vague wanderings and become more or less settled on definite territory of their own. Thence they might still indeed raid their neighbours, but they had made a step from a nomad towards a settled life. The inland regions of Phrygia, inhabited by a peasantry in scattered villages, long accustomed to bow to foreign masters, Persian and Macedonian, lay an easy conquest. And here the Galatians began to make themselves at home. Their bands had consisted of men of three tribes or nations, and each of these took to itself a special territory. They lay one beside another along the north of the central table-land, around the ancient Phrygian towns and the monuments of old Asiatic religions. The Trocmi came to possess the most easterly territory with its centre across the Halys at Tavium; the next tribe, the Tectosages, had their centre in Ancyra; the third, the Tolistoagii[2] in Pessinūs, where from time immemorial the Great Mother of the Phrygians was worshipped with fanatic rites. It was with the last, as the most westerly, that the Greeks had most to do.[3]

[1] Just. xvii. 2, 13; Lucian, *Zeuxis*, 8.

[2] So the inscriptions; writers call them Tolistobōgii.

[3] There is some divergence in the account of these settlements. The statement above, being that generally accepted, is taken from Strabo xii. 567; Plin. v. § 146. Livy (xxxviii. 16, 12) gives the Trocmi *the shore of the Hellespont*. Memnon gives the Tolistobogii Tavium, the Trocmi Ancyra, and the Tectosages Pessinus. Pliny, who gives the towns as above, contradicts himself in another sentence by saying that the territory of the Tectosages lay to the east in Cappadocia, and giving the Trocmi Maeonia (*sic*) and Paphlagonia. Possibly all this confusion arose from the Galatians changing their seats repeatedly before

We can no longer trace the process by which the Galatians were brought to settle down, nor say when or by what steps the organization sketched by Strabo[1] took shape. When the Galatians first came to Asia, they were led, according to Memnon,[2] by seventeen chiefs, of whom Leonnorius and Lutarius were the first in rank. In Strabo a much more regular organization appears. Each of the three tribes is subdivided into four *tetrarchies*; every tetrarchy has a chief ($\tau\epsilon\tau\rho\acute{\alpha}\rho\chi\eta s$) of its own, and, under him, a judge ($\delta\iota\kappa\alpha\sigma\tau\acute{\eta}s$), a marshal ($\sigma\tau\rho\alpha\tau o\phi\acute{\upsilon}\lambda\alpha\xi$), and two under-marshals ($\dot{\upsilon}\pi o\sigma\tau\rho\alpha\tau o\phi\acute{\upsilon}\lambda\alpha\kappa\epsilon s$). The twelve tetrarchs are supreme as a body over the whole nation, and are associated with a Council of 300 men, who meet in a certain sacred place ($\Delta\rho\upsilon\nu\acute{\alpha}\mu\epsilon\tau o\nu$). The Council alone has jurisdiction in cases of murder; in all other cases, the tetrarchs and judges. The organization of the horde must have been much looser when it first overspread Asia Minor.

The house of Seleucus played an honourable part in these days as the champion of civilization against the Gauls. It was a *rôle* in which all the Greek kings were anxious to shine. Even Ptolemy II, when he contrived to make away with a mutinous contingent of Gallic mercenaries, was depicted by his court-poet as sharing with the Delphic god himself the glory of vanquishing these "late-born Titans from the utter West."[3] To such a glory Antiochus might have made out a better claim. It was indeed as *Soter*, the "Saviour," or even (if we may judge by his cult at Seleucia-in-Pieria[4]) as Apollo Soter, that he was remembered.[5] He was so called, says Appian, because "he drove out the Galatians who invaded Asia."[6] This Antiochus did not do, but he did win one or more victories, which doubtless had an effect in stemming the

---

they finally settled down, or fractions of the three different nations may have remained mingled with each other, just as in Asia Minor to-day Turks, Armenians, Kurds, Kizil-bashis, etc., live side by side.

[1] xii. 567. [2] Ch. 19 = *F.H.G.* iii. p. 536.

[3] ὀψίγονοι Τιτῆνες ἀφ' ἑσπέρου ἐσχατόωντος, Callim. *Hymn.* iv. 174; cf. Schol.

[4] *C.I.G.* 4458.

[5] It is not proved that he bore the surname during his life; on the other hand, the argument from silence against his having done so is worth very little, where our documents are so scanty.

[6] App. *Syr.* 65.

Galatian raids on the coast and relieving certain districts. His Gallic War seems to have been sung in an epic by Simonides of Magnesia,[1] but without thereby securing any immortal record. Only the story of one battle, in which the Galatians were scared by the sight of the King's elephants, is preserved in its popular form by Lucian.

On the night before the battle (so it runs) the King dreamed a dream. He saw the great Alexander standing beside him, and then and there Alexander himself gave out the password for the coming day: "Health!"—the ordinary word at parting.[2] Antiochus' heart failed him as the battle drew on. The host of the Galatians counted forty thousand horse and a great array of chariots, eighty of them scythed, and against all this he had only a small body of troops to set, hastily collected and for the most part light-armed. But the tactician, Theodotas of Rhodes, bade him be of good cheer. The King had sixteen elephants, and Theodotas instructed him to set these in the fore-part of the battle. The device answered. For when the elephants moved out, the Galatian horses became mad with fear and swerved backwards. The scythed chariots tore their own ranks. The Macedonians and Greeks followed up with an immense slaughter. Only a few of the Galatians escaped into the hills. The Macedonian army gathered about their King and crowned him victor, raising the shout of *Kallinikos*. But the eyes of Antiochus were full of bitter tears. "Shame, my men," he broke out, "is all that we have got this day. Our deliverance we owe to these sixteen brutes. But for them, where should we have been?" And the King commanded that the trophy should bear nothing but the figure of an elephant.[3]

Whether the action was quite as great an affair as it appears through this epic medium may be questionable. But we may believe that Antiochus did win a notable victory. Against such an enemy as the Galatians, however, one victory is not likely to have gone far, and what the success of

---

[1] Suid. Σιμωνίδης Μάγνης Σιπύλου, ἐποποιός, γέγονεν ἐπ' Ἀντιόχου τοῦ Μεγάλου κληθέντος καὶ γέγραφε τὰς Ἀντιόχου τοῦ Μεγάλου πράξεις καὶ τὴν πρὸς Γαλάτας μάχην, ὅτε μετὰ τῶν ἐλεφάντων τὴν ἵππον αὐτῶν ἔφθειρεν. Obviously this is the celebrated battle fought by Antiochus *the First*, not by Antiochus the Great.

[2] Lucian, *Pro Lapsu inter Salut.* 9.   [3] *Ibid. Zeuxis*, 8.

Antiochus was in other parts of the war we can only divine from the reputation he left behind him. Whatever it may have been, it was anything but thorough. The Galatians continued to be a menace to the inhabitants of the sea-board, and, according to Livy [1] not only the small communities, but even the Seleucid government was reduced at last to pay blackmail.

§ 3. *Foreign Policy : Antigonus and Ptolemy*

A connected narrative of the reign of Antiochus I after the Gallic invasion can hardly be pieced together out of our fragmentary materials, but the general lines of its policy may be discerned. As in Asia Minor, so in the neighbouring realms the Gallic invasion *marks the end of an epoch.* The chaotic struggle between the five Macedonian houses is concluded. Two Macedonian kingdoms with firm outlines are now the principal foreign powers with which the house of Seleucus has to do. The houses of Antipater and Lysimachus are heard of no more after the confusion which follows the death of Ptolemy Keraunos in Macedonia (278-276), when Ptolemy, the son of Lysimachus, and Antipater, the grandson of the old Antipater, appear for a moment among the ephemeral kings.[2] Then Antigonus Gonatas strikes in from Central Greece and gradually brings under all hostile elements in Macedonia—rival factions and Gallic swarms.

By 276 he stands before the world as acknowledged King in the Macedonian fatherland. The object for which the first Antigonus had vainly striven his grandson now finally attains. The house of Antipater disappears, except in so far as Antigonus may claim by virtue of his mother Phila to represent that also, or those kings of the Seleucid house who descend from Phila's daughter Stratonice.[3] The house of

---

[1] xxxviii. 16, 13.   [2] Diod. xxii. 4.

[3] That such claims were considered is shown by the cases in which names characteristic of one house appear in another house connected with it by female descent, *e.g.* the name Lysimachus in the Ptolemaic royal family, the name Antipater in the Seleucid ; especially by the names Demetrius and Philip (*i.e.* the Antigonid names), which we shall find the later Seleucids taking as family names of their own.

Lysimachus also disappears. It has been conjectured that the Ptolemy son of Lysimachus, whose daughter is appointed high-priestess of the Seleucid queen in Asia Minor about thirty years after,[1] is the man who had once been for a few days King of Macedonia.

Henceforth the house of Antigonus takes root in Macedonia, as the house of Ptolemy has done in Egypt and the house of Seleucus in Asia. These are the three powers who play the leading part in the lands of the eastern Mediterranean during the rest of the third century before Christ, till all relations are changed by being drawn within the widening sphere of Rome.

If these powers grouped themselves in two opposing camps it meant that two of them must gravitate together against the third. We accordingly find a close understanding during all this period between the Seleucid and the Antigonid houses against the Ptolemaïc, with which one or other of them, if not both together, is continually at war.

They were, as we have seen, already connected in the person of queen Stratonice. The beginning of this period of friendship is marked by another marriage. The daughter whom Stratonice, before being passed on to Antiochus, had borne to Seleucus was now of marriageable age. She was called Phila, after her maternal grandmother, the daughter of Antipater. Soon after her uncle Antigonus had established himself on the Macedonian throne she was sent over to Macedonia to become his wife. It was a wedding distinguished apparently by the illustrious throng of philosophers and poets whom the Stoic king called together, a company in which Aratus of Soli made a brilliant figure.[2]

Ptolemy II Philadelphus occupied a strong position which both his brother-kings felt as a menace to themselves. He had in Egypt a territory which experience had shown to be fenced against all attack, and which by its natural wealth and its position on the world's highways, brought him an immense revenue, while its limited area allowed it to be held in the grip of a far more thorough centralization at a far less expense than the sprawling provinces of the Seleucid. But if his realm

---

[1] See p. 178.   [2] Diog. Laert. vii. 1, 8; *Vit. Arat.*; Michel, No. 1295.

had been confined to Egypt the other courts might have regarded him as inoffensive. It was as the great naval power that he aroused their hostility. As a naval base for the eastern Mediterranean, Egypt under the conditions of those days was unmatched. It had in Alexandria one sufficient harbour, and the rest of its short coast protected by lagoons.

For the timber indeed necessary to ship-building, Egypt had to look without, but in the dependent island of Cyprus, the southern Lebanon, and the coasts of Asia Minor, Ptolemy possessed an ample supply. A power which created a sea-empire, spreading its influence over all the coasts and islands of the Levant, and interfering in the politics of Greece and Ionia, was not a power which either Seleucid or Antigonid could tranquilly behold.

It is no longer possible to trace the stages by which the house of Ptolemy acquired its possessions over-seas. A beginning had already been made by the first king. Ptolemy Soter had finally reannexed Cyprus about 294, and had brought under his protectorate the Confederation of the Cyclades.[1] It was in war with Antiochus, doubtless, that Ptolemy II won many of the strong places along the coasts of Asia. The immediate origin of war between the two kingdoms is shrouded in obscurity. The relations between them at Antiochus' accession were friendly and regulated by an express treaty made under Seleucus. It seems to have been on the side of Antiochus that the *status quo* was first disturbed.

One of his daughters, called after her Bactrian grandmother Apama, Antiochus had given in marriage to Magas, the half-brother of Ptolemy, who ruled the Cyrenaïc province as viceroy.[2] Some time after the Gallic invasion[3] Magas declared himself independent and took up an attitude hostile to Egypt.

---

[1] Michel, No. 373. Niese (ii. p. 101 f.) supposes that Ptolemy I also reannexed after Ipsus the places he had occupied in 309 on the coast of Asia Minor. For his possessions in Caria, Niese cites Jerome on Daniel, 11, 5, "tantae potientiae, ut . . . Cariam quoque obtineret, et multas insulas urbesque et regiones, de quibus non est huius temporis scribere." For his possession of Halicarnassus, Niese cites *Inscr. of the Brit. Mus.* No. 906 (Michel, No. 1198). But is it certain that this inscription belongs to the reign of the Ptolemy I?

[2] At the accession of Antiochus, Apama cannot have been more than ten or eleven, Wilcken in *Pauly-Wissowa* under "Apama" (3).

[3] Because Ptolemy has a corps of Gallic mercenaries.

Antiochus soon after abjured his neutrality and drew his sword against Ptolemy in alliance with his son-in-law.[1]

Such is the order of events in the sketch of Pausanias, but of their real connexion, the diplomatic to-and-fro which accompanied them, we can only guess. We do not know whether it was Antiochus or Magas to whom the initiative in the rupture with Egypt should be assigned. There were at any rate more selfish reasons to make Antiochus break with Ptolemy than sympathy with his daughter's husband, and it may well be that Apama carried with her to Cyrene the instigations to revolt.

The date of the beginning of hostilities between Antiochus and Ptolemy is fixed by Babylonian inscriptions to the year 38 of the Seleucid era (October 274-October 273 B.C.).[2] Its effects were abundantly felt in the country beyond the Taurus, upon whose coasts Ptolemy was able, in virtue of his supremacy at sea, to throw his armies, or at any rate swarms of privateers.[3] It was a war in which neither struck a vital part of his adversary, which dribbled on, with pauses and local variations, till it must have seemed the normal state of things.

To the house of Seleucus it meant a fresh complication in the Trans-Tauric problem. There was now an external foe pressing from without, to add to the rebellious elements within. It was such a complication as the house of Achaemenes had found in the attack of the European Greeks. That had compelled them for long periods to abandon the coasts which the Asiatic Greeks inhabited, and the house of Seleucus now found its hold on the coasts become exceedingly precarious and interrupted. Ptolemy, of course, could use the old cry of Hellenic autonomy against the master in possession.

To attempt a chronology of such a war—a multitude of local struggles, strong places wrested now by one side, now by the other, factions oscillating in the cities—would probably be difficult if we had all the facts. Under the circumstances all one can do is to indicate the traces of Ptolemaïc rule along the coasts. Our chief literary authority is unfortunately a

[1] Paus. i. 7, 3.
[2] *Zeitschr. für Assyr.* vii. p. 232. The era in use in Syria had as its starting-point the autumn of 312; that of Babylonia the autumn of 311.
[3] Paus. i. 7, 3.

court-poet, whose phrases cannot be taken too severely. When Theocritus says that Ptolemy "gives the signal to all the Pamphylians and the spearmen of Cilicia, to the Lycians and the war-like Carians,"[1] it need mean no more than that Ptolemaïc garrisons were posted at strong points along the southern coast—places like Selinus and Coracesium—and that many of the cities of Lycia and Caria had been drawn into the Ptolemaïc alliance.

To begin with the east, with Rough Cilicia—the end, as the ancients reckoned, of the Taurus barrier—the struggle between Seleucid and Ptolemy has here left its mark in the names of the coast towns. Near the river Lamus, after which, to the west, Rough Cilicia was held to begin,[2] we hear of an Antioch.[3] Then we have Seleucia on the Calycadnus (mod. Selefkeh), where there is still room between mountains and sea for a large city—founded, according to its legend, by Seleucus Nicator himself.[4] Next come Ptolemaïc towns, Berenice,[5] called after the wife of the first or the third Ptolemy, and Arsinoë,[6] called after Arsinoë Philadelphus, the sister-wife of Ptolemy II, the sometime wife of Lysimachus, or possibly after the sister-wife of Ptolemy IV. Then again we have a Seleucid foundation in Antioch-near-Cragus.[7]

On passing to Pamphylia we are confronted at the entrance by a Ptolemaïs,[8] and then again in the plain about the mouth of the Eurymedon comes a Seleucia.[9]

In Lycia the Ptolemaïc influence seems to have become especially consolidated. Patara, the harbour-town of Xanthus, was enlarged by Ptolemy II as another Arsinoë, though in

---

[1] *Idyl.* xvii. 88, 89.   [2] Strabo xiv. 671.

[3] Antioch, Ἰσαυρίας ἡ Λαμωτίς, Steph. Byz. see Droysen ii. p. 724. This *may*, of course, be a foundation of Antiochus Epiphanes or one of the later kings. [Ramsay identifies it with Antioch-on-Cragus, *Hist. Geog.* p. 380.]

[4] Steph. Byz.; Strabo xiv. 670; Amm. Marc. xiv. 8, 2.

[5] Steph. Byz.; *Stadiasmus Maris Magni* (Müller, *Frag. Geog. Graec.* i.), § 190.

[6] Steph. Byz.

[7] Ptolemy v. 8. 2; for Cragus, Strabo xiv. 669. The site of this Antioch is thought to be marked by the remains of an aqueduct between Selinti and Kharadran [Murray, *Asia Minor* (1895), p. 176]. Droysen gives further an Antioch παράλιος and another Antioch which appear to belong to Cilicia and be different from any of those mentioned above, but whose sites cannot be fixed.

[8] Strabo xiv. 667.   [9] *Stadiasmus,* § 216.

this case, no less than when her former husband called Ephesus after her, the queen's name had too famous a name to compete with ever to obtain currency.¹ The possession of Patara probably implies authority over the whole Lycian Confederation.² Caria is named by Jerome among the possessions of the second Ptolemy.³ The towns, more strictly Carian, lying inland, were, as we shall see, held by Antiochus, but we can prove Ptolemaïc possession in the chief Greek towns of the coast and some of the adjoining islands. Caunus is found as the station of a Ptolemaïc fleet at a moment soon after the marriage of Ptolemy and his sister Arsinoë (before 274).⁴ Cos, together with the shrine on the Triopian promontory, the religious centre of the Dorian Body, received special attention from Ptolemy, as befitted his birthplace.⁵ At Halicarnassus the Ptolemaïc supremacy is evidenced by inscriptions.⁶

The Ionian cities Antiochus I seems, as a whole, to have been able to retain. Samos, indeed, had been acquired by Ptolemy some time before 274,⁷ and gave the Egyptian fleets an important station in the Aegean, and even on the mainland Miletus, in spite of the favours which the house of Seleucus had showered upon it, had to yield to the superior force of the king of Egypt. The day came when it was the Ptolemaïc house whom the obsequious *demos* honoured at Branchidae.⁸ At the neighbouring Heraclea also the ascendancy of the Ptolemaïc house is indicated by an inscription assigned to the

[1] Strabo xiv. 666.

[2] I know of no other traces of Ptolemaïc rule in Lycia except this regeneration of Patara which can be *certainly* ascribed to the time of the second Ptolemy, *i.e.* of his wars with Antiochus I and Antiochus II. Niese (ii. p. 102, note 3), Mahaffy (*Empire of the Ptolemies*, p. 487), Haussoullier (*Revue de Philol.* xxiv. (1900), p. 324, note 2) hold that the two decrees of Lissa (Michel, Nos. 548, 549), dated the eighth and eleventh years of Ptolemy, the son of Ptolemy, belong to the reign of Philadelphus, *i.e.* to 278-277 and 275-274 B.C., not to that of Ptolemy III Euergetes, as Hicks (*J.H.S.* ix. (1888) 88 f.) and Michel (*loc. cit.*) suppose. Niese argues from the formula describing the King, but it seems to me not improbable that a shorter formula might still be used locally when a longer one had come into use in more central quarters.

[3] *Comment. on* Daniel, 11.

[4] Athen. xiv. 621 *a*. [5] Theoc. *Idyl.* xvii. 66.

[6] Michel, Nos. 595, 1198. [7] See Niese ii. 104, note 2.

[8] This inscription, recently published by Haussoullier (*Revue de Philol.* xxiv. (1900), p. 323), is the first clear evidence which has turned up of Ptolemaïc influence at Miletus under Philadelphus.

reign of the second Ptolemy.¹ But north of the Latmian Bay evidences of Ptolemaïc rule are not found till Antiochus II sits upon the Seleucid throne. In an inscription,² which must be later than 269,³ the Ionian Body addresses itself to the Seleucid court.⁴

This arrest of the Ptolemaïc conquest at the Latmian Bay was no doubt due to the action of the Antigonid king. In 272, or soon after,⁵ Antigonus joined in the war, and his fleets proved themselves more than a match for the Ptolemaïc. His great victory off Cos⁶ created a balance of power in the Aegean, where hitherto Ptolemy had been sole master. This diversion naturally weakened the pressure of the Ptolemaïc forces in Asia Minor.

§ 4. *Government of the first Seleucids in Asia Minor*

We turn now from considering how Asia Minor was affected by the foreign relations of the Seleucid court to examine what can still be deciphered of the workings of Seleucid government within.

It is perhaps not merely due to the imperfection of our evidence, to the fact that the part of Seleucid history which affected the Greeks stood the best chance of being recorded, that Asia Minor rather than Syria or the East seems, till after Magnesia, the chief sphere of Seleucid activity. One may well believe that it was the part of their dominions to which the Seleucid kings attached the greatest value. It is never

---

[1] Rayet, *Revue de Philol.* xxiii. (1899), p. 275 : Haussoullier, *ib.* xxiv. (1900), p. 323.

[2] Michel, No. 486.

[3] Because the young Antiochus appears in it as co-king, and Babylonian inscriptions of the year 269 show Seleucus still associated with his father. Wilcken, *Pauly-Wissowa*, i. p. 2452.

[4] The thirteen cities (see Michel, No. 485) which formed the Ionian Body were Miletus, Myus, Priene, Ephesus, Colophon, Lebedus, Teos, Clazomenae, Phocaea, Samos, Chios, Erythrae, Smyrna. Of these Miletus, Samos, and perhaps Erythrae (see Niese ii. p. 79, note 2) were or had been in Ptolemaïc possession, but the *majority* of the cities must be represented in an embassy to Antiochus, which claims to speak in the name of the Body. The inscription was found at Clazomenae ; the list of the envoys has perished after the first two, the envoys of Ephesus and Lebedus.

[5] Just. xxvi. 1, 1. [6] The references in Niese ii. p. 131.

ANTIOCHUS I (SOTER)

so inappropriate to speak of the dynasty as "Syrian" as in these earlier reigns. We cannot even perceive that Antioch on the Orontes held at that time any primacy over the capitals of the West and the East, over Sardis and the Babylonian Seleucia.[1]

Sardis since the days of the Lydian kingdom had held the position of capital of the country north of the Taurus. It had always been the chief seat of the power ruling the interior, Persian or Macedonian, unless perhaps it was superseded by the Phrygian capital, Celaenae, under Antigonus. Under the house of Seleucus, Sardis enjoyed its old dignity. It was there that the government archives were kept.[2] It had been transformed from a barbarian to a Hellenic city.[3]

In the absence of the King, the governor of Lydia exercises a general authority over the whole Trans-Tauric domain.[4]

Of the satrapies into which that domain was divided under the Seleucids we have no complete statement. According to the system which Alexander took over from the Persians, it would have formed six, Greater Phrygia, Hellespontine Phrygia, Lydia, Caria, Lycia, and Cappadocia. Of these only two can be proved by express mention under the Seleucids, Hellespontine Phrygia (ἡ ἐφ' Ἑλλησπόντου σατράπεια)[5] and Lydia.[6] We have also a satrapy mentioned, which appears to be that of Greater Phrygia.[7]

There is no reason to suppose that the Seleucids, while

---

[1] It would therefore be as appropriate to call the Seleucid kings *Lydians* as Syrians. An expression in Justin, if it corresponds with anything in his sources, tends to show that Asia Minor was in fact considered the real home of the earlier Seleucids. Seleucus II, after being driven across the Taurus and compelled to make Syria his chief seat of government, is said to have "lost his kingdom" and to be "an exile." "Seleucus quoque isdem ferme diebus *amisso regno* equo praecipitatus finitur, sic fratres quasi et germanis casibus *exules ambo* post regna scelerum suorum poenas luerunt" (xxvii. 3, 12).

[2] εἰς τὰς βασιλικὰς γραφὰς τὰς ἐν Σάρδεσιν, *Revue de Philol.* xxv. (1901), p. 9.

[3] Its hippodrome, Polyb. vii. 17, 2; its theatre, *ib.* 18, 3. We hear (after 188) of the *demos* of Sardis (ὁ δᾶμος ὁ Σαρδιανῶν) sending envoys to Delphi, *Bull. corr. hell.* v. (1881), p. 385.

[4] See Appendix G.

[5] Michel, No. 35.   [6] Polyb. xxi. 16 (13), 4.

[7] ἐν τῇ σατραπείᾳ, Michel, No. 40. The inscription was found in Phrygia.

they continued to hold territory in Caria, Lycia, and Cappadocia, modified the system which they found existing.[1]

While "satrapy" continued to be the official name for the province, the governor in official documents is called by the Greek title of *strategos*.[2] In popular language he was still spoken of as satrap.[3] He was the intermediary in all transactions between the central government and the province. It was to him that the King addressed his rescripts, which the *strategos* communicated in his turn to the subordinate officials who would be concerned with their execution.[4]

What the lower officials were who made up the machine of government in Asia Minor under the Seleucids we are only imperfectly informed. Each satrapy seems to have had a special controller of the finances (ὁ ἐπὶ τῶν προσόδων).[5] An *oikonomos* is mentioned in an inscription recently published, where his duty is to pass on to a district officer an order received by the *strategos* from the King relating to the alienation of a piece of the royal domain.[6] The same inscription gives the title of this district officer as *hyparchos*. This word, of course, in popular speech was quite a vague one, meaning any one who bore authority under any one else, and was even used as a translation of the Persian *satrap*.[7] In the official language *hyparchos* meant the governor of one of those

---

[1] There may be some doubt whether Caria continued to form a separate satrapy or was amalgamated with Lydia, since one would expect to hear something of the satrap of Caria, if there was one, at the time of Philip's operations in that region (see vol. ii. p. 33). Pamphylia, on the other hand, may have been separated from Lycia, since it is mentioned separately in the inscription of Ptolemy III (Michel, No. 1239), but the regions mentioned there need not necessarily be *satrapies*.

[2] Michel, No. 526; *Bull. corr. hell.* x. (1886), p. 515; cf. Haussoullier, *Revue de Philol.* xxv. (1901), p. 21.

[3] Polyb. xxi. 16 (13), 4.

[4] *E.g.* Michel, Nos. 35, 40; cf. Haussoullier, *Revue de Philol.* xxv. (1901), p. 22. The form of these rescripts is given us in the inscriptions cited; they open with a plain salutation, in which the name of the governor appears without the mention of his office, Βασιλεὺς Ἀντίοχος Μελεάγρῳ χαίρειν. The rescript to Zeuxis begins Βασιλεὺς Ἀντίοχος Ζεύξιδι τῷ πατρὶ χαίρειν (Joseph. xii. § 148). The rescripts to Meleager close with the word ἔρρωσο.

[5] *Bull. corr. hell.* xv. (1891), p. 556; cf. Arr. *Anab.* i. 17, 7; iii. 16, 4.

[6] Haussoullier, *Revue de Philol.* xxv. (1901), p. 9.

[7] *E.g.* Diod. xix. 48, 5; Arr. *Anab.* iv. 18, 3, and generally in Herodotus.

smaller districts, *hyparchies*, into which the satrapy was divided.[1]

Such is about all we know of the framework of government. In what relation did the different elements which made up the population stand to the Seleucid power?

§ 5. *The Native Powers and Antiochus I*

First we notice that *the north of the peninsula has now been finally abandoned*. The native dynasties, the houses of Mithridates, of Ariarathes and of Zibœtes—these and the Galatian tribes are left in unchallenged possession of all that lies to the north of the central plateau.

Of the two principalities of Persian origin that of Mithridates soon showed itself the more important. Mithridates already assumed the name of *king* in 281 or 280,[2] and coined in gold—a mark of absolute independence. Neither of these things did Ariarathes venture to do. The kingdom of Mithridates seems from the first to have admitted the lustre of Hellenism; his father indeed and grandfather in the fourth century had been ardently phil-Hellenic, and received the honorary franchise of Athens.[3] The territory he now ruled had bordering upon it Greek cities like Trapezus and Sinope, and Mithridates was in diplomatic connexion with Heraclea.

The principality of Ariarathes, on the other hand, has an out-of-the world, antiquated air about it. Ariarathes II continues to stamp his money with an Aramaïc legend.[4] His court was a region which the vagrant *literati* of Greece, who were found everywhere else, did not explore.[5] It must have seemed by contrast a strangely silent place. A primitive domesticity is the impression we gather from the family annals till Seleucid princesses come to trouble the house with the spirit of a

---

[1] See Appendix H.   [2] T. Reinach, *Trois royaumes*, p. 161.

[3] Demosth. *in Aristoc.* § 141, 202. His father may be meant by the Mithridates, son of Rhodobates (*sic*), who presented the Athenian Academy with a statue of Plato, Diog. Laert. iii. 20 (25). See Marquart. *Philologus*, liv. (1895), p. 491.

[4] Reinach, *Trois royaumes*, p. 29.   [5] Diod. xxxi. 19, 8.

less simple and kindly sphere. The only thing we know as to the part taken by the Cappadocian court in history for a hundred years is that it seems the place where a fugitive Seleucid prince can best efface himself from the sight of the world.

Whether Antiochus I, having recognized the impossibility of ejecting Mithridates and Ariamnes, who seems to have succeeded his father Ariarathes II about the same time that Antiochus succeeded to the Seleucid throne,[1] adopted that policy of close friendship with the two Persian courts which was afterwards the tradition of the Seleucid house we are not told. From faint indications we may conjecture that the tradition goes back in its origin to his reign. The only piece of information we get as to the history of Mithridates I after the accession of Antiochus is that some Galatian bands, whom Mithridates and his son Ariobarzanes had taken into their service, drove a Ptolemaïc force which had endeavoured to penetrate into the interior back to the sea, and took the anchors of the Egyptian ships. Whatever historical foundation the story may have, it goes to show the Mithridatic house as an ally of the Seleucid.[2]

In the case of the South Cappadocian court it may show close relations with the house of Seleucus that Ariamnes begins to put a Greek instead of an Aramaïc legend upon his coins.[3]

In the hills between Bithynia and the valley of the Amnias the chiefs of the native tribes perhaps already began to assert their independence of any of their great neighbours. It was the country in which Mithridates had first grounded his power, but in the course of the century which succeeded his establishment as king farther east, Paphlagonia seems to have

---

[1] The dates of Ariamnes are extremely uncertain, Reinach, *Trois royaumes*, p. 14, note 1.

[2] Apollonius of Aphrodisias, ap. Steph. Byz. s.v. Ἄγκυρα. The story is an aetiological legend to account for the name of the city Ancyra. The place of the incident which it is supposed to reflect is thought by Droysen (iii. p. 264) to be the shores of the Black Sea, by Niese (ii. p. 129, note 9) Caria.

[3] "Ce prince est le premier de la série qui ait fait reproduire son portrait sur ses monnaies; il est aussi le premier qui ait substitué l'écriture grecque à l'écriture araméenne. Ces innovations indiquent un rapprochement avec la civilization héllénique." Reinach, *Trois royaumes*, p. 31.

PLATE I

1. SELEUCUS I NICATOR. (From a coin of Pergamos.)
2. DEMETRIUS (POLIORCETES).
3. ANTIOCHUS I SOTER.
4. PHILETAERUS OF PERGAMOS.
5. MITHRIDATES II OF PONTIC CAPPADOCIA.
6. APOLLO ON THE *OMPHALOS*, THE CHARACTERISTIC REVERSE TY
   ON THE TETRADRACHMS OF ANTIOCHUS I, ANTIOCHUS
   SELEUCUS III, ANTIOCHUS III AND SELEUCUS IV, FOUND AL
   ON MANY TETRADRACHMS OF ANTIOCHUS IV.
7. ANTIOCHUS II THEOS.
8. PTOLEMY III EUERGETES, OF EGYPT.
9. DIODOTUS OF BACTRIA.
10. SELEUCUS II KALLINIKOS (young).
11. THE SAME (bearded).
12. SELEUCUS III SOTER (KERAUNOS)

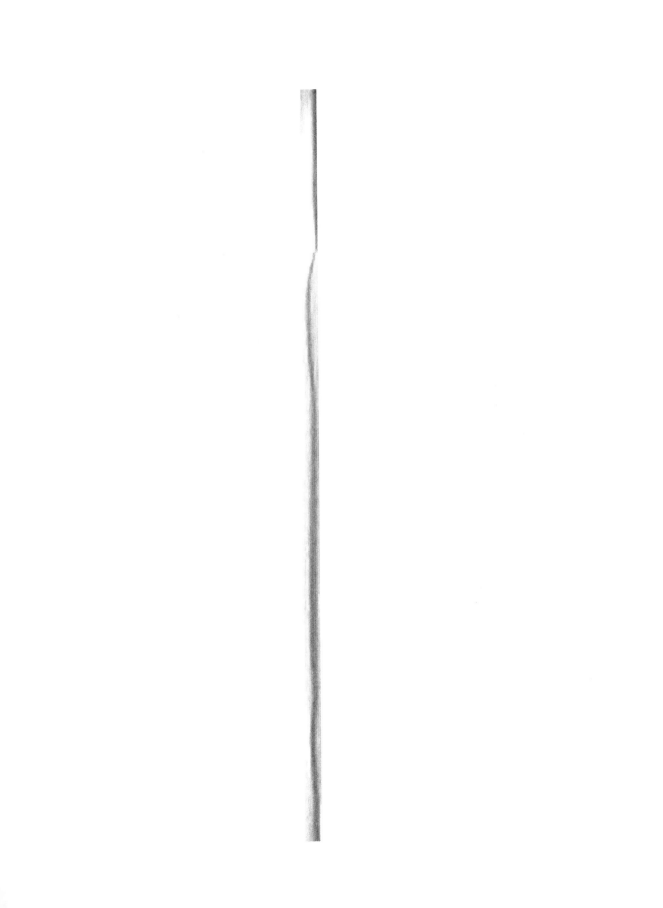

fallen back to the same condition as under the Persian Empire. In the earlier part of the second century before Christ a native chief, Morzias, has his seat at Gangra (mod. Changra).[1]

The war between Antiochus and Nicomedes of Bithynia seems never to have been renewed after the Gallic invasion. *That war was the last attempt made by a Macedonian ruler to humble the house of Dœdalsus.* Under Nicomedes the Bithynian kingdom passes from a mere barbaric chiefship to a state of the approved Hellenistic pattern. Zibœtes had already founded a city; under Nicomedes the transformation of Bithynia was carried through. Nicomedes, the " executioner of his brothers," had a heart as cruel as any barbarian sultan's, but an unregenerate heart has never prevented a barbarian, then or now, from assuming the externals, and even some of the tastes, of a higher civilization. The coins of Nicomedes—for now the Bithynian principality begins to have a coinage—show him a regular Greek king, with the smooth-shaven face which had become the vogue since Alexander, and the simple band of riband to show his royalty. In the great Hellenic centre, Olympia, his form figured in ivory.[2]

In 264 Nicomedes founded the city which was to perpetuate his name. At the end of the most northern of the two inlets on the east side of the Propontis had stood the Greek city of Astacus. The situation was an important one, lying on the road between the Bosphorus and the interior of Bithynia, just as Nicaea, the city of Antigonus and Lysimachus, lay on the road between the Bosphorus and Phrygia. Astacus had been demolished by Lysimachus perhaps in the interests of Nicaea. Since then its citizens had been homeless. Now, near the vacant site, but on the opposite side of the inlet,[3] enjoying the same advantages of situation as the old city, rose the new Nicomedia. The population of the

---

[1] Strabo xii. 562; cf. Polyb. xxv. 2, 9.

[2] Paus. v. 12, 7. At least it was the local tradition that a certain ivory statue represented this Nicomedes. It may have been he, too, who offered to pay off the whole public debt of Cnidus if they would let him have the Aphrodite of Praxiteles, but it may equally well have been one of the later Bithynian kings (Pliny, *N.H.* vii. § 127; xxxvi. § 21).

[3] ἀντικρὺ Ἀστάκου, Memnon 20 = *F.H.G.* iii. p. 536.

old city, was settled in the new. In course of time Nicomedia came to be one of the great cities of the world.¹

But although hostilities between Nicomedes and Antiochus appear to have ceased, the war had left behind it a feeling of estrangement. It was probably believed at the Bithynian court that the house of Seleucus wanted only some accession of good fortune to become again its aggressive enemy. Antiochus on his part may have smarted under some sense of dishonour not wiped away. At any rate Nicomedes at his death committed his infant children to the protection, not of the Seleucid King, but of Antigonus, Ptolemy, and the neighbouring cities.²

At Pergamos, during all the time that Antiochus, the son of Seleucus, was combating Ptolemaïc and barbarian enemies in Asia Minor, the astute eunuch Philetaerus remained master of citadel and treasure. He seems to have seen his interest in maintaining to the end his policy of friendship with the house of Seleucus. The earliest coins of the Pergamene dynasty, those probably which were struck under the rule of Philetaerus, exhibit the head of the deified Seleucus.³ And Antiochus on his side probably thought it wise to purchase the adherence of Philetaerus by moderating his claims.⁴ So that all through the twenty years of his rule Philetaerus was able to go on quietly consolidating the power of his house. At the very beginning of the reign of Antiochus, when Pitane contracted a debt of 380 talents to the King, we find Philetaerus forward to advance them a portion of the sum, and thereby secure some influence over that city.⁵ An inscription just published (1902) records his gifts to the city of Cyzicus, to make good the losses it had suffered in some war (with the anti-Seleucid Northern League?) and from the ravages of the Galatians.⁶ And his family, drawing no doubt on his support, were meanwhile acquiring power in the country. The Eumenes who was in possession of Amastris about 280 (see page 134) was probably his brother, and by the time that Philetaerus

---

¹ Liban. *Orat.* vi.   ² Memnon 22=*F.H.G.* iii. p. 537
³ Imhoof-Blumer, *Die Münzen der Dynastie von Pergamon*, p. 26.
⁴ Strabo xiii. 623.   ⁵ Fränkel, *Inschrift. von Pergamon*, No. 245.
⁶ *J.H.S.* xxii. p. 194.

came to be an old man of eighty, the son of this Eumenes, called also Eumenes, had established himself as dynast in the region adjacent to Pergamos. The other brother of Philetaerus, Attalus, contracted a marriage which must have advertised to the world the standing which the house of Philetaerus had attained. His wife was Antiochis, the daughter of Achaeus, a cousin of the Seleucid King.[1]

In 263-262 Philetaerus died at the age of eighty,[2] and Pergamos passed to his nephew Eumenes, who now united with it the principality of which he already stood possessed. This concentration of power in the hands of a younger ruler than the old eunuch was followed by a rupture with the house of Seleucus. It was probably inevitable that the Seleucid King should not suffer this new power to grow up without first testing his ability to prevent it. Eumenes, when hostilities had once been opened, struck straight for the Seleucid capital. A battle was fought in the neighbourhood of Sardis, at which Antiochus would seem to have commanded in person. It issued in a decisive victory for the Pergamene forces.[3] This happened only a short while before Antiochus I died.

Of the way in which Antiochus dealt with the free tribes of the Taurus, of any action of the Seleucid house in Lycia or Pamphylia, we know nothing except what can be inferred from the names which stamp some cities as Seleucid foundations.[4]

§ 6. *The Greek Cities and Antiochus I*

The relation between the King and the Greek cities was still formally what it had been since Alexander. They did not in theory form a part of his dominion, but a series of independent states, with whom the King, the lord of the barbarian interior, had entered into *alliance*. The Empire was not in this view a monarchy, but a federation, of which the King and a number of free republics were members.[5] It was

---

[1] Strabo *loc. cit.*   [2] Lucian, *Macrob.* 12.
[3] Strabo *loc. cit.*   [4] See Appendix I.
[5] ἐν τῇ χώρᾳ τε καὶ συμμαχίᾳ, Michel, No. 35, l. 46; *ib.* l. 58.

unnecessary for official language to take account of the fact that one member of the federation was so immensely more powerful than the rest that his sole word was law. Still, as under Alexander, the King's territory was distinguished from the territory of the cities.[1] Of the occupiers of his own land, the Phrygian and Lydian villagers (βασιλικοὶ λαοί), the King, as supreme proprietor, exacted regular tribute.[2] He had no such rights over the territory of the Greek cities. The frontiers between these two spheres underwent continual modification. Of instances in which the King acquired or seized territory belonging to the cities there is no record;[3] such an act there would be little motive to register. On the other hand, it was in the interest of the new possessors to have clear documents to point to in cases where the King alienated some parcel of his domain. Of these, therefore, some trace has survived. The alienation is seen taking place in two ways. Sometimes the King makes it an affair of business, raising money by a sale. At the very beginning of his reign Antiochus I sells a piece of ground to the city of Pitane for 380 talents; the transaction is engraved on stone, and records of it laid up in the temples of Ilion, Ephesus, and Delos.[4]

Another instance of sale is that recorded in a recently published inscription.[5] It was perhaps a somewhat abnormal case, for the purchaser is here not a Greek city or a citizen of one, but the sister-wife herself of King Antiochus II, Laodice. Whether it was usual for Seleucid queens to buy themselves appanages with money paid into the royal treasury, or whether the transaction in question sprang from the peculiar state of things, when Queen Laodice was living in divorce, we do not know. In this case also the sale was to be recorded not only

---

[1] Haussoullier (*Revue de Philol.* xxv. (1901) p. 27) makes the royal domain (ἡ βασιλικὴ χώρα), if I understand him rightly, to be special lands belonging to the crown within the realm, the *paradeisoi* inherited from the Persian kings, and so on. It appears to me rather to be the realm itself distinguished from the territory of the Greek cities, which were, in theory, *outside the realm*.

[2] ἡ φορολογουμένη χώρα is used by Antigonus as equivalent to ἡ ἡμετέρα in distinction from the territory of Teos, Michel, No. 34, l. 84, 85.

[3] Seleucus II promises Smyrna τὴν πατρίδα (χώραν) ἀποδώσειν, Michel No. 258. This may point to a seizure of some of the city's territory by a former king.

[4] Fränkel, *Inschr. von Pergamon*, No. 245 C.

[5] Haussoullier, *Revue de Philol.* xxv. (1901), p. 9.

in the government archives at Sardis, but by *steles* in the temples of Ilion, Samothrace, Ephesus, Branchidae, and Sardis.

At other times the kings alienate parcels of their territory by way of *grants* to individual Greeks. Such grants of land to reward good service were an old custom of the Macedonian monarchy.[1] The hordes of adventurers from all corners of the Greek world who flocked to the Seleucid court had in view similar rewards among the rich fields of Asia. But any one who found himself in possession of land *within* the King's realm would of course have to pay the tribute which was ordinarily paid by the barbarian cultivators. To do this would injure not only the pocket, but the dignity, of a Greek. In the cases, therefore, which we can examine of such alienations the territory is removed from the realm altogether. The new possessor is allowed to annex it to the domain of one or other of the allied cities, to hold it as a citizen or *metoikos* of that city, not as the subject of a king, and to pay money only indirectly into the royal treasury, in so far as he contributes to whatever the city is obliged, as an ally, to furnish. Both Laodice and Aristodicides of Assos—in the two cases under our observation—are allowed great latitude in choosing the city to which their property is to be attached. It need not necessarily be a city of the immediate neighbourhood. There are in fact known cases in which cities possessed lands (*enclaves*) altogether detached from their main territory, and surrounded by the possessions of other states.[2]

To what extent the reality answered to the form by which the Greek cities took the rank of free states, we have not the means to determine. We find at any rate many of the cities still disposing of military and naval forces of their own. Two inscriptions from Erythræ contain honours voted to the civic *strategoi* for organizing the city's forces, and from one of them we learn that these forces consisted to some extinct, like all armies of the time, of mercenaries.[3] An inscription of Priene seems to indicate a mercenary force maintained by the people

---

[1] Cf. Michel, No. 321; Demosth. *De Fals. Leg.* § 145.
[2] Haussoullier, *Revue de Philol.* xxv. (1901), p. 32.
[3] Michel, Nos. 503, 504.

in the citadel.¹ Smyrna has troops in the middle of the third century with which it can garrison neighbouring towns.² Alexandria Troas in 216 can launch a force of 4000 men against a Galatian horde.³ Calymna about the same time possesses a fleet.⁴

With the means of levying war on their own account, the cities to some extent pursue an independent policy. In the disturbed times which immediately preceded the conquest of Asia Minor by Seleucus we hear of a petty war between Magnesia-on-the-Meander and Priene.⁵ There were probably various gradations of freedom, depending partly on geographical position, partly on the circumstances of the moment, between the complete liberty of great states like Heraclea or Rhodes and the subjection of a royal residence like Ephesus under Antiochus II.

In whatever cases the King was strong enough, if he chose, to demand tribute, to set a garrison, to meddle with the constitution, the city lived with an uneasy sense of holding all that it most valued on sufferance. The inscriptions which record the benefactions of the kings say nothing of the cases where he used his power to curtail liberty. But the effusion with which they acknowledge his moderation is significant. Priene, a story says, was "enslaved" by Antiochus I for a time, and liberated again through the influence of its citizen, Sostratus the dancer.⁶ Perhaps already the exaction of tribute (φόρος), which under Alexander had been, as we have noted, only an exceptional punishment, was becoming common, as it appears to have been in the time of Antiochus III,⁷ or it may have been that the name of tribute began to be bluntly applied to the forced benevolences. For demanding such contributions the Seleucid kings had a good pretext in the Galatian peril; it was indeed only fair that the cities should pay their quota towards the cause which was theirs as well as the kings'; but the pretext may have been used im-

---

¹ Michel, No. 483; cf. Lenschau, *De rebus Prienensium*, p. 207.
² Michel, No. 19, l. 100.   ³ Polyb. v. 111, 4.
⁴ *Inscr. in the Brit. Mus.* No. 259. The date of the inscription is unknown.
⁵ *Inscr. in the Brit. Mus.* Nos. 401, 402.
⁶ Sext. Empir. *adv. gramm.* 293 = p. 667, 15, Bekker.
⁷ Polyb. xxi. 43, 2.

moderately; whether it was or not, the cities felt the demand a burden.

To judge, however, by the inscriptions, Antiochus I and Antiochus II were ready enough to meet the wishes of the Greeks. In a somewhat ambiguous phrase the envoys of the Ionian Body to Antiochus I are instructed to exhort the King "to take the Ionian cities under his most earnest care, in order that henceforth, enjoying free and popular government, they may at last be secure in the possession of those constitutions which their fathers have handed down to them; and the envoys are further to represent to the King that in so doing he will confer great benefits upon the cities and will also adhere to the policy of his ancestors."[1] It does not read as if a danger to the laws and liberties of the cities were apprehended from the King himself; it seems rather as if it were against external enemies that the Seleucid is entreated to become protector. One might guess that the occasion of the decree was some withdrawal of the Ptolemaïc forces, or a defeat of the Galatians, or the suppression of some local tyrants. In the case of one of the Ionian cities, Erythrae, an inscription informs us that its freedom was respected by Antiochus I, as it had been by Alexander, Antigonus, and Seleucus; Antiochus even remitted the contribution to the Galatian war.[2]

There were two ways by which the cities might bring influence to bear upon the King. There was firstly the direct method of diplomatic intercourse. Envoys were continually going to and fro between the several cities and the court. The royal embassies were given precedence of all others in the cities save the sacred ones.[3] The kings, on their part, appear continually receiving embassies from the

---

[1] παρακαλείτω]σαν δὲ οἱ πρέσβεις τὸμ βασι[λέα Ἀντίοχον πᾶσαν ἐπιμ]έλειαν ποιεῖσθαι τῶμ πόλε[ων τῶν Ἰάδων ὅπως ἂν τὸ λοιπὸ]ν ἐλεύθεραι οὖσαι καὶ δημο-[κρατούμεναι βεβαίως ἤδη πολι]τεύωνται κατὰ τοὺς πατρί[ους νόμους, ἀποφαινέτωσα]ν δὲ αὑτῷ οἱ πρέσβεις διότι [τοῦτο ποιῶν πολλῶν τε ἀγαθ]ῶν αἴτιος ἔσται ταῖς πόλε[σιν καὶ ἅμα ἀκολουθήσει τῇ τ]ῶν προγόνων αἱρέσει. Michel, No. 486. "His ancestors," as we see by another inscription is simply a court phrase for Seleucus, his father; what is meant, of course, is "the traditional policy of his house," as we should put it.

[2] Michel, No. 37. See Appendix J.   [3] Michel, Nos. 367, 457.

cities. The expenses of this intercourse formed a very serious item in the civic budgets. The ambassadors to court could not go empty-handed. Those, for instance, sent by Erythrae to Antiochus I have to carry a crown, presumably of gold, and gold for presents (εἰς τὰ ξένια).[1] The expenditure on such embassies ranked with that on theatres, temples, and great public works.[2] The other, and probably more effectual, means of securing their ends the cities found in obtaining the advocacy of persons powerful at court. This advocacy had often without doubt to be purchased, and the presents to the King's friends were perhaps as severe a drain on the city's resources as the presents to the King himself.[3] Sometimes, however, there was no necessity to pay for the services of an advocate. Civic patriotism was an unfeigned virtue among the Greeks, and those who won influence over the King no doubt thought in the first place of exercising it for the benefit of their native city. The case of Sostratus the dancer has been already mentioned. Demodamas, the explorer of the Far East for Seleucus and Antiochus I, did not cease to act as a citizen of Miletus.[4]

It was specially as arbitrator in the quarrels between city and city, or faction and faction, that the King was appealed to. We find the Seleucid King intervening in the intestine feuds of Bargylia,[5] and perhaps in the secular quarrel between Samos and Priene.[6] It was of course not absolutely necessary that the King to whose empire cities at variance were attached should be the arbitrator chosen; it might be a neutral city.[7]

---

[1] Michel, No. 37.

[2] The patriotic Malusius lends money largely without interest to the Ilian Body, 300 gold pieces for an embassy to Antigonus, Michel, No. 522.

[3] Haussoullier thinks that the Arrhidaeus honoured by Ephesus (*Inscr. of the Brit. Mus.* No. 451) was the *oikonomos* of the property of Laodice, and that he championed the cause of Ephesus at her court, *Revue de Philol.* xxv. (1901), p. 20.

[4] Haussoullier, *Revue de Philol.* xxiv. (1900), p. 245 f.

[5] Michel, No. 457. The rescripts relating to a quarrel between Priene and Miletus, of which fragments remain (*Inscr. in Brit. Mus.* Nos. 412, 414), may emanate from a Seleucid king (Lenschau), but are probably later (Haussoullier, *Revue de Philol.* xxv. (1901), p. 141).

[6] *Inscr. in the Brit. Mus.* No. 403, l. 132 f. (the King is Antiochus II).

[7] Michel, No. 417; *C.I.G.* No. 3184; Sonne, *De arbitris externis* (*Quaest. epig. Gott.*), 1888.

The usual course seems to have been for the King, even when appealed to, not to adjudge the disputes himself but to nominate a neutral party, some friendly city, as arbitrator.[1]

The relations, however, between the earlier Seleucids and the old Greek cities do not exhaust the relations of that house with Asiatic Hellenism. For Hellenism was spreading far beyond its original sphere. It was under these Greek kings — perhaps it was their greatest glory, though historians were far more interested in their battles, their vices and their *amours*—it was under them that the process went on by which Hellenism pushed its way far into the interior. Cities with Greek names, of Greek speech and life, rose one by one where before only ignoble Phrygian or Cappadocian towns had huddled round temples and bazaars.

Antiochus I has been described by a well-known authority as that "great city-builder who has almost faded out of our tradition."[2] A view of that work we shall never recover, except imperfectly. From time to time archaeology will fill in fresh details of that mighty plan by which the successors of Alexander, Greek and Roman, multiplied the centres of Hellenism in the land. It is part of the difficulty that even when we have ascertained the existence of a Greek or Macedonian colony in a particular place it remains in a large number of cases doubtful who planted it there, and when.[3]

A certain mark of Seleucid foundation (or refoundation) is given by the names of some of the cities, Seleucia, Antioch, Laodicea, and so on. The cities so named are found to go mostly along the two main lines of communication between Syria and the Aegean, the water-way along the coast — where we have seen the Seleucid competing with Ptolemaïc foundations—and the great high-road which ran from the Cilician Gates westward between the inner steppe and the Pisidian hills to Lydia and Ionia.

---

[1] So in the case of Bargylia the King nominates Teos, which deputes one of its citizens to try the cases on the spot. Cf. the action of Antigonus (Michel, No. 34, i. 30).

[2] "... dem grossen aber in der Ueberlieferung fast verschollenen Städtegründer," E. Meyer, *Hermes* xxxiii. (1898), p. 643.

[3] See the examination to which E. Meyer (*loc. cit.*) submits the catalogue of Radet (*De coloniis a Macedonibus in Asiam cis Taurum deductis*, Paris, 1892).

The Seleucid cities on this road are placed, as no doubt had been the native settlements before them, at the points of junction where other roads run in from either side.

First, going from the east, is the Laodicea called "the Burnt-up" (Κατακεκαυμένη), where a road comes in from Cappadocia, the realm of Ariarathes, and the Upper Euphrates. Then after turning the northern end of the mountain obstacle, Paroreia (now called Sultan Dagh), the highway ran on to the Phrygian capital, Apamea. Its predecessor was the Phrygian town of Celaenae, a strong mountain city of the old-world sort in whose very market-place the Marsyas rushed from a sacred cavern to join the Meander, that river also having its source in a neighbouring tarn. Here roads came in from all sides, from Northern Phrygia and from Pisidia; it was the central point of the interior. Here Antigonus had had his seat of government at a time when he aspired to rule Asia. Perhaps he had already begun the new Greco-Macedonian city lower down towards the foot of the hills, which from the time that Seleucus conquered Asia Minor was known as Apamea, a memorial of the Irânian queen. From Apamea the great high-road ran down the Lycus valley. Where that valley opens out before the junction of the Lycus and Meander, in the fat plains which nourished innumerable flocks and yielded the softest wool to the Greek market,[1] two chief roads diverged. One ran north-west to the valley of the Hermus and the royal city of Sardis, the government centre of Asia Minor; the other led the trains of merchantmen down the Meander valley to the commercial centre, Ephesus.

Above the plains of the Lycus where these roads diverged we find the third great Seleucid city, Laodicea, rich and increased with goods from the traffic which passed through it and the exchange of its wool,[2] looking on the one hand down the Meander to the Aegean, and on the other through the "Syrian" Gate down the long road that led ever eastwards. On the

---

[1] Strabo xii. 578.

[2] The region in which Laodicea lay was peculiarly subject to earthquake and volcanic disturbances, and was hence called *Katakekaumene*, "Burnt-up." A confusion therefore of this Laodicea with the other easterly Laodicea is to be avoided, which was itself distinguished as Katakekaumene. Laodicea Katakekaumene was not in the *region* called Katakekaumene.

road between Laodicea and Sardis no certain trace of a Seleucid foundation has been discovered, though such there may have been. The traffic on the other road to Ephesus was no doubt much greater, and here the Seleucid foundations succeeded one another at short intervals. First came an Antioch, Antioch-on-Meander, a place that gave its name to a brand of dried figs,[1] then a day's journey brought one to Nysa, which was for a time renamed Antioch, and another day's journey to Tralles, to which the same undiscriminating name as well as the other of Seleucia was attached. From Tralles Ephesus was only thirty-five miles by road.[2]

Such were the cities with Seleucid names through which the main artery of commerce between the Ionian coast and the Farther East ran. It remains to enumerate those which commanded the side lines.

The main road, as we have seen, turned the north of the Paroreia (by Philomelium, Holmi, Chelidonia, and Metropolis[3]); on the south side of the range was set an Antioch, from which a side-road ran into the main road at Apamea.[4]

Whether at the time when this Antioch was founded there was an alternative road to the main road on the south of the Sultan Dagh, leaving the main road at Iconium and rejoining it at Apamea, or whether Antioch was rather the terminus of a road pushed out from Apamea, an outpost of the Seleucid power towards the Pisidian hills, we do not know. Antioch in Pisidia was one of those cities which succeeded an older religious centre of the Phrygians, in this case a sanctuary of the Moon god, endowed with a great property in lands and slaves. The new settlers, planted presumably by some Seleucid king to form the substance of his Greek city, were drawn from Magnesia-on-Meander.[5] Another road came into Apamea from a Seleucia, surnamed "the Iron" (Σελεύκεια σιδηρᾶ), planted

---

[1] Strabo xiii. 630.

[2] It is probable that the refoundation of these towns as Antiochs belongs to the time of Antiochus III.

[3] Strabo xiv. 663; cf. Ramsay, *Historical Geography of Asia Minor*, p. 171.

[4] Kiepert, connecting Antioch and Philomelium by a road across the Paroreia, makes them both stations on the main road, but there appears to be no possibility of more than a rough bridle-path over the mountain. Ramsay, *Church in the Roman Empire*, p. 28; Murray, *Asia Minor*, p. 148.

[5] Strabo xii. 577.

on the western side of Lake Egirdir (its name still survives as Selef). This may also have been intended to keep a watch on Sagalassus and the Pisidian towns to the south.[1] Still more to the west we find a city whose foundation is fixed by its name of Themisonium (mod. Kara-euyuk Bazâr) to the reign of Antiochus II, accessible by a roughish pass from Laodicea on the Lycus, and looking across the valley of the Indus towards the mountain state of Cibyra. A station of guard-troops or constabulary (φυλακῖται) and settlements of military colonists, probably Seleucid, is proved by an inscription to have existed in the valley below on the road to Cibyra, at Eriza (near Dere-Keui) and the neighbouring villages.[2]

Going westward still, we find a road connecting Tralles-Antioch on the main road with the harbours of Southern Caria, Physcus, and Caunus. It was the further connexion of these harbours with a great commercial state like Rhodes, which indeed came to possess them as dependencies, that the importance of this road across Caria lay. It passed through the old centres of Carian life, through Alabanda and by the temple of Zeus Chrysaoreus, the religious centre of the Carian people, in which the federal parliament assembled, composed of delegates from the various groups of villages.[3]

In both places the Seleucid government made establishments. Alabanda for a time became Antioch.[4] By the temple of Zeus Chrysaoreus arose a new Macedonian city, Stratonicea, founded no doubt by Antiochus I in honour of his wife. The Macedonian settlers took part in the national assemblies and cults at the neighbouring temples.[5]

To find the other colonies, which are certainly Seleucid, we must go northwards to those roads which bind the capital, Sardis, to the Troad—the highway, that is, between Sardis

---

[1] This colony is omitted, perhaps by an oversight, in Radet's catalogue.

[2] Berard, *Bull. corr. hell.* xv. (1891), p. 556. Haussoullier, *Revue de Philol.* xxv. (1901), p. 24. Mr. Mahaffy (*Empire of the Ptolemies*, p. 492) says that this inscription "shows that the sway of Egypt extended up the mountain passes" from the coast. That the inscription is Egyptian is the very thing which requires to be proved. It is more probably Seleucid. The well-known inscription containing the decree of Antiochus II (Michel, No. 40) was found at Durdurkar in this neighbourhood.

[3] Strabo xiv. 660; cf. *C.I.G.* 2691 f.; *Revue des Études Grecques*, xii. (1899), p. 345 f.   [4] Steph. Byz.   [5] Strabo xiv. 660.

and Europe—and to the Propontis.¹ Travellers to either destination would go in company till a place was reached some ten miles from the ridge which divides the waters of the Hermus from those of the Caïcus. Thence the roads forked, one entering the Caïcus valley and running down it to Pergamos, the other crossing the valley higher up and striking over the hills to Cyzicus. It was at this point that a colony of Macedonians took possession of the native town of Thyatira.² These Macedonians claimed the great Seleucus as their founder, but the story they told of the city's origin is discredited by modern etymology, and the real founder may have been Antiochus I.³

The road from Thyatira down the Caïcus valley was the thoroughfare between Sardis and Pergamos, continued beyond Pergamos in the coast road of the Troad. On this no Antiochs or Seleucias are to be found. In this region the earlier Seleucid kings were willing to tolerate the authority of the rulers of Pergamos. Already, in the reign of Antiochus I, there rose a Philetaeria under Ida and an Attalia.⁴

A rupture between the courts of Sardis and Pergamos must have broken communication between the Seleucid government and the Hellespont by the natural way that followed the Caïcus. Under such circumstances the road leading north from Thyatira to the district of the modern Balikisri,⁵ whence

¹ The Stratonicea πρὸς τῷ Ταύρῳ, mentioned by Strabo (xiv. 660), and described as πολίχνιον προσκείμενον τῷ ὄρει, is still unidentified.

² Strabo xiii. 625.

³ Steph. Byz. ἀπὸ Σελεύκου τοῦ Νικάτορος Λυσιμάχῳ πολεμοῦντος καὶ ἀκούσαντος ὅτι θυγάτηρ αὐτῷ γέγονε τὴν πόλιν ὠνόμασε Θυγάτειρα. The name is a native one, "teira" being supposed by S. Reinach and Ramsay (*Historical Geography*, p. 114, note) to mean "town." As a matter of fact, the legend does not seem to me to be *proved* baseless by this; a Greek might well have retained the native name because of its ominous coincidence with the birth of a daughter, and it must be admitted to be curious that in the case of a colony so important as Thyatira there is no attempt to replace the native name by one borrowed from the royal house. But it is the general untrustworthiness of such legends which makes this one suspected.

⁴ Michel, No. 15. The site of Philetaeria is unidentified. There was an Attalia on the Lycus about ten miles north of Thyatira (Radet, *Bull. corr. hell.* xi. (1887), p. 168 f., p. 397 f.), but it seems to me unlikely that the Pergamene authority stretched so far east in 263.

⁵ Identified by Ramsay with Hadrianūthērae, which itself no doubt succeeded an earlier Greek town.

one can reach the Troad by striking off to the west, must have assumed great importance. It is on this road that we find a Stratonicea where it crosses the Caïcus valley.[1] It remains only to note that in the Troad itself the town of Cebrene is proved at one period by its coins to have entitled itself Antioch. It must have recovered an independent existence after Antigonus had transferred its population to Ilion, thanks possibly to the good-will of a Seleucid king.[2]

The new cities of the Greek kings differed generally from the old native towns in being on lower ground. The old towns had been rather citadels than dwelling-places, fortresses perched on the edge of precipices, to which the cultivators of the neighbouring fields might flee in stress of war. Considerations of commercial convenience and easier living made it a point to have the new cities accessible rather than inaccessible. The new cities seemed to have slid down from the heights to come into touch with the plains. It was still unusual to build them in an altogether exposed position, although in a country securely pacified like Lydia it might be done. Thyatira lay flat upon the marshes of the Lycus.[3]

But the favourite position was the foot of some hill half plain and half slope, a compromise between convenience and security. This was notably the case with the colonies along the great eastern highway, Laodicea the Burnt-up in a bare "theatre-shaped recess in the outer skirt of the mountains,"[4] Apamea below the old Celaenae, set on a foot-hill where the Marsyas breaks into the plain, Laodicea on the Lycus on the slopes which rise from the river to Mount Salbacus.

§ 7. *The End of Antiochus I*

Between July 262 and July 261 Antiochus Soter died, after having wrestled with the task bequeathed him by Seleucus for nineteen years. He was sixty-four years old.[5]

---

[1] At modern Seledik, Radet, *Bull. corr. hell.* xi. (1887), p. 108 f.

[2] Imhoof-Blumer, *Numism. Zeitschr.* iii. p. 306.

[3] Radet, *De coloniis*, p. 67; Foucart, *Bull. corr. hell.* xi. (1887), p. 101; Murray, *Asia Minor*, p. 85.

[4] Ramsay, *Historical Geography*, p. 86.   [5] Eus. i. p. 249.

ANTIOCHUS I (SOTER)

We hear of six children, the two sons of Stratonice, Seleucus and Antiochus; the two daughters of Stratonice, Apama, who had married Magas of Cyrene, and Stratonice, who was still unmarried at her father's death; and, lastly, we hear of a son and daughter of Antiochus by another (perhaps earlier) wife, Alexander and Laodice. This daughter was destined to play a prominent part in Asia Minor; she became the wife of her half-brother Antiochus.[1]

Already in the reign of Antiochus I an evil had appeared in the Seleucid house, to which no less than to any overmastering circumstances its ultimate ruin was due — the division of the house against itself. The elder son of Antiochus I, bearing the name of his grandfather Seleucus, had been designated the successor. From the earlier years of the reign of Antiochus till some time between 269 and 265 he had been associated with his father as joint-king,[2] and had perhaps been given the government of Babylon and Irân.[3] Then there came a dark suspicion between father and son. Antiochus gave command that the prince was to be put to death; and it was done.[4] His younger brother Antiochus stepped into his place and was made partner in the throne.[5]

It is hardly possible from our scanty materials to arrive at any idea of the personality of the first Antiochus, to penetrate to the real man whose work we have been attempting to follow. He seems indeed to be typical of his house, indefatigably busy in keeping the unwieldy empire together, hurrying from one end of it to the other, fighting almost incessantly. Nor was he a mere spectator in the battles fought under his conduct. At Ipsus, a young man of twenty-five, he had commanded the wing attacked by Demetrius

---

[1] The marriage of the children of one father, if the mothers were different, but not of *uterine* brothers and sisters, was allowed by Attic law. The marriage of full brothers and sisters, which was of course incestuous to the Hellenic conscience (Athen. xiv. 621 *a*) is not proved in the Seleucid family till 196 B.C., although the second Ptolemy had begun it in Egypt.

[2] *Zeitschr. f. Assyr.* vii. pp. 226, 234; viii. p. 108; Schrader, *Keilschr. Biblioth.* iii. 2, p. 136.

[3] This is probable, since it was in accordance with the arrangement made by Seleucus I in the case of Antiochus.

[4] John of Antioch, frag. 55 = *F.H.G.* iv. p. 558; Trog. *Prol.* xxvi.

[5] Michel, No. 486.

Poliorcetes; and even as King he took his share of danger like the Macedonian and Irânian chiefs from whom he sprang. A stone found at Ilion contains a decree of that city conferring honours on the physician Metrodorus of Amphipolis because he had successfully treated King Antiochus for a wound in the neck, got in battle.[1] He may also be credited with a prudent sense of the limits of his power, an honest recognition of facts, abandoning, for instance, a useless hostility to the Persian houses which had cut off for themselves provinces of the realm, and holding out to them instead the hand of friendship. His coins show us a homely face, practical, unideal, of a sort of wizen shrewdness, the eyes somewhat screwed up, the lips pursed together. The gossip that caught at any suggestion of irregular *amours* did not fail to detect a side of weaker sensuality in Antiochus; it dwelt on the story of his enervating passion for his stepmother, on the influence exerted upon him by the flute-player Sostratus.[2] But there were not many princes of whom gossip did not find similar stories to tell.

[1] Michel, No. 526. Cf. Wilcken, *Pauly-Wissowa*, i. p. 2454.
[2] Hegesander ap. Athen. i. 19 *d*; Aristodemus ap. Athen. vi. 244 *f*; Sext. Emp. *adv. gramm.* 293.

CHAPTER IX

ANTIOCHUS II (THEOS)

It was Antiochus II, now a young man of about twenty-four,[1] who took up the Seleucid inheritance in 262.

In him, the grandson of Demetrius Poliorcetes, the sensual strain was more strongly pronounced than in his father. At least the scandal-mongers found him a richer theme. He was a hopeless drunkard; he slept off his morning bouts, only to begin again in the evening. Those admitted to his presence on official business rarely found him in anything but a shocking condition. Vile creatures ruled him by the most discreditable sort of influence, such as the Cypriot Aristus and his brother Themison.[2] Themison assumed the name and insignia of Heracles and became the object of a regular cult. When he entered the lists at public games he was proclaimed as Themison a Macedonian, the Heracles of King Antiochus. When any person of distinction offered sacrifice on his altar, he condescended to reveal himself, disposed on a couch with a lion-skin thrown about him, a Scythian bow and club at his side.[3] Two other persons who enjoyed high consideration at the court of Antiochus were Herodotus the buffoon and Archelaus the dancer.[4] The face of Antiochus upon his coins, with its full protruding chin and gross jaw, betrays the sensual element in his character;[5] but we should do well to

---

[1] Wilcken, *Pauly-Wissowa*, i. p. 2455.
[2] Phylarch. ap. Athen. x. 438 *c*; Aelian. *Var. Hist.* ii. 41.
[3] Pythermus ap. Athen. vii. 289 *f*. It may be more than a coincidence that some of the coins of Antiochus II have a type representing Heracles seated on a rock, holding his club, Babelon p. lx, f. [4] Hegesander ap. Athen. i. 19 c.
[5] These characteristics are less seen in the coin given on Plate I than in some others.

accept the stories of the scandal-mongers with some reserve, or at any rate to remember that there was probably a great deal more that might have been said about Antiochus II. What sort of idea should we have of Philip of Macedon or Julius Caesar if all we knew about them were the stories on which gossip loved to dwell?

In Asia Minor the reign of the second Antiochus seems, from what we can see, to have been till the peace with Egypt merely a continuation of the reign of Antiochus the First. There were the same questions for the Seleucid court to deal with—the internal ones presented to it by the lesser principalities, Cappadocian, Bithynian, Pergamene, by the hill-tribes of the Taurus and by the Galatians, by the Greek cities, and the external ones constituted by the relations of the Seleucid court with Ptolemy and Antigonus. It is not possible to discover anywhere a change of policy consequent upon the new reign, except that the quarrel with Eumenes of Pergamos seems to have been dropped and a *modus vivendi* to have been discovered which allowed the ruler of Pergamos to hold his extended principality as a subordinate or ally of Antiochus. With the two dynasties in Cappadocia the relations of the Seleucid court continued friendly. To the house of Ariarathes indeed it gave its recognition in the way that was most impressive by uniting it with the Seleucid house in marriage. The Greek king recognized a brother in the barbarian prince. It was during the first four or five years of the reign of Antiochus II[1] that Ariamnes began to be styled *king*.[2] It was about the same time that his son, Ariarathes, whom he had associated with himself on the throne, married the daughter of Antiochus II, Stratonice.[3] A passage of Strabo seems to indicate that the region of Cataonia was ceded by Antiochus to the new Cappadocian kingdom as his daughter's dowry.[4] In the case of the dynasty of Pontic Cappadocia it is to be observed that after Mithridates the Founder, who was succeeded by his son Ariobarzanes in 266,[5] the kings cease to

---

[1] Between 260 and 256, Reinach, *Trois royaumes*, p. 17.
[2] Syncell. i. p. 523.   [3] Eus. i. p. 251; Diod. xxxi. 19. 6
[4] Strabo xii. 534; cf. Reinach, *Trois royaumes*, p. 18.
[5] Reinach, *Trois royaumes*, p. 161.

coin in gold—an indication that they are willing to purchase the friendship of the Seleucid house by some formal recognition of its suzerainty.

Of the relations of Antiochus and Bithynia we are told nothing. About 250 Nicomedes died, and fresh family feuds distracted the princely house. He left a wife, Etazeta, and some infant sons, but besides these he had by an earlier wife, a Phrygian, Ditizele, a grown-up son called Ziaëlas.[1] Under the *régime* of Etazeta, Ziaëlas had been discarded; he had even found his father's court no safe place for him and had vanished out of the land. Nicomedes left his kingdom to Etazeta's children, placing them by his will under the protection of Ptolemy and Antigonus, of Byzantium, Heraclea, and Cius. But now Ziaëlas, who had been living all this time with the king of the Armenians, suddenly reappeared in Bithynia at the head of a body of Galatians, Tolistoagii. A civil war at once raged over the country. The adherents of Etazeta were supported by troops from the states under whose protection her children had been placed. Ziaëlas succeeded, however, in conquering first a part, and then the whole, of his father's realm. Heraclea, which had taken a prominent part in opposing him, was raided by his Galatians. We hear presently of a son of Nicomedes called Zibœtes[2] as an exile in Macedonia; this is no doubt one of the sons of Etazeta who had taken refuge with his guardian, King Antigonus.[3]

With the two other Macedonian kingdoms the relations of the Seleucid continued to be the same under Antiochus II as under Antiochus I—friendship with the house of Antigonus, a state of war with Ptolemy. The former was to be still more complicated with the house of Seleucus by another marriage. Demetrius, the son of Antigonus Gonatas and Phila, fetched in his turn a bride from the Seleucid court, Stratonice, the daughter of the elder Stratonice and Antiochus the First, a princess who—so involved were now the relations—was at

---

[1] On his coins ΖΙΑΗΛΛ.

[2] Polyb. iv. 50, 9. *Tibœtes* is obviously another way of writing in Greek the same Bithynian name.

[3] Memnon, 22 = *F. H. G.* iii. p. 537; Tzetzes, *Chil.* iii. 950 f.; Plin. *N. H.* viii. 144; Polyb. iv. 50, 1; cf. Reinach, *Trois royaumes*, p. 100 f.

once the half-sister and the niece of his mother and the niece of his father.[1]

The war with Ptolemy was still, as far as Asia Minor was concerned, a war of which the Greek states of the coast and the neighbouring islands were both the theatre and the prizes of victory. It continued to fluctuate without discoverable progress. In the latter years of Antiochus I, or early in his son's reign,[2] Ephesus, the commercial centre of Asia Minor, passed from Seleucid to Ptolemaïc possession. A son of King Ptolemy's, himself called Ptolemy, commanded the garrison which held it — a garrison composed largely, we understand, of half-wild men from Thrace.[3] This gain, however, to the Ptolemaïc side was quickly overbalanced by losses. Miletus, which we saw lately obsequiously dedicating an image of Ptolemy's sister, about this time fell away under a tyrant called Timarchus. It has been suggested that this man was the Aetolian *condottiere* who once descended on the coast of Asia and defeated a general of King Ptolemy's.[4] This is very probable, and if so, Timarchus must have seized Miletus by a *coup de main*. At any rate Timarchus the tyrant had no idea of being subordinate to either Ptolemy or Seleucid. It seemed possible at that moment that the rivalry of the two houses might allow petty princes to maintain their independence in the midst. At Ephesus the young Ptolemy abjured his allegiance to his father and set up for himself. He and the tyrant of Miletus made common cause.[5] But they had miscalculated the forces with which they had to do. Miletus was recaptured by Antiochus II, and the *demos* now turned the stream of its flattery upon the Seleucid house. The surname of "God," by which Antiochus II was afterwards

---

[1] Eus. i. p. 249; Justin xxviii. 1, 2; Agatharchides, frag. 19 = *F.H.G.* iii. p. 196. The mistake in Justin, "ad fratrem Antiochum" (1, 4) is to be explained, not as Beloch explains it, by making it refer to Stratonice's *nephew* Antiochus Hierax, but by supposing that Justin found her described, quite correctly, as the sister of King Antiochus (the Second), who was reigning *at the time of her marriage*.

[2] After the Decree of the Ionian Body (Michel, No. 486, see p. 150), where an Ephesian appears among the envoys.

[3] Athen. xiii. 593 *a*.

[4] Polyaen. v. 25; Frontin. *Strateg.* iii. 2, 11; cf. Niese ii. p. 134, note 6.

[5] Trog. *Prol.* xxvi.

distinguished, is said to have been first pronounced in Miletus.¹

The rule of young Ptolemy² at Ephesus also came to an abrupt end. His Thracian guards, knowing the weakness of his position, broke out in mutiny. Ptolemy fled with his mistress Irene to the great temple of Artemis. The Thracians, undaunted by its sanctities, followed him up and there slew him. Irene, holding with one hand to the knocker of the door, so as herself also to claim the protection of the goddess, with the other sprinkled her lover's blood upon the holy things till she too was cut down.³ Ephesus passed once more to the Seleucid.⁴ There are two isolated notices which our ignorance of the time does not allow us to bring into relation with each other or with contemporary events, but which seem to show that at some time under Antiochus II the activity of the Seleucid house extended to Europe. One of these is the statement abstracted from Memnon⁵ that at one moment hostilities were on the point of breaking out between Antiochus and Byzantium. The Northern League, which we saw combating Antiochus I, seems to have been still in existence. For at

---

¹ App. *Syr.* 65.
² H. von Prott [*Rhein. Mus.* liii. (1898), p. 471 f.] identifies Ptolemy, the commandant in Ephesus, with the Ptolemy who appears as joint-king in papyri before 259-258, but who vanishes after that date. This seems probable. When, however, von Prott goes on to identify him also with Ptolemy, the son of Lysimachus, who had once sat for a moment on the Macedonian throne, and with Ptolemy the father of the high-priestess, Berenice (see p. 178), and to tell us that he followed his mother Arsinoë to Egypt, and was there adopted by King Ptolemy as his son, and recognized as heir, he seems to propose a theory which is not favoured by the evidence. A fact so momentous as the house of Lysimachus coming in this decisive way to the front again could not have failed to leave some trace even in our fragmentary records. The Ptolemy at Ephesus could not be referred to in both cases simply as the son of his adopted father when his real parentage was so illustrious and full of consequence.
³ Athen. xiii. 593 *b*.
⁴ Niese (ii. p. 135) refers to this occasion the conquest of Ephesus by an Antiochus described in Frontin. *Strateg.* iii. 9, 10. Niese (ii. p. 135) cites *Inscr. in the Brit. Mus.* Nos. 403, 423, to prove that Antiochus II gave judgment in the dispute between Priene and Samos, and that *Samos* therefore was at one time under him. But there is nothing about Samos at all in No. 423, and it is not clear to me that Antiochus is mentioned in No. 403, except *to date certain events by his reign*, which might be done because *Priene* was within his sphere.
⁵ Memnon 23 = *F.H.G.* iii. p. 538.

this juncture Heraclea sent a contingent of forty triremes to Byzantium, and the war "advanced as far as threats only."[1]

The other notice[2] is one which shows us the Seleucid King in person on European soil. He is besieging or has taken[3] the Thracian town of Cypsela. Numbers of the old Thracian nobility have rallied to his side. Antiochus had perhaps espoused the native cause against the new-come Galatians who had founded a separate kingdom in this region.[4] He gave at any rate princely entertainment to the Thracian chiefs who joined him. When the Thracians of Cypsela see their countrymen walking about the Greek king, ablaze with ornaments of gold and silver arms, they declare themselves ready, not only to submit, but to fight under his banners. [Against whom? Byzantium? the Gauls of Tylis? Ptolemaïc forces?]

We have no details as to the treatment of the Greek cities by Antiochus II except his liberation of Miletus. In that city a hundred years afterwards the day still lived in the imagination of the citizens when Hippomachus the son of Athenaeus, an Erythraean who had found favour at the Seleucid court, appeared clothed with the royal authority to restore freedom and democracy.[5] When Rome had come to bear rule in Asia, the Ionian Greeks still spoke of Antiochus II as "the God," and appealed to the decrees by which he had granted them constitutions, as if in fact he were the author of their liberties.[6] Nevertheless, it is under Antiochus II that we find the most opulent and splendid of the Ionian cities, Ephesus, after it has been recovered from

---

[1] Niese (ii. p. 137) brings this dispute between Antiochus and Byzantium into connexion with the war by which Byzantium had some time before broken the strength of Callatis, a city, Niese supposes, under Seleucid protection. If, however, Antiochus intervened as the patron of Callatis, there is some improbability that he would have found Heraclea, the mother-city of Callatis, so strenuously opposing him.

[2] Polyaen. iv. 16.   [3] The readings differ between ἐπολιόρκει and ἐπόρθει.

[4] The "friendly relations" of these Gauls with Byzantium spoken of by Niese (ii. p. 138) seem to have consisted in their exacting an increasingly heavy blackmail, or threatening to destroy the fields (Polyb. iv. 46).

[5] ἀπόγονος ὑπάρχουσα Ἱππομά[χου] τοῦ Ἀθηναίου, ὃς κατήγ[α]γεν τ[ὴ]ν τ[ε ἐλ]ευθερίαν καὶ δημοκρατίαν παρ[ὰ β]ασ[ιλέως Ἀντι]όχου το[ῦ] θεοῦ, Haussoullier, Revue de Philol. xxv. (1901), p. 6.   [6] Joseph. Arch. xii. § 125.

Ptolemy, subjected to direct control. It has been suggested[1] that Laodice after her divorce maintained at Ephesus a separate court of her own. There appears at any rate at the time of Antiochus' death a royal official who is expressly spoken of as being "set over Ephesus."[2]

It is to the reign of Antiochus II that the important inscription found eighteen years ago (1884) at Durdurkar (near the ancient Eriza) belongs.[3] It is the one document we possess which tells us something of the worship of the sovereign established by imperial authority in the realm. The cities, as we saw, already offered divine honours to Alexander and his successors of the first generation. And instances of such civic cults recur during our period. There was a priest of Antiochus I at Ilion[4] before 277; the Ionian Body joined the worship of Antiochus I, his son and joint-king Antiochus and Stratonice to that of "the god Alexander";[5] and games were celebrated by Erythrae in honour of Antiochus I after his death, in which he was worshipped by his divine name of Saviour.[6] At Smyrna, Stratonice was worshipped as Aphrodite Stratonicis, and her son Antiochus II was in course of time joined with her;[7] Miletus, as we saw, hailed Antiochus II as "God." But all these were cults established by the *cities*; they were not organized by the imperial government. We have no mention of an *imperial* cult of the King and Queen except in the inscription of Durdurkar, and hence it is often inferred to have been an *innovation* of Antiochus II. The accidental fact, however, that our one document belongs to his reign is not sufficient to establish such an inference; it may indeed have been so; on the other hand, such a cult may quite well have existed as early as the reign of the first Seleucus. The document in question is a rescript of Antiochus II to Anaximbrotus, presumably the satrap of Phrygia, which Anaximbrotus forwards with a covering letter to the district officer Dionytas. The King's rescript states that his worship is already established in the several satrapies of the realm,

---

[1] Haussoullier, *Revue de Philol.* xxv. (1901), p. 20.

[2] ὁ ἐπὶ τῆς Ἐφέσου, Phylarch. ap. Athen. xiii. 593 b. Whether he was a civil governor or commander of a royal garrison we do not know.

[3] Michel, No. 40. [4] *Ibid.* No. 525. [5] *Ibid.* No. 486.
[6] *Ibid.* No. 457. [7] *Ibid.* No. 19.

under a high-priest in each satrapy, by whom legal instruments are dated, and whose office is therefore probably annual. The King has now determined to institute a similar worship of the queen Laodice, for which each satrapy is to have a special high-priestess. For the satrapy of Anaximbrotus the high-priestess appointed is Berenice, the daughter of Ptolemy the son of Lysimachus, and in her grandfather we *may perhaps* see the great Lysimachus.

Suddenly in the last years of Antiochus II we find a complete revolution in the relation of the powers. The dreary war between Seleucid and Ptolemy, which had seemed to have become a permanent feature of the world, ceased. It not only ceased, but was succeeded by close alliance. Things had not gone altogether well with the house of Ptolemy. Its successes had been in many cases evanescent. We have seen the case of Ephesus and Miletus. It had had another disappointment which touched it more nearly. The rebel viceroy of Cyrene, Magas, Ptolemy's half-brother, who had been the ally of Antiochus I, had been brought to a composition with the King of Egypt about 258. His daughter by Apama, Berenice, was betrothed to the young Ptolemy, the heir of the Egyptian throne—an arrangement by which the Egyptian and Cyrenian kingdoms would once more coalesce. Unfortunately for Ptolemy, Magas, after making this treaty, almost immediately died, and the Queen-Mother, Apama, coming thereby to power, immediately abjured the compact and fetched a husband for her daughter from the anti-Ptolemaïc court of Macedonia. Demetrius the Fair, the brother of King Antigonus, came to reign in Cyrene. The influence of the Seleucid queen-mother continued paramount, for Demetrius, although nominally the husband of Berenice, formed a *liaison* with Apama herself. Cyrene was still a thorn in the side of Egypt.[1]

It is implied that Ptolemy took the initiative in proposing a peace to Antiochus. He seems to have made it worth the Seleucid King's while. He offered the hand of his daughter, another Berenice, to Antiochus, who undertook on his part to

---

[1] Just. xxvi. 3. Apama is here called Arsinoë by a characteristic slovenliness of Justin.

repudiate in her favour his present queen, Laodice. The hand of Berenice was to bring with it large advantages; *phernophoros*, dowry-bringing, became her popular description.[1] What these advantages were one can only speculate. They may not improbably have included territorial concessions. By comparing the list which Theocritus gives of the countries under Ptolemaïc influence with those which Ptolemy III states (in the description of Aduli) that he inherited from his father, it is observed that Cilicia and Pamphylia, which appear in the former, are absent from the latter. It is therefore likely that the Ptolemaïc claims to these regions were abandoned in this treaty; Ptolemy indeed may have already been obliged to evacuate them.

An immediate change came over the Seleucid court. Laodice disappeared; a rival appeared to her sons, Seleucus and Antiochus, in a child whom Berenice bore to Antiochus. It may be that the residence of the court was now more regularly fixed at the Syrian Antioch, towards the Ptolemaïc realm, instead of in Asia Minor, where Laodice was strong. Friendly offices between the houses became at any rate the order of the day. The physician, Cleombrotus of Ceos, sent possibly from the medical schools of Alexandria, was rewarded by Ptolemy with a hundred talents because he had treated Antiochus successfully.[2] Casks of Nile water were carried systematically to Berenice in her new home;[3] it has been pointed out[4] that it had a great reputation for rendering fertile.[5]

All seemed to go smoothly. But the divorced queen was not a woman to sit down tamely in her humiliation. She worked fiercely to be reinstated, and at last succeeded, for if policy bound Antiochus to Berenice, his heart, it is said, belonged to Laodice. In 246 Berenice was sitting solitary in Antioch, and the King was across the Taurus living once more with his former queen. Then he suddenly died at Ephesus.[6]

---

[1] Jerome *in Dan.* 11.

[2] Plin. vii. § 123. The story is told by an error of Erasistratus, Plin. xxix. § 5.

[3] Athen. ii. 45 *c*.   [4] Mahaffy, *Empire of the Ptolemies*, p. 171.
Plin. vii. § 33.   Eus. i. p. 251.

Laodice (or so it was believed) had cut short his life by poison, to prevent the succession of her children being any more endangered by the fluctuations of his mood.[1]

The peace of Asia, so recently secured, instantly vanished.

[1] App. *Syr.* 65; Val. Max. ix. 14; Plin. vii. § 53; Jerome *in Dan.* 11, 6.

CHAPTER X

SELEUCUS II (KALLINIKOS) AND SELEUCUS III (SOTER)

§ 1. *The War of Laodice*

THE Seleucid power had ceased to be a unity. It was represented by two rival Queens, both masculine, resolute women, after the fashion of these Macedonian princesses, Laodice across the Taurus, Berenice in Syria. The son of Berenice, who was probably proclaimed King in Antioch, was of course an infant in arms; the eldest son of Laodice, Seleucus, was a youth nearing manhood.[1]

Seleucus was proclaimed King in Ephesus and Asia Minor. To support his right, as against the child of Berenice, Laodice resorted, according to one story,[2] to the device of dressing up a certain Artemon, who bore a close resemblance to King Antiochus, and causing him to be laid in the royal bed before the King's death was known, in order that in the presence of the magnates of the court he might solemnly declare his son Seleucus the true heir. Laodice proclaimed her son King, but she kept the reins of government in her own hands.

It must come of course to an internecine struggle between the two Queen-mothers. In the kingdom itself Laodice, the old Queen, was the stronger; Berenice had at her back the might of Egypt. It all depended on whether Laodice could strike quickly enough. Even in Antioch she had partizans,

---

[1] He was old enough to take a personal part in war a few years later. His younger brother Antiochus is said at a date about 240 to be fourteen (Just. xxvii. 2, 7). On this reckoning he would be eight in 246.

[2] Val. Max. ix. 14; Plin. vii. § 53.

among them Genneus or Caeneus,[1] one of the chief magistrates of the city. She hit on the bold thought of kidnapping the child of her rival. Her emissaries, flying perhaps to Antioch almost with the post that brought the news of the King's death, arranged the plot. It succeeded. The young prince vanished.

In this extremity Berenice showed the spirit of a lioness. The child was believed to have been carried to a certain house. Berenice instantly mounted a chariot, took in her own hand a spear, and galloped to the spot. On the way Caeneus met her. The Queen aimed her spear at him. It missed. Nothing daunted, Berenice followed it with a stone, which brought her enemy down. A crowd, partly hostile, surged about the closed doors, behind which the prince was understood to be. But they fell back before the fierce approach of the Queen. And here the story is broken off.[2] Another author[3] takes it up at a later point. The fate of the young prince is still mysterious; it is not known whether he is alive or dead. Obviously the popular feeling in Antioch is so strongly on the side of Berenice that the murderers dare not avow what they have done. To this body of sentiment Berenice appeals. She shows herself to the people in the guise of a suppliant, and the storm of public indignation is so strong that the guilty magistrates are obliged to dissemble. A child is exhibited to the people as the infant King and surrounded with all the due pomp; they have still authority enough to keep this child in their own hands. But they are obliged to come to some agreement with the Queen and allow her to establish herself in a defensible part of the royal palace at Daphne[4] with a body of Galatian guards.

This was an awkward turn for the plans of Laodice. Everything depended on crushing Berenice before the Egyptian force could be brought to bear in her favour. And shut up in the palace at Daphne, Berenice could gain time. The Ptolemaïc power was at this moment in a position to strike strongly. The Cyrenaean difficulty had been at last settled

---

[1] Jerome *ad Dan.* xi. 6 mentions Icadion and Genneus; this latter is probably the same as the *Caeneus* of Valerius.
[2] Val. Max. ix. 10.   [3] Polyaen. viii. 50.   [4] Just. xxvii. 1, 4.

to its satisfaction. The young Queen, Berenice the daughter of Magas, had discovered the relations of her husband Demetrius with her mother, and displaying the characteristic spirit of her race, caused him to be assassinated in Apama's bed under her own eyes. She had then renewed her interrupted betrothal with the heir of the Ptolemaïc throne. About the time that the other Berenice, her cousin, was defying siege at Daphne, the old King of Egypt died; the government passed into young and vigorous hands. Ptolemy III ascended the throne, married Berenice of Cyrene, and prepared to intervene with the whole force of his kingdom in his sister's defence. At the same time the struggle between the two Queens was being watched breathlessly throughout the Seleucid realm. A number of the Greek cities of Asia [1] declared for Berenice, and put on foot the civic forces.[2] Contingents began to glide out of their harbours or to move along the road to Antioch. Berenice had only to sit still in her fortress and wait.

The hope of Laodice to reach her seemed desperate. But even so she succeeded. It seems an incredible folly on the part of Berenice that she exposed herself—to be instantly cut down. But she was led to trust to the oath of her enemies, and her physician Aristarchus, by whom she was guided, was really Laodice's tool. And here we are told another of those strange impersonations which give the whole story of these events such a mythical complexion. Berenice's women, it is said, after they had done their best to shield her with their own bodies and several of them had fallen, concealed her corpse, and put one of their number who was wounded, but not mortally, in her place, keeping up, till the advent of the King of Egypt, the delusion that the Queen and her son were still alive.[3]

Meantime Laodice was strengthening herself in Asia Minor. Miletus is found hastening to declare its adherence to Seleucus II; its embassy conveys to the young King a wreath of bay

---

[1] It is impossible to say which, except that Magnesia-on-Sipylus seems to have been one; not Smyrna or Magnesia-on-the-Meander (Michel, No. 19), not Miletus (Haussoullier, *Revue de Philol.* xxv. (1901), p. 125 f.), not Ephesus (*Flinders Petrie Papyr.*). Laodice was strong in Asia Minor; it may rather be the cities of Syria which are in question.

[2] Just. xxvii. 1, 5.   [3] Polyaen. viii. 50; Just. xxvii. 1, 7.

leaves, plucked in the sacred enclosure of the Didymaean temple.[1] Many of the other Greek states must have acted likewise. But the attack of Ptolemy III came with terrific effect upon the divided kingdom. He appeared at the head of his army in Syria, before the death of Berenice and her son was certainly known, and in many quarters was regarded rather as an ally than a conqueror.[2] The states which had flown to arms in Berenice's defence, finding themselves too late, had no option, now that they had compromised themselves, but to join him.[3]

The great events of the following years are obscured by the character of our sources. In their loose description we seem to see a conquest of Asia which goes beyond the old invasions of Tothmes, and even resembles the triumphant march of Alexander. If we look more closely, however, we shall form, I think, a more moderate estimate of the exploits of Ptolemy Euergetes. The war called by contemporaries the "Laodicean War" (Λαοδίκειος πόλεμος)[4] falls into two divisions—the maritime war and the land war. Of these the maritime is really the more important, and here the successes of Ptolemy are more solid. It was on the sea that the Ptolemaïc power really lay; it had already, as we have seen, secured a number of *points d'appui* over the coasts and islands of the Levant, and what Ptolemy Euergetes did was to carry to its farthest extent the traditional policy of his house. On the coasts of Phœnicia, Lycia, and Caria, Ptolemy was already predominant; he possessed Cyprus and the federated Cyclades.[5] The maritime war of Ptolemy III rounds off the work of his father and grandfather. What had been lost in recent years, the Cilician coast, for instance, and Ephesus, are recovered. The line of Ptolemaïc power is carried still farther along the coasts. Even the acquisitions of the house of Seleucus in Thrace, from which it was necessarily cut off by a power dominating the sea, pass to Egypt.

A moment of this war is lit up for us in a curious way. The commander of a Seleucid squadron on the coasts of Asia

[1] Haussoullier, *Revue de Philol.* xxv. (1901), p. 126.
[2] Polyaen. viii. 50. [3] Just. xxvii. 1, 8.
[4] *Inscr. in the Brit. Mus.* No. 403, l. 134. [5] Michel, No. 1239.

sent home a sheet of papyrus giving a narrative of his operations. This paper, or pieces of it, worn but still partly decipherable, came the other day into the hands of modern archaeologists.

Where the dispatch begins to be decipherable the capture of some town by a detachment of the Ptolemaïc forces is described, apparently one of the towns of Cilicia. A party among the inhabitants seem to have had an understanding with the attacking force, and the town was taken by a night surprise. A garrison was put in to hold it under an officer called Epigenes. Then, after a gap, the document seems to speak of a squadron of five ships in the Seleucid service, who, acting on the orders of " the Sister," *i.e.* Laodice, had collected all the money they could along the coast and deposited it in (the Cilician) Seleucia—1500 talents in all. In Seleucia the Seleucid governor of Cilicia (ὁ ἐν Κιλικίᾳ στρατηγός), Aribazus, was commanding, and his purpose was to forward the moneys now collected to Laodice at Ephesus. Before, however, he could do so, the town of Soli and the subordinate *strategoi* of Cilicia, the district officers, went over to the Ptolemaïc side, and in concert with them a Ptolemaïc force, under Pythagoras and Aristocles, attacked Seleucia. The town, even the citadel, was stormed. Aribazus essayed to escape across the Taurus, but fell into the hands of the native tribes who lived about the passes; they cut off his head and brought it presently to Antioch.

The rest of the document narrates operations on the Syrian, not the Cilician, coast, in which the writer would seem to have taken part in person. A Ptolemaïc squadron of as many sail as the harbour of (the Syrian) Seleucia was understood to be capable of holding, puts to sea in the first watch of the night. Its place of starting is conjectured by Köhler to be Salamis in Cyprus. About three o'clock the following afternoon it strikes the Syrian coast at Posidium, a fort some twenty miles south of Seleucia. There it remains for the night, and at the next daybreak moves to Seleucia. Here it is received with open arms. The priests, the magistrates, the populace, the troops of the garrison flock down the road to the harbour to meet it in festival array.

From Seleucia the Ptolemaïc force moves upon Antioch itself, which was in those days accessible by water. In Antioch there is a considerable military force, and the district officers, the "satraps" of the neighbouring country, seem to have gathered within its walls. And it looks as if Antioch had thought at first of offering some defence. But the sight of the Ptolemaïc force convinces it that to do so is hopeless. Antioch, like Seleucia, receives the invader. A procession of the chief men, satraps, captains, priests, and magistrates, accompanied by the "youths from the gymnasium" and the populace, all wearing crowns, comes to meet the Ptolemaïc force. "They brought all the animals for sacrifice into the road without the gate; some shook our hands, and some greeted us with clapping and shouting." There the document leaves off, having shown us the chief city of Seleucid Syria in the hands of King Ptolemy.[1]

For the land war our chief authority is the *Monumentum Adulitanum*, an inscribed stone seen at Aduli in Abyssinia in the seventh century A.D. by Cosmas Indicopleustes, who has left us a copy of it.[2] It was a monument put up by some Ptolemaïc official at that remote station on the Red Sea giving an account of the King's conquests. It describes how he advanced upon Asia with foot and horse and ships, "and elephants," the official is careful to note, whose chief business in Aduli was no doubt to replenish the supply, "from the Troglodyte country (*i.e.* the Red Sea coast) and Aethiopia, which his father and he himself were the first to cause to be captured in these parts and brought down to Egypt, and to train for service in war," how he "made himself master of all the country this side of the Euphrates (*i.e.* Northern Syria), Cilicia, Pamphylia, Ionia, the Hellespont and Thrace, and of all the forces in these countries and the Indian elephants, and made all the petty despots in these regions subject to him," and then how he crossed the Euphrates and plunged into the distant world of Irân.

It will be observed that till the passage of the Euphrates

---

[1] *Flinders Petrie Papyri* (Mahaffy), Part II. No. 45; Köhler, *Sitzungsb. der königl. Akad. zu Berlin*, 1894, p. 445 f.; Wilcken, *Griechische Papyri*, p. 52.

[2] Michel, No. 1239.

no country is mentioned as conquered which is not open to attack by sea. *The Ptolemaïc land forces never crossed the Taurus.* Having once secured the road through Northern Syria (Antioch itself succumbed, as we saw, to an attack *from the sea*) they passed east. In Asia Minor, which hitherto rather than Syria had been the Seleucid base, the court of Laodice and Seleucus was safe from molestation, except on the coast. And even the coast was only partially conquered by the Ptolemaïc fleet. Ephesus indeed, where Laodice was still established when the Ptolemaïc captain penned his dispatch, passed before long to Ptolemy, the Seleucid court returning, no doubt, to the safer distance of Sardis. But Miletus and Smyrna remained in the Seleucid alliance.

The loss of Ephesus can perhaps be traced in the story taken from Phylarchus.[1] The court is residing at some place other than Ephesus, which is not mentioned, but which must surely be Sardis. Ephesus, however, is still held, as Sophron, the governor of the city (ὁ ἐπὶ τῆς Ἐφέσου), has been called to the royal presence. He has somehow incurred the displeasure of Laodice, and she has determined to make away with him. Among Laodice's women, however, is Danaë, the daughter of that famous courtesan Leontion who had shone among the companions of Epicurus: Danaë is always at the Queen's side; all the Queen's purposes are open to her. In past days Sophron was her lover. When Sophron stands before the Queen, Danaë is sitting by the Queen's side. As Laodice and Sophron talk, the truth breaks upon Danaë that Laodice is inviting him to his destruction. She makes him a quick imperceptible sign. It is understood. He feigns to agree generally with the Queen's proposals but asks for two days further to consider. Laodice assents. The next night Sophron flies for his life to Ephesus. Then Laodice understood what Danaë had done. Instantly old friendship was swallowed up in vindictive fury. Danaë was haled as a criminal before her, but the questions which Laodice put to her she met with disdainful silence. She was led away to be hurled from a high place. As she went she made an utterance which those about her thought worthy of record. "The common run of

---

[1] Athen. xiii. 593 c.

men make small account of religion, and they are quite right. I saved the man that was my lover, and this is the recognition I get from the Powers which dispose of us. Laodice killed hers, and she is thought to deserve all that honour."

Sophron fled to Ephesus. That was no safe place, if it was still to be in Laodice's possession. It was probably Sophron who now called in the Ptolemaïc forces. It is found at any rate a few years later occupied by a Ptolemaïc garrison, and a Sophron appears in command of a Ptolemaïc fleet.[1]

The young king Seleucus seems early to have gone at the head of an army across the Taurus to defend or to regain the Syrian and eastern provinces.[2] It went hard in his absence, and the absence of the troops which followed him, with the adherents of his house along the coast. Smyrna, for instance, was exposed to attack, not only from the Ptolemaïc fleets, but from its neighbour, Magnesia-on-Sipylus, where there was a great military settlement which declared against Laodice and Seleucus and harried its fields.[3] Smyrna, at any rate, stood fast, and in this region the Seleucid cause held its own. The Magnesian colony was compelled to return to the old alliance, and at some subsequent date was incorporated by the Smyrnaeans in their own state.[4]

On Smyrna in return for its fidelity the King was concerned to shower favours. He gave the usual promise that the city should continue autonomous and be free of tribute.[5] He also guaranteed it in the possession of all the territory it already stood possessed of, and promised to restore any it had formerly owned. More than this, he interested himself warmly in what was the chief interest of the city, its great temple of Aphrodite-Stratonicis. Smyrna would secure a great advantage if it could shield itself by the sanctity of its shrine, if it could be treated as "holy and inviolable" (ἱερὰ καὶ ἄσυλος). It could only obtain this advantage in so far as the independent powers of the world, any who had the material

---

[1] Trog. *Prol.* xxvii. reading "Antigonus Andro proelio navali Sophrona vicerit" (C. Müller) for MS. "Antigonum Andro proelio navali oprona vicerit."

[2] See Appendix K.

[3] Smyrnaean Inscr. (Michel, No. 19), l. 1-3 ; l. 42, 43.

[4] Smyrnaean Inscr. l. 19, 20.

[5] Michel, No. 258, Smyrnaean Inscr. l. 11, 12.

force to molest it, would consent to recognize its sanctity. To obtain this recognition was the object it had in view. It began by procuring a pronouncement of the Delphic oracle in favour of its claims. Armed with this, it approached the Seleucid king. Seleucus threw himself heartily into the cause of the faithful city. He addressed letters to all the states of the Greek world, "to kings and rulers and cities and nations,"[1] asking them to recognize the temple of Aphrodite-Stratonicis as a sanctuary and Smyrna as a city holy and inviolable. One of the answers has been preserved, that of the city of Delphi, which, as the original oracle had proceeded from them, is naturally favourable. It charges the *theoroi*, who were sent round the Greek states to invite them to the Pythian games,[2] to bestow special commendation on King Seleucus both for his piety in obeying the oracle and his honourable treatment of a Greek city.[3]

Ptolemy did not continue to direct the Asiatic campaigns in person. After his raid into the eastern provinces he returned to Egypt, where troubles had broken out which called for his presence.[4] But the war did not thereby come to an end. Ptolemy left officers to govern in his name both in the West and in the East, in Cilicia his "friend" Antiochus, in the provinces beyond the Euphrates "another general, Xanthippus."[5] One would like to know on what principle Ptolemy at this juncture framed his policy. He has been commended for wise moderation in withdrawing after his triumphal march. And indeed the traditional policy of his house was to set a prudent limit to ambition. But the texts hardly show the action of

[1] Smyrnaean Inscr. l. 11.

[2] Haussoullier supposes that the celebration of the games in question is that of the year 238. It might be the one before, that of 242.

[3] Michel, No. 258.   [4] Just. xxvii. 1, 9.

[5] "Ciliciam autem amico suo Antiocho gubernandam tradidit et Xanthippo alteri duci provincias trans Euphraten," Jerome *in Daniel*, 11, 9. The theory of Niebuhr and Droysen that this Antiochus is Antiochus Hierax, the younger brother of Seleucus, has now been generally abandoned (Beloch, Wilcken, Bouché-Leclerq, Niese, Haussoullier). A probable conjecture (Lenschau, *De rebus Prienensium*, p. 204) identifies him with the Antiochus ὑπὸ τοῦ βασιλέως Πτολεμαίου τεταγμένος, who appears in the affair of Samos and Priene (*Inscr. in the Brit. Mus.* No. 403, l. 153). If so, Haussoullier is probably right in conjecturing that the province of Antiochus was the whole strip of coast, so far as it was subject to Egypt, from Cilicia to Ionia *Revue de Philol.* xxv. (1901), p. 145.

Ptolemy III in this light. *His personal return is no evacuation of the conquered countries.* In that moment of intoxicating glory, in the prostration of the rival house, Ptolemy III seems really to have contemplated making himself king of Asia as well as of Egypt. He actually intends to govern Irân from Alexandria as a dependency. It is not his prudence, but the force of circumstances, which makes him abandon the idea.

But although the return of Ptolemy to Egypt did not mean a suspension of hostilities, the absence of the King relaxed the pressure upon his enemies. Seleucus now took strenuously in hand the reconquest of Northern Syria and the revolted cities of the coast. A great armada was fitted out in one of the harbours of Asia Minor, and presently took the sea. It met, however, with a storm which completely shattered it—as the fleet of Seleucus' son was later on shattered in the same dangerous waters—and few, according to Justin, beside the King himself escaped to land.[1] After this, Justin goes on, the cities were so sorry for him that they joined him of their own accord—a passage over which modern writers make very merry, perhaps undervaluing the part which sentiment plays even now in human politics. As a matter of fact, it seems probable that the cities of Northern Syria were really attached to the house which had planted and fostered them, and that they had conceived themselves, not so much to be revolting against that house, as standing by its wronged representatives, Berenice and her son, in whose name the King of Egypt had summoned them. It would therefore be natural that as soon as it became apparent that the house of Seleucus was to be crushed altogether, and that they were to be annexed to Egypt, a great wave of compunction should sweep over them.

Of this phase in the war, that which is marked by the Seleucid house recovering Northern Syria, no detail is preserved except the bare statement of Eusebius that in the year 142-141 (Olym. 134. 3) Orthosia on the Phœnician coast, which was being besieged by a Ptolemaïc force, was relieved by Seleucus, who brought up reinforcements.[2]

---

[1] Just. xxvii. 2, 1.

[2] Eus. i. p. 251. A notice of the *Chronicum Paschale* (p. 330, Bonn) assigns to about the same time the foundation of Kallinikon on the Euphrates,

In the next phase of the war Seleucus passes from recovering his father's share of Syria to attacking the Ptolemaïc. The war of defence became a war of reprisals. An encounter, somewhere in Palestine, took place between the two hosts. Seleucus was completely beaten. He withdrew the shattered remnant of his army of invasion to Antioch. His position was once more critical, for he had no force left wherewith to meet the counterstroke of his enemy.[1]

The operations in Syria had drawn the Seleucid King for the most part to the regions south of the Taurus; they had made Antioch on the Orontes rather than Sardis or Ephesus the pivot of his kingdom. But meantime the Queen-Mother, Laodice, was still reigning in Asia Minor, and had her younger son, Antiochus, joined with her, a boy at that time of some fourteen years. In his extremity Seleucus now addressed an entreaty to his brother to cross the Taurus to his assistance.[2] This request seems to show that a certain independent authority was exercised by Antiochus in Asia Minor, or rather by those who governed in the boy's name, his mother Laodice and her friends.[3] And this inference finds a separate confirmation in an inscription from the temple at Branchidae,[4] which contains a list of offerings made to the shrine by "the kings Seleucus and Antiochus." The Antiochus here is therefore one who shares the royal authority; that he does so as a subordinate is shown by the fact that the letter accompanying the gifts runs in the name of King Seleucus alone.[5]

but, as Niese remarks, the *Chronicum* is so full of blunders that not much weight can be attached to it. In this notice some confusion at any rate is evident. It dates Ol. 134. 1 (244-243), but gives the consuls of 242.

[1] Just. xxvii. 2, 4.   [2] *Ibid.* 2, 6.

[3] This conclusion was drawn from the text by Niebuhr, and although his identification of Antiochus Hierax with the friend of King Ptolemy be dropped, this conclusion appears to me to hold good still. The alternative interpretation (Wilcken, *Pauly-Wissowa*, i. p. 2457) that what Seleucus besought was only that Antiochus should personally come to his help at the head of the Seleucid forces in Asia Minor seems unsatisfactory. That the forces should be led by a child of fourteen would be no great thing for Seleucus to secure; the forces themselves were what he wanted; if they were subject to no authority but his, he had but to order his generals to bring them up.   [4] Michel, No. 39.

[5] I follow Haussoullier (*Revue de Philol.* xxii. (1898), p. 121; xxiv. (1900), p. 257) in adhering to the older view that these kings are Seleucus II and Antiochus Hierax, not Seleucus I and Antiochus I (Soldau, Wilcken, etc.).

To secure the co-operation of his brother's court, Seleucus offered to make a partition of the Empire, to cede the trans-Tauric country to Antiochus. Whether the cession was to be absolute or whether he reserved to himself any right of suzerainty we are not told.[1] If his mother and her friends were already the real rulers of that region, the offer of Seleucus amounted simply to a recognition of existing facts. The events which followed this proposition are touched on so summarily by Justin that it is scarcely possible to follow the connexions between them. At first the court of Sardis closed, or feigned to close, with it. The forces of Asia Minor were set in motion to join those in Syria. This co-operation between the two Seleucid courts seems not to have entered into Ptolemy's calculations, although why it should not have done so, when it seems the most natural thing to expect, we cannot say. Perhaps there were already signs of rivalry and dissension between them. At any rate, on getting word of the advance of the trans-Tauric army, Ptolemy, instead of following up his recent victory, concluded a peace for ten years with Seleucus.[2]

§ 2. *The Fraternal War*

Antiochus, however, did not join his forces with those of Seleucus. The concession made by the elder king seems to have been used to bring all power in Asia Minor more absolutely into the hands of the court of Sardis. As soon as that had been done, the mask was thrown off and a claim was advanced to the whole Seleucid Empire.[3] The people,

On the other hand it appears to me more likely that the dedication was made before the formal cession of the trans-Tauric country to Antiochus than after it, as Haussoullier (*Revue de Philol.* xxv. (1901), p. 140) supposes. Surely a letter to a city of Asia Minor could not have run in the name of King Seleucus alone when once Asia Minor had been made over to Antiochus.

[1] Just. xxvii. 2, 6.

[2] *Ibid.* 2, 9. Beloch conjectures that Justin has here misunderstood his authority, which said that Ptolemy concluded a peace *after a war of ten years*, not a peace for ten years. That, of course, is possible; but so are many other mistakes possible in our texts, which we cannot, however, correct at pleasure without losing ourselves in unlimited scepticism.

[3] Just. xxvii. 2, 7.

who were acting behind the boy Antiochus, were of course the Queen-Mother Laodice[1] and her friends. Amongst these the chief place was held by the Queen's brother, Alexander, who probably performed the functions of viceroy of the trans-Tauric country.[2]

With this breach between the brother kings there began for Asia Minor a period of civil war which must have dealt the country far deeper wounds than the war between Seleucid and Ptolemy, which affected only its seaward fringes. Seleucus, crippled as he had been by his recent defeat in Palestine, had still enough authority in the Empire to gather a force about him with which he crossed the Taurus to crush this new rebellion. Nowhere along the great high-road did the partizans of Antiochus arrest his march onwards. He was already in Lydia before his army met that of his brother. The first battle went in his favour. He fought another, and again successfully. But his victory was stayed by the strong city of Sardis, where the party of Antiochus found a sure retreat.[3]

It was now, however, seen what danger to the central government lay in all those independent elements in Asia Minor. A disturbance such as the rebellion of Antiochus Hierax[4] communicated unrest to all the peninsula. The task of Seleucus was indefinitely complicated. Antiochus had only to hold up his hand to bring up hordes of Galatians. In some quarters the cause of Antiochus and the Queen-Mother was more favourably regarded than that of the elder king, who indeed had been for much of the time since his accession absent from the country.

We last saw the dynast of Pontic Cappadocia employing Galatian bands against the Ptolemaïc forces, apparently in alliance with the Seleucid King (p. 154). Since then Mithridates the Founder had died in a good old age of eighty-four years,[5] and had been succeeded by his son Ariobarzanes (in 266). Of the reign of Ariobarzanes we know nothing except

---

[1] καὶ τὴν μητέρα συλλαμβάνουσαν εἶχεν, Plutarch, *De frat. amore*, 18.
[2] See Appendix L. [3] Eus. i. p. 251.
[4] Hierax, of course, is not an official surname, but a popular nickname, the "Hawk." [5] Lucian, *Macrob.* 13.

that he got into difficulties with his Galatian mercenaries[1] and has left no coins. He died about 250,[2] and was followed by another Mithridates, who at his father's death was still a boy. Under such circumstances the Galatian troubles grew worse, and the Pontic territory was so harried that famine stared the population in the face. Heraclea, whose friendly connexion with the Mithridatic house continued, sent what help it could, and had in consequence to bear a Galatian attack in its turn.[3] And now, some ten years later, the breach in the Seleucid house brings the Pontic king once more upon the stage. With this Irânian dynasty also, as with that in Southern Cappadocia, the great Macedonian house had mingled its blood. One sister of Seleucus II was the wife of Ariarathes; the other sister he gave in marriage to Mithridates II, with Greater Phyrgia (or so the Pontic house afterwards asserted) for dowry.[4]

At this juncture Mithridates declares in favour of his younger brother-in-law, Antiochus, and enters the field at the head of a great army of Galatians.

The intervention of the Pontic king and his fierce mercenaries gave a new turn to the struggle. A great battle, one of the landmarks of that confused epoch, took place near Ancyra.[5] The forces of Seleucus were swept down by the Galatian onset. Twenty thousand are said to have perished. At the end of that day of blood Seleucus himself was nowhere to be found. The news ran through the host of the victors that he was dead. The youth who by such an event became the sole and unrivalled possessor of the Seleucid throne displayed or affected great sorrow. Antiochus put on the garb of mourning and shut himself up to bewail his brother. Then the tidings came that he had lamented, or rejoiced, too soon. Seleucus was still alive. He had disguised himself as the

---

[1] Memnon 24 = *F.H.G.* iii. p. 538. [2] Reinach, *Trois royaumes*, p. 164.
[3] Memnon 24 = *F.H.G.* iii. p. 538.
[4] Eus. i. p. 251; Just. xxxviii. 5, 3. See Appendix M.
[5] Eus. says "in Cappadocia." The explanation probably is that Ancyra was in that part of Phrygia which Seleucus had allowed Mithridates to annex to his Cappadocian realm. The battle taking place here seems to show an attempt on the part of Seleucus to cut the communications between Sardis and the Pontic kingdom.

armour-bearer of Hamactyon, who commanded the Royal Squadron (βασιλικὴ ἴλη), and had escaped so from the fatal field. He was now beyond the Taurus, safe in Cilicia, rallying once more about him what remained of his power. Antiochus came out of his retirement, offered a sacrifice of thanksgiving for his brother's welfare, decreed public festivities in the cities subject to him, and sent an army to cross the Taurus and crush Seleucus before he had time to recover.[1]

One story which the Greeks remembered in connexion with this battle was that of Mysta, Seleucus' concubine. Like the old Persian kings, the Seleucids took women with them in their camps. As soon as she saw the day was lost, Mysta also disguised herself. She had been dressed as a queen; she now put on the habit of a common serving-maid and sat among the huddled women, who fell after the battle into the victor's hands. She was put up for sale with others, bought by some slave-merchant, and carried to the great market of Rhodes. Rhodes was soil friendly to Seleucus, and once there she made herself known. The Rhodian state instantly paid her price to the merchant and sent her back with every due observance to the King.[2]

§ 3. *Antiochus Hierax and Attalus of Pergamos*

The battle of Ancyra shattered the cause of Seleucus II in Asia Minor. It would be out of the question for some time to come for him to attack his brother. But the disappearance of Seleucus meant less the reign of Antiochus than anarchy. The Galatians knew their power; it was easy by their help to overthrow any existing authority, but it was not possible to base upon it any secure throne. Antiochus himself found his life full of vicissitude enough; at one moment marching over the Phrygian uplands at the head of his Galatian bands, levying a blackmail which can only by courtesy be described as the tribute due to the royal treasury;[3] at another moment

---

[1] Eus. i. p. 251; Just. xxvii. 2, 10; Trog. *Prol.* xxvii.; Plutarch, *De frat. amore*, 18.
[2] Polyaen. viii. 61; Athen. xiii. 593 c, both from Phylarchus.
[3] Eus. i. p. 251.

bargaining for his life with the same bands,[1] or by hairbreadth escapes breaking away from them and throwing himself into friendly cities, like Magnesia;[2] then meeting and beating them in open battle; then again raiding, as before in their company.[3]

The unhappy Greeks of Asia looked round for a deliverer from the deluge of anarchy and barbarism. This then was what the Macedonian rule, which had ousted the Persian with such fair promises, had come to. There were two powers which seemed to offer resistance to the barbarian storm in the land of the Asiatic Greeks, the Ptolemaïc and the Pergamene. Ptolemy saved at least the cities he held, like Ephesus and the Carian harbours, from barbarian dictation. We even hear, on an occasion when Antiochus had broken with his mercenaries, of help being sent him from a neighbouring Ptolemaïc garrison.[4] But it was Attalus of Pergamos who now came forward as the main champion of Hellenism and order.

The figure of this man, who had succeeded his cousin Eumenes in 241-240, embodying so much of that age, is obscured for us by the defects of our tradition. And yet even so he is significant for us, connecting in his person an epoch that was passing away with one that began a new state of things. Now when he first appears in the eye of the world, the great Macedonian houses, the heirs of Alexander, are the cardinal powers of the Eastern Mediterranean; his last breath is spent in exhorting the peoples of Greece to accept the hegemony of Rome. It was his wars on behalf of civilization in Asia Minor against the barbarian tribes which first made him a name. These wars are a glorious, but almost forgotten, episode of Greek history. We may indeed believe that they were somewhat artificially magnified by the Pergamene court, which loved to put them in the same order as the classical struggles between light and darkness, order and chaos, Hellenism and barbarism, to set them beside the battles of Gods and giants, of Athenians and Amazons, of Greeks and Persians. It was these scenes, together with those of the Galatian wars, which the sculptors commissioned by the rulers of Pergamos had to

---

[1] Just. xxvii. 2, 11. [2] Eus. *loc. cit.*
[3] Just. xxvii. 2, 12. [4] Eus. i. p. 251.

set before the eyes of the Greek cities.[1] But that the glory claimed by Attalus he did to a large extent deserve, there is no reason to deny. A genuine sentiment seems to have thrilled the Greek world as the contest was victoriously carried on. A current oracle, cited by Pausanias, represents Attalus as a deliverer divinely raised up for the Asiatic Greeks, almost a demi-god himself—

> Then having crossed the narrow strait of the Hellespont
> The destructive army of the Gauls shall pipe; they shall lawlessly
> Ravage Asia; and God shall make it yet worse
> For all who dwell by the shores of the sea
> For a little while. But soon the son of Kronos shall stir up a helper for them,
> A dear son of a Zeus-reared bull,
> Who shall bring a day of doom on all the Gauls.[2]

In days when art had begun to languish because the old enthusiasms were dying away, the struggle with the barbarism of Asia Minor called a new and original school into being, not indeed reaching the serene heights which the children of those who had fought at Marathon and Salamis attained, but displaying a vigorous realism, a technical mastery and a lively feeling for dramatic effect.

No narrative of these wars remains. Historians mention them summarily. When even the Seleucid house had come to pay blackmail to the Gauls, "Attalus," says Livy, "first among all the inhabitants of Asia refused. His bold resolution was, contrary to the expectation of all, backed by fortune. He met them in fair field and came off victor."[3] "His greatest achievement," Pausanias says, "was compelling the Gauls to retreat from the coast into the territory which they still occupy."[4] Sometimes a particular battle is spoken of,[5] a "great battle," Strabo calls it;[6] a battle "at Pergamos" is mentioned in a *Prologue* of Trogus.[7] According to the text of Justin[8] the battle took place immediately after the battle

---

[1] E. Gardner, *Handbook of Greek Sculpture*, p. 452 f.
[2] Paus. x. 15, 3, trans. Frazer.   [3] Liv. xxxviii. 16, 14.
[4] Paus. i. 8, 1 (trans. Frazer, vol. i. p. 11).
[5] νικήσας μάχῃ Γαλάτας (Polyb. xviii. 41, 7), as Livy (xxxiii. 21, 3) translates "victis deinde *proelio uno* Gallis."
[6] xiii. 624.   [7] *Prol.* xxvii.   [8] xxvii. 3, 2.

of Ancyra, before the victors had had time to recover from the effects of that great day, Antiochus himself being still with the Galatians—if indeed it be the same battle which is meant in the narrative of Justin and in the *Prologue*, or the phrase "saucios adhuc ex superiore congressione integer ipse" be not an antithesis thrown in for mere rhetorical effect. It is difficult to see how the victorious army of Ancyra should have engaged Attalus at Pergamos, more than 250 miles away, before they had recovered from the wounds of their former battle.

When, however, we turn from the historians to what remains of the stones of Pergamos, the wars of Attalus appear no affair of one battle and instant victory. They show Attalus making dedication to the gods of trophies from a great number of battles. Sometimes the state of the stone allows us to read the denotation of the enemy and the site of the battle, sometimes both are conjectural. It is at any rate impossible to arrange the battles in any connected narrative or even to fix their order in time. In one Antiochus and two of the Galatian tribes, the Tolistoagii and the Tectosages, are coupled together; it is the battle fought "near the Aphrodisium";[1] unfortunately it is impossible to identify the Aphrodisium in question. In another the Tolistoagii are mentioned alone, the battle "by the sources of the Caïcus."[2] In another Antiochus is mentioned alone, the battle in Hellespontine Phrygia.[3] One inscription speaks of a battle in which Attalus defeated the Tolistoagii and Antiochus *a second time*,[4] whether identical or not with any of those just mentioned we do not know. From all this we can gather little except that the struggle of Attalus with the forces of anarchy was prolonged and swept over the country between the valley of the Caïcus and Bithynia.[5]

This contest lifted the Pergamene dynast to an altogether new position in Asia Minor. As he had taken over from the

---

[1] Fränkel, *Inschrift. von Perg.* No. 23 = *C.I.G.* 3536.
[2] Fränkel, Nos. 20, 24.   [3] *Ibid.* No. 22.   [4] *Ibid.* No. 247.
[5] A somewhat idle question (as it seems to me) has been debated whether Attalus combated the Gauls "as a nation" or as the mercenaries of Antiochus. The Gauls did not form a compact state but a free element, which was equally mischievous whether the hordes raided on their own account or in the name of a Seleucid, Bithynian, or Pontic prince. Even when they let out their swords,

house of Seleucus the work which they professed to perform in that country, the protection of Hellenism and civilization, so he stepped into their dignities. After the battle of Ancyra indeed, with the elder Seleucid king driven across the Taurus, and the younger turned into a captain of freebooters, Seleucid authority ceased in Asia Minor. In that part of the country which had once obeyed mandates from Sardis or Antioch it was now the armies of Attalus who marched along the roads, and his officers who began to claim the tribute of Lydian and Phrygian villages. From this time the dynast of Pergamos assumed the title of King.[1]

To the Greek cities the substitution of the Pergamene for the Seleucid house was probably welcome. The Aeolian cities at any rate, as well as Alexandria, Ilion and Lampsacus, became his cordial allies. Even Smyrna, which had been so eminent for its loyalty to the Seleucid house, now changed about, swore fidelity to Attalus, and was henceforward altogether alienated at heart from the Seleucid cause.[2] Attalus presented himself to the Greeks in the most attractive light. Not only was he their champion against barbarism, as indeed the house of Seleucus in its better days had been, but he did everything to show himself an ardent Hellenist and to exhibit at his court a wholesome family life which would form a contrast in the eyes of the Greek *bourgoisie* to the barbaric vice and cruelty which were rife in the Seleucid and Ptolemaïc courts. His mother Antiochis was a kinswoman of the Seleucid house,[3] and his maternal aunt Laodice was the wife of Seleucus II, but Attalus himself elected for his queen Apollonis, the daughter of a plain citizen of Cyzicus, "a woman," says Polybius, "deserving for many reasons remark and admiration," who "rose from a private station to royalty, and kept her high place to the last by means of no meretricious seductions, but by a plain and sober dignity and

they, rather than their employers, seem to have been the masters. Attalus, it is true, employed Gallic bands himself on occasion (Polyb. v. 77 f.), but he does not seem to have fallen under their domination, and for that very reason had to part with them.

[1] Strabo xiii. 624.   [2] Polyb. v. 77 f.
[3] As is shown by her name, by the name of her sister Laodice, and by the fact that the Seleucid king chooses his wife from this family.

goodness."[1] Instead of the fraternal feuds and family murders which seemed to be elsewhere the rule in royal houses, the children of Attalus and Apollonis showed the world a delightful picture of simplicity and natural affection. And whilst the house of Attalus recommended itself to the moral sentiments of the Greek republics, it did so equally to their literary and artistic susceptibilities. "Pergamos," says the historian of Alexandrine literature, "was in all probability the source of that renewal of Atticism to which we owe in great part the preservation of the masterpieces of Attic prose."[2] Attalus maintained close relations with a number of the great literary men of his time, especially with the philosophers of Athens. An Athenian poet, Ctesiphon, was given a high place in his civil service.[3] Research into the peculiarities of his own dominion was encouraged. Polemon of Ilion cast his essay on the local cults and deities into the form of a "Letter to Attalus." Attalus himself wrote; from one work of his a fragment is still preserved, describing a certain pine-tree in the Troad.[4] The school of artists, which developed under his patronage, has been already mentioned. And not only did Pergamos itself become a city gloriously beautified to the eyes of the Greeks with the monuments and altars which commemorated the Galatian wars, but works of art in other cities testified to the munificence of the Pergamene king. Athens especially he delighted to honour.[5] If the ideal of the phil-Hellenic king, which had been more or less pretended to by all the successors of Alexander, was capable of realization at all, it seemed to be realized in Attalus.

On some points we are imperfectly informed. What were the relations between this new-grown power in Asia and the house of Ptolemy, which had so many footholds on the coast? We do not even know what the relations were between Attalus and Seleucus. Was the king who reigned on the Orontes content to see a new king arising in Asia Minor to counterbalance Antiochus Hierax, and the territory which he himself

---

[1] Polyb. xxii. 20.
[2] Susemihl, *Geschichte der griech. Lit. in der Alexand.* vol. i. p. 4.
[3] δικαστὴς βασιλικῶν τῶν περὶ τὴν Αἰολίδα, Demetrius of Scepsis ap. Athen. xv. 697 c.
[4] Strabo xiii. p. 603.   [5] See Frazer, *Pausanias*, vol. ii. p. 322.

could not wrest from his brother passing at any rate out of his brother's hands?[1]

All this time Sardis continued to maintain the semblance of a Seleucid capital. How long Laodice reigned there we do not know. According to Appian[2] her end was to be killed by Ptolemy Euergetes.[3] The court over which she had presided continued to subsist as that of King Antiochus.[4] If Attalus was supported by the Hellenic element in Asia Minor, Antiochus was in close association with the barbarian powers. He married a daughter of Ziaëlas, the Bithynian king.[5] He was also, as we have seen, in alliance with Mithridates, and seems to have contemplated at some time before his death marrying a daughter of the Pontic king, whether in succession to, or side by side with, the Bithynian queen we do not know. A daughter of Mithridates, at any rate, whom we may by her name, Laodice, conjecture to be the issue of Antiochus' sister, is found to be at one time in his hands.[6] Among the Pisidians Antiochus had his friends; Logbasis, a prominent citizen of Selge, was among his familiars, and it was at Selge, among the Pisidian hills, that Laodice, the Pontic princess, whom he probably intended to marry, grew to womanhood.[7] Even with an Armenian petty king, Arsames, he had relations of close friendship.[8]

---

[1] Niese (ii. p. 156, note 1) adduces it as evidence that Attalus was allied with Seleucus that in the Smyrnaean Inscription it is provided that one of the copies of the alliance between Smyrna and Magnesia is to be put up in the temple at Gryneum in Pergamene territory. If, however, the Smyrnaean Inscription belongs to a date before the battle of Ancyra, this would not be strong evidence for a time when the situation in Asia Minor had been vastly modified.

[2] *Syr.* 65.   [3] See Appendix N.

[4] The coins commonly assigned to Antiochus Hierax cannot, Mr. Macdonald tells me, be his, since they are found, not in Asia Minor, but in the far east of the Empire. This confronts numismatists with a double problem, (1) Whose are these coins? and (2) Where are the coins of Antiochus Hierax? These questions, in Mr. Macdonald's view, have not yet been satisfactorily answered.

[5] Eus. i. p. 251.   [6] Polyb. v. 74, 4; cf. viii. 22, 11.

[7] Polyb. v. 74, 4 f. According to one restoration of Fränkel, *Inschr. von Perg.* No. 25, we have an epigraphical record of the alliance between Antiochus and the Pisidians. ἀπὸ τῆς παρ[ὰ τῆς πρὸς . . .] καὶ τοὺς Σελ[γεῖς καὶ ᾿Αντίοχον μάχης]. But we should more probably restore τοὺς Σελ[εύκου στρατηγούς]. See Gäbler, *Erythrä*, p. 48.

[8] Polyaen. iv. 17, φίλος ὢν ᾿Αρσάβης MSS. The form ᾿Αρσάμης is got from the coins, Babelon, *Rois de Syrie*, p. cxciii.

Pushed on the west by the victorious arms of Attalus, Antiochus began to think of restoring his fortunes at his brother's expense in the east. He attempted to turn the position of Seleucus in Syria by crossing the Euphrates high up and then descending upon Mesopotamia by way of the friendly kingdom of Arsames. But in the plain the armies of his brother were waiting to receive him. They were led by Achaeus and his son Andromachus, two persons of the highest rank in the kingdom, for Achaeus was the father-in-law of King Seleucus.[1] Antiochus fared badly at their hands. After his defeat a discreditable abuse of those courtesies which in ancient warfare were connected with the burial of the dead enabled him to cut down four thousand of his brother's troops unarmed; but his cause was none the less lost.[2] He took refuge at the court of Ariamnes in Cappadocia, where his sister Stratonice was queen.[3] But he had not been there long before he discovered that though all was smiles about him, his host had an understanding with Seleucus, and was preparing to deliver him up.[4] He once more fled. It seems that he made one last desperate attack upon Attalus (229-228). We hear of four battles, two "in Lydia," one by Lake Coloë, and one in Caria.[5] They only served to complete his ruin. Nowhere in Asia did he now seem safe from capture by either Attalus or his brother. He crossed into Europe, to Thrace, which had been held since the Laodicean War by Ptolemaïc forces, and threw himself upon the generosity of the King of Egypt (228-227). On the orders of the Alexandrian court he was held under close guard. By the help, however, of some girl, whose heart had been won by the captive prince, he eluded his keepers. But the wild mountains of Thrace were no safe

---

[1] Another daughter of his was the mother of King Attalus, so that he mus have been now an old man. We are told at least by Strabo (xiii. 624) tha Antiochis, the mother of Attalus, was "the daughter of Achaeus," and it i generally assumed that the Achaeus in question is the father of Andromachu and Laodice, the wife of Seleucus II. It may, of course, have been an earlier Achaeus, the father of the father of Andromachus.

[2] Polyaen. iv. 17 ; Trog. *Prol.* xxvii.

[3] It is probably this affinity which was in Justin's mind when he described Ariamnes as "socerum suum."

[4] Just. xxvii. 3, 7 ; Trog. *Prol.* xxvii.

[5] Eus. i. p. 253 ; cf. Fränkel, *Inschr. von Perg.* Nos. 26-28.

place for fugitives. His little company encountered a marauding band of Gauls, and by the hand of the Gauls, with whom he had had all his life long so much to do, Antiochus Hierax came to his end. A story was told by the contemporary historian Phylarchus that the horse of Antiochus, when the Gallic chief Centaretus mounted it, leaped over a precipice and avenged its master.[1]

The disappearance of Antiochus Hierax from the scene extinguished the separate Seleucid court in Asia Minor. Attalus was left in possession of what had once been the Seleucid domain north of the Taurus. It remained for Seleucus Kallinikos to decide whether he would acquiesce in the severance of that country from his house or demand its restitution by force of arms from the Pergamene king. What he actually did we do not know with certainty. He was given but little time to do anything. A year after the death of his brother, Seleucus II perished by a fall from his horse (227-226).[2] He had never come to his own again in the land where his reign had begun.[3]

§ 4. *Seleucus III Soter*

The task of restoration, which devolved upon his successor, was a hard one. The geographical centre of the Empire, Syria, Babylonia, and the nearer Irânian provinces, were still held, but in the west and east great members had been broken away. The Ptolemaïc power ruled the coasts of southern Asia Minor, even to some extent of Syria, possessing Seleucia and the mouth of the Orontes; the Pergamene power ruled the Ionian and Aeolian coasts, and as much of the interior as was not in the hands of barbarian princes. For this task the youth who succeeded Seleucus Kallinikos was little fitted. He was the elder of the two sons of Seleucus II by Laodice, the daughter

---

[1] Eus. i. p. 253; Trog. *Prol.* xxvii.; Just. xxvii. 3, 9 f.; Ael. *Hist. An.* vi. 44; Solin. 45; Plin. *N.H.* viii. § 158.

[2] Eus. i. 251, 253; Just. xxvii. 3, 12.

[3] At one period of his reign Seleucus II, as his coins show, wore a beard. This, of course, was not usual among the upper classes of the Greek world in that age, except in the case of philosophers and poets, or as a sign of mourning. The beard of Seleucus got him the popular nickname of *Pogon*, Polyb. ii. 71, 4.

of Achaeus. He had hitherto been known as Alexander, but on ascending the throne assumed the dynastic name of Seleucus. Seleucus Soter was his official style. He was of weak bodily constitution, liable, if one may judge by the nickname of Keraunos, which the soldiers gave him, to fits of uncontrolled passion. He seems, however, to have addressed himself without delay to the work of recovering his kingdom in the west. His younger brother Antiochus was apparently sent to represent the royal authority in the eastern provinces.

Of the two enemies in the west, the Pergamene king is the only one whom Seleucus III is said to have directly attacked. He seems to have prepared to strike a blow from the instant of his accession.[1] The inscriptions of Attalus record victories over the "generals of Seleucus."

Presently the young King himself crossed the Taurus with a large army. From this time to the day of his death he was warring in Asia Minor. Was anything done meantime against the Egyptian power? In the Book of Daniel (11, 10) *both* the sons of Seleucus II are said to be "stirred up," *i.e.* against the King of Egypt, and to "assemble a multitude of great forces." If we had any ground for supposing an alliance between Pergamos and Egypt, the attack on Attalus might be considered an indirect attack on Ptolemy. But we have no ground. Niese supposes that hostilities between the Seleucid court and Egypt had again broken out before the death of Seleucus Kallinikos, and that they were closed by a definitive peace under Seleucus Soter.[2] It is at any rate likely that preparations were made by Seleucus III for a renewal of the war with Egypt, especially as his chief minister, Hermīas the

---

[1] Polyb. iv. 48, 7.

[2] The grounds for the supposition of new hostilities are (1) that Seleucia-in-Pieria was in Seleucid possession at the time of Stratonice's insurrection, but was again in Ptolemaïc hands at the accession of Antiochus III ; (2) that Andromachus, the brother of Seleucus II's queen, was commanding against Antiochus Hierax about 230, but had been captured by the Egyptians some time before 220. Neither of these grounds is certain evidence. The ground for supposing a definitive peace is the fact that Polybius (v. 67) calls the attempt of Antiochus III to conquer Cœle-Syria προφανὲς ἀδίκημα, and speaks of the Egyptian envoys as εἰς παρασπόνδημα τὴν Θεοδότου προδοσίαν καὶ τὴν ἔφοδον ἀνάγοντες τὴν Ἀντιόχου. It is to be noticed, however, that Polybius implies that in doing so they *exaggerated*, τὸ παρὸν ηὔξον ἀδίκημα.

Carian, was the main advocate of an aggressive policy against Egypt a few years later under Antiochus III. If Seleucus III made the war with Pergamos take precedence of the war with Egypt, it may have been that the attack on the Ptolemaïc power was left by an understanding to the allied court of Macedonia. About the same time that Seleucus engaged Attalus in the interior of Asia Minor, Antigonus Doson, reigning as Regent in Macedonia for the infant Philip, whom the death of Demetrius about 230-229 had made King, descended upon the coasts of Caria and expelled the Ptolemaïc garrisons.[1]

How the war between Seleucus III and Attalus went we do not know. Seleucus was at any rate unable to maintain order in his own camp. The result was a conspiracy against the King's life, of which the leading spirits were Nicanor, no doubt a Macedonian officer of the King's *entourage*, and Apaturius, a chieftain of the mercenary Gauls. Seleucus was in Phrygia in the summer of 223, when the design against him was brought to pass. His life was suddenly cut short, by poison according to one account.[2] One disaster after another had come upon the house of Seleucus, and its extinction must have seemed at that moment a possibility of the near future.

[1] This war in Caria is known only by two notices: Ἀντίγονος . . . τὸν προκείμενον ἐτέλει πλοῦν εἰς τὴν Ἀσίαν, Polyb. xx. 5, 11. Quo (*i.e.* Demetrio) mortuo tutelam filii eius Philippi suscepit Antigonus, qui Thessaliam, Mœsiam, *Cariam* subegit, Trog. *Prol.* xxviii. [Beloch (*Beiträge zur alt. Gesch.* ii. 1902) puts the expedition before the death of Antiochus Hierax.]

[2] App. *Syr.* 66; Polyb. iv. 48; Eus. i. 253; Jerome, *in Daniel*, 11, 10; Trog. *Prol.* xxviii.

The confused period covered by this chapter has been specially treated by U. Köhler, *Die Gründung des Königreichs Pergamon-Histor. Zeit.* xlvii. (1882), p. 1 f.; Koepp, *Rhein. Mus.* xxxix. (1884), p. 209 f.; Beloch, *Histor. Zeit.* lx. (1888), p. 500 f.; Bouché-Leclercq, *Le règne de Séleucus II* (an admirable summary and discussion of the various theories), reprinted from the *Revue d. Universités d. Midi,* iii. (1897), and by Haussoullier, *loc. cit.*

CHAPTER XI

SYRIA

THE reigns of the first Seleucids have hitherto been traced in regard to Asia Minor; they have appeared but as a long struggle for the possession of that country. But while it is in this light that the surviving records show them, while this perhaps they principally were, the successors of Seleucus wished also to preside over the life of that remoter world which the Greek had come to know beyond the Taurus, to be the sovereign power over the ancient Aramaean and Babylonian peoples, over the husbandmen and horsemen of Irân. But of the work they did there, of the cities they built, of the Hellenic communities they planted far and wide, of the way in which the native peoples looked upon this new element thrust into their midst and upon their alien overlords—of all that what memorial is left?

The Seleucid domain towards the east consisted, as we have seen, of three main divisions, the lands immediately to the south of the Taurus—that is Cilicia, Northern Syria, and Mesopotamia—the lands of the lower Euphrates and Tigris—that is, the Assyrio-Babylonian country—and lastly, Irân. We will take each of these separately and see what can be made out of Seleucid rule there up to the accession of Antiochus III. For all of them our evidence is two-fold, literary and archaeological, both sorts scanty enough. In the remains of historians only a notice here and there occurs relating to some part of these countries, as they were touched by the interminable wars; from the geographers the names of cities can be gathered which bear witness to the Hellenizing activity of the Seleucid kings, and sometimes show on what main pivots geographically the life of those days turned. The archaeological evidence may be multiplied in time by the traveller and excavator; but at present practical difficulties have prevented the examination of most of this field, and we have no series of Seleucid inscriptions, as in Asia Minor. The coins, lastly, can tell us something, although the extreme uncertainty which hangs about their places of minting makes this line of evidence a seductive, rather than a safe, guide.

The land which we call Syria is created by the line of mountain which goes from the Taurus on the north as far as the Gulf of 'Akaba in the Red Sea. These mountains prevent the Arabian desert, traversed by the Euphrates and Tigris, from extending quite to the eastern shore of the Mediterranean. They interpose a belt of habitable country between the expanse of sea and the expanse of sand. From its position Syria has always been the bridge between Egypt and Asia. But it was not only traversed by a world-route going north and south, it was crossed east and west by the routes from Babylon and the Further East, which found on its coasts their nearest outlet to the Mediterranean, and in the Cilician Gates their natural door into Asia Minor. *It belongs to the Mediterranean lands, and at the same time is of those lands the most closely connected with the great seats of Asiatic civilization.*

The line of mountain on which Syria is formed is a double one. From end to end a depression divides two parallel ranges. Sometimes the floor of the depression rises with the mountains to a considerable height above the sea, as in Al-Biká' (Cœle-Syria in the narrow sense) between the Lebanon and Antilibanus; sometimes it sinks even below sea-level, as in the Jordan valley. The mountains themselves have different names in different parts of their line. Sometimes they are too high and rugged to be habitable near the summit; in that case they come as a barrier between the people who inhabit the depression and those of the outside slopes; sometimes they are low enough to be habitable in all their breadth; Judaea covers the high ground between the Mediterranean and the Dead Sea. The depression makes the bed of different rivers, the Orontes, Al-Litânî, the Jordan; the two former burst through the western range to the Mediterranean; the Jordan ceases before finding an exit.

The name of Syria, however, extends somewhat farther than the two parallel ranges and the lands which thence draw their water. It covers those adjoining lands on the north which receive their water from the Taurus and its foot-hills, and which extend eastwards as far as the Euphrates, where it most nearly approaches the Mediterranean. They rise above the level of the desert, and of the plains in which the depression just spoken of ends to northward. Between these plains and the Euphrates they intervene as a sort of plateau pushed out from the Taurus. The plains are the natural centre of Northern Syria, receiving the Orontes from the south as well as streams from the Taurus on the north, communicating through the gorge of the Lower Orontes with the coast and by an easy ascent with the plateau of inner Syria. The climate of the plateau is other than that of the plains and coast. It is a more arid and barer world. The soil yields under labour, but is apt to be stony. There are here longer winters and more parching summers. But it is crossed by the roads to the Euphrates, and it is in Aleppo that the life of modern Syria finds its centre.

The administrative system according to which Northern Syria was divided under Seleucus and his first successors cannot be traced with any clearness. We know that the Seleucis consisted of the four satrapies of Antioch, Seleucia, Apamea and Laodicea,[1] and outside of this there lay to the north Cyrrhestice and Commagene. To the south the frontier between Seleucid and Ptolemaïc Syria was probably, on the coast, the river Eleutherus,[2] and in the interior some point in the valley called Marsyas or Massyas.[3]

In this country the invasive Greek element soon made itself thoroughly at home. Syria became a "new Macedonia." Its districts and rivers were renamed after those of the motherland. The mountain region north of the mouth of the Orontes, perhaps from some resemblance to the mountains north of Tempe, became Pieria, the Orontes itself Axius, and so on. Local attachments had to be found for the old Greek legends.

[1] Strabo xvi. 749 f.   [2] *Ibid.* 753   [3] Polyb. v. 45, 8; Strabo xvi. 753.

At Daphne, four miles from Antioch, the place was shown where the nymph Daphne, pursued by Apollo, was changed into a bay-tree. It was in this region that Typhon was blasted by Zeus; the river-bed, in fact, had been formed by his writhings. The wandering heroes of Greek mythology were especially useful in making these connexions. On the Amanus mountains Orestes had been delivered from his madness, as the name proved—Amanus, "a-mania." Io naturally had left traces of herself, and Triptolemus, as we shall presently see.

The establishment of Hellenic communities in barbarian Asia was not, of course, the outcome of spontaneous immigration only; we see in it rather the fixed policy of the kings. A Greek population could not exist except as grouped in Greek cities, and these cities the kings were zealous to build. Their citizens, no doubt, were to a considerable extent Greeks driven from their old homes by political or economic causes, or drawn by hopes of advantage, but they consisted also of soldiers, Greek and Macedonian, settled by royal order, and also, one must believe, of natives and half-breeds, who had put on the externals of Hellenism. The lower classes were perhaps frankly barbarian; but whatever the real parentage of the citizen-body, it was in theory and guise Macedonian or Greek. It was in the Orontes valley that the life of Seleucid Syria pulsed most strongly. Of the four great cities established by Seleucus Nicator, three were here, Seleucia, Antioch, and Apamea.

Seleucia-in-Pieria guarded the mouth of the river. The coast of Northern Syria, ramparted by hills which jut out to sea in rocky promontories, offers little friendliness to ships. But where the Orontes breaks through this wall, a bay, some ten miles across, reaches from Mount Coryphaeus (mod. Jabal Mûsâ) on the north to the great landmark of the coast, the towering Mount Casius (mod. Al-Akra') on the south. Along the inner recess of the bay lies a crescent-shaped plain, presenting to the sea a fringe of sand-dunes and salt pools, but a little inland covered with corn-fields, with figs and pomegranates, and enfolded by the rich background of wooded hills. At the southern extremity of this plain, close under Mount

Casius, the Orontes flows into the sea; at the northern extremity, about five miles off, was built the city of Seleucia, above what was in those days the principal harbour of the coast. The mountain here rises from the sea in a series of ledges or terraces. From the quay[1] one ascended to a level which stood some 20 or 30 feet above the waves, beyond which a much higher shelf rose in rocky walls of 400 or 500 feet. It was on this shelf that the upper city of Seleucia lay. Behind it were the wild contours of the Pierian range. At its feet along the level was the lower city, containing the harbour, the warehouses, and the "outer town" (προάστειον). Set upon precipices, Seleucia was remarkable for its strength.[2] Mighty walls, the work of kings, supplemented the cliffs. Climbing streets and rocky stairways connected its upper and lower parts. Its temples and buildings were displayed in their full magnificence by the rising ground. It was worthy to be the gateway of a great kingdom.[3]

The legend of the founding of Seleucia by Seleucus Nicator after sacrifice on Mount Casius is given by a late writer.[4] That it was really the first Seleucus who founded it is open to no doubt. Bearing his name, the city worshipped him as its god. It was granted the possession of his body by Antiochus I, and a temple was built over his sepulchre, with a sacred precinct attached, the Nicatoreum.[5]

It was not necessary for those voyaging to Antioch to disembark at Seleucia. Till as late as the Crusades the Orontes was navigable as far as Antioch itself. From the mouth of the river the traveller would ascend, having on his left the plain of Seleucia and on his right the base of Mount Casius. This region was once full of human life. Casius was vested in immemorial sanctity as the holy mountain of some Semitic Baal whom the Greeks, of course, called Zeus. Its summit was too sacred to be mounted.[6] The festivals of the god periodically called forth gay throngs of worshippers from the capital. To-day it is a wilderness, given up to the jackal, though the remains of ancient works and once well-

---

[1] Polyb. v. 59, 9.   [2] ἐρυμνοτάτη, Strabo xvi. 749.
[3] Strabo xvi. 749; Polyb. v. 59   [4] Malalas, p. 198 (Bonn).
[5] App. *Syr.* 63.   [6] Ael. Spart. *Hadr.* 14.

trodden roads can still be found among its growth of oleanders. Presently, as the traveller continued to ascend the river, the mountains would close in on the left as well; he would be in the gorge, some six miles long, by which the Orontes cuts through the coast range to the sea, a place of extraordinary and romantic beauty, not unlike the Thessalian Tempe. From the gorge he emerges upon the plains of inner Syria. The spur of Casius, however, on his right, continues to keep close to the bank, splendidly covered with timber and flowering shrubs, and sending down a thousand torrents into the river. The chain ends in Mount Silpius, round which the Orontes makes its westward bend, coming from the south. Beyond Mount Silpius to the east is open country, the plain of Amyce (עמק),[1] with the great levels of the lake of Antioch beginning some ten miles farther on.

Under the northern slopes of Silpius rose the new Seleucid city. The beauty for which Antioch was notable was derived in part from its setting, the near background of wild mountain contrasting delightfully with the rich culture of its well-watered plain. Its position was favourable to growth in greatness and riches. The climate, except in the matter of some malignant winds from the north, was excellent; the soil was very fertile; and, in addition to these advantages, it was admirably placed with regard to the commerce of the world. The Orontes valley here opens out into the plains which, as has been said, are the natural centre of Northern Syria. Along this way went the regular land-routes from Babylonia and Irân to the Mediterranean. It suffered indeed from certain inconveniences. The most serious was the frequency of earthquakes in Northern Syria. Besides this the numerous torrents from Silpius, which added to the city's charm and made it singularly fortunate in its supply of good water, had the drawback of being sometimes swollen and intractable, when they spread devastation on the slopes.

Before Seleucus, Antigonus had chosen this region as the site of one of his principal cities. But the two designs did not exactly correspond. Seleucus found the infant city of Antigonia *north* of the Orontes on a stream (Arceuthus, mod.

[1] Polyb. v. 59, 10.

Kara-su) which carried to the Orontes the overflow of the Lake of Antioch.[1] He marked out Antioch along the *southern* bank of the Orontes on the level strip, two miles broad, between river and mountain. He avoided building on the slope for fear of the torrents. The city was designed by the architect Xenarius,[2] according to the practice of the time, on a regular plan with straight-ruled thoroughfares. It formed an extended oblong, the main street running through it parallel with the river, and making a long vista from end to end.

The legend of the foundation of Antioch, as given by Malalas, represents what the Antiochenes liked to be believed as to the origin of their city. In naming the different constituents of which the first population was formed it perhaps reflects some historical facts. According to this legend Antioch had a claim to be held one of the first-born Greek colonies, no *parvenue* of Macedonian creation. It claimed affinity with Athens and Argos; Io, the daughter of Inachus, had died there, and the party of Argives, led by the Attic Triptolemus, who had gone in quest of her, had settled on Mount Silpius, and their descendants had made the nucleus of Antioch. They appealed to the name which the native Aramaeans gave the great city, *Ione*, as the Greeks pronounced it;[3] it meant, of course, in reality no more than "city of the Greeks (Javan)." That there was an Athenian element in the population first settled by Antigonus at Antigonia and transferred by Seleucus to Antioch is quite possible;[4] both the coins and the monuments of Antioch put forward the connexion with Athens. It is allowed by Malalas that a good part of the original colonists were Macedonians. Cretans and Cypriots are also mentioned.

During the reigns of the first successors of Seleucus Antioch grew. To the original city of Seleucus a second city was added with its own separate wall—a foundation, according to Strabo, "of the resident population," whatever that may mean.[5] A third quarter was founded on an island in the Orontes

---

[1] The lake of Antioch is not mentioned before Malalas, but the argument from silence cannot be pressed against its existence in earlier times.

[2] Malalas, p. 200. [3] Strabo xvi. 750; Libanius, *Antioch.* p. 289.

[4] Malalas, p. 201.

[5] τοῦ πλήθους τῶν οἰκητόρων ἐστι κτίσμα, Strabo xvi. 750.

opposite the existing double city, when Seleucus II, driven from Asia Minor, made Antioch his residence. It was perhaps in this island quarter that the palace of the later Seleucids lay. A bridge, of course, connected it with the mainland, and Antioch was thus become a *tripolis*. Seleucus II probably only began to build, since the island city is represented by Libanius[1] as the work of his son, Antiochus III.

It would seem that at the foundation of the new cities of that age a cult was instituted of the *Fortune* of the city, that is, the spiritual personality of the city, and an image of it was set up. According to stories told in later times a virgin was actually sacrificed, and thereby identified in some way with this soul of the city; but the stories possibly have no basis but the image itself. The image of Antigonia, when Seleucus destroyed the foundation of his rival, was transferred to Antioch and worshipped in the new city till it was again removed to Rhossus on the coast.[2] But Antioch had a Fortune of its own. The sculptor, Eutychides of Sicyon, a pupil of the great Lysippus, was commissioned to make its image.[3] Of all the great works of art with which Antioch the Beautiful was adorned this is the only one which retains a visible form for us to-day. A copy of it in marble exists in the Vatican, just as it is shown on many of the coins of Antioch.[4] The personified Antioch sits with a certain noble freedom, holding an ear of corn in her hand, her head crowned with flowers, and a small figure, representing the river Orontes, rising out of the ground at her feet. The original must have had all that dramatic effectiveness which stamps the products of Greek sculpture in the third century B.C.[5]

A chief glory of Antioch was the paradise of Daphne, which lay between river and mountain some four or five miles below the city. The place to-day is notable for its rich greenery

[1] *Antioch.* p. 309.

[2] By Demetrius the son of Antigonus Poliorcetes after the death of Seleucus, says Malalas; what sense is to be extracted from this confusion is problematical.

[3] Paus. vi. 2, 4.

[4] See the reverse of the coin of Tigranes on Plate IV.

[5] For Antioch the standard work is Karl Ottfried Müller's *Antiquitates Antiochenae* (1839), but an important addition to the literature on the subject is made by R. Förster's article in the *Jahrbuch d. kaiserl. deutsch. archäolog. Instituts*, xii. p. 103 (1897).

and rushing streams—the "House of the Waters" (Bait-al-Mâ). In ancient times these streams ran through the gloom of giant cypresses which encompassed the temple of the Pythian Apollo. Under their shadow, or among the bay-trees and oleanders, the population of Antioch spent their hours of pleasure. A course for games, of which the god was patron—an imitation of the *Pythia* of Greece—was made near the temple, and Daphne was continually filled with the noise of festivals and the glitter of gay processions. The image of Apollo, put up by Seleucus I, was the work of the Athenian Bryaxis. It represented Apollo in his form as Musagetes with the lyre and the long garment down to the foot. Other lesser temples rose among the trees. The place was a sanctuary, and as such, one would think, did not tend to diminish the criminality of the great city close by. Its whole circuit was eighty *stadia*.[1]

The high-priesthood of Apollo at Daphne was a position of ease and dignity. It seems not to have been annual but permanent, since we find Antiochus III conferring it upon a distinguished servant who, after the long campaigns in Asia Minor, was too broken for further fatigues.[2]

The third great city of Seleucus, Apamea, dominated the middle Orontes. The course of the river between the neighbourhood of Apamea and the point where it issues from the mountains to make its westward bend round Silpius is very ill known. About Apamea the valley widens out into a swampy basin. Continual streams fall into it from the hills on the east and produce a rank vegetation. Alongside of the river stretch reedy lagoons. It is a district which seems hardly to belong to dry Syria. Apamea stood on the lower slopes of the eastern hills. South of it comes one of those depressions in the range which opened out easy communications between the Orontes valley and the east. Seleucus seems to have found here an earlier settlement of Macedonian soldiers, who called their city Pella after the Macedonian capital.[3]

[1] Strabo xvi. 750, and the references in Müller, *Antiq. Antioch.* p. 46; see also Ritter, *Erdkunde*, viii. 2te Abtheil. 3ter Abschnitt.

[2] *Philologus* xvii. (1861), p. 345. An interesting and little known inscription.

[3] Strabo xvi. 752. Malalas (p. 203) says oddly that Seleucus called Apamea Pella because the *Tyche* of Apamea bore this name, and adds as a further explanation that Seleucus himself was a native of Pella. If there was an earlier

Whether the altar of the Bottiaean Zeus, at which the city worshipped, was really put up by Alexander himself, as the tradition asserted, may be questioned. Apamea became the military headquarters of Syria, if not of the Empire. Here was the central office for the army (τὸ λογιστήριον τὸ στρατιωτικόν) and the military schools. Here were the government studs, which embraced at one time more than 30,000 mares and 300 blood stallions. Here Seleucus placed the 500 elephants which he got from the Panjab.

The neighbourhood of Apamea seems to have been dotted with settlements of soldiers, which formed petty townships dependent upon the great city. Strabo gives the names of Casiani, Megara, Apollonia, and Larissa. The sites of none of these are known except that of Larissa. This was the modern Shaizar, set upon a rock of reddish-yellow limestone, which stands up precipitously above the Orontes on its western bank. Just south of this the river issues out of a narrow gorge that has been compared to the Wye at Chepstow, and Larissa is thus a position which must have been always strategically important as guarding the entrance into the Apamea basin. The settlers in Larissa were Thessalians, and it was after the Thessalian Larissa that the township on the Orontes was called. They furnished horsemen to the first *agema* of the royal cavalry, and their descendants seem to have kept up for more than a hundred years at least after the death of Seleucus the tradition of horsemanship and prowess.[1]

The remaining one of the four great cities was not in the Orontes valley, but at one of the few safe harbourages along the rocky coast—Laodicea, called after Laodice, the mother of Seleucus. It stood on the coast about in a line with Apamea in the Orontes valley, and communicated both with it and Antioch by roads across the mountain. These roads, however, are said to be difficult in winter, and Laodicea did not possess the advantages of Seleucia and Antioch in standing on a great commercial route between the Mediterranean and the East.

Macedonian settlement called Pella, with a worship of its patron-goddess as the *Tyche* of Pella, Seleucus may have authorized the old name to be still used for ritual purposes from superstitious reasons.

[1] Diod. xxxiii. 4 *a*.

It offered, however, a good harbour, nearer than Seleucia, to ships coming from the south or from Cyprus, and it had its own produce to export. This consisted mainly in wine. The hills behind the city were terraced almost to the top with vineyards, and Laodicean wine found a large market in Egypt.[1]

These four cities show us the chief centres of life in the Seleucis. But they were only the first of a growing number of communities, Greek in speech and structure, which overspread the country during the rule of Macedonian kings and Roman emperors. The hills and valleys are full of the remains of this departed life. But the very names of the towns have mostly perished. A few gathered from ancient authors cannot in most cases be certainly fixed to particular sites. On the coast in the Bay of Issus was a foundation of Alexander's, Alexandria, the modern Alexandretta. Its relative importance, of course, was not so great as it is to-day, when it is the main port of Northern Syria. We hear of a Heraclea and an Antioch in Pieria,[2] of Meleagrū-charax in the plain of Antioch,[3] of Platanus on the road through the hills from the great Antioch to Laodicea,[4] of Lysias[5] and Seleucobelus,[6] which seem to have been among the dependent townships of Apamea. The ancient Arethusa, a colony of Seleucus I according to Appian,[7] is represented by Ar-rastan. In the region of the Upper Orontes and the Lake of Kadesh, round which are the remains of a once numerous population, some of them classical, we have Laodicea-on-Lebanon.[8] South of it the Lebanon and Antilibanus close in and make the narrow valley, called by the ancients Marsyas. In this there was a Chalcis,[9] and near the sources of the Orontes, Heliopolis (mod. Baalbek).

The great desert east of the Orontes valley made a blank for civilization. Only in the neighbourhood of the hills which divide the desert from the valley is a strip of country, treeless

---

[1] Strabo xvi. 752.   [2] Steph. Byz. s.v.   [3] Strabo xvi. 751.
[4] Itiner. Anton.   [5] Strabo xvi. 760.
[6] Steph. Byz. s.v.; Hierocl. p. 712; Σελεύκεια πρὸς Βήλῳ, Ptolem.; Seleucia ad Belum, Plin. v. § 82; Σελευκόβολος, Theoph. Chron. p. 533 (Bonn). Perhaps the same as Σέλευκος πόλις περὶ τῇ ἐν Συρίᾳ Ἀπαμείᾳ, Steph. Byz.
[7] Syr. 57.
[8] Λαοδίκεια ἡ πρὸς Λιβάνῳ, Strabo xvi. 755; Itiner. Anton.; Polyb. v. 45, 7.
[9] Strabo xvi. 755; Joseph. Arch. xiv. § 40, etc.

and bare-looking, but covered in the spring with grass and flowers, and repaying the toil of irrigation. Along this also are abundant remains of the people who dwelt here in the days of Greek and Roman ascendancy—their sepulchres, their buried cities, and dry cisterns. Towards the north the desert ceases as the land begins to rise. We reach the plateau of inner Syria. Here the traces of a great population are thicker than ever. In Al-Jabal al-A'lā, the most northerly of the hills which bound the Orontes valley to the east, merging on the side away from the valley by gradual declivities with the plateau, there are "twenty times more Greek and Roman antiquities than in all Palestine." The road from Antioch to the modern Dâna, to the north-east of Al-A'lā, is one series of ruins on both sides of the way. It is here that a traveller asserts he was never out of sight of architectural remains, of which he could sometimes see from ten to twelve heaps from a single point of view.[1]

The plateau is divided by the river Chalus (mod. Kuwaik), which flows from the hills of Cyrrhestice[2] and loses itself in a salt swamp on the confines of the desert. From the hills which divide the plateau from the plain of Antioch as far as the Chalus valley, the undulating country is capable of cultivation, and was once populous. It is now neglected and to a large extent waste. The valley of the Chalus is much more fertile. Where it opens out into a rich plain, stood, no doubt, long before Seleucus, the Syrian city of Chalep. This became a new Greek city with the name of Beroea. The route from Antioch to Hieropolis passed through it, and it must have drawn its resources from the road as well as from its fields. Aleppo, as we call it, is to-day the most important centre in Northern Syria. Near Beroea, and apparently to the north of it, Strabo mentions a Heraclea whose site has not been identified. Beside the route from Antioch to the Euphrates, which crossed the Chalus valley at Beroea, there was one more to the south, reaching the Euphrates at Barbelissus (mod. Bâlis). This route crossed the Chalus only one mile above

---

[1] Walpole, *The Ansayrii*, iii. p. 246.

[2] In Strabo (xvi. 751) Cyrrhestice does not seem to include the plateau of Beroea.

the salt marsh in which it ends, and here on a lower terrace of the hills which overlook it was the city of Chalcis. The modern Kinnasrîn, the frontier town towards the desert, which corresponds in position to Chalcis, holds a very inferior place with respect to Aleppo. Under the Seleucids the relative importance of the two cities was perhaps reversed. We know almost nothing of the life of inner Syria in those days, but we may conclude something from the fact that the region of the lower Chalus was called, not after Beroea, but Chalcidice.

Between the Chalus and the Euphrates the country is to-day almost unoccupied, one "level sheep-tract." We hear of a Seleucid colony, Maronea or Maronias, which seems to have been on the road from Chalcis to Barbelissus.[1] But the great place of this region was the ancient Syrian town Mabog, about twelve miles from the Euphrates. It stands in the centre of a rocky plain, some 600 feet above the river, without running water or any advantage likely to create a place of importance. Its greatness had a religious ground. Men had congregated here about a famous temple of the Mother-goddess, whom under different names the Semites adored, here as Atargatis. Under Greek rule its name was temporarily Hieropolis, Seleucus himself according to one statement having made the innovation.[2] It strikes coins under Antiochus IV, and had therefore been certainly Hellenized before that time. Its old name in the Greek form of Bambyce was still in use, and survives as Mambij to this day.

The plateau of Beroea stood to the east of the plain of Antioch; to the north of the plain rose the lower spurs of the Taurus. The upland tracts among them were not an unfavourable field for Hellenic colonization. Although the soil was generally light and stony, the spring crops were productive, and the climate was healthier than in the plain. At the beginning of the reign of Antiochus III the troops drawn from this region, consisting no doubt of Macedonian and Greek settlers, numbered 6000 men, and formed an element of account in the royal army.[3] The whole political situation in Syria might be affected by the disposition of these colonies.[4]

[1] Ptolem. v. 15, 18; App. *Syr.* 57.
[2] Ael. *Hist. An.* xii. 2.
[3] Polyb. v. 50, 7 f.
[4] *Ibid.* v. 57, 4.

These things would point to a liberal plantation of Hellenic communities in the region in question. We cannot, however, get from our authorities the names of the new foundations, except one or two. Cyrrhus, the city after which the whole region was called Cyrrhestice, borrowed its name from Cyrrhus in Macedonia.[1] Later on, another city, Gindarus, in a valley opening out into the plain of Antioch, seems to have taken the first place. Strabo calls it the "acropolis of Cyrrhestice."[2] In the disordered times of the later Seleucids it probably became what Strabo describes it, a robber-hold. One Greek city of these hills goes back perhaps to Alexander himself, Nicopolis. It stood on the eastern slopes of the Amanus, in the valley of the river now called Kara-su, on the place where Darius had pitched before he crossed the Amanus to meet Alexander at Issus.[3] North of Cyrrhestice the hill country of Commagene lay above the Euphrates. Here Hellenism was probably later in establishing itself. How soon Samosata, the capital, became a Greek city we do not know. The Antioch ἐπὶ τῷ Ταύρῳ mentioned in Commagene may have been founded by one of the later Seleucids, or even by the semi-Irânian dynasty which reigned here in the last century B.C. and used Antiochus as a royal name to show its affinity with the house of Seleucus. Whether Doliche and Chaonia were Greek cities is a question.

There is a line of Greek foundations along the Euphrates at the places of passage, and in coming to those on the eastern bank we enter upon the province of *Mesopotamia*. By this name the Greeks understood the country between the Euphrates and Tigris above Babylonia. Only that part of Mesopotamia which lay far enough north to receive water from the Taurus was habitable land, and this region was divided from Babylonia by the great desert. From Syria on the other hand it was separated only by the Euphrates, and thus by geographical position, as well as by the homogeneity of their population, Syria and Mesopotamia formed almost one country.

The most northerly place of passage on the Euphrates was

---

[1] Its site is that of the village of Kûrus, 40 miles N. by W. from Aleppo on the slopes of the Taurus.   [2] xvi. 751.
[3] Droysen ii. p. 663, note 10. It is curious that its coins describe it as Σελευκίδος. "Seleucis" must be used in a sense which includes Cyrrhestice.

at Samosata in Commagene, and here on the Mesopotamian bank opposite Samosata stood a Seleucia.[1] A much more important passage was that where a bridge of boats crossed the river on the direct route between Antioch and Edessa. Either head of the bridge was held by a Greek town, a foundation of the first Seleucus. On the Syrian bank was Zeugma, called after the bridge, on the Mesopotamian Apamea (mod. Birejik), with a rocky fortress of exceptional strength. Where the road from Syria to the East by way of Hieropolis struck the Euphrates was a Europus, called after the native city of Seleucus I,[2] and near it a Nicatoris.[3] The ancient route between Syria and Babylon crossed the Euphrates at Thapsacus,[4] and some twelve miles lower down, on the opposite bank, was Nicephorium, founded, according to Isidore and Pliny, by Alexander, and according to Appian by Seleucus I.[5] Whether the Kallinikon, said by the *Chronicon Paschale* (Olymp. 134) to have been founded by Seleucus II Kallinikos, was identical with Nicephorium is a matter of dispute.[6] There seem to have been other Greek cities in this neighbourhood. The immense importance of the ford at Thapsacus, as one of the cardinal points in the traffic of the world, no doubt made the Greek rulers wish to secure it strongly. Amphipolis, described as a foundation of Seleucus I,[7] is identified by Pliny with Thapsacus.[8] It was perhaps adjacent to the old native town. A city called Aenus is also mentioned as opposite or close by.[9] Near Nicephorium, a Zenodotium is mentioned.[10] On the Euphrates below Thapsacus we can point to no more Greek cities till we reach Babylonia except one, Europus, about half-way between Nicephorium and Babylonia. It was the native town of Dura Hellenized, and the old name continued in use with the people of the land.[11]

[1] Droysen (ii. p. 728) suspects that Strabo (xvi. 749) is confusing the Zeugma at Samosata with *the* Zeugma lower down, but it appears to me without adequate reason.

[2] Plin. v. § 86; Procop. *De aedific.* ii. 9; Lucian, *Quom. hist. conscrib.* 24, 28.
[3] Steph. Byz.   [4] The Ten Thousand; Alexander.
[5] Isidore 1; Pliny vi. § 119; App. *Syr.* 57.
[6] Droysen (ii. p. 742) thinks it was not, and suggests that Kallinikon may have been at a place called Harugla (*i.e.* Heraclea) and Nicephorium at Ar-Rakka, a little lower down. Kallinikon and Nicephorium are identified on Kiepert's map.
[7] Steph. Byz.; App. *Syr.* 57.   [8] Plin. v. § 86.   [9] κατὰ Θάψακον. Steph. Byz.
[10] Steph. Byz.; Plutarch, *Crass.* 17; Dio Cass. xl. 13.   [11] Isidore 1.

We come now to the Greek cities of the interior of Mesopotamia. Their appearance gave the country a new character. Under the old Oriental empires the immemorial village life had predominated, although there had been towns like Haran and Nisibis. Now new centres of life sprang up everywhere in the Greek cities.[1] It was along the river valleys, as we saw in Syria, that these cities were for the most part built. In Mesopotamia, the most westerly of the streams sent down from the Taurus and its foot-hills combine in the Belichas (mod. Al-Balîkh) before they fall into the Euphrates by Nicephorium. Moving up the Belichas from the Euphrates, we come, at a point where another stream comes into the Belichas from the west, to Ichnae, called after a city of Macedonia, and described as "a Hellenic city, a foundation of the Macedonians."[2] At the time of the campaign of Crassus it was apparently little more than a fortress ($\tau\epsilon\hat{\iota}\chi o\varsigma$).[3] In the valley of the western tributary we have Batnae, a gathering-place of merchants, since here the great eastern road from Hieropolis crossed the valley, described as a Macedonian colony,[4] and near the source of the tributary Anthemusias, the first station on the road from Apamea to Babylon.[5] In the valley of the Belichas itself, understood to include that of the Scirtus (mod. Daisân), we have the two important cities of western Mesopotamia. They were both old native towns transformed. The more northern, Urhai, or as the Greeks wrote it, Orrhoë, was given the new Macedonian name of Edessa. The native element was allowed to retain its place here to a larger degree than was usual in the new cities. According to Malalas, Seleucus first made it an Antioch with the distinguishing appellation of $\mu\iota\xi o\beta\acute{a}\rho\beta a\rho o\varsigma$. In later times it was one of the chief seats of Syriac letters,

---

[1] "Mesopotamia tota Assyriorum fuit, vicatim dispersa praeter Babylona et Ninum. Macedones eam in urbes congregavere propter ubertatem soli." Pliny vi. § 117.

[2] Isidore 1.   [3] Dio Cass. xl. 12.

[4] Municipium . . . conditum Macedonum manu priscorum. Amm. Marc. xiv. 3, 3.

[5] Isidore 1; Tac. Ann. vi. 41. In Strabo and Ptolemy, Anthemusias is the name, not of a city, but of the district. When Strabo says of the Aborras that it is $\pi\epsilon\rho\grave{\iota}\ \tau\grave{\eta}\nu\ \text{'}A\nu\theta\epsilon\mu o\nu\sigma\acute{\iota}a\nu$ (xvi. 748) he probably is speaking carelessly, meaning only that it is a river of N.W. Mesopotamia.

proud of its pure dialect. In the modern Urfa the old name survives. The other city on the Belichas was Haran, associated in our minds with the story of Abraham. Its transformation to the Macedonian colony of Carrhae seems to be rightly attributed to Alexander himself. Seleucus, as we saw,[1] found a body of Macedonian soldiers settled here in 312. It became one day tragically famous by the disaster of Crassus.

In the valley of the Chaboras (Al-Khâbûr), and along those many streams which go to form it, we cannot show Greek cities as we can to the west. That they existed is highly probable, but if so, their names have perished. There is one exception, Nisibis. It became an Antioch.[2] Part of the new population is said to have consisted of Spartans.[3] An inscription speaks of it as the "holy city, which Nicator built, upon the stream of Mygdon, in a land of olives."[4] It was a great junction of roads. The highway of communication between Syria and lands beyond the Tigris ran through it.[5] In this case also the old name prevailed in the long run over the new. The district, in which Nisibis-Antioch was, got from the Macedonians the name of Mygdonia after their home. Antioch-in-Mygdonia was the city's official name. We may perhaps infer that the district was more completely appropriated by the new civilization than we could guess from the one city, whose existence is established.[6]

We have followed what can still be traced of the network of Greco-Roman cities cast by the new rulers of the East over the country of the Aramaeans (Syria and Mesopotamia). We should like to know more than we do of the inner life of these communities. The political forms of the Greek city-state were, of course, maintained. We should have found in each

[1] P. 53.
[2] Joseph. *Arch.* xx. § 68; Plutarch, *Lucull.* 25; Strabo xvi. 747; Theophylact. iii. pp. 123, 134.   [3] Plutarch, *Ser. num. vind.* 21.
[4] *C.I.G.* No. 6856.   [5] Polyb. v. 51, 1.
[6] Some of the places mentioned by Pliny (vi. § 118), Dios-pege, Polytelia, Stratonicea, and (if not identical with Antioch-Nisibis) Antioch Arabis, may belong to this region. Of the names given by Appian (*Syr.* 57) as of cities founded in Syria and "the barbarians further inland" (including perhaps Western Irân, but not Parthia) the following are otherwise unknown—Perinthus, Callipolis, Achaïa (unless this is Heraclea in Media), Astacus, Tegea, and Heraea.

the periodically elected magistrates,[1] a *boule* and a *demos* passing decrees after the usual pattern and inscribing them on tables of brass and stone.[2] The social organization of the citizens also probably followed the Greek type. At Antioch the people was divided into tribes,[3] and we may infer the same thing in the other cities. The gymnasium, with the body of *epheboi* attached to it, was an essential feature.[4] But to what extent the old Hellenic spirit survived in these forms, to what extent the new settlers preserved their type in the new environment, escapes our discovery. According to a speech which Livy puts into the mouth of Manlius (189 B.C.) there had been rapid degeneracy. "Just as in the case of plants and live-stock, breed alone will not maintain the quality against the influences of soil and climate, so the Macedonians of Alexandria in Egypt, of Seleucia and Babylonia, and all the other scattered colonies throughout the world, have degenerated into Syrians, into Parthians, into Egyptians."[5] Titus Flamininus said of the armies of Antiochus III that they were "all Syrians."[6] Whether this testimony is biassed, or again whether there was the same degeneration in the smaller cities as in great cosmopolitan centres like Antioch, we have not the means of making out. The Syrian Greeks were regarded as inferior by the Greeks of the motherland.[7]

[1] I do not know that we can exactly *prove* this, but it may be taken for granted, since the system belongs to the essence of the city-state. We hear of τὰ τέλη at Seleucia in Pieria (Gurôb papyrus, *Sitzungsb. der Akad. z. Berlin*, 1894, p. 445 f.), of the συναρχίαι at Antioch (*ib.*), at Damascus of the ἐγχώριοι ἀρχαί, Suidas s. Antipater of Damascus. The title borne by the chief magistrates was that of *strategoi* in the case of Antioch (Michel, No. 550), but the decree in which it occurs is of the time of Antiochus IV Epiphanes.

[2] The *boule* is mentioned at Antioch (Michel, No. 550), and at Gaza (consisting of 500), which, of course, was not under the Seleucids till the time of Antiochus III (Joseph. *Arch.* xiii. § 364).

[3] Müller, *Antiq. Antioch.* p. 30.

[4] At Antioch, οἱ ἀπὸ τοῦ γυμνασίου νεανίσκοι (Köhler, *Sitzb. Berl.* 1894, p. 445 f.), who are no doubt identical with the ἔφηβοι (Polyb. xxxi. 3, 12). The party at Jerusalem, who wish to transform the city into a Hellenic Antioch, regard the gymnasium as almost the principal thing (1 Macc. 1, 14 ; ἐὰν ἐπιχορηγηθῇ διὰ τῆς ἐξουσίας αὐτοῦ γυμνάσιον καὶ ἐφηβίαν αὐτῷ συστήσασθαι, καὶ τοὺς ἐν Ἱεροσολύμοις Ἀντιοχεῖς ἀναγράψαι, 2 Macc. 4, 9).

[5] Liv. xxxviii. 17, 10. [6] *Ibid.* xxxv. 49, 8 ; Plutarch, *Titus*, 17.

[7] παραγενόμενος εἰς τὴν Συρίαν καὶ καταφρονήσας τῶν ἀνθρώπων, Polyb. xxxii. 6, 6.

It must be admitted that we do not get a favourable picture of them from their fellow-countryman, Posidonius of Apamea (*circ.* 135-51 B.C.); and even if his description be true only of the later days of the Seleucid dynasty, the decline must have begun long before. "The people of these cities are relieved by the fertility of their soil from a laborious struggle for existence. Life is a continuous series of social festivities. Their gymnasiums they use as baths, where they anoint themselves with costly oils and myrrhs. In the *grammateia* (such is the name they give the public eating-halls) they practically live, filling themselves there for the better part of the day with rich foods and wine; much that they cannot eat they carry away home. They feast to the prevailing music of strings. The cities are filled from end to end with the noise of harp-playing."[1] Consonant with this picture is the account Posidonius gives of the war between Apamea and Larissa—some petty war of two neighbour cities which is not otherwise known.[2] He narrates the setting out of the Apamean force. "They had caught up poignards and javelins which were indistinguishable in rust and dirt. They wore hats with broad brims, exquisitely adjusted so as to shade the neck without keeping off the cool breeze. Behind them trailed a string of asses, laden with wine and all sorts of viands, alongside of which might be seen pipes and flutes, the instruments of revelry, not of war."[3]

It is possible, of course, that Posidonius caricatured his countrymen. The fact that he himself was of Apamea shows that the stock could still produce men capable of taking the highest place in the literary and scientific world. But the traces of intellectual activity among the Syrian Greeks are, it must be admitted, scanty. The only way in which we can estimate it is by noting which of the memorable names are coupled with a Syrian origin. And this is an unsure method. For the literary world was cosmopolitan, and a man's activity might not lie in the place where he was born. There is, how-

---

[1] Posidonius ap. Athen. v. 210 *f*, and xii. 527 *e*.

[2] Larissa, whose citizens seem to have maintained their manly character (see page 215), had probably revolted from dependence upon Apamea.

[3] Posidonius ap. Athen. iv. 176 *b*.

ever, this to be said, that some degree of culture must be supposed in the early environment of men who left their native place to seek learning or literary fame, something to have stimulated them to such a quest.

Looking, then, at the list of remembered names in all departments of culture, we find that Antioch, the greatest of the cities, contributes during the Seleucid epoch only a Stoic philosopher, Apollophanes, and a writer on dreams, Phœbus. Cicero describes Antioch as a "city once much resorted to, and abounding in men of the highest education and in the pursuit of liberal learning."[1] Seleucia-in-Pieria produced Apollophanes, who was body-physician to Antiochus III, and made some valuable contributions to ancient medicine. The only Syrian city to whose name any literary lustre attaches is one which did not pass under Seleucid supremacy till the time of Antiochus III, Gadara. This is leaving out of count the Phœnician cities, to which we shall come presently.

One question which naturally suggests itself about this Syrian Hellenism is whether the newcomers were influenced to any extent by the people of the land, whether they adopted their traditions and modes of thought. We have very few data to go upon. The matter of language, which is a capital point, must be largely conjectural. The educated classes in the cities of course spoke Greek. But was it usual for them to have any real knowledge of the native language, without which a communication of ideas must have been very scanty? That they picked up common words and phrases, as an Anglo-Indian does of Hindostani, is to be taken for granted,[2] but does not prove much. It is somewhat more significant that the nicknames of some of the later Seleucids (Balas, Siripides, Zabinas) are Aramaïc. The Antiochene populace with whom they started was, no doubt, bilingual.

The only distinct borrowing of native tradition which we can point to is in the cults. The ancients thought it prudent to honour the gods of a land into which they came, even

[1] Cicero, *Pro Arch.* 3.
[2] Meleager of Gadara (who was, it is true, of Syrian origin) in one of his epitaphs asks to be greeted in whichever language is the mother-tongue of the passer-by, with the Aramaïc "*Salam,*" the Phœnician "*Audoni*" (?), or the Greek "*Chaire,*" *Anth. Pal.* vii. 419.

when they came as conquerors. Most, if not all, of the new cities stood where native towns or villages had stood before them, each with its local Baal or Astarte. These cults were, no doubt, in most cases retained, the Greeks, of course, giving to the native deities the names of their own gods.

At Antioch there was a temple of Artemis Persike, that is, one form of the great Mother-goddess worshipped by the Semites and peoples of Asia Minor.[1]

At Seleucia-in-Pieria there appears from the coins to have been a temple whose deity was represented by a conical stone, and that it was an old local god is shown by the name of Zeus Casius, which is often attached to the symbol. Zeus Casius was the god of the neighbouring mountain,[2] worshipped from time immemorial by the Phœnician coasters. Sometimes the epithet on the coins is not Casius but Keraunios, and this suggests that the thunderbolt, the sacred emblem of the city, may be connected with the old worship, and the Greek story of the foundation of the city have been invented later to explain it.

At Laodicea-on-the-Sea the coins show an armed goddess, identified by numismatists as Artemis Brauronia, whose image had been carried away from Attica by the Persians in 480, was found by Seleucus at Susa, and presented to his new colony.[3] This does not exclude the possibility that in the native township, Ramitha,[4] or Mazabda,[5] which had preceded Laodicea, a goddess of this type had been worshipped, and that this was the motive which led Seleucus to choose Laodicea as the recipient of the venerable idol; or the whole story of the image may even have been invented in later times by the Laodiceans to give an Oriental cult a respectable Attic parentage.

The great example of an ancient cult continuing to flourish under Greek rule was in Bambyce-Hieropolis. The deity here was Atargatis, *i.e.* Astarte (the wife) of 'Atch. The temple and ritual are described at length by Lucian in a special work, *De Syria Dea.* According to the story told him by the priests,

[1] Libanius, *Antioch.* p. 291.
[2] I do not know whether it has been suggested that the conical symbol may be meant for an image of the mountain in miniature.
[3] Paus. iii. 16, 8.   [4] Steph. Byz. *s.v.* Laodicea.
[5] Malalas, p. 203.

the actual building was the work of Stratonice, the queen of Seleucus I and Antiochus I. The story told about her is certainly fabulous, and it is therefore possible that an old legend may have become accidentally attached to her name from its resemblance in sound to that of Astarte. A prominent feature of the religion of Atargatis was the sanctity of fish. There was a pond with the sacred fish beside the temple, some of them with pieces of gold attached to their fins. On certain holy days the images of the gods were carried down to the pond.[1] The priests were, of course, native Syrians, and there was a great body of consecrated eunuchs.

A goddess of the same type as the Ephesian Artemis, certainly a form of the Mother-goddess, is seen on coins of one of the late Seleucids; she was, no doubt, worshipped in the place where these coins were minted.[2] On other coins of the same epoch is a bearded deity in a conical cap, holding an ear of corn in his hand.[3] The Baal of Doliche in Cyrrhestice did not only continue to be worshipped by the Greeks, but his cult, as that of Zeus Dolichenus, was spread into foreign lands, and became one of that farrago of Oriental superstitions, cults of Sarapis, of Isis and Mithra which were so much in vogue throughout the Roman Empire in the latter time of paganism. The same thing happened in the case of another Syrian god, Baal Markod, the "lord of dancing." At the village of Baetocaece there was a miraculous shrine of the local god (Zeus Baetocaeceus), which obtained from a King Antiochus a grant of land and a sanction of its inviolability, as his letter (of which a copy made in Roman times was found on the spot) declares at large.[4]

It is difficult to trace the action of their new environment upon the Greeks and Macedonians of Syria; it is no easier to follow the workings of the old Aramaean civilization and life under the strange forces which now came to bear upon them. The country-side retained its old speech, this much we know.[5] In the cities the populace was largely, and perhaps mainly,

---

[1] Lucian, *De Syr. Dea* 45-47.   [2] Babelon, p. clxx.
[3] *Ibid.* p. clxxiii.   [4] *C.I.G.* No. 4474.
[5] Becker-Marquardt, *Handb. d. röm. Alt.* iii. p. 258, note 1801.

Aramaean.[1] Even as an official language Aramaïc did not quite die out, as is shown by its use later on in Palmyra and among the Nabataeans. There were still circles, in such places presumably as Edessa, in which Aramaïc literature continued to be cultivated. The oldest works in Syriac which have come down to us (Christian) show the language in a fixed and developed form. They were not first essays in a new medium.

But although Aramaïc speech and literature survived, they were discredited among the upper classes. They shrank with a sense of inferiority from contact with the Muses of Greece. Greek throughout Seleucid Syria was the proper language of official documents, of literature and of monuments. The Syrian youth, who aspired to be counted wise, found the wisdom of his fathers no longer of any savour, when he might put on the Hellenic dress and talk Zeno or Epicurus in the porticoes of the new cities. Meleager of Gadara seems to have been of native Syrian origin.[2] Even where the old language of the land was used, the thought was, no doubt, largely Greek, as is the case with the dialogue *On Fate*—one of the oldest Syriac works we possess, written early in the third century A.D. by a disciple of the heretic Bardesanes, and continuing possibly a pre-Christian tradition. It is not really surprising that that literature should have perished. Driven into the background by Greek literature as barbarian during the pagan period, it was annihilated in the Christian period as pagan.[3]

We have hitherto left aside that Semitic people of whom we know more than the Aramaeans, the Phœnicians of the coast. Greeks and Phœnicians had known each other since the prehistoric centuries. The Phœnicians, like the coast-peoples of Asia Minor, had already undergone some degree of Hellenic influence before Alexander. They had also before Alexander had a long experience of foreign rule.

---

[1] The references in Müller, *Antiquitates Antiochenae*, p. 29; see also Philostr. *Apoll.* i. 16. A curious custom is mentioned by Malalas, p. 29, by which on a certain day every year the Aramaean population at Antioch went along knocking at the doors of the Greeks and saying something which is rendered, ψυχὴ Ἰοῦς σωζέσθω. [2] *Anth. Pal.* vii. 417.

[3] Nöldeke, *Ueber Mommsen's Darstellung der römischen Herrschaft im Orient. Zeitschr. d. deutsch. morgenl. Gesell.* xxxix. (1885), p. 331 f.

But under their various foreign masters, Assyrian, Babylonian, Persian, the Phœnicians had maintained from time immemorial their nationality and local independence. The cities had their own constitutions or kings. In opposition to Alexander, to the advent of a power far more penetrating and transforming than that of the earlier monarchies, history sees the national spirit of the Phœnicians blaze up for the last time in its original seat. In Africa, indeed, it was still to meet Rome for life or death. But the siege of Tyre, which delayed Alexander for some eight months in 332, was the last of those sieges of Phœnician cities of which history remembered so many, the last in which the defenders were the natives themselves, animated by a national or civic spirit against a foreign king. Sidon had been crippled twenty years before by the fearful vengeance taken by Artaxerxes Ochus for its revolt; Tyre was crushed finally by Alexander. With some few exceptions, all its inhabitants who could not escape were killed or sold for slaves. Some of the old population may have drifted back, strangers came in to fill the gaps, Tyre became again a great commercial town,[1] but the old spirit never returned, the ancient tradition was broken for ever.

In the new population the Hellenic element was probably considerable. At any rate the old Phœnician cities now undergo the same sort of transformation into Hellenic cities as we have seen in the case of the Aramaean cities. The Phœnician tradition would seem, however, to have been less completely suppressed by the new culture. Not only are Phœnician inscriptions put up by private citizens under the Macedonian rule, but the coins of Tyre, Sidon, Aradus, Laodicea-Berytus and Marathus bear Phœnician legends alongside of Greek legends and the heads of the Macedonian rulers. As late as the Christian era there were many people in Tyre who did not even understand Greek.[2] At the same time, the Hellenism which took root here became in time more vigorous and productive than that in the Aramaean domain. Several of the prominent philosophers of the last centuries B.C. are described as being of Tyre or of Sidon.[3] In the closing

---

[1] Strabo xvi. 757.   [2] Socrates, *Hist. ecc.* i. 19.
[3] See Susemihl, *Geschichte der griech. Lit. in d. Alexandrinerzeit;* Zeno of

century before Christ, the development of the Greek epigram, "when it had come to a standstill in Alexandria, reached its completeness on the Phœnician coast, on a soil, that is, properly Semitic but saturated with Greek culture and civilization."[1]

There is another region which we have to consider in connexion with Syria.

We have seen that *Cilicia* went, according to ancient geography, rather with Syria than Asia Minor. The Seleucid kings who wished to reign in both naturally looked upon Cilicia as theirs. As a matter of fact the Cilician plains were cut off both from Syria and from the rest of Asia Minor by tremendous mountain barriers, communicating with Asia Minor only by the narrow doorway of the "Cilician Gates," with Syria by a pass equally narrow between mountain and sea, the "Syrian Gates," or by the difficult roads over the Amanus. Cilicia, whose native population was probably akin to the Aramaeans of Syria, had a history which went back like that of Syria into the days of Assyrian supremacy, and had, like Syria, its cities of old fame, Soli, Mallus and Tarsus, the seat under the Achaemenians of those semi-independent native princes who bore the name of Syennesis. But the Hellenic influence had come to work earlier in this region; the old cities had already become more than half Hellenized by the time that Alexander arrived, and thought it decent to appear as Greek colonies. Actual Greek colonists may indeed have come to settle in them. Soli claimed Argos and Rhodes as its mother-cities.[2] Tarsus called sometimes the Greek hero Triptolemus, sometimes the Assyrian king Sardanapallus its founder.[3] Mallus had been founded in the dim days of Greek legend by Mopsus and Amphilochus.[4] Mopsus, indeed, as a wandering hero figured largely in the myths of the Greek colonies along the south coast of Asia Minor, and the most

---

Sidon (Stoic), i. p. 73; Diodorus of Tyre (Peripatetic), i. p. 154; Antipater of Tyre (Stoic), ii. p. 247; Zeno of Sidon (Epicurean), ii. p. 261; Diotimus of Tyre (Democritean), ii. p. 279; Boëthus of Sidon (Peripatetic), ii. p. 307.

[1] Susemihl ii. p. 551.
[2] Strabo xiv. 671; Mela i. § 71. [3] Strabo xiv. 672, 673.
[4] *Ibid.* 675; Arrian *Anab.* ii. 5, 9.

important town of the interior of Cilicia after Tarsus bore in Greek the name of Mopsū-hestia, the Hearth of Mopsus.

The Hellenism of the cities of Cilicia vindicated itself in the third century by its fruits. Just as at the very beginning of Greek philosophy, in the case of Thales, there had been matter supplied to Hellenic thought by the Phœnician tradition, so now it was on this ground, where Hellenic cities had grown up among a Semitic people, that the great philosophic school of later Hellenism, the Stoic, took its rise. The founder, Zeno, was a native of Citium in Cyprus, the Phœnician Chittim; but his follower, Chrysippus, who developed and systematized the doctrine, the "second father" of the school, was a Cilician Greek,[1] of Soli, born just about the time that Seleucus Nicator wrested Asia Minor from Lysimachus. Tarsus became a principal seat of the Stoic school. Zeno, the successor of Chrysippus, was of Tarsus,[2] so was Antipater, head of the school somewhat later;[3] the fellow-pupil of Antipater, Archedemus;[4] the disciple of Antipater, Heraclides,[5] and Nestor.[6] Among the Stoics of a still later generation we hear of the Cilicians, Crates of Mallus,[7] and his disciple, Zenodotus of Mallus,[8] and several of those philosophers who were associated as friends and teachers with the leading men of Rome in the last age of the Republic were natives of this region.[9] Some of the Cilician philosophers inclined to other schools than the Stoic. One of the greatest names among the leaders of the Academy in Athens was that of Crantor of Soli,[10] and we hear of a Diogenes of Tarsus as an Epicurean.[11] Tarsus by the last century B.C. had become one of the great "universities" of the Greco-Roman world. "Such an enthusiasm for philosophy and all the other parts of a liberal education has been developed in the people of this city," says Strabo,[12] "that they have surpassed Athens and Alexandria and all other places one might mention as seats of learning and philosophical study.

---

[1] Susemihl, *Gesch. d. gr. Lit.* i. p. 75 f.   [2] Susemihl i. p. 82.
[3] *Ibid.* p. 84.   [4] *Ibid.* p. 85.
[5] *Ibid.* p. 87.   [6] *Ibid.* ii. p. 243.
[7] *Ibid.* p. 4.   [8] *Ibid.* p. 14.
[9] Athenodorus (called Cordylio) of Tarsus (Susemihl ii. p. 246); Athenodorus of Cana (*id.* p. 248); Xenarchus of Seleucia (*id.* p. 321).
[10] Susemihl i. p. 118.   [11] *Ibid.* ii. p. 258.   [12] xiv. 673.

Here all the students are natives, and strangers do not readily come to reside. . . . They have schools for all branches of literary culture." It is not only in philosophy that Cilicia produced great names. Soli, whose Hellenic character was of an older standing than Tarsus, produced men of letters in the first century of Macedonian rule who attained world-wide fame. Castorion of Soli was even commissioned at Athens (309-308) to compose hymns for public festivals.[1] A still greater name is that of Aratus, the author of the astronomical poem which we still possess, the model for numerous imitations by later writers, Greek and Roman.[2] The tragic poet Dionysiades of Mallus or Tarsus is by some reckoned among the "Pleiad" of Seven which shone at the court of the second Ptolemy.[3] Apollodorus of Tarsus was known as a commentator on Euripides and Aristophanes.[4]

As to the working of native Cilician influence upon Cilician Hellenism, we have the same indications as in Syria of the continuance of the old cults. On coins of Mallus, struck under the Seleucids and Romans, appears the goddess of the neighbouring Megarsus, the usual Semitic Mother-goddess, whom the Greeks here called Athene.[5] So, too, on the coins of Tarsus a common type is a curious pyramidal monument or shrine with a barbarian male-deity depicted upon it, whom Babelon conjectures to be Zeus Dolichenus.[6]

Of the events which took place in Syria and the adjoining provinces under Seleucus and his earlier successors we know almost nothing. These regions had, of course, formed part of the realm of Antigonus till the battle of Ipsus. After that Syria passed to Seleucus, but Cilicia was at first handed over to Plistarchus, the brother of Cassander, and the garrison set by Antigonus in Tyre and Sidon held firm for Demetrius when the news of Ipsus reached them. As we saw,[7] Demetrius expelled Plistarchus from Cilicia and occupied the country in 299, at the time when Seleucus and Demetrius were friends.

[1] Susemihl ii. p. 518.   [2] *Ibid*. i. p. 284 f.
[3] *Ibid*. p. 280.   [4] *Ibid*. ii. p. 178.
[5] Babelon, p. cxxxii.   [6] *Ibid*. p. clvi. f.
[7] P. 63.

But it was exactly because Seleucus wished himself to be master both in Cilicia and on the Phœnician coast that the rupture between them occurred. Demetrius refused on any terms to part either with Cilicia or the Phœnician cities. Then in the following years, whilst Demetrius was busy in Greece and Macedonia, Seleucus succeeded in making Cilicia his. At the same time Demetrius lost Tyre and Sidon. Into whose hands did they fall? They lay close both to Northern Syria, which belonged to Seleucus, and to Palestine, which had been occupied by Ptolemy. We have not yet any conclusive evidence to show which of the rival houses at this juncture obtained possession of them.[1]

The score of years, however, during which Seleucus Nicator ruled Syria, if they have furnished no matter to the historians, were far from unimportant. A great work of organization, of Hellenization, as to which the historians are silent, must have been carried through. The four great cities of Seleucid Syria, Antioch, Seleucia-in-Pieria, Apamea, and Laodicea, as well as a large number of the lesser Greek communities, were founded and started in life. The division of the country into districts, such as Seleucis, Cyrrhestice, and Commagene, and of Seleucis again into the four satrapies corresponding to the four great cities,[2] presumably goes back to the reign of Seleucus. Thenceforth these Greek communities were the active and determining element in the population.

As soon as the death of Seleucus became known, a faction hostile to his house raised its head in the Syrian cities. Antiochus I found the Syrian Macedonians and Greeks largely in arms against him. "In the beginning of the reign of King Antiochus," says the Sigean Inscription,[3] "at the instant of his accession he adopted an honourable and glorious policy, and whereas the cities in Seleucis were troubled in those days by those who had made insurrection, he sought to restore them to peace and their original well-being, to do vengeance on the

---

[1] See Appendix O.

[2] Strabo xvi. 749. That *satrapy* really was the official name for these subdivisions of Seleucis is confirmed by an inscription, *C.I.G.* No. 4474.

[3] Michel, No. 525.

rebellious, as justice would, and to recover his father's kingdom. So, cherishing an honourable and just purpose, and not only finding the army and the court (τοὺς φίλους) zealous to carry his cause to victory, but having the favour and assistance of heaven, he brought back the cities to a state of peace and the kingdom to its original well-being." Through these high-sounding official phrases we must see all that can be seen of the truth.

From this moment till Seleucus II is driven out of Asia Minor by the battle of Ancyra, the history of Syria is a blank, except in so far as it is involved in the long wars between Seleucid and Ptolemy. War indeed seems to have been opened by a battle, in which the Seleucid army was commanded by King Antiochus I in person, somewhere in Syria—although, if Antiochus was the aggressor, most probably in the Ptolemaïc province south of the Lebanon. At least, a Babylonian inscription says that in the year 274-273 B.C. King Antiochus, who had come east of the Euphrates, returned to the "land beyond the River"[1] against the army of Egypt. Ptolemy's strength lay on the sea, and perhaps the interior of Syria was less involved in the war, even on the frontier, than the coasts. The only recorded incident of which inland Syria is the scene is the capture of Damascus. Damascus was held by a Ptolemaïc garrison under Dion; King Antiochus (the First, no doubt) was with an army at some days' distance. Antiochus knew that Dion was receiving intelligence of his movements, and accordingly caused his army to celebrate a Persian festival and in appearance give themselves up to jollity. This deceived Dion and threw him off his guard. Antiochus crept round upon Damascus by mountain and desert solitudes, fell upon it unawares, and took the city.[2] In 242 Damascus is in Seleucid possession.[3] Whether the Seleucid kings kept their hold on this important place all the time from its capture by Antiochus till that date, or whether it changed hands with the varying fortunes of the war we do not know.

---

[1] This, of course, was the ordinary designation of Syria in the official language of the old Persian Empire, Ezra 4, 10; Babelon, *Perses Achéménides*, p. xlv.   [2] Polyaen. iv. 15.   [3] Eus. i. 251.

It is in the provinces open to the sea that the struggle was probably fiercest. The possession of Cilicia and the Phœnician coast, with their wealth in timber, was especially important to a power like the Egyptian.

Cilicia seems to have changed hands at least three times. If the poem of Theocritus is any evidence, the second Ptolemy before 271[1] had ousted the Seleucid. He "gives the signal to the warriors of Cilicia."[2] Then Antiochus II seems to have recovered it, since it is not among the countries inherited by Ptolemy III in the Inscription of Adule. Then again it is conquered by Ptolemy III in the campaign for which we have the Ptolemaïc officer's dispatch.[3] And in Ptolemaïc possession it still was on the accession of Antiochus III.

From the Gurôb papyrus we get a fragmentary view of the organization of Cilicia as a Seleucid province in 246. It is, as we saw, under the *strategos* Aribazus, divided into smaller districts with *hyparchs* of their own, whom the Ptolemaïc captain describes likewise as *strategoi*; that is, the same general form of government appears as we find in the rest of the Empire. The town of Seleucia is, for the moment at any rate, the headquarters of the administration. Soli is seen to take a line of its own, shifting its allegiance to the house of Ptolemy at discretion.

From the outbreak of the war, during the time of the two first Antiochi, Tyre and Sidon are under Ptolemaïc influence. Tyre strikes coins of Ptolemy with an era dating from 275-274, that is, from about the time when hostilities were opened in Syria.[4] Sidon also strikes coins of Ptolemy II with dates which run from 261 to 247.[5] A certain Philocles, son of Apollodorus, who commands Ptolemaïc forces in the Aegean, is described as "king of the Sidonians."[6] Phœnicia is mentioned on the monument of Adule as one of the countries inherited by Ptolemy III from his father. The more northern Phœnician cities, on the other hand, were probably

---

[1] See v. Prott, *Rhein. Mus.* liii. (1898), p. 475.
[2] Παμφύλοισι τε πᾶσι καὶ αἰχμηταῖς Κιλίκεσσι | σαμαίνει, Theoc. xvii. l. 87.
[3] See p. 185.
[4] Head, *Hist. Num.* p. 675.   [5] *Ibid.* p. 672.
[6] Michel, No. 373; cf. Winckler, *Altorientalische Forschungen*, 2te Reihe, ii. p. 295.

Seleucid from the battle of Ipsus. Some of the coins of Antiochus I bear the monogram of Aradus.[1] The year 259-258 is the starting-point of a new era for Aradus,[2] and this is generally thought to show the concession of complete autonomy to the city by Antiochus II. In the "Laodicean War" an attempt was made by Ptolemy to capture these northern Phœnician cities, but unsuccessfully. Orthosia, which was beleaguered by his forces, was relieved by Seleucus Kallinikos in 242-241.[3] Later on Aradus secured fresh privileges by declaring for Seleucus against Antiochus Hierax. In recompense for this, the obligation to deliver up fugitives from the Seleucid realm was remitted, and such right of sanctuary, in times when political fugitives of wealth and influence were numerous, proved extremely profitable to the city.[4]

We have already in a former chapter dealt with the occurrences on the coast of Cilicia and Syria in the opening stage of the Laodicean War.[5]

The expulsion of Seleucus Kallinikos from the country north of the Taurus shifted the centre of gravity in the Empire. The disreputable court of Antiochus Hierax at Sardis could not claim equality with the court of the elder brother, which was now fixed in the Syrian Antioch. By this change Antioch rose at once in dignity. And the change made itself apparent in the outward aspect of the city. Seleucus Kallinikos added a new quarter.[6]

Of the events which took place in Syria in these days we know only the incident of Stratonice and her rebellion. Stratonice was that aunt of Seleucus who had been married to Demetrius, son of the King of Macedonia. In 239 Demetrius succeeded to the throne and was moved to contract a new marriage with an Epirot princess. To Stratonice the idea of remaining at the Macedonian court under the new *régime* was not unnaturally repugnant. She departed, studying revenge, for the court of her nephew. Her scheme was that he should marry her and declare war on her late husband. When,

---

[1] Head, p. 666.   [2] Droysen iii. p. 312 ; Head, p. 666.
[3] See p. 190.   [4] Strabo xvi. 754.   [5] See p. 185 f.
[6] Strabo xvi. 749.

however, she proposed it to Seleucus he displayed a mortifying unwillingness to marry his aunt. For this attitude on his part Stratonice had been wholly unprepared. But her spirit was not broken. She waited her time. The Antiochenes came to know the figure of an unfortunate princess who moved amongst them as an injured and angry woman. Her opportunity came about 235, when the King was absent on an expedition into Irân. She then summoned the city to revolt, and so well had she played her game that the city responded and took up arms on her behalf against Seleucus. When the King returned from the East he was reduced to the necessity of recapturing his capital. Stratonice was unable to offer a prolonged defence. When she saw that the city must fall she fled to Seleucia. Thence she might have escaped, but was induced by an adverse dream to put off sailing. As a result of this delay she was caught by the people of Seleucus and put to death.[1] The story certainly proves that the restiveness which the Syrian Greeks had shown at the accession of Antiochus I was not extinct under Seleucus Kallinikos.

[1] Just. xxviii. 1 ; Agatharchides ap. Joseph. *Con. Ap.* i. § 206 f. (*F.H.G.* iii. p. 196). This story is commonly adduced as evidence that Seleucia was at this moment in Seleucid possession (so Niese ii. p. 168). That it was momentarily recaptured by Seleucus is of course possible, but the story does not say so. The delay of Stratonice at Seleucia might have been the cause of her being captured by the pursuers, even if it were not in Seleucia itself that she was captured.

CHAPTER XII

BABYLONIA

At a time beyond the vision of history some members of the human family found the country about the lower reaches of the rivers Euphrates and Tigris—then a swampy wilderness—good to live in. They began to cast seed into the black earth and to dry lumps of it in the sun for the building of houses. Presently they went on to improve Nature's distribution of the water, digging new channels which carried it from the swamp, where there was too much of it, to the desert, where there was too little. The area of serviceable land gradually extended. Here and there the mud-brick houses clustered into villages. Then the villages became cities, with great temples and palaces and towers for star-gazing. Society became more complex; there were rich and poor; rich, who wanted a variety of things to make their life easeful and beautiful; and poor, whose myriad hands were busied in their manufacture. The communication of thought between man and man or between one generation and another, which the complexity of society now required, was made possible by the fixing of speech in written signs. All this process was already accomplished by the time history becomes cognizant of human things. The cities and their civilization were already there; not Babylon only—for Babylon was but one of many sisters and not the first-born, though in time she eclipsed them all—Ur, Eridu, Uruk, and many others stood once on an equal footing. Who the people were, who first lived in these cities, what their affinities were with other branches of the human race, history cannot say. The people who possessed the land later on were

Semites, cousins of the Jew and the Arab, but these Semites, it is believed, were not the original inhabitants; they broke in from the desert upon the older people and overwhelmed them, but became themselves assimilated in manners and traditions to the conquered race, using its old-world tongue as a sacred language alongside of their own living Semitic idiom.

This branch of the Semitic peoples did not occupy the alluvial country about the lower Euphrates only—the seat of that primeval civilization of which we have just spoken. Its settlements were pushed up the Tigris to the point where it issues from the Armenian highlands. At intervals on its banks cities arose whose language and culture did not differ essentially from those of Babylon. In process of time two great monarchical states shaped themselves: a northern one, whose centre was first at Asshur and then at Nineveh— what we know as the Assyrian kingdom—and a more southern one, in the alluvial country about the lower Euphrates, whose centre was in Babylon. In the day of their greatness the northern Semites, the Assyrians, were able to subjugate their cousins of the south; but the yoke was impatiently borne. At last it was finally broken. About 607 B.C. the Assyrian kingdom succumbed to a combined attack of Babylonians and Medes. Nineveh fell. Under Nabopolassar (625-605) and Nebuchadnezzar (605-562) Babylon had a new period (brief enough) of independence and glory.

During all these centuries the Semitic kingdoms on the Euphrates and Tigris had been the focus of civilization in the East. They were to the peoples of mountain and desert round about them what the Roman Empire was afterwards to the peoples of Central Europe. There was no other area of cultivation in Western Asia so wide and productive as Babylonia; there were no other cities so large and populous as those on the banks of the two rivers; no centres of industry to compare with those great hives of labour; no wisdom like the wisdom of the Chaldaeans; no king so exalted as the "King of kings." The influence of Babylon radiated as far as the Mediterranean on the west and India on the east. From all parts of the world there was a demand for its wares, especially for its embroideries and rich tissues, "goodly Babylonish garments." The river, which created its fertility, made at the same time a great highway through the desert, by which it communicated with the lands to the north and west, with Syria and Asia Minor and Egypt; on the east roads ran from it through Assyria or through Elam up to the Irânian plateau. And by these routes Babylon not only exported its own products; it was the central mart, through which the products of one end of the world found their way to the other. In its bazaars merchants perhaps chaffered for wares of India which were destined to be used by the peoples of the far-away Aegean.[1] Babylon was thus the commercial capital of the world, the heart in which all the arteries of traffic met. Its unit of weight, the *manah*, set the standard for all nations; the Greeks measured by the *mná*, the Indians of the Rigveda by the *maná*—a witness to the universal authority of Babylon.

It was not commerce only which brought Babylon into contact with foreigners, but in a lesser degree war as well. The Babylonians, being an industrial not a martial people, were obliged to have most of their fighting done for them, like the Carthaginians. Hard by on the east the lower slopes of the Irânian border range nourished a people who made excellent soldiers, and could be hired for money, predecessors of the modern Bakhtiaris. From how far afield they drew their mercenaries under the second Babylonian Empire is shown by the case already mentioned of the brother of the Lesbian poet Alcaeus.

Men from every quarter were thus drawn to Babylon and the other great cities of the Euphrates and Tigris, Phœnician merchantmen, nomads of the desert, and hardy fighting men from the hills of Asia Minor and Irân. Before their eyes were displayed the riches and glory, the handicraft and science of these settled kingdoms. It is no wonder that many nations learnt in their infancy from Babylon, that traces of Babylonian influence may be found in the primitive traditions of Canaan and India and Irân.

---

[1] The question whether there was any *maritime* trade between Babylonia and other lands before Greek rule is a controverted one; see Speck, *Handelsgeschichte des Altertums*, §§ 107, 135.

BABYLONIA

In the sixth century B.C. the long dominion of the Semites in Western Asia came to an end. Kurush, whom we call Cyrus, the chief of a Persian clan, led his countrymen forth from their mountains to seize, first the hegemony of the Irânian race, and then the empire of the world. On the 3rd of Marheshwân (about October 20) 539 Cyrus entered Babylon as a conqueror. But Babylon did not thereby lose its imperial dignity. Its greatness was too well based on its old renown, its geographical position, its immense population, its commercial and industrial supremacy. It could not but be still the capital of the world, the seat of the " King of kings," even though that title now belonged to a foreigner. During the hot Babylonian summer indeed the Irânian monarch used to withdraw to his own high country, to Persepolis or Ecbatana; but for the seven cooler months of the year the Persian court resided at Babylon.[1]

The Babylonians did not think without regret of the days of Nebuchadnezzar. They were troubled with memories of old empire. More than once they rose in revolt—in vain revolt. It was this disposition which moved the Persian kings to break their spirit by a series of rigorous measures.[2] The Babylonians looked on ruined temples, the evidence of their master's vengeance, or saw their golden images carried off to satisfy his greed.[3] Xerxes, after one of their revolts, forbade altogether the carrying of arms; let the Babylonians keep themselves to their harps and flutes, the life of the brothel and the bazaar.[4] But although under unsympathetic rule, Babylon continued to be the greatest of cities, "not so much a city in dimensions as a nation."[5] The population of Babylonia was the densest known,[6] with elements drawn from every nation under heaven.[7] Agriculture, manufactures and trade, three unfailing springs of wealth, made Babylonia the richest province of the Empire.[8] As to the first, it was a chief duty

---

[1] Xen. *Cyrop.* viii. 6, 22 ; Plutarch, *De exilio*, 12, etc.
[2] Arist. *Pol.* iii. 13.
[3] Hdt. i. 183 ; Arr. *Anab.* iii. 16, 4.
[4] Plutarch, *Apophth.* Ξέρξου, 2.
[5] Arist. *Pol.* iii. 3. [6] *Ibid.* ii. 6.
[7] Βαβυλὼν δ' ἡ πολύχρυσος πάμμικτον ὄχλον πέμπει σύρδην, Aesch. *Persae*, 52.
[8] Xen. *Cyrop.* vii. 2, 11.

of the satrap to regulate that elaborate canal system upon which Babylonian agriculture depended, and immense bodies of men were employed upon the works.[1] Herodotus tells us what Babylonia was like in the middle of the fifth century, after a hundred years or so of Persian rule. He saw its flat expanse, intersected by canals, stretching away in endless fields of wheat and millet and sesame, dotted with clumps of palm. For corn, "the fruit of Demeter," he knew no land like it. Wheat crops yielded from two to three hundredfold, and the size which millet and sesame attained, "I *could* say, but I will not, because I know very well that even what I have already said about its corn has gone far beyond the bounds of belief of such persons as have not been to the land of Babylon."[2] The industries of Babylon were still busily plied. Its many-coloured embroidery was as much in demand under the Persians as centuries before in the time of Joshua, or centuries after under the Roman emperors.[3]

With regard to trade, Babylon held its place as the great mart of Asia. Herodotus[4] describes the boats which regularly brought merchandize down the river and unloaded in Babylon. In the hot summer nights merchants from cooler lands could be seen in its crowded *khans*, trying to secure a little relief by lying on skins filled with water.[5] The traffic with India naturally continued under an empire which extended over all the intervening country.

There are nevertheless indications that the conditions were not as favourable to trade under Persian rule as they might

---

[1] Arr. *Anab.* vii. 21, 5; Strabo xvi. 739, 740.   [2] Hdt. i. 193.

[3] Arr. *Anab.* vi. 29, 5, 6; Philostr. *Vita Apoll.* i. 25; Plin. *N.H.* viii. § 196; Paus. v. 12, 4; Plutarch, *Cato Major*, 4; Mart. viii. 28, 17; Justinian, *Pandect.* xxxiv. 2, 25; Reber, *Ueber altchaldäische Kunst, Zeitschr. f. Assyr.* i. (1886), p. 291 f. It seems also to have produced a special sort of red or purple (Philostr. *Epist.* 54). We hear a good deal of Babylonian ungents and perfumes, but it is doubtful how far they were actually made up there, and how far imported into Babylon from India. It was at any rate the fashion for every Baylonian to scent his whole body (Hdt. i. 195; Athen. xv. 692 c; Pollux vi. 104; Hor. *Odes* ii. 11, 16; Tibull. iii. 6, 63. Cf. Aesch. *Ag.* 1271, Σύριον ἀγλάϊσμα, *i.e.* Ἀσσύριον = Babylonian). The other industries, which can be gathered from scattered allusions, such as the manufacture of seals and carved work (Hdt. i. 195), of reed-baskets (Strabo xvi. 740), and beds of palm-branches (Theophr. *Plant.* ii. 6, 6), do not appear to have been of more than local importance.

[4] i. 194.   [5] Plutarch, *Symp.* 2, 2, 12.

have been. The important water-way of the Tigris was blocked by "cataracts," which Alexander found it an easy matter to level, and which the local tradition asserted to have been made by the King's order, on purpose to bar the way to hostile ships.[1] The sea-route, again, between the Persian Gulf and India seems to have been forgotten; one would gather, from the accounts of Nearchus' voyage, that it was of the nature of a re-discovery, and this is all the more remarkable since these waters had been explored for Darius Hystaspis by the Greek Scylax, and Herodotus expressly declares that the sea-route was thereafter in use.[2] One might conclude that a weak commercial policy had marked the Persian government only in its declining days. We have an incidental sign of its slipshod administration at the end of the dynasty in the circumstance that a law which imposed a duty of 10 per cent on imports into Babylon, although it had never been repealed, had fallen into general neglect by the coming of Alexander.[3]

Some estimate of the relative importance of the Euphrates and Tigris regions to the Persian king can be formed from the revenue table of Darius, as given by Herodotus.[4] The Empire is divided for purposes of revenue into twenty districts, of which Babylonia and "the rest of Assyria" form one. When we deduct from the total annual revenue of the King the tribute in gold-dust, 360 talents, from the Indian district, we get a total of 7600 talents of *silver* (about 19,773,848 rupees) from the remaining nineteen districts. And of this the single district of Babylonia and Assyria yields 1000 (about 2,864,980 rupees). Egypt alone competes with it, yielding 700 talents.[5] Besides this tribute in money, the various provinces were required to make contributions in kind to the support of the King and his army. The part taken in this by Babylonia exhibits its importance in a more striking way still. "There being twelve months to the year," says Herodotus, "for four of them the land of Babylon supports him, and for the other eight all the rest of Asia. Thus the

[1] Arr. *Anab.* vii. 7, 6. [2] Hdt. iv. 44.
[3] Arist. *Oec.* ii. 34. [4] iii. 89 f.
[5] I have given the equivalents in rupees, because the fluctuating relation of silver and gold makes the comparison with a gold standard misleading.

Assyrian country is according to its capacities a third part of Asia."[1] The governorship of this province, he goes on to say, was the most lucrative appointment in the Empire. One satrap, whom he mentions, drew from it a daily income of an *artabe* (a bushel and a half) of silver.

Closely associated with Babylonia in past history was a land to the east of it, the torrid river-country which intervenes between the ramparts of Irân and the Persian Gulf, watered by the Choaspes (Kerkha), the Copratas (Dizfûl), and the Eulaeus (Karûn). It is described to-day as "a malarious labyrinth of meandering rivers and reedy swamps."[2] Once it was the seat of a unique civilization, of a people as alien from the Semites of Babylonia as from the races of Aryan speech on the farther table-land. According to one theory, they had come across from Africa. For centuries their kings were the antagonists, sometimes the conquerors, of the neighbouring Semitic powers. They were known by many names, to the Semites as Elam, to the Persians as Hûzha, to the early Greeks (Herodotus, Aeschylus) as Kissioi. When the Macedonians appeared in this part of the world, some of the Hûzha maintained themselves as a robber people among the hills,[3] but the Elamites of the lowland had probably forgotten the far-off days of their independence and glory. For hundreds of years they had borne the yoke of the stranger, Assyrian, Babylonian, Persian. So completely had they been assimilated to their rulers that the Greeks could see no difference between their manners and customs and those of the Persians.[4] Their country became in fact almost the central province of the Persian Empire. Its favourable position, near the cradle of the ruling race, and yet enough removed to free the monarch from the inconvenient aristocratic tradition of Irân and to overlook the western half of the Empire, led the Persian kings to make Susa ("Shushan the palace") a chief residence of the court during the delicious Elamite spring and one of the principal treasuries of the realm.[5]

---

[1] i. 192. [2] D. G. Hogarth, *The Nearer East*, p. 134.
[3] See p. 23. [4] Strabo xv. 732.
[5] Strabo xv. 728; Xenophon, *Cyrop.* viii. 6, 22.

BABYLONIA

In the autumn of 331, two hundred and eight years after the triumphal entry of Cyrus into Babylon, the city witnessed another triumphal entry. This too registered a new epoch in human history: after the Persian the man of Javan, the Hellene, the progenitor of the modern world, had come to reign in the seats of the old civilization. Alexander had two courses open to him after the victory of Gaugamela, to pursue Darius into his native Irân, or, in the first place, to seize Babylon. The latter was the course which Darius had rightly conjectured he would take; to possess the capital of the Empire was the thing most immediately essential; the rich cities of the plain, Babylon and Susa, were the real "prize of the war."[1] Therefore Alexander pressed on south. Mazaeus,[2] the greatest of the western satraps, who united under his governorship Cilicia, Syria and Mesopotamia, and to whom the disastrous battle of Gaugamela (Arbela) had only brought fresh credit, had thrown himself into Babylon with the wreck of his forces. But on Alexander's approach he at once surrendered; no assault had to be made upon the famous Babylonian wall. Mazaeus was rewarded by being made satrap of Babylonia under the new Great King.

Babylon thus passed under Greek rule, just ten years before Seleucus came to govern it. The change did not make much difference in the appearance of things there. A Persian grandee still held the place of satrap. It was rather as the restorer of the old order than as an innovator that Alexander presented himself to the Babylonians. He ordered the ruined temples to be rebuilt as in the days of Nebuchadnezzar, and in thirty days was gone again for fresh conquests. Only among the motley crowd of the bazaars one might now see here and there the mailed figure of a Macedonian soldier;[3] and behind the caparisoned Persian satrap stood the real holders of power, Apollodorus of Amphipolis, the commander of the military forces of the province; Agathon of Pydna, the commandant of the citadel; Asclepiodorus, who was over the tribute.

[1] τοῦ πολέμου τὸ ἆθλον, Arr. *Anab.* iii. 16, 2.

[2] On his coins he writes his name, in Aramaïc, Mazdai, מזדי. Babelon, *Les Perses Achéménides*, p. xliii. f.

[3] A garrison of 700 Macedonians was left in the citadel, Diod. xvii. 64 : cf. Curt. v. 1, 43.

Whether Alexander intended Babylon to be ultimately capital of his Empire, or Alexandria in Egypt, or Pella in Macedonia, we do not know—whether even he intended to make one capital for the whole. Babylon, at any rate, seems to have been regarded as the capital for Asia from its conquest to the time of his death. It was the headquarters of Harpalus, chief treasurer of the Empire;[1] and Alexander returned there in 323 to plan a new scheme of enterprise, and to make a new organization of the imperial army. Then Babylon, which had seen the glories of the oldest conquerors remembered by man, saw the youngest conqueror die. In Babylon the army and its chiefs made a new settlement for the Empire.

We proceed to inquire how the conquering European race and this most ancient world acted upon each other. Alexander, as we saw, presented himself here, as in Egypt, as the restorer; the evidences of Persian tyranny, ruined and impoverished temples, were to be no more seen. The gods of Babylon were to share in the impartial liberality of the universal King. But his magnificent projects were slackly prosecuted in his absence; the Babylonian priests enjoyed the temple revenues, so long as the temples lay waste, and they felt a tenderer interest in their money-bags than in the honour of their gods.[2] Here, too, Alexander had time only to adumbrate his policy.[3]

The pupil of Aristotle and the educated men who accompanied him looked with interest at the physical character of the lands into which they came. In Babylonia they were drawn to experiment in the acclimatizing of the plants of their native land. In this they had been anticipated to some extent by the old Eastern kings, who were zealous to collect the fauna and flora of remote countries in their gardens.[4]

---

[1] Harpalus had charge of the other treasuries as well as the Babylonian, that of Ecbatana, for instance (Arr. *Anab.* iii. 19, 7), and his authority extended to Northern Syria and Cilicia (Athen. 595 *d*), but Babylon, one gathers, was his headquarters (Diod. xvii. 108; Plutarch, *Alex.* 35; Athen. 595 *a, b, c*). Diod. is incorrect in speaking of him as *satrap*.

[2] Arr. *Anab.* vii. 17.   [3] Strabo xvi. 738.

[4] Tiele, *Babyl.-assyr. Gesch.* p. 603; cf. Michel, No. 32.

Now under the Macedonian supremacy the culture of the vine was attempted in Babylonia and the land of Elam on a new method adapted to the peculiarity of the soil.[1] Harpalus vainly attempted to make ivy grow in the gardens of Babylon.[2]

But in a much more vital respect the aspirations of the old national kings were fulfilled in the larger and more systematic designs of the man of the West. Nebuchadnezzar, according to an account which perhaps emanates from Berosus, had shown interest in the coast traffic of the Gulf. He had attempted to make solid harbours in the swamp, and had built the town of Teredon towards the land of the Arabs.[3]

The Persian government, as we have seen, had cared little for such things. But now in the mind of Alexander the idea of a mighty sea-traffic between Babylon and India shaped itself. The expedition of Nearchus from the Indus to the Persian Gulf subserved this policy. The latter months of Alexander's life were almost entirely taken up with examining the water-ways of lower Babylonia, regulating the canal system, and framing a scheme for the exploration of Arabia. Near Babylon itself he began to dig a gigantic basin capable of containing a thousand vessels of war with the corresponding docks.[4] New cities of Greek speech even in this overpowering climate began to rise, one among the pools west of the Euphrates, in which a number of Greek mercenaries and broken veterans were planted,[5] another to the east on the lagoons of the lower Eulaeus (Karûn)—an Alexandria populated partly with natives from an old "royal town," partly, like the other city, with broken soldiers.[6]

Babylonia and the land of Elam, called by the Greeks Susiana, from Susa, its capital, formed two satrapies under Alexander.

In 321-320 Seleucus becomes satrap of Babylonia, and Antigenes, who commands the Silver Shields, satrap of Susiana. Till 316 Seleucus governs Babylonia. Of his administration

---

[1] Strabo xv. 731. [2] Theophr. ix. 4, 1.
[3] Abydenus, frag. 8, *F.H.G.* iv. p. 284.
[4] Arr. *Anab.* vii. 19. [5] *Ibid.* vii. 21, 7.
[6] Plin. *N.H.* vi. § 138. A very full discussion of the site of this city by Andreas will be found in *Pauly-Wissowa*, s. "Alexandreia, No. 13."

during those four years we know next to nothing. One thing had become clear: in the dissensions of the Macedonian chiefs the native element was not a negligible quantity. It was largely owing to the support of natives that Docimus had overthrown Archon.[1] To this fact Seleucus was no more blind than Antigonus or Ptolemy or Pithon in the case of their respective provinces. The one point told us as to his first period of rule is that "he bore himself honourably towards all men, evoking the good-will of the people, and preparing long beforehand partizans to help him, should he ever get an opportunity of striking for power."[2]

Can we form any idea of Babylon, as it appeared in the last days of its greatness, when Seleucus reigned as satrap in the palace of Nebuchadnezzar?

Babylon had many features in common with London—if we can think of London under an Oriental sun—its size, its industrial ferment, its great brick wharves with a *babel* of foreign seamen.[3] It lay on either side of a river, a flat city of brick (so much more prosaic than a city of stone), with straight streets and houses three or four stories tall.[4] Unlike London, it was protected by a system of enormous walls from an invader. The whole province of Babylonia in the first place was shut off from Mesopotamia by the "Median Wall," which ran across the neck of land between the Euphrates and Tigris, 20 feet broad and 100 high, according to Xenophon.[5] Coming down the left bank of the Euphrates, one passed through it by the "Babylonian Gates,"[6] out of the Mesopotamian desert into the rich fields of Babylonia.[7] Dominant in this expanse, the mighty circumvallations and towers of Babylon soon showed themselves. In the days of Nebuchadnezzar the city had lain in a square tract enclosed by an outer and an inner wall, known respectively as Nimitti-Bel ("Foundation of Bel") and Imgur-Bel ("May Bel show mercy"). But

---

[1] See p. 38.   [2] Diod. xix. 91, 2.

[3] Babel, the Hebrew form of Bab-ilu, the city of the confusion of tongues.

[4] Hdt. i. 180, 3.

[5] *Anab.* ii. 4, 12. This wall is probably identical with the Σεμιράμιδος διατείχισμα of Strabo (ii. 80; xi. 529).

[6] Steph. Byz. Χαρμάνδη.   [7] Xen. *Anab.* i. 5.

under the Persians the outer wall had been breached and suffered to fall into decay; Imgur-Bel was still standing when Mazaeus delivered up the city to Alexander.[1] Its compass is given by the Greeks as 360 stadia,[2] or $38\frac{1}{2}$ miles; its height as 50 cubits, or about 75 feet,[3] and its breadth as 32 feet, so that two chariots of four horses could pass each other upon it. All the space within this immense barricade of brick, over 90 square miles, was not taken up by building. It embraced royal hunting grounds and pleasances, and even tracts of corn-land, which might make the city independent, if need should be, of external supplies.[4]

The flatness of the city had been redeemed under the Babylonian kings by artificial erections. The Babylonian plain-dwellers delighted above all things in gigantic towers. Their temples took this form; their citadels were not nature's work, but piles of brick; in the famous "Hanging Gardens" art had striven to reproduce by a series of ascending terraces, supported on arches and covered above with mould, the aspect of a mountain with all its romantic caverns and waving trees [5] —the work of one of the old kings, tradition asserted, whose queen had come from a land of hills. Another great pile was the palace on the right bank of the river—a city in itself, shut off from the common gaze by a wall of its own, and connected with the tower-temple called E-sagila. This inner "Royal City" was doubtless one of the two "citadels" which are spoken of in the days of Seleucus.[6] Where the other citadel is to be placed is more questionable. But there is a strong presumption that, since we hear in the story of Alexander's last days of two "palaces," the other citadel is the same as the other palace. And this is borne out by the description of Diodorus, who says (following Ctesias) that the

---

[1] Abydenus, frag. 8, *F.H.G.* iv. p. 283.

[2] Diod. ii. 7, 3. Curtius says 365 (v. 1, 26); the MSS. in Strabo xvi. 738 give 385, but this is generally supposed to be a copyist's error.

[3] Curt. v. 1, 26; Strabo xvi. 738. Diod. (ii. 7, 4), following Ctesias, says *fathoms*, not feet, but that is only the sort of inept mendacity one expects in Ctesias.

[4] Curt. v. 1, 26 f.; Arr. *Anab.* vii. 25.

[5] Diod. ii. 10; Curt. v. 1, 32 f.; Strabo xvi. 738; Berosus, frag. 14 (*F.H.G.* ii. p. 507); Abydenus, frag. 8 (*F.H.G.* iv. p. 284).

[6] Diod. xix. 100, 7; Plutarch, *Dem.* 7.

two palaces were built in order that from them the sovereign might "overlook the whole city, and hold the keys of its points of vantage."[1] Now the local relation of the two palaces is fixed beyond mistake. They lay over against each other on opposite banks of the Euphrates,[2] joined, according to one account, by a tunnel which ran under the river.[3] Each of these palaces was fenced off from the city of the people, one of them by as many as three walls. They rose, these walls, the second above the first, and the inmost above the second, their faces of brick variegated with hunting scenes in bright enamels, and above all the copper roofs under a Babylonian sun crowned the Royal City with a crown of fire.[4] It was in one of these palaces that Alexander was stricken with his mortal sickness; in the other he died.[5]

Below these palace-citadels the city of the common people spread on either side of the river. Although the days were long past when the Babylonians had borne rule in Asia, and history, concerned almost entirely with courts and wars, has little to say about them, the Babylonian people and the Babylonian civilization existed still. The cities which had been cities when Ecbatana and Persepolis, when Athens and Pella were not, were still hives of busy life. In Babylon itself, in Barsip (Greek Borsippa), Erech, Sippar, the old life went on and the old industries were plied. All over the Mediterranean lands, in the temples and houses of the new rulers of the world, might be seen splendid fabrics, covered with strange beasts and fantastic branchwork, upon which brown hands in the cities of the Euphrates had laboured after an immemorial tradition.[6] Borsippa hummed with a multitude of looms which turned the flax of the Babylonian plains into

---

[1] Diod. ii. 8, 3.

[2] Diod. *loc. cit.*; Arr. *Anab.* vii. 25; Plutarch, *Alex.* 76.

[3] Cf. Philostr. *Vit. Apoll.* i. 25.

[4] Diod. *loc. cit.*; Philostr. *loc. cit.*; Berosus, frag. 14; cf. Perrot et Chipiez, *L'art dans l'antiquité*, ii. p. 703 f.; Delitzsch, *Babylon* (Leipzig, 1901).

[5] The objection which might be raised to the view just given is that while the mound called El Kasr certainly represents the palace on the eastern bank, there is no corresponding mound on the western. But the river appears here to have changed its course towards the west, and thus obliterated the traces of the other palace.

[6] See the references on p. 242.

linen cloth for the merchantmen.[1] The old formalities of law and business were observed; those stamped clay tablets which record transactions done under Macedonian kings are of the same type as those made under Nebuchadnezzar.

The old gods, although they could no more give their people the lordship of the nations, had not ceased to be served with sacrifice and prayer. The learned and priestly caste—Chaldaeans the Greeks called them—continued to hand down the ancient lore—theology, mythology, astrology, magic—and to write in the cuneiform character. Schools of them seem to have been connected with some of the great temples; we hear of such in Borsippa, Erech and Sippar.[2] How far the Babylonian (Semitic) language remained in popular use cannot be exactly known. It had, to a large extent at any rate, been supplanted by Aramaïc, the *lingua franca* of Western Asia. For legal and priestly documents the old language and character were employed as late as the last century before Christ.[3]

Babylon had a bad name for its moral atmosphere. There was all the vice inseparable from a great city, made more rank by the absence of national or civic enthusiasms, by an enervating climate, by an abundance of the means of luxury. There in the warm nights, while eye and ear were allured by flame-lit colours and artful music, sensuality put on its most seductive glamour. The lascivious city threatened to engulf the northern soldiery of Alexander like an evil morass.[4]

Seleucus reaped the fruit in 312 which he had sown during his first administration. Babylon received him back with open arms. As we saw, he had soon brought the neighbouring Susiana also under his authority, and after conquering the East was satrap of Babylonia no longer, but King. From 312 for 175 years Babylonia and Susiana were under the house of Seleucus. We still have only fragmentary information of the Hellenic rule in this quarter.

Babylonia and Susiana[5] continued to be two satrapies.

---

[1] Strabo xvi. 739.   [2] Strabo xvi. 739; Plin. *N.H.* vi. § 123.
[3] Schrader, *Zeitschr. d. deut. morg. Gesell.* xxiii. (1869), p. 371; Nöldeke, *Die semit. Sprachen*, p. 41 f.; Gutbrod, *Zeitschr. f. Assyr.* vi. (1891), p. 26.
[4] Curt. v. 1, 6; Plutarch, *Apophth.* Ξέρξου, 2.   [5] See Appendix P.

The extent of Babylonia is, so far as I know, quite uncertain. In the district between the rivers it was, of course, divided from Mesopotamia by the desert, and the actual frontier was perhaps the Median Wall. But on the east of the Tigris lay a long strip of land from Susiana in the south to Armenia in the north—the country of the Assyrians—and it is nowhere said in our authorities under what government it was placed. From the fact, however, that Babylonia as a geographical term is sometimes found to include this country, it may be inferred as probable that the satrap of Babylonia had under him Assyria east of the Tigris as well.[1] This strip of land is sometimes called Parapotamia, and it had perhaps by 218 a separate *strategos* from Babylonia.[2]

To the south of Babylonia the region next to the sea appears to have been detached before the time of Antiochus III as a separate province, called after the "Red Sea" (*i.e.* the Persian Gulf).[3] This seems to be identical with the region which we find later called Mesene (in Syriac Maisân).[4]

There was one respect in which Seleucid rule left a conspicuous and lasting impress upon the country — the destruction of Babylon. Sennacherib had razed it to the soil, and it had risen again to new glory. Cyrus and Alexander had conquered it, and it was still the capital of the world. But Seleucus Nicator brought its doom upon Babylon at last. It had subsisted, we have seen, through all changes of empire owing to a prerogative which was founded upon natural conditions. But the prerogative belonged to the land rather than the particular city. It was a natural necessity that there should be in this alluvial region a great centre of human life, and if Babylon were merely dispersed, as by Sennacherib, the human swarm again

---

[1] In Strabo xvi. 745 Adiabene is τῆς Βαβυλωνίας μέρος. See *Pauly-Wissowa*, art. "Babylonia."

[2] Polyb. v. 69, 5; cf. 48, 16. There is some doubt, owing to the suspicion of a confusion in the latter passage, and to the fact that the name of Parapotamia was applied to other districts, Strabo xvi. 753.

[3] Πυθιάδην τὸν τῆς Ἐρυθρᾶς Θαλάσσης (ἔπαρχον), Polyb. v. 46, 7; cf. 48, 13; 54, 12.

[4] Numenium ab Antiocho rege Mesenae propositum, Plin. vi. § 152. See Saint Martin, *Recherches sur l'histoire et la géographie de la Mesène et de la Characène* (1838); E. Schwartz in Kern's *Inschrift. v. Magnesia* (1900), p. 171.

gathered. There was only one way by which Babylon could really be undone—by the creation of another centre. This was what Seleucus did. Forty miles north of Babylon, on the Tigris, about fifteen miles below Baghdad, Seleucus marked the foundations of a new city, Seleucia-on-the-Tigris. It was a favourable position for commanding the traffic of both rivers, for it was here that the space between the rivers narrows to twenty-five miles. It was a better "focus of continental trade" than a city on the Euphrates.[1] From this moment Babylon was doomed.

The legend of the founding of Seleucia, as narrated by Appian,[2] represents the wise men of Babylon as being conscious of all that the marking out of the new walls meant for them. When they were required by King Seleucus to fix the lucky day and hour for beginning to build, they purposely gave him a wrong time. Only when the lucky moment came, a sudden inspiration thrilled through the Greek and Macedonian troops, so that with one accord and in disregard of the royal heralds they flung themselves upon the work. Then the wise men saw the finger of God. "O King, there is neither man nor city that can change the thing decreed. Even as men, cities have their hour and their appointed end."

Seleucia, chosen for the capital of the eastern half of the Empire, grew apace. It was soon what Babylon had been, one of the largest cities of the world. The estimate of its *free* population, preserved in Pliny, made how soon after its founding we do not know, is 600,000.[3] Elements from all quarters must have entered into the human mass which jostled in its streets. Its prevailing tone, no doubt, was Greek; in later times, under barbarian rule, it prided itself on keeping the Hellenic tradition.[4] But the native population of old Babylon, no doubt, were driven or drifted into the new city.[5] In a way, therefore, what Seleucus did was less to destroy Babylon than transfer it to another site. It was usual, as Strabo observes, to

---

[1] Hogarth, *The Nearer East* (1902), p. 261.
[2] *Syr.* 58.   [3] Plin. vi. § 122.
[4] "Neque in barbarum corrupta, sed conditoris Seleuci retinens," Tac. *Ann.* vi. 42.   [5] Paus. i. 16, 3.

describe a man of Seleucia as a "Babylonian."[1] Perhaps no city has left so little memory of itself in proportion to its size and consequence as Seleucia. Babylon and Baghdad are both familiar names to our ears with great associations, but to how many people does Seleucia mean anything? So little trace is left of those great multitudes, akin in civilization to ourselves, who for centuries lived and worked beside the Tigris.[2]

As to the political constitution of Seleucia, some people called *Adeiganes* are mentioned, who are taken to be a magisterial body of some sort. If so, it is significant that their title is not Greek.[3] But Seleucia, as a royal capital, had its autonomy openly curtailed by its being put under an *epistates*,[4] and watched by a garrison. The *strategos* of the province (Babylonia) sometimes holds the office of *epistates* of the city as well. Democrates the son of Byttacus is *strategos*, *epistates* of the city, and commander of the garrison all at once. But the inscription which mentions him proves at any rate that Seleucia could, as a city, pass honorary decrees.[5]

---

[1] Strabo xvi. 743. It seems that a similar usage is found under the Sassanians: by "Babylon" was understood Ctesiphon, Winckler, *Altor. Forsch.* 2te Reihe, iii. p. 529.

[2] Winckler, *Altor. Forsch.* 2te Reihe, iii. (1901), p. 509, should be consulted. With much that appears to me doubtful conjecture, it is made probable that Opis, the great town on the lower Tigris in Assyrian and Persian days, was near the site of Seleucia, so that the new foundation of Seleucus absorbed this old city as well as Babylon.

[3] Polyb. v. 54, 10. A suggested derivation is from the Aramaic *dîn* with the article prefixed (Pauly-Wissowa), or the word is explained as equivalent to the Persian "*dihkane*" (Saint Martin). But the single reference to them in Polybius does not make it certain that they were *magistrates* at all; one might equally conclude from that passage that they were a *political party*.

[4] Polyb. v. 48, 12.

[5] Ἡ πόλις
Δημοκράτην Βυττάκου
τὸν στρατηγὸν καὶ ἐπιστά-
την τῆς πόλεως, τεταγμέ-
νον δὲ καὶ ἐπὶ τῶν ἀκρο-
φυλακίων καλοκαγαθίας
ἕνεκεν.

Haussoullier, *Rev. d. Philol.* xxiv. (1900), p. 332. [It is to be noticed that U. Köhler questions the Babylonian origin of this inscription. He thinks that it was put up by Antioch-on-the-Orontes under Antiochus IV, "*Zwei Inschriften aus der Zeit Antiochos IV*," reprinted from *Sitzungsb. Berl.* 1900.]

And while Seleucia grew, the old Babylon decayed. The famous walls, slowly crumbling, enclosed deserted, crumbling streets. Only in the midst of the desolation the huge temples still rose, and societies of priests clustered about them, performing the ancient rites and cultivating the traditional wisdom.[1] The policy of Alexander in honouring the gods of the nations was followed by Seleucus and his house. In March 268 Antiochus I laid the foundation for the rebuilding of the temple of Nebo at Borsippa. His inscription proclaims: "I am Antiochus, the Great King, the Mighty King, the King of the armies, the King of Babylon, the King of the lands, the restorer of the E-sagila and E-zida, the princely son of Seleucus, the Macedonian King, the King of Babylon."[2]

It was not Seleucia only which displayed in this quarter the colonizing activity of the new rulers. There were the Alexandrias founded by Alexander near the coast (*i.e.* in Mesene). There was an Apamea also in Mesene.[3] The Assyrian country east of the Tigris got its complement of new foundations. Opposite Seleucia was Ctesiphon, under the Seleucid kings apparently only a place of cantonments,[4] but destined to be refounded by the Arsacids as their chief city. Sittace is described by Pliny as of Greek origin, but we hear of Sittace in Xenophon as a great city,[5] so that it was only a case of Hellenization. In the same region as Sittace (Sittacene) was an Antioch and an Apamea,[6] Apollonia, Artemita, and perhaps a Laodicea.[7] A Seleucia-on-Hedyphon,[8] a Seleucia-on-the-Red-Sea, and a Seleucia-on-the-Eulaeus[9] are also mentioned.

---

[1] Strabo xvi. 739; Paus. i. 16, 3; viii. 33, 3.

[2] *Keilscriftl. Biblioth.* iii. 2, 136 f.

[3] Droysen ii. p. 745; *Pauly-Wissowa*, i. p. 2664; Schwartz in Kern's *Inschr. v. Magnesia*, p. 171. [4] Polyb. v. 45, 4.

[5] Plin. vi. § 132; Xen. *Anab.* ii. 4, 13.

[6] Plin. vi. § 132; Schwartz, *loc. cit.*

[7] The region was sometimes called Apolloniatis instead of Sittacene, Strabo xv. 732; Polyb. v. 43 f.; Isidore, 2. This Apollonia is mentioned in Steph. Byz., and is perhaps intended in App. *Syr.* 57. Artemita, which took the place of an old native town, Chalasar, seems to have become the chief city of the district, Strabo xi. 519; xvi. 744; Plin. vi. § 117.

[8] Strabo xvi. 744; Plin. vi. § 135.

[9] Kern, *Inschr. v. Magnesia*, No. 61. Are these two last Seleucias the Alexandrias renamed?

The Greeks of Babylonia seem to have contributed their proportion of great names to Hellenic literature and science. Diogenes of Seleucia, called "the Babylonian" (about 243-155) listened to Chrysippus, and became in time head of the Stoic school.[1] Apollodorus of Artemita was in Strabo's time the great authority for Parthian history.[2] But what is above all interesting is to see the ancient Babylonian mind caught in the movement of new ideas and exercising itself in the field of Hellenic culture. Berosus, the priest of Bel, aspires to the distinction of a Greek historian, and writes the fables and the history of his race for these Western people to read, encouraged by the grace of King Antiochus I. From the work of Berosus almost all that was known of Babylonian history, till the inscriptions were found and deciphered, was ultimately derived.[3] There is another figure of peculiar interest in this connexion. A native of lower Babylonia, of the region near the sea, he is drawn to the great centre of Seleucia, takes the Macedonian name Seleucus, and goes deep into the mathematical science of the Greeks. His writings were given to the world about the middle of the second century B.C.; they were still known to Strabo and Plutarch. They seem to have been indeed of a high scientific order. Not only did he advance true views about tides, but he set about proving that the earth and the planets really go about the sun. The Babylonian, quickened by contact with Hellenism, anticipates Copernicus.[4]

While the Babylonians were drawn to the light of Hellenism, the Greeks on their part were sensible of that fascination which the darkness of the ancient East has often had for the children of light. Alexander paid attention to the counsels of Babylonian magic; so did his successors. When Alexander fell ill, a number of the Macedonian chiefs, among them Seleucus, consulted a Babylonian oracle.[5] Antigonus changes his mind at once on a warning from the "Chaldaeans."[6] Seleucus, as we saw, is represented by the legend as applying to the Babylonian wise men to fix the lucky hour for his city's foundation. Throughout the later epoch of classical paganism

---

[1] Susemihl, *Gesch. d. griech. Lit.* i. p. 82.
[2] Susemihl, ii. p. 385.   [3] *Ibid.* i. p. 605.
[4] *Ibid.* i. p. 763.   [5] Arr. *Anab.* vii. 26.   [6] Diod. xix. 55, 7.

the roving Babylonian enjoyed great prestige as a diviner. Such men were found, no doubt, in all the great Greek cities, muttering strange words and magical formulae under the patronage of rich women, very much as the Indian *guru* may get a circle of curious listeners in the drawing-rooms of Europe and America to-day.

CHAPTER XIII

IRÂN

THE plains of the Euphrates and Tigris are bounded on the east by the long mountain walls which, one behind the other, fence the tableland of Irân. This name, of course, belongs to an ethnological, rather than a physical, demarcation of the earth —the country possessed by Irânian man. And in this sense Irân embraces more than the tableland; it includes the mountainous country which forms a bridge between the tableland and the Pamir; it includes also the regions to the north of the bridge as far as the Jaxartes (Syr-daria); to use modern political divisions, it includes, besides the kingdom of Persia, which coincides with the tableland, the principalities of Afghanistan and Bokhara. Within this region, in the dim centuries which precede recorded time, a peculiar national type had shaped itself as distinctive as that of the kindred Indians farther east, or as that of the Semitic kingdoms on the west. Into this old Irân, when the tribal organization of society had not yet been overlaid by an imperial system after the Assyrian model, we can get barely a glimpse. The Greek historians and Old Testament writers, to whom well-nigh everything we know of the Median and Persian Empires is due, show us almost exclusively the Irânian monarch in his relation to the foreign peoples dwelling west of Irân, his subjects, his enemies, or his allies; they show us the Achaemenian court established for the most part outside Irân on the ground of those older monarchies which it imitated, in Babylon, or in Susa; beyond the court, into Irân itself, into the land and the life, in which the Achaemenian house had its roots, they give us little insight.

The Irânian people, before Deïoces[1] the Mede built an Empire, were split into a number of small princedoms and clan chieftainships. Their necks had not been bent under the yoke of a Great King. They stood in very much the same stage of social development as Macedonia up to the days of Philip, or as the mediaeval princedoms of Europe. We see in all of these an aristocracy of great houses, of chiefs ruling by virtue of blood and inherited authority in the tribe, the clan, or the family.[2] The typical Persian nobleman was known for his magnificent airs. His manner of life was very like that of his Macedonian counterpart. He had the same passion for dogs and horses, for hunting and the profession of arms. He had the same love of wine and night-long wassails, although he combined this with a great capacity for abstinence, where need was, in forced marches through the starved regions of Irân.[3] Lying was the cardinal sin, and the chaffering of the market-place he held a thing with which only lower breeds of men would have to do.[4] But to till the ground in ancestral fashion and tend flocks and herds was labour honourable and well-pleasing to God.[5]

None of these qualities are, however, very distinctive. Most warlike aristocracies are proud in bearing, devoted to sport and good company, and contemptuous of trade. To find the distinctive expression of the old Irânian spirit we must turn to the Zoroastrian religion. It is certainly impossible to determine how far the actual religion of Achaemenian days conformed to the true Zoroastrian type. The royal houses of Media and Persia, as we can gather from some of the proper names in use, from the fact that the Achaemenian kings worship Ahuramazda as the One Creator, were professed Zoroastrians. But certain salient differences appear between their practice and what was, later on at any rate, held orthodox —their custom of *burial*, for instance. In the worship of the

---

[1] Dayaukku is not a proper name, but = "lord of the district (Gaugraf)." Tiele.   [2] Spiegel, *Eranische Alt.* ii. p. 237 f.
[3] Xen. *Cyrop.* viii. 8, 11.   [4] Hdt. i. 153.
[5] Justi, in Geiger's *Grundriss der iran. Philol.* vol. ii. p. 395 f.

clan deities we may see a survival of old pre-Zoroastrian heathenism, in the cult of Anahita the adulteration of the Faith through foreign influences. But even if we cannot infer that this or that prescript of Zoroastrianism was observed in the Persia of Darius Codomannus, the Avesta sheds a flood of light on the fundamental religious conceptions, on the peculiar religious temperament of old Irân. And we are led, I think, to place it high in the scale. The earliest form of Zoroastrianism to which we can get back is practically monotheistic. And not only is God one God—the Egyptians and Indians spoke sometimes of the One in a pantheistic sense —Ahuramazda is a Person, a strongly moral Person. He differs altogether from the old non-moral nature gods whom even the ordinary Greek still worshipped, and equally so from the non-moral abstractions into which the old nature-gods became resolved by the speculative thought of Greek and Indian philosophers. And with such a God, the attitude of the Irânian to the world and its ways formed a strange contrast to that which we loosely talk of as "Oriental," to the attitude of his Indian kinsman, for instance. The material world was not a vain process, a burden from which the wise man would, as far as possible, withdraw himself; it was that which Ahuramazda created good, though the wicked spirits were now doing their best to spoil it. We speak of the "brooding East"; the religion of Zarathushtra was above all things a religion of honest work. Its supreme object was that "the Cow" (*i.e.* agriculture generally) should no longer, through the craft of lying spirits, suffer neglect. It is true that the piety required by Ahuramazda was to some extent narrow and formal, that no voice in old Irân proclaimed, "Bring no more vain oblations; incense is an abomination unto me; your new moons and your appointed feasts my soul hateth." But it is also true that in the Zoroastrian conception of God and His service we, who have derived our thoughts of God from Jerusalem, find something strangely responsive.[1]

Two centuries of empire made indeed a great difference in the aristocracy of Irân. The Persian nobles who fought against Alexander were very unlike the rude highland chiefs who had

[1] Tiele, *Geschichte der Religion im Altertum* (Gotha, 1895), vol. ii.

gathered round the standard of Cyrus. The good things of the world, the riches and refinements of great industrial cities, the precious wares of India and Ionia, had not been laid open to their fathers in vain. Even in the time of Cyrus the Persians had discarded their primitive kilts for flowing robes, such as the Medes had already borrowed from Assyria,[1] for the purples of Tyre, and the rainbow embroideries of Babylon. Their inbred passion for carousing and hunting was gratified in artificial modes on a magnificent scale. A Persian banquet became to the Greeks the type of extravagant luxury. All Asia was ransacked to furnish the table of the Great King.[2] Armies of cooks, confectioners, and butlers waited on a Persian nobleman.[3] His banqueting hall must be richly hung, and blaze with gold and silver plate.[4] The couches must be overlaid with gold and spread with costly fabrics. In fact, the art of spreading couches was brought to such nice perfection that to satisfy the Persian sense required a special training, and when the King made a present of valuable carpets to Greek visitors, the couch-spreader was an indispensable adjunct.[5] So too with the Persian love of hunting. Huge parks were now enclosed, stocked with all manner of game, for his diversion—a declension, it seemed to the fine instinct of the sportsman Xenophon, from the true spirit of the field, " like slaying beasts chained up."[6] Horse-breeding was passionately studied, and horses, in the estimation of a Persian, among the most honourable presents he could give or receive.[7] The Indian hounds kept, in the time of Herodotus, by the satrap of Babylon were so numerous that their maintenance was the sole charge laid upon four substantial villages.[8]

And yet, sumptuous as the Irânian nobility had grown in its style of living, much of the old spirit survived. There was still a social code which prompted the Persian baron to adventure himself hardily in battle and to close with great beasts. The fresher spirits of the Greek world,

---

[1] Xen. *Cyrop.* viii. 1, 40 ; 3, 1 ; Diod. ii. 6, 6.
[2] Xen. *Ages.* 9, 3 ; Strabo xv. 735.   [3] Xen. *Cyrop.* viii. 2, 5 f.
[4] Xen. *Cyrop.* viii. 8, 15 f. ; Strabo xv. 734 ; Hdt. ix. 80.
[5] Plutarch, *Pelop.* 30 ; *Artax.* 22.
[6] *Cyrop.* i. 4, 11.   [7] *Anab.* i. 2, 27 ; *Cyrop.* viii. 2, 8.
[8] Hdt. i. 192.

men like Xenophon and Alexander, found much in the better type of Persians to admire. There was indeed such a fundamental resemblance between the tastes and ideals of the Macedonian and Irânian aristocracy as to naturally create a kind of fellow-feeling. And the struggle which brought Macedonian and Persian into close contact led, as we know, in the case of Alexander himself, and those of his *entourage* who were in sympathy with him, to a generous eagerness to make friends. It is no part of Alexander's policy in the latter years of his life to depose the Irânian race from its position as the ruling race of Asia. He aspired to make of Irânian and Macedonian and Hellene one people. Device after device is put forth in order to promote their fusion—intermarriage, association in the army, transportation in the mass. When his schemes are cut short by his death, the situation in Irân is one of counterpoise. Some of the satraps are natives, some are Macedonian. A Hellenic element has been introduced by the planting of new cities; in the villages, no doubt, and along the country-side the authority of the old families is still cherished.

The great geographical divisions into which Irân, according to the usage prevalent at the time of the Macedonian conquest, fell were twelve: two on the west and south-west of the central desert—(1) Media (Mâda) and (2) Persis (Pârsa, mod. Fârs); two to the north and north-east of it, (3) Hyrcania (Varkâna) and (4) Parthia (Parthava); on the east of the desert, adjoining the mountain country which connects Irân with Central Asia, came (5) Arīa (Haraiva) and (6) Drangiana (Zaranka); the mountain-country itself fell into the two divisions of (7) Paropanisidai on the north, including the Cophen (Kabul) valley, and (8) Arachosia on the south; the region which sloped down, north of the Paropanisidai, to the Oxus formed (9) Bactria (Bâkhtrish, mod. Balkh); the country between the Oxus and Jaxartes (10) Sogdiana (Suguda, mod. Sughd); and, lastly, along the south of the Irânian plateau lay (11) Gedrosia and (12) Carmania (mod. Kirmân). The number of administrative provinces or satrapies which these twelve regions constituted varied naturally according to the convenience of the hour. At Alexander's death we can probably make out eight: Parthia and Hyrcania were under one satrap, so were Aria and Drangiana, Arachosia and Gedrosia, Bactria and Sogdiana.

Of the rule of Alexander's successors in this part of the world we know even less than of their rule in Syria. The native tradition, as it was gathered in later centuries under Mohammedan rule, had forgotten even the names of the kings who ruled Irân between Iskander and the Sassanians. We can discern the work of the Seleucid house only in the Greek cities which here also are shown us by the geographers. But we can gather further from the history that this Greek element was an extremely important political factor in Irân.

Media, as has been said, was the most important of the Irânian provinces. Alexander had put in a native nobleman as satrap, controlling him by the presence of Macedonian commanders. At his death this arrangement was changed by the chiefs in Babylon. Media was now divided into two satrapies. The principal part of it, from Persis northward as far as the river Amardus (mod. Kizil Uzen), containing Ecbatana and Rhagae, its two most illustrious cities, was made over, as we saw, to Pithon the son of Crateuas. The northernmost part, the country at the corner of the Irânian plateau, about Lake Urumiya, was divided off as "Lesser Media" and left in the hands of Atropates, the satrap appointed by Alexander.

Lesser Media is a lovely "Alpine" land, belonging by its character to Armenia almost as much as to the Irânian plateau. By the action of the chiefs it was abandoned more or less to native government. Atropates was the father of a dynasty, and the country came to be called *Atropatene* after him, a name which still cleaves to it in the form Âdharbaijân, although Atropates and his house have long been forgotten there. It is a holy land in Zoroastrian tradition. When Kai-Khosrū, the legend ran, destroyed an idol-temple in the land, the divine fire, Âdar-Gushasp, played about his person—an occasion commemorated by the great temple of Adar-Gushasp upon Mount Asnavanta (mod. Savelan). There were other religious centres in the land, Vesaspe (mod. Ardebil), called after the heavenly Being worshipped there, and the great fire-temple, Âdaraklish, at Gazaca (mod. Takht-i-Sulaimân), the capital of Atropatene, and, according to one tradition, the birthplace of Zoroaster.

Whether this prestige of Atropatene is due to the dynasty of Atropates, or whether it is of earlier date, has not, as far as I know, been determined.

In the other part of Media, "Greater Media," the work of Hellenization was prosecuted vigorously. The hills, indeed, were left to the warlike Kurdish tribes who inhabited them. It was, in fact, their neighbourhood which led Alexander and his successors to protect civilization in these parts by multiplying new foundations, although the hill-tribes, it must be remembered, did not only appear to the kings as a menace, but as a valuable element to be incorporated in their own armies.[1] The case of the Greek cities of Media shows with peculiar force how unsafe it is in this department to be guided by the fulness with which our fragmentary authorities inform us of any matter in estimating the real proportions of things. It is not possible to gather more than the names of one or two cities. And yet Polybius expressly tells us that "Media was covered with Greek cities after the plan prescribed by Alexander, to form a defence against the neighbouring barbarians."[2] Whether Ecbatana received a Greek colony is doubtful. Polybius makes it an exception, but he may mean no more than that it was not a *new* foundation of the Macedonians. Pliny says that "King Seleucus built it."[3] The magnificent cedar palace of the Achaemenians, covering over twenty-five acres with its colonnades, was left standing, and was an occasional residence of the Seleucid kings.[4] Rhagae (mod. Rhei), the older capital of Media, is distinctly said by Strabo to have been refounded by Seleucus Nicator as a Greek city, and given the name of Europus—his own birthplace.[5] Appar-

---

[1] Just in the same way the Gauls in Asia Minor were regarded both as the most valuable mercenaries and, when left to themselves, the greatest menace to order and civilization. But the free fighting tribes in Asia have always appeared in this double light to the rulers of the lands. It is exactly the same in the case of the tribes of the North-West frontier in India to-day. They enrol themselves under the British standards or raid the British dominions with equal readiness.

[2] Polyb. x. 27, 3.   [3] Plin. vi. § 43.   [4] Strabo xi. 524.

[5] Strabo xi. 524. Droysen (ii. p. 749) questions Strabo's identification of Rhagae, Europus, and Arsacia. The old Median city, the Greek, and the Parthian one may have been locally distinct and yet near enough to be sometimes regarded as one.

ently near Rhagae was the Heraclea founded by Alexander, and restored by Antiochus (the First, presumably) with the new name or surname of Achaïs.[1] We hear further of a Laodicea[2] and an Apamea Rhagiana.[3]

The course of things in the province which adjoined Media on the south-east, *Persis*, where lay the seats of that part of the Irânian race which had so long held the supremacy, and the royal burg in which the Achaemenian kings had been at home, is involved in complete darkness during the rule of the Seleucid house. That the national or tribal feeling was strong in these valleys we may see by the case of Peucestas, who found it good policy to adopt the guise of a Persian when satrap, and the bold declaration of the native nobleman in the council of Antigonus, that if Peucestas were deposed no other Macedonian governor would be accepted. And that this feeling continued under Seleucid dominion we may see by the fact that as soon as the authority of that house weakens, the country is found under the government of native princes. The work of the Seleucids can be discerned only in the frontier city of Laodicea, founded by Antiochus,[4] the Antioch-in-Persis of which we know by a decree which its citizens once passed in their *ekklesia*,[5] the Stasis, "on a huge rock," which again is connected with the name of Antiochus I[6] and, if we can argue from its Greek name, Methone.[7] At some time or other a revolt seems to have broken out among these soldier-colonists ($\kappa \acute{a} \tau o \iota \kappa o \iota$) in Persis, like the revolt among the Bactrian Greeks after Alexander's death. The stratagem is described by which Oborzus, apparently a Persian employed by the Seleucid government, had 3000 of them put to the sword.[8]

On the north the Irânian plateau is fenced by the high

---

[1] Plin. vi. § 48; Solin. 48; Amm. Marc. xxiii. 6. 39.
[2] Strabo xi. 524; Steph. Byz.; Eustath. ap. Dion. Perieg. 918.
[3] Plin. vi. § 43; Strabo xi. 524.   [4] Plin. vi. § 115.
[5] Kern, *Inschr. v. Magnesia*, No. 61.   [6] Steph. Byz.   [7] *Ibid.*
[9] Polyaen. vii. 40. The only reason for putting this incident under the Seleucid kingdom is its resemblance to the preceding story of Siles and the 3000 Persians. It *may*, however, refer to the time when native princes ruled in Persis, and it would be in favour of this supposition that the rebels are colonists and the suppressor of the revolt an Irânian.

line of the Elburz range from the Caspian. Along the southern, that is, the interior, face of this range runs a narrow belt of habitable country which forms the connexion between Western and Eastern Irân. Here the province of Media adjoined *Parthia*, the country which included the easternmost part of the belt just named as well as the mountains which bend southwards in a sort of crescent from the Elburz to meet the mountains of Aria. It corresponded with the modern Khorassan, or the northern part of it. It is a country of which the greater part is barren—sterile ranges bordering the great desert, but with tracts here and there in the valleys of extreme fertility. Such was the region of Nisa—one of the places cited as especially blessed in the Zoroastrian scriptures, in which an Alexandropolis is mentioned by Pliny as having been founded by Alexander.[1] Hecatompylus, the capital of the province, owed its name, according to Polybius,[2] to the roads from all quarters which here converged; in a land where the lines of communication are so restricted the centre of a road-system is all the more important. That such a point, therefore,[3] should have been secured by the Macedonian kings is a matter of course. And indeed we find Hecatompylus reckoned among the foundations of Seleucus Nicator.[4] The only other Greek city in Parthia whose name has come down to us is Calliope, likewise founded, according to Appian, by the first Seleucus.[5] It must have been on the extreme west of the province, since it is said by Pliny to have been at one time a frontier fortress against the Medes.[6]

Closely connected in the administrative system with Parthia was the country on the northern side of the Elburz range along the southern shore of the Caspian, *Hyrcania* (mod.

---

[1] Plin. vi. § 113. See Tomaschek (*Pauly-Wissowa*, i. p. 1408).

[2] x. 28, 7.

[3] The modern Shah-rûd is supposed to correspond in site to Hecatompylus.

[4] App. *Syr.* 57; cf. Curt. vi. 2, 15, "Hecatompylos condita a Graecis."

[5] App. *Syr.* 57; cf. Steph. Byz.

[6] Plin. vi. 15, § 44. Droysen conjectures that this refers to the frontier between the Arsacid kingdom and the realm of Atropates. It may equally refer to the older time of the Median Empire. That the Greek name Calliope was given because the original native name had a somewhat similar sound, as Brunnhofer asserts, is possible, but by no means "without any doubt" (*Irân und Turan*, p. 41).

Mâzanderân). Physically, no contrast could be greater than that between the regions to the north and those to the south of the Elburz. Instead of the arid terraces of the Parthian side, the Hyrcanian slopes, receiving moisture from the Caspian, are clothed with rank forest. The sea-board at their feet has an almost Italian character. The exuberant fertility of the country is described by Strabo.[1] Its inhabitants were perhaps of another stock than the Irânians, and the hills were tenanted here, as elsewhere, by unruly tribes, Mardi and Tapyri. Several "considerable cities" (πόλεις ἀξιόλογοι) are mentioned by Strabo as being in Hyrcania, and as the names are native, we may perhaps infer that the fertility of the country had favoured the growth of larger communities even before the Macedonian conquest. The chief place at the time of Alexander is Zadracarta (probably where the modern Asterabad stands). Polybius in the time of Antiochus III speaks of Sirynca as the seat of government (βασίλειον),[2] and Strabo uses the same expression of Tape.[3] Whether these are different names of the same place is impossible to say. Of Greek towns in this region, although such must needs have existed, in view of the country's richness and the interest taken by Seleucus and his son in the navigation of the Caspian, we have no names given us except that of Eumenea.[4] It is noticeable, however, that there was a community of resident Greeks at Sirynca in 209.[5]

Hyrcania and Parthia, by the system which obtained at the death of Alexander, were under a single satrap, a native, who was replaced by the Macedonian Philip in 321.[6] This was the man whom Pithon killed in 318 in order to put in his own brother Eudamus. Eudamus was almost immediately ejected by the confederate satraps, and after the triumph of Antigonus in 316 the province seems to have been annexed

---

[1] xi. 508.   [2] Polyb. x. 31, 6.   [3] Strabo xi. 508.
[4] Steph. Byz.   [5] See vol. ii. p. 20.
[6] Justin (xiii. 4, 23) says: "Parthos Philippus, Hyrcanos Phraphernes (sortitur)." If this is not a mere confusion of the partition of Babylon with that of Triparadisus, it suggests that at the time of Philip's appointment the native satrap was allowed to retain Hyrcania, just as Atropates kept Lesser Media when the Greater Media passed to Pithon.

to Bactria, and to have formed part of the governorship of Stasanor.[1] A few years later it passed with the rest of the East to Seleucus.

The eastern half of the Irânian upland consists, as we have said, not of a central desert surrounded by mountains, but of a mountain mass pushed out from Central Asia. The backbone of this mass is formed by the Paropanisus (Hindû-Kush), and round about it are the provinces fed by the rivers which it sends down. On the west of it, adjoining Parthia, was the province which drew its life and its name from the river Arius (mod. Harê-Rûd), the province of *Aria* (old Pers. Haraiva).[2] The name bears witness to the grateful contrast of its well-watered valleys with the neighbouring desolation of mountain and desert. It was a land of vineyards, among the six blessed regions of the Vendîdâd. Here Alexander began the work of colonization by planting an Alexandria, and the old capital Articoana was rebuilt in more splendid fashion by Antiochus I.[3] From Alexandria-of-the-Arians two important roads diverged. One ran round the north side of the mountain mass to Bactria, the other went south to Drangiana, and thence reached India by way of Alexandria Arachōtōn (Kandahar).[4] Alexandria Ariōn was thus a station through which all traffic between Western Irân and the lands farther east must almost

---

[1] This seems to be the best interpretation of Justin xli. 4, 1. "Post mortem Alexandri . . . nullo Macedonum dignante, Parthorum imperium Stagnori, externo socio, traditur." In xiii. 4, 23, professing to give the partition of Babylon, Justin says, according to our present text, "Sogdianos Sulceus Stagnor." Stasanor was of Soli in Cyprus (Strabo xiv. 683), and "Sulceus" should no doubt be "Soleus." He was transferred *at Triparadisus* from Aria to the governorship of Bactria and Sogdiana. By the partition of Babylon he had been left in command of Aria. Justin, confounding the two partitions, reduplicates Stasanor, giving him Aria under his proper name, and Sogdiana under the corruption "Stagnor."

[2] It is perhaps unnecessary to say that the name of the province Aria has nothing to do with Arayana, mod. Irân, Greek 'Αριανή, the name of the whole plateau. [To be strictly accurate, I should have written Îrân.]

[3] Plin. vi. § 93. "Artacabene" is obviously only another way of writing the same Persian name which is represented by "Artacoana." That Pliny gives both as two distinct towns is nothing against this, since his perspicacity often does not reach to detecting identity under slight variations of form in his different authorities. A few lines below, for instance, we find Drangae and Zarangae mentioned separately.

[4] Strabo xi. 514 ; xv. 723.

necessarily pass, a knot where the great lateral lines of the world's communications were drawn together.[1]

Two other Greek cities are found in Aria bearing witness to the activity of the Seleucid government, Achaïa, whose founder Achaeus[2] was no doubt the general and father-in-law of Seleucus II, or an elder Achaeus of the same family,[3] and Sotira, called probably after Antiochus I Soter.[4] The Charis mentioned by Appian[5] must also have been either in Parthia or here.

Two regions geographically distinct from the valley of the Arius seem to have been included in the satrapy as it was marked out under Alexander and his successors. Somewhat east of the Arius, another river, the Margus (mod. Murghâb), comes down from the mountains and flows out into the desert parallel with the Arius, where it meets with the like fate, perishing in the sand. But it does not disappear before it has created in mid-desert the oasis which the ancients called *Margiana* and the moderns call Merv. Under careful irrigation this spot was turned into a paradise. It also was among the blessed lands of the Vendîdâd. "Report affirms," said Strabo, "that vines are often found whose stock it takes two men to compass, with clusters two cubits long."[6] To balance its advantages, the oasis was by its position more than ordinarily exposed to be ravaged by the nomads of the desert. The

---

[1] Artacoana and Alexandria are obviously not *identical* in Pliny, or the passage of Strabo, where he writes πόλεις δὲ 'Αρτακάηνα καὶ 'Αλεξάνδρεια καὶ 'Αχαΐα (xi. 516). But they may have been close together, perhaps on opposite banks of the river, and commonly spoken of together as Alexandria. It is otherwise difficult to see how it should come about that Alexandria should be the great place on the high-road, and yet Artacoana "multo pulchrius sicut antiquius" and of larger extent. It must be remembered that the question of the identity of a new city in the East with one it replaces is often an ambiguous one, since the new city may be even at a considerable distance from the old, and yet called by the same name. According to Tomaschek (*Pauly-Wissowa* 'Artakoana') Artacoana corresponded with the *citadel* of the modern Herat, and Alexandria with the *lower town*. [2] Strabo xi. 516.

[3] This city tends to prove the existence of an *elder* Achaeus, which there is reason on other grounds to suppose (see p. 202), since a Seleucid foundation in this region must have preceded the Parthian revolt (250). Of course, if Appian is right in assigning the foundation of Achaïa to the time of Seleucus Nicator, the elder Achaeus is a necessity.

[4] App. *Syr.* 57; Ptolem. vi. 17, 7; Amm. Marc. xxxiii. 6, 69.
[5] App. *Syr.* 57. [6] Strabo xi. 516.

Alexandria placed here by Alexander was actually overwhelmed within a few years of its foundation.[1] The city rose again under the hand of Antiochus I as an Antioch, "Antioch-in-the-waters,"[2] standing among its network of canals. Its new founder took the precaution of surrounding the whole oasis with a wall, 1500 *stadia* long (about 173 miles).[3] Thenceforward Merv, under various masters, Macedonian, Parthian, Mohammedan, maintained its contest with the children of the desert. These in the long run got the better of every wall. Century after century the swarms broke upon it, till at the coming of the Russians the other day it was found little better than a heap of desolations.[4]

The other region attached to Aria lay to the south of it. The rivers on the southern slopes of the Afghan country tend south-westerly, and find their ultimate meeting-place in the swampy basin of Seistân, where they form a lake of varying extent. This lake, which is now called Hamûn, was known to the old Irânians as Daraya, the "Sea," in the eastern dialect Zaraya, and the people who dwelt about it were called Daranka or Zaranka, the dialectical variation giving rise to the two Greek names of Drangai and Zarangai (in Herodotus Σαράγγεες). The chief city of *Drangiana* became already under Alexander a Greek colony,[5] with the name Prophthasia, which at once commemorated the discovery of the plot of Philotas and rendered something of the sound of the native name, written by Stephen of Byzantium as Phrada. It was the principal station on the road to India between Alexandria of the Arians (Herat), and Alexandria of the Arachosians (Kandahar).[6]

Aria, together with Drangiana, and presumably Margiana, had at Alexander's death Stasanor, a Cypriot of Soli, for governor. By the partition of Triparadisus, when Stasanor was transferred to Bactria, his place in Aria was taken by another Cypriot, Stasander. This man appears among the confederate satraps who were beaten by Antigonus in 316, and in

---

[1] Plin. vi. § 47.
[2] Ἀντιόχεια ἡ καλουμένη ἔνυδρος (MS. ἄνυδρος), Isidor. 14.   [3] Strabo xi. 516.
[4] There was perhaps another Greek city, a Seleucia, higher up the Murghâb, where it issues from the mountains. Droysen ii. p. 673.
[5] Plutarch, *De fort. Alex.* 5.   [6] Strabo xi. 514; xv. 723.

the case of Aria, Antigonus was able after his victory to make a change of satrap in his own interest. The province, being next to Parthia on the main road east and west, was perhaps more accessible than Carmania and Bactria. Nominees of Antigonus, first Euitus and then Euagoras,[1] replaced Stasander. Whether Seleucus found Euagoras still installed in Alexandria-Arion when he brought the province under his authority we do not know.

On the east of Drangiana came *Arachosia*. The Erymanthus (Haitumant, mod. Hilmend) perhaps constituted the frontier for part of its course.[2] Arachosia, corresponding to the southern part of modern Afghanistan, is a land of mountain ranges running south-west from the watershed, which divides the tributaries of the Kabul and the Hilmend. On its eastern sides the valleys run steep down to the Indus. Its inhabitants, like their descendants, the Afghans of to-day, formed a connecting link between the pure Irânians and the races of India.[3] They called themselves, as the Afghans do now, Pakhtûn (Pushtoo: Πάκτυες, Herodotus). The Greek name Arachosia, in use after Alexander, was taken from the main eastern tributary of the Hilmend, the river *Harahvati*, which the Greeks called Arachotus (mod. Argandâb). Here, too, the hand of Alexander was busy. Kandahar was once undoubtedly an Alexandria. Through Alexandria of the Arachosians, the capital of the province, went the great road to India.[4]

We know of only one satrap of Arachosia between the death of Alexander and the rise of Seleucus, Sibyrtius. He was among the confederate satraps, but having conspired to supplant Eumenes, he was accused before the army and barely escaped with his life. Antigonus naturally looked upon him as an ally, and restored him to his province in 316. Megasthenes, the historian of India, had resided at the court of Sibyrtius before he was employed as the ambassador of King Seleucus to the Indian king.[5]

Not only Arachosia, but the country to the south as far

---

[1] Diod. xix. 48, 2.
[2] It is assigned sometimes to Drangiana (Arr. *Anab.* iv. 6, 6; cf. iii. 27, 4; Ptol. vi. 19, 4), sometimes to Arachosia (Polyb. xi. 34).
[3] They were called "White Indians," Isid. 10.
[4] See Appendix Q. [5] Arr. *Anab.* v. 6, 1.

as the sea, belonged to the province of Sibyrtius. This country consisted of *Gedrosia* (Beluchistan) and the coast, inhabited by races different from those of the interior. The Irânian plateau falls to the sea in wastes of shifting sand. Although Gedrosia has its habitable valleys and its caravan routes, "in which one can always rely after a day's march, at least, on a well of brackish water and a little fodder for the camels,"[1] in an area of 100,000 miles there are less than 500,000 inhabitants. The prevalence of desert all along the sea-board from the Indus to the Persian Gulf diverted commerce to other roads. Gedrosia seems, therefore, to have been an unknown land to the Greeks before Alexander. Herodotus calls the people of this part of the world Parikanioi, a Greek form of the Persian term, which described them as "worshippers of the Pairikâ," the unclean spirits of the desert. After Alexander the Greeks called them Gedrōsoi, a name of unknown origin and meaning. They were of another stock, probably, than the Irânians. The Beluchis, who now inhabit the land, do belong to the Irânian family, but they represent a drifting of the Irânian race eastwards in later centuries. There is, however, a people of darker skin, the Brahui, who live alongside of the Beluchis in the land, and these are supposed to be the remnant of the ancient Gedrosians. Their affinity is with the black Dravidian peoples of India. An extension of the Aryan civilization of India to this country in ancient times is indicated (if it is safe to build anything upon a proper name) by the name of the chief city of the Gedrosians, Pûra, which seems to be good Sanskrit for "city."

But whilst Gedrosia was of little consequence for land traffic, the coast formed part of the maritime high-road between India and the West. It was inhabited by different peoples again from the Gedrosians, Arbies and Oritae, belonging, like the Gedrosians, to the Indian group,[2] and west of these, in what is now called the Mekrân, people whom the

[1] Reclus, *Geograph. Univ.* ix. p. 119.
[2] According to Arr. *Ind.* 25, the dress and weapons of the Oritae were Indian, but their language and customs not. Of course no very great weight can be attached to what the ancients state with regard to linguistic or ethnographical affinities.

Greeks described simply as Ichthyophagoi, Fish-eaters—a race of squalid beings living in huts by the shore and catching the fish in which that sea is peculiarly rich. The intense interest taken by Alexander in the sea-route to India could not fail to stir his activity in this region also as a city-builder. But here, too, the scattered notices of the ancients do not make clear how many cities were founded by Alexander and his captains, or even satisfy us to which of the landmarks of to-day the names they use refer. Rambacia, the principal village of the Oritae, was transformed into a city by Hephaestion on Alexander's direction, a city for which Alexander divined a great future;[1] an Alexandria rose on the coast near a place of good harbourage;[2] Nearchus founded a city at the mouth of the river Arbis;[3] but whether all these passages as well as the statement of Curtius[4] refer to one city, or to several, is debatable.[5] Distinct, at any rate, must be the Alexandria in Macarene (Mekrân), near the river Maxates (Mashkid).[6]

The mountain-mass of Afghanistan north of Arachosia is cloven from its centre down to the Indus by the valley of the river Kabul. This valley must always be important as the main way of entrance from the west into India, its door being familiar to English ears as the Khaibar pass. By it Alexander entered, and the highway of traffic under the Macedonian kings struck north from Kandahar (Alexandria) across the hills to Kabul, instead of following the directer, but more difficult tracks by the valleys of the Bolan or the Gumal.[7] From Kabul (the ancient name is written by the Greeks as Ortospana) a road ran down the valley to the Khaibar. Another great road entered the Kabul valley from the north, from Balkh, making by its junction with the Kandahar-Kabul-Khaibar road the "Three-ways from Bactra" (ἡ ἐκ Βάκτρων τρίοδος). The importance of holding strongly this country north of the Kabul valley, the Paropanisus (old Persian, Paruparanisana; mod.

---

[1] Arr. *Anab.* vi. 21.   [2] Diod. xvii. 104, 8.
[3] This is following Detlefsen's text of Plin. vi. § 97, "Haec tamen digna memoratu produntur: Arbis (MSS. abhis or abies) oppidum a Nearcho conditum in navigatione et (MS. omit 'et' or read 'ea') flumen Arbim (MSS. 'nabrum' or 'nabrim') navium capax."
[4] ix. 10, 7.   [5] See Appendix R.   [6] Steph. Byz.
[7] Strabo xi. 514; xiv. 723.

Hindû-Kush), with its passes commanding the communication between the Kabul valley and Bactria, led to its being constituted a separate satrapy, described as that of the *Paropanisidai*.[1] At the death of Alexander the satrap was Oxyartes, the father of Roxane; he continued to hold his place through the partitions both of Babylon and of Triparadisus, and was even unmolested by Antigonus in 316, although he had sent troops to the confederate army. It is after this that the cloud comes down upon the East, in which the conquests of Seleucus Nicator are involved.

Here, too, as in Beluchistan, the people of Irânian stock (Afghans), who are the ruling race to-day, are late-comers. At the time of Alexander the population of the Kabul valley was Indian, Gandara; the hills, of course, were then as now held by fierce fighting tribes, who gave Alexander considerable trouble on his way to India. It was their neighbourhood, like that of the Kurds in Media, which led presumably to the multiplication of new foundations, which we seem to discern in the Paropanisus. The chief of these, Alexandria-on-the-Caucasus,[2] seems to have stood in one of the side valleys leading up from the Kabul to the passes into Bactria.[3] In the old Buddhist books Alasandâ is spoken of as the chief city of the Yonas (Ionians, Greeks).[4] The other cities mentioned[5] are Cartana, afterwards called Tetragonis,[6] Cadrusi,[7] and Asterusia, a settlement of Cretans, called after the Cretan mountain.[8]

---

[1] That the satrapy of the Paropanisidai did not extend south of the Kabul, this river being apparently the frontier between it and Arachosia, is indicated by the expression of Arrian (*Anab.* iv. 22, 5); σατράπην δὲ Τυριάσπην κατέστησε τῆς τε χώρας τῆς Παραπαμισαδῶν καὶ τῆς ἄλλης ἔστε ἐπὶ τὸν Κωφῆνα ποταμόν.

[2] The companions of Alexander identified the Hindû-Kush with the Caucasus.

[3] Fifty miles from Ortospana (Kabul) according to Plin. vi. § 61. There are no data to fix its site. The principal conjectures are Bamian (Ritter), the neighbourhood of Charikar and Ghorband (Wilson, Droysen, Kaerst), Parwân (Tomaschek). Tomaschek (*Pauly-Wissowa*, i. p. 1389) seems to make a mistake in saying that Strabo puts *Alexandria* at the τρίοδος.

[4] Mahâvança, chap. 29, p. 171.

[5] In Diod. xvii. 83 the readings vary between ἄλλας πόλεις and ἄλλην πόλιν.

[6] Plin. vi. § 92. Tomaschek (*Pauly-Wissowa*, i. p. 1389) conjectures that Gariana should be read for Cartana, as a Gariana is named in this region by the Arab geographers.

[7] "Oppidum ab Alexandro conditum," Plin. *ib.*   [8] Steph. Byz.

North of the Hindû-Kush lay the last region towards the wildernesses of Central Asia, in which the Irânian man had, till the coming of the Greeks, borne rule. Beyond was the outer darkness of Turanian barbarism. So long as the great rivers, the Oxus (Amu-daryâ) and Jaxartes (Syr-daryâ), are accompanied by offshoots of the mountain mass whence they take their rise, the country about them can nourish a settled population. This land of hills between the sand-wastes on the west and the mountains on the east formed the two outlying provinces of *Bactria* and *Sogdiana*, Bactria being in fact the lower slopes of the Hindû-Kush towards the Oxus, and Sogdiana the country between the two rivers.

In both these provinces the ruling race at any rate was Irânian. They formed not only a genuine part of Irân, but a most illustrious part. According to one view here were the oldest seats of the Irânian civilization. The Zoroastrian religion had perhaps its cradle in this region; at any rate its stronghold was here. Nowhere else did the Irânians offer so desperate a resistance to Alexander. Again and again cities like Cyrescheta on the Jaxartes rose in rebellion. Intersected, too, as the country was by spurs of the lofty ranges to the south and east, it furnished the great lords like Oxyartes with castles lodged high on precipitous crags where they could long defy the Macedonian. The two provinces were similar in their physical character and their population. In Sogdiana there seems, as one might expect to have been the case, some infusion of Turanian elements. Under the Achaemenian kings their governor was commonly a son of the Great King, or a prince of the blood-royal. Even so the great resources of the country and its outlying position had tempted the rulers of Bactria and Sogdiana to revolt from the central authority on almost every opportunity. The case was not altered when a Seleucid was substituted for an Achaemenian king.

Bactria (the northern part of the principality of Afghanistan), although it contains some barren tracts, and the lowlands by the river have a bad name for malaria, is on the whole singularly favoured by nature. Strabo describes it as producing everything, except the olive, and quotes Apollodorus of Artemita, who called it the "pride of all Irân" ($πρόσχημα$

τῆς συμπάσης Ἀριανῆς).[1] Its eastern end, the modern Badakshan, is rich in minerals, in rubies, and lapis lazuli. But its special fame has in all times rested upon its breed of horses. In the old Indian epics we hear of the "Turanian," (*i.e.* the Bactrian) steeds, and to-day the horses of Andkhoi are a name in Asia.[2] The ancient capital Zariaspa itself recalls by its name (açpa, a horse) the prominent place of the horse in Bactrian life. And it was not only from its own soil that Bactria drew its wealth. It was well placed for commerce, one of the countries binding India to the West. For besides the road we have seen, skirting the southern side of the mountains of Afghanistan and reaching the Kabul valley by way of Kandahar, there was an alternative road from Alexandria-Ariōn (Herat) by way of Bactria and the passes of the Hindû-Kush.[3]

The country on the other side of the Oxus, included under the name Sogdiana, is divided into three strips by the double range of mountains sent through it lengthwise from the mass of Central Asia. The southern strip slopes down to the Oxus, and coincides with the modern Bokhara, the northern to the Jaxartes, and between these lie the parallel ranges, making a sort of trough down which the river Polytimetus (mod. Zarafshan) flows toward the desert, where it disappears. This middle district, the valley of the Polytimetus, is the most fertile of the province. Here was the capital Maracanda, destined, as Samarkand, to bear the finest flower of Mohammedan learning.

In these two provinces, so important from their resources and their character as frontier provinces against the Scythians, and yet so difficult to hold because of their remoteness and the proud spirit of their inhabitants, Alexander established masses of Greeks. Strabo[4] gives the number of cities as eight, Justin[5] as twelve. But the most striking figures are those of the army formed by these colonists, when after Alexander's death they attempted to return—more than 20,000 infantry and 3000 horse.[6] The names of most of the new cities are

---
[1] Strabo xi. 516.
[2] Five hundred horses are included in the annual tribute sent to the Amir of Afghanistan from Badakshan.
[3] Strabo xi. 514 ; xv. 723.   [4] xi. 517.   [5] xii. 5, 13.
[6] Diod. xviii. 7, 2.

no longer recoverable. We know of an Alexandria Eschate on the Jaxartes (mod. Khojend) looking across the river into the illimitable wilderness[1]—the last outlying station of Hellenism, in whose market-place, in the centuries after Alexander, the Greek trader from the West saw the Indian caravans which had come across the snowy ridges of the Tian-shan mountains, bringing the new substance of silk and stories of the great cities of the Silk-people, which lay in some distant world far away to the east. We hear also of an Alexandria Oxiana,[2] of an Alexandria-by-Bactra (κατὰ Βάκτρα),[3] of perhaps another Alexandria Eschate on the upper Oxus towards the Pamir,[4] and of an Antioch in Scythia.[5] Lastly, the capital of the southern province, Zariaspa, or, as the Greeks called it, Bactra, was in all probability occupied by Greek colonists even before a separate Greek kingdom came to exist in this quarter, when indeed Bactra was a royal capital,[6] fortified so strongly as to make its siege by Antiochus III one of the great sieges of the age.[7]

At the death of Alexander a certain Philip is over both Bactria and Sogdiana. The experiment of leaving the farther province under a native satrap had not succeeded, and since the first revolt of the Greek colonists in 325 Philip had governed both provinces. By the partition of Triparadisus (321), Stasanor, the Cypriot of Soli, was transferred from Aria to Bactria and Sogdiana. It may well have been that a governor *who was a Greek*, not a Macedonian, was more likely to manage the restive Greek colonists. In fact we are told expressly that in 316 Antigonus did not dare to disturb Stasanor; "it was not easy to depose him by a letter, as he had dealt adroitly with the natives, and he would have many friends to fight in his cause."[8] It has been noticed[9] that the "one piece of information on record as to the way in which

---

[1] Arr. *Anab.* iv. 1, 3; Plin. vi. § 49. Cf. Ptol. i. 11, 7.

[2] Ptol. vi. 12, 6. It is identified by Tomaschek (*Pauly-Wissowa*, i. p. 1389) with Beikend or Nakhsheb in Bokhara. [3] Steph. Byz.

[4] Ptol. vi. 12, 6; viii. 23, 14. It is possible that Ptolemy means the city ordinarily called Alexandria Eschate on the Jaxartes. [5] Steph. Byz.

[6] On the identity of Zariaspa and Bactra see Kaerst, *Gesch. d. hellenist. Zeitalt.* i. p. 345, note 4. [7] Polyb. xxix. 12, 8.

[8] Diod. xix. 48. [9] Gutschmid, *Irân*, p. 23.

Seleucus Nicator came into possession of the Upper Satrapies is that he subdued the Bactrians by force of arms."[1]

We have still one province of Irân to speak of, that which lies on the south side of the plateau between Persis and Gedrosia, the province of *Carmania*, corresponding with the modern Kirmân and Laristân. The description of Carmania closely coincides with that of Bactria. It is a land of hills and rivers. Here, too, everything prospered, according to Strabo, except the olive. It was famed for its noble trees, and a sort of vine with immense clusters. Here, too, was much mineral wealth, river-gold, and mines of silver, of copper, and vermilion.[2] The division between Carmania and Persis was probably an artificial one; the physical character of the two regions is similar; the Carmanians did not differ sensibly from the Persians of Persis, except that they maintained less impaired the fighting qualities of their ancestors.[3] The only Greek town which we know of for certain in Carmania is an Alexandria.[4] Harmuza, the port, whose name was to become famous in the markets of the world,[5] was perhaps a foundation of the Greeks; at any rate it would seem that Nearchus found no settlement here in 325.[6] Carmania, as has been remarked, was not on the principal line of traffic between east and west, which went along the north of the Irânian plateau. It remained undisturbed by the political convulsions which followed Alexander's death. The satrap appointed by Alexander in 325, Tlepolemus, continued to hold his position till the cloud comes down upon the East after the departure of Antigonus in 316. Tlepolemus had taken part, indeed, with Eumenes and the confederate satraps, but he also, like Stasanor, had rooted his position too well in his province for Antigonus to overthrow him by a letter from Persepolis.

---

[1] Principio Babylona cepit; inde auctis ex victoria viribus Bactrianos expugnavit, Just. xv. 4, 11.

[2] Strabo xv. 726.

[3] The name Carmania seems to have been coined by the Greeks from the name of the chief town, Carmana; the native name for the Carmanians was Jûtija.

[4] Plin. vi. § 107. Identified by Tomaschek (*Pauly-Wissowa*, i. p. 1390) with the modern Gulashgird.

[5] As Hormuz. "The wealth of *Ormus* or of Ind," Milton. [6] Arr. *Ind.* 33.

Such fragments can still be made out of that system of Greek cities with which Irân, like Syria and Babylonia, was overspread by Alexander and his first successors. Besides the name of Alexander himself, two others recur among the founders, those of Seleucus Nicator and his son, the first Antiochus. It may not be mere chance that while Alexander appears as founder over the whole tract, Seleucus and Antiochus (except in the case of Antioch in Scythia) do not leave traces east of Merv and Herat. That the further provinces were under their authority is of course unquestionable, but their main activity as founders was perhaps in Media, Parthia, and Aria. It is impossible to draw a line between the foundations of Seleucus and those of Antiochus. The activity of Antiochus in Irân belonged, no doubt, in great measure to the time when he reigned in the East as viceroy, and his acts might be indifferently ascribed to himself or to the father whom he represented.

Of the elements of which the population of the new cities was composed we have some sparse indications. It is noteworthy that in some of the foundations of Alexander a body of natives is said to have been incorporated with those Greek or Macedonian soldiers who were to give the city its Hellenic character. In the case of Alexandria Eschate we are told that the population was composed (1) of a body of Greek mercenaries (settled, no doubt, by compulsion); (2) of all the natives who voluntarily associated themselves in the new city; (3) of the Macedonian veterans who were past service.[1] The population of the city or cities near Alexandria-on-the-Caucasus consisted of (1) 7000 natives; (2) 3000 of the camp followers, and (3) all the Greek mercenaries who wished to join.[2] So too we are told of the city founded among the Oritae that a body of Arachosians were settled there.[3] That the Hellenic character, however, continued in the case of these cities to be dominant may be inferred from the way in which Alexandria-on-the-Caucasus is referred to, as we saw in the Buddhist books, as a city of the Ionians. The European colonists were, of course, either Macedonians or Greek mercenaries—the latter therefore, no doubt, of those Greek races in the main which

---

[1] Arr. *Anab.* iv. 4, 1.
[2] Diod. xvii. 83, 2.
[3] Curtius ix. 10, 7.

sent out most soldiers of fortune, Cretans, Arcadians, Aetolians, and so on, or men of the Thessalian horse,[1] or, thirdly, they belonged to some of those less civilized nations of the Balkan peninsula, Thracians and Illyrians, which furnished contingents to the Macedonian king.[2] It was not for the first time in these cities that a Greek population and a barbarian coalesced.[3]

An extremely interesting document in this connexion is the decree passed by Antioch-in-Persis, which a stone found in Asia Minor has preserved for us. It is dated by the eponymous magistrate of the year, who in this city is the priest of the deceased Seleucid kings and the reigning kings, Antiochus III and his son Antiochus, and shows the normal forms of the Greek city-state, a *boule* and an *ekklesia*, a γραμματεὺς τῆς βουλῆς, who introduces the decree in the popular assembly, and πρυτάνεις, who put it to the vote. The occasion is a request sent by Magnesia-on-the-Meander to the cities of the eastern provinces to recognize as a festival of Panhellenic standing that celebrated by Magnesia in honour of Artemis Leucophryene. To this Antioch gives a cordial answer, and praises Magnesia for its zeal in Hellenism and its loyalty to the Seleucid King. It also recalls the old ties of kinship between the Greeks of Antioch-in-Persis and the Greeks of Magnesia, and in so doing throws light upon the procedure of colonization. The city of Antioch was called after Antiochus I Soter; whether it was his own foundation or an earlier colony renamed we do not know; but Antiochus at any rate was concerned to increase it by a fresh body of colonists. To do this he makes an appeal to Magnesia-on-the-Meander (and others, presumably, of the Greek cities of the west) to send out some of their citizens. It is a matter which touches the glory of Hellenism, and the Magnesians respond by sending out men "adequate in number and distinguished for virtue," who go to reproduce the Hellenic

---

[1] A settlement of Cretans we saw in the Hindû-Kush. The leader of the Greek insurgents in Bactria was an Aenianian, Diod. xviii. 7, 2.

[2] The Thracians of the eastern colonies (Θρᾷκες ἐκ τῶν ἄνω κατοικιῶν) are mentioned, Diod. xix. 27, 5.

[3] See Strabo iii. 160. He is speaking of the city Emporium in Spain, where this had happened in the old days. τῷ χρόνῳ δ' εἰς ταὐτὸ πολίτευμα συνῆλθον μικτόν τι ἔκ τε βαρβάρων καὶ Ἑλληνικῶν νομίμων, ὅπερ καὶ ἐπ' ἄλλων πολλῶν συνέβη.

life among the hills of Irân.¹ And locked within those hills, we cannot doubt, are many similar decrees, awaiting the modern European excavator to reveal the European civilization which once flourished there.

Once, then, in its long past has Irân—including regions which to-day are a shut-up land to Europeans—been for a brief space under "western" rule. And it is striking to observe how the ancient world was as conscious of the essential difference between this rule and the spirit of Oriental government as we are in our own time. Then also it was the characteristic of the western rulers that they must be carrying things forward, curious to discover the nature and conditions of the country under their hands, restless to develop and improve. "Considerate management" ($\epsilon\pi\iota\mu\acute{\epsilon}\lambda\epsilon\iota\alpha$) was what the countries got from them, and could not get from Asiatic kings. In speaking of Hyrcania and the Caspian, Strabo describes their undeveloped resources. The considerate management has here been lacking. "And the reason is that the rulers have here always been barbarian (*i.e.* non-Hellenic), Medians, Persians, and, last and worst of all, Parthians." In this long history the period of Macedonian rule was a momentary taste of better things, but too brief, and spoilt by the continual wars.²

We may then probably think of the reigns of Seleucus Nicator and Antiochus Soter as a period when a new spirit of inquiry and enterprise was active in Irân. Obscured as those days are for us, we have seen some indications of that activity in the building of cities and such works as the great wall of Merv. We have further evidence of it in the work of exploration and research connected with the two names of Patrocles and Demodamas. Already under Alexander the best information as to the measurements and local conditions of the Empire had been collected by qualified agents and laid up in the royal archives. This valuable body of documents was in time handed

[1] Kern, *Inschr. v. Magnesia*, No. 61.
[2] Strabo xi. 509. Cf. the expressions of Isocrates, anticipating the Macedonian conquest of the East, ἢν γὰρ ταῦτα πράττῃς, ἅπαντές σοι χάριν ἕξουσιν, οἱ μὲν Ἕλληνες ὑπὲρ ὧν ἂν εὖ πάσχωσι . . ., τὸ δὲ τῶν ἄλλων γένος (*i.e.* the Orientals), ἢν διὰ σὲ βαρβαρικῆς δεσποτείας ἀπαλλαγέντες Ἑλληνικῆς ἐπιμελείας τύχωσιν, *Philip.* 154.

over by Xenocles, Alexander's treasurer, to Patrocles, the minister of Seleucus.¹ Patrocles carried the work further. We have already seen this man taking a prominent part in the affairs of the kingdom. At one time he held a command in the eastern provinces,² when he was commissioned to explore the coasts of the Caspian, and report on the possibility of a northern waterway to India. The development of trade-routes was a main concern of the Hellenic kings. Alexander had ordered the exploration of the Caspian shortly before his death with this end.³ An exploration, imperfect indeed and obviously provisional, was actually carried out by Patrocles. Patrocles seems to have made two voyages from some port at the south-west extremity of the sea, one in which he proceeded as far north as the mouth of the Cyrus (mod. Kur), another in which he sailed up the east side of the Caspian to some point impossible to determine with certainty. He embodied the result of these voyages in a book, a *Periplus*, which was thenceforward the standard authority for these regions. Strabo speaks of Patrocles with great respect, of his trustworthiness and knowledge of scientific geography, and contrasts his sober report with the fabulous stories of Megasthenes and Deïmachus.⁴ The curious thing is that this authority, so conscientious and intelligent, should have fixed for generations the error that the Caspian *did* communicate with the ocean, and that it was possible to sail that way to India.⁵

While Patrocles explored the Caspian, his contemporary, Demodamas of Miletus, was employed by Seleucus or Antiochus to investigate the course of the Jaxartes. As in the case of

---

[1] Strabo ii. 69.

[2] ὁ τῶν τόπων ἡγησάμενος τούτων Πατροκλῆς, Strabo ii. 74. He is called "praefectus classis" in Plin. vi. § 58.

[3] Arr. *Anab.* vii. 16, 1.   [4] Strabo ii. 68, 70.

[5] Müller, *F.H.G.* ii. p. 442 f.; Neumann, *Hermes* xix. (1884), p. 165 f.; Susemihl, *Gesch. der griech. Lit. in d. Alex.* i. p. 657 f.; W. W. Tarn, *Journ. of Hell. Stud.* xxi. (1901), p. 10 f. The subject of the voyages and theories of Patrocles will be found fully discussed in the learned and valuable article last mentioned. Mr. Tarn holds that Patrocles only asserted a connexion between the Caspian and the Aral, and that the geographers misunderstood him. In spite, however, of his arguments, it seems to me rash to correct the geographers in this way, seeing that they had the work of Patrocles before them, and we have not.

the Caspian, commercial interests were no doubt largely the motive of the enterprise. The Jaxartes might be a waterway, connected with a landway from India across Central Asia. That India, at any rate, fell within the purview of Demodamas is suggested by the fact that the one express quotation from his writings refers to a town in India.[1] By the side of the Jaxartes, on the edge of the Scythian waste, Demodamas erected altars to the Didymaean Apollo, the god of his home.[2]

Of a piece with this policy of discovering or opening trade-routes along the north of Irân is the intention which is ascribed to Seleucus Nicator at the end of his reign of making a canal between the Caspian and the Black Sea.[3] It may well be[4] that the first voyage of Patrocles to the mouth of the Cyrus had relation to this scheme, and that it was his discoveries which showed its impracticability. But in fact it was not one scheme only, it was the whole system of policy, which collapsed with the Bactrian and Parthian revolts. The exploration of the Caspian was only begun by Patrocles; had Seleucid rule lasted in these regions the work would surely have been completed, but the great Hellenic Empire was broken up before it could bring its vast designs to accomplishment.

The danger from the unsettled peoples beyond the pale—this constituted the main preoccupation of civilized rule in Irân, just as in the West a similar danger was forced upon the attention of the Greek kings in the irruption of the Gauls. The danger in the East confronted the heirs of Seleucus in an ominous form when an independent dynasty established itself, defying their authority, in Parthia. We have very divergent statements as to the rise of this Parthian dynasty; when it became great in the world, its origins gathered round them a

---

[1] "Ἄντισσα, πόλις . . . Ἰνδικῆς, ἣν ἀναγράφει Φίλων καὶ Δημοδάμας ὁ Μιλήσιος, Steph. Byz. (*F.H.G.* ii. p. 444, frag. 2).

[2] Plin. vi. § 49. Haussoullier has recently published a Milesian inscription (*Revue de Philol.* xxiv. 1900, p. 245), in which the proposer of the decree (a decree in honour of Antiochus during his father's lifetime) is Demodamas the son of Aristides. There can be little doubt that this is the explorer of the Jaxartes.

[3] Plin. vi. § 31. The statement is given on the authority of the Emperor Claudius; it cannot be traced farther.

[4] As W. W. Tarn suggests in the article just cited.

halo of mist. Its rise also proceeded gradually, by successive advances, and it was possible, no doubt, for different traditions to take different moments in this process as its true beginning. But certain facts stand out. It was not a revolt of the native Parthians. That province, consisting, as we saw, of sterile mountains, with a few fruitful valleys and plains, could not nourish a large population. Its inhabitants were homogeneous with the other peoples of Irân; they are mentioned in the inscriptions of the Achaemenian kings as one of the peoples of the realm; in the revolt they play, as far as our existing records show us, a merely passive part. The blow is struck by a tribe issued out of the dim wilderness to the north, who seize the Parthian country and reduce the natives to the position of serfs.[1] It was no doubt by continual reinforcement from the north that the power of the invading tribe grew. It consisted of Parni, a division of the people whom the Greeks called Daae, and who ranged the steppes to the east of the Caspian. The Daae are described as a "Scythian" people, but this tells us nothing of their affinities, since the name *Scythian* was applied by the Greeks to all the peoples of Russia and Turan indiscriminately. When they entered the Parthian province and wrested it from the body of the Seleucid Empire, a separate *Parthian* dynasty may be said to begin, in the sense of a dynasty with its basis in that province, but that moment had been led up to both by events in Parthia and by the earlier history of the family which now came to rule there. Parthia itself had showed a tendency before the Scythian irruption to break away from the Empire; at least something of the sort is to be inferred from the coins which Andragoras, the satrap, strikes in his own name.[2] On the other hand the Scythian chief Arsaces[3] seems, before his invasion of Parthia

---

[1] Just. xli. 2, 5 f.

[2] Niese ii. p. 141. Andragoras is a person who presents great difficulties. An Andragoras is said by Justin to have been made governor of Parthia by Alexander, and he is described as a "Persian noble" (xii. 4, 12). We hear no more of this Andragoras. He appears neither in the partition of Babylon in 323, nor in the partition of Triparadisus. But the satrap of Parthia at the time of the Scythian invasion is called in Justin's account Andragoras (xli. 4, 7).

[3] The name is Irânian; so, according to Gutschmid, is the name of the nation Daae and of its tribes, Parni, Xanthii, and Pissuri. We must, therefore, either infer a close kinship between those nomads and the settled Irânians, or suppose

proper, to have established a petty sovereignty in the neighbouring region of Astabene, with his seat at a place called Asaak.[1] The conquest of Parthia did not, apparently, take place till the battle of Ancyra (soon after 240) had crippled the Seleucid power in the West.[2] It was, however, an earlier moment in the history of the dynasty, perhaps that of the establishment of Arsaces at Asaak, or some victory won over the army of a satrap, that the later reckoning fixed upon as the birth-year of the Arsacid power.[3] And this much is at any rate plain, that as the difficulties of the house of Seleucus in the West had not begun with the battle of Ancyra, but for the thirty years preceding it the wars with Egypt and the Gauls drained its strength, its hold upon the East had already begun to relax under Antiochus II, and that the earlier stages in the formation of the Arsacid power go back to his reign.

It is these earlier stages which the later tradition wrapped in an atmosphere of romance, through which it is difficult to detect the truth of things. Beyond the Arsaces who conquered Parthia looms the shadowy figure of another Arsaces, his brother, whose image, as that of the divine founder of the kingdom, all the Parthian drachmae bear;[4] he sits, bow in hand, upon the *omphalos*, from which he has ousted the Seleucid Apollo. Only two years did this first Arsaces reign on the confines of the desert. He was succeeded by his brother, whose personal name was Teridates, but who assumed his

that they had come under Irânian influence strongly enough for their nomenclature to be affected.

[1] Isidor. 11.

[2] "Hic (Arsaces) solitus latrociniis et rapto vivere, accepta opinione Seleucum a Gallis in Asia victum, solutus regis metu, cum praedonum manu Parthos ingressus Andragoran oppressit sublatoque eo imperium gentis invasit," Just. xli. 4, 7. Παρθυαῖοι τῆς ἀποστάσεως τότε ἦρξαν (*i.e.* the time of Seleucus II) ὡς τεταραγμένης τῆς τῶν Σελευκιδῶν ἀρχῆς, App. *Syr.* 65.

[3] The official era in the Arsacid kingdom dated from Olymp. 133, 1 (Eus. i. 207 f.; cf. G. Smith, *Assyrian Discoveries*, p. 389), *i.e.* 248-247 B.C. Justin gives another self-contradictory statement. "A cuius (*i.e.* Nicatoris Seleuci) pronepote Seleuco primum defecere primo Punico bello, L. Manlio Vulsone, M. Atilio Regulo consulibus." These are the consuls of the year 256-255 B.C., and Seleucus II did not come to the throne till 246. It is generally thought that *C.* Atilio should be read for *M.* Atilio, which would make the year 250-249. This would agree with the date Olymp. 132, 3, given by Eus. *Canon.* (Schoene ii. p. 120). [4] Percy Gardner, *Parthian Coinage*, p. 18.

brother's name, Arsaces, on his accession, this becoming thenceforth the royal name of all the dynasty. It was this second Arsaces, Teridates, who conquered Parthia soon after 240.[1]

It may, however, be questioned whether, in the case even of the first shadowy king, Arsaces was a personal name, and not rather adopted deliberately in order to affiliate the new dynasty to the old Achaemenian house. For Arsaces had been the name of Artaxerxes II (Mnemon) before his accession,[2] and we are expressly told that the Arsacid dynasty drew their descent from "the Persian king Artaxerxes."[3] It was the same motive which made the court tradition give five companions to the brothers Arsaces and Teridates in their assault upon the Macedonian power,[4] their enterprise being thus assimilated to the overthrow of the False Smerdis by the Seven.

The story of their rebellion, as we have it in a mutilated form, says that in the reign of Antiochus II they attacked Pherecles, the satrap appointed by the Seleucid government, because he had offered a gross insult to Teridates, the younger of the two brothers, and slew him. Of what province, however, Pherecles was satrap the abstract of Arrian given by Photius does not specify; we may presume he was really eparch or hyparch of the district in which Asaak was situated.[5] That the establishment of the Scythian tribe in this region involved some collision with the Macedonian officers, especially if it maintained itself by marauding, is no doubt true.

About the same time that the house of Arsaces emerged from the wilderness, the provinces of Bactria and Sogdiana ceased to obey the Seleucid King. We have already seen that the new colonies in this region, being mainly composed of Greeks, had shown themselves impatient of Macedonian rule, and a leader who could play upon this national feeling could

---

[1] Arr. *Parth.* frag. 1 (*F.H.G.* iii. p. 586 f.).

[2] ὁ δὲ Ἀρτοξέρξης Ἀρσίκας πρότερον ἐκαλεῖτο, Plutarch, *Artox.* 1.

[3] Syncell. p. 539. Arrian, as represented by Photius, calls the Arsacids τοῦ υἱοῦ Ἀρσάκου τοῦ Φριαπίτου ἀπόγονοι, which the state of our knowledge does not allow us to explain. [4] Arr. *Parth.* frag. 1.

[5] Syncellus, who also professes to be following Arrian, substitutes for Pherecles an Agathocles, ἔπαρχος τῆς Περσίδος. He is probably more correct than Photius in the *title*; the province mentioned is, of course, absurd.

make himself very strong. Diodotus the satrap, probably a Greek like his predecessor Stasanor and his successor Euthydemus, abjured allegiance to his Seleucid master and declared himself an independent king.[1]

We do not know whether the revolt of Diodotus preceded or followed the appearance of Ptolemy III in the eastern provinces,[2] which must have loosened the whole fabric of Seleucid government in that part of the world.[3] Nor do we know what order of things Ptolemy left here on his retirement, except for the statement that he confided the government of the East to his general Xanthippus.[4] If his conquest consisted in little but his obtaining the recognition of his authority from the existing administrators of the country, the Seleucid authority, such as it was, would be quietly re-established so soon as the provincial magnates thought it advisable to regard Seleucus once more as their overlord. In this way the Egyptian conquest would be a mere transitory phase, which, except in weakening the power and prestige of the Seleucid court, would not permanently modify the situation.

This situation, then, as it appears in the early years of Seleucus II, presents three more or less independent powers in the Far East, that of Andragoras in Parthia, of Diodotus in Bactria, and of Arsaces in the region of Astabene. The relations of the three to each other cannot be distinctly made out. Arsaces seems to have been regarded by Diodotus as one would expect the Hellenic ruler of Bactria to regard the marauding chiefs of the wilderness. The fields and villages, no doubt, suffered. The district of Astabene was perhaps one which had been attached to the Bactrian province, and was considered by Diodotus part of his legitimate domain. One account, Strabo tells us, spoke of Arsaces as "a Bactrian,"

---

[1] Strabo xi. 515 (οἱ περὶ Εὐθύδημον is a slip of the pen; cf. τῶν περὶ Διόδοτον a little farther on), Just. xli. 4, 5; Trog. Prol. xli.

[2] See p. 186 f.

[3] It is not expressly said that Ptolemy himself went as far as Bactria, διέβη τὸν Εὐφράτην ποταμόν, καὶ τὴν Μεσοποταμίαν καὶ Βαβυλωνίαν καὶ Σουσιανὴν καὶ Περσίδα καὶ Μηδίαν καὶ τὴν λοιπὴν (γῆν) πᾶσαν ἕως Βακτριανῆς ὑφ' ἑαυτῷ ποιησάμενος κτλ. Michel, No. 1239. If Ptolemy only went personally as far as Seleucia-on-the-Tigris, and there received acknowledgment of his authority from the satraps of the further provinces, the phraseology of the inscription would be justified.

[4] Jerome on Daniel 11.

and asserted his attack on Parthia to have been due to the pressure of the power of Diodotus.[1] The relations of Arsaces to Andragoras are still more problematical. On the one hand, Andragoras is spoken of as holding Parthia against Arsaces and his Scythians till he is swept away by their onset;[2] on the other hand, Justin says elsewhere that from Andragoras, the satrap put over Parthia by Alexander, the "kings of the Parthians" professed to descend.[3]

The conquest of Parthia by Arsaces Teridates made the situation in the East far more grievous for the house of Seleucus. The province was of great importance as the link between western and eastern Irân. And if Andragoras had been semi-independent, the new ruler of the country was not only independent but aggressive, and already styled himself king. He had soon conquered, not only Parthia proper, but Hyrcania, so that his power reached from the interior desert to the Caspian. Seleucus Kallinikos had not long rallied in Syria the broken forces left him by the battle of Ancyra before he set out to win back the East. About this time Diodotus of Bactria died and was succeeded by his son Diodotus II. The Greek ruler of the lands by the Oxus had now to choose whether he would range himself with Seleucus or Arsaces. On either side there was danger: Seleucus would hardly allow a rebel to retain his authority, and the re-establishment of Seleucid rule must probably mean the disappearance of Diodotus; on the other hand, by the Scythian occupation of Parthia, Bactrian Hellenism was cut off from connexion with the Hellenic powers of the West, and left isolated among barbarians. Arsaces feared that Diodotus would make his peace with the Seleucid King, and that he would be attacked on both sides. The elder Diodotus had

[1] Strabo xi. 515. Syncellus himself is probably responsible for the confusion when he makes the first Arsaces and Teridates *satraps of Bactria*, Syncell. p. 539. That Arsaces was first known to the world as the ruler of a district in Bactria may be the truth behind these statements.

[2] Just. xli. 4, 7.

[3] xii. 4, 12. It is perhaps possible that the authority followed by Justin was speaking, not of the Arsacid dynasty, but of *the semi-independent dynasty in Parthia which the Arsacid replaced*. Justin, in his speaking of "the kings of the Parthians," must, of course, have understood the Arsacids. The coins which bear the name of Andragoras do not give him the title of *king*.

been his enemy, but the accession of the son seems to have brought a change of policy. Diodotus II granted the new Scythian power a treaty which left Arsaces at rest as to his eastern frontier.[1]

Seleucus advanced. Before the disciplined armies of Macedonian Syria the barbarian chief thought it the better strategy to vanish into the desert out of which he came. He took refuge in the camping grounds of a tribe whose name is given as Apasiacae.[2] It was the eternal trick by which the arm of Oriental governments is evaded. Whether Seleucus plunged into the waste in pursuit of him we do not know. Some fighting between his army and the Scythian hordes took place, but it can hardly have been the desire of Arsaces to come to close quarters, unless he had got his pursuer in a tight place. In after times the anniversary of some encounter was celebrated in the Parthian kingdom as of the victory which had been "the beginning of liberty."[3] Whether it was in reality a skirmish or a great battle we do not know. No decisive result had been obtained when troubles in the West compelled Seleucus to withdraw.[4] This was equivalent to complete failure. Diodotus, as far as we know, he never reached.

Immediately, of course, that Seleucus was gone, Arsaces reoccupied Parthia, and there was none now to hinder the consolidation of his power. He worked hard at putting the country into a thorough state of defence, organizing his rude Scythians as a regular army and fortifying strongholds. Among the latter Dara in the region of the Apaorteni is especially mentioned.[5] Any new attempt to establish Seleucid

---

[1] Just. xli. 4, 9. It is to be noted that numismatists are sceptical as to the existence of a second Diodotus. Only one portrait appears on the coins. But this does not seem to me very strong evidence.

[2] Strabo xi. 513. [3] Just. xli. 4, 10.

[4] These are ordinarily taken to be the insurrection in Syria fomented by Stratonice. Agatharchides ap. Joseph. c. Apion. i. § 206 = F.H.G. iii. p. 196. This is supposing that ἡ ἀπὸ Βαβυλῶνος στρατεία of that passage is the expedition of Seleucus against Arsaces. Justin (xli. 5, 1) says "Revocato deinde Seleuco novis motibus in Asiam" (i.e. Asia Minor), and would rather point to some developments in the fraternal war.

[5] Just. xli. 5, 2. The name of this region is preserved in the town of Bâvard in Khorassan, the original Irânian name being, according to Brunnhofer (Iran u. Turan, p. 40), Apavarta or Apavorta.

authority in the East was not likely to find the task any easier for the expedition of Seleucus Kallinikos. And with his retirement we leave Irân in obscurity till we follow Antiochus, the son of Seleucus, into the eastern provinces some twenty-five years later.

It remains to ask what traces we have of the relations of the native Irânians to the Hellenic kings. The indications do not point to altogether friendly ones. In Alexander, as in the British rulers of India, the "western" spirit had to deal with practices which are abhorrent to it, and with a great desire in both cases to show extreme tolerance, there are certain limits beyond which the superior civilization has to repress by force. The British have abolished Sati (Suttee); Alexander prohibited the custom, which the extravagant form of Zoroastrianism followed in Bactria prescribed, of exposing persons at the point of death, while still alive, to the sacred dogs.[1] It is perhaps due to this and similar actions on the part of the Greek rulers that we find Alexander appearing in the Zoroastrian tradition in a light which is strangely at variance with his main policy. Alexander, who was concerned above all things to patronize the national cults and conciliate the native priesthoods, here figures as the great enemy of the religion, the destroyer of the sacred books.

Perhaps this conflict between Hellenic humanity and barbarian religion was confined to the east of Irân; but in the west the memories of their former position must have worked in the hearts of Medes and Persians. Of actual revolts we are not told much. Thespias, the native nobleman, threatened Antigonus with one in Persis, under any other satrap than Peucestas.[2] The revolt which broke out in Media after Pithon's removal, although led by the Macedonian and Greek adherents of Pithon and Eumenes, drew in a part of the natives and may have been supported by the national feeling. One, at any rate, of the leaders themselves was a native Mede.[3]

We are told definitely of one revolt among the Persians under the house of Seleucus. Siles, the officer representing

---

[1] Strabo xi. 517. [2] Diod. xix. 48, 5. [3] *Ibid.* 47.

the Macedonian king (whether it was the first Seleucus or the second there is no indication, and does not much matter), enticed 3000 of them into a village called Rhanda among marshes, where he surrounded them with Macedonian and Thracian troops and made away with them all.[1]

On the other hand, numbers of Persians served both as administrators and soldiers under Seleucus and his successors. The satrap of Cilicia at the beginning of the reign of Seleucus Kallinikos is proved by his name Aribazus to have been an Irânian.[2] Another Aribazus is the governor of Sardis under Achaeus.[3] Oborzus, who crushes the revolt of *katoikoi* in Persis, is by his name a Persian.[4] The Smyrnaean inscription mentions "Omanes and the Persians under Omanes" among the troops stationed in the neighbourhood.[5] A force commanded by Antiochus I in Syria celebrates a Persian festival.[6] There was a Zoroastrian temple on Mount Silpius at Antioch —a temple of the Eternal Fire.[7] Considering that our whole knowledge of the organization of the Seleucid kingdom is derived from chance notices gathered here and there, such references as those above indicate a larger Irânian element than we can actually trace with our imperfect sources. These references are enough to prove that the policy of Alexander, which set Macedonian and Irânian side by side, was not altogether abandoned by those who inherited his throne.

[1] Polyaen. vii. 39.   [2] See p. 185.
[3] See vol. ii. p. 7.   [4] Polyaen. vii. 40.
[5] Michel, No. 19, l. 104.   [6] Polyaen. iv. 15.   [7] Malalas, p. 38; cf. p. 119.

CHAPTER XIV

INDIA

THE realm of Seleucus and his successors did not include the Indian provinces of Alexander's Empire; but with the princes who ruled there they had to do as neighbours, and it is therefore part of our business to inform ourselves of what was going on in this region in the century after Alexander's death. In doing so we enter a field which has a peculiar interest for Englishmen.

In the year 326 B.C. a glitter of strange spears, a mailed line of men, issued out of the Khaibar pass into the land of the Five Rivers. These men had trodden, step by step, the whole way from the shores of the Mediterranean, and for the first time Greek and Indian looked upon each other's face. Many things in the India discovered to Alexander and his soldiers were like the things seen in India to-day—the wide dusty plains, the naked ascetics sitting by the wayside. But in some respects the aspect of things was different. None of those intricate carven temples or figures of curious gods which we associate with the India of to-day were to be seen; the sculptured rocks were then plain; it was from this new people that the Indian would get the impulse to build and carve in stone.

No kingdom of any large dimensions existed in India. The peoples were divided into hundreds of petty principalities, often at war with one another. The two most considerable princes with whom Alexander had to do were those whom the Greeks called Taxiles and Porus. The principality of Taxiles lay between the Indus and Hydaspes (mod. Jehlam), that of

# INDIA

Porus farther east, between the Hydaspes and Acesines (mod. Chenab). Taxiles from the outset made friends with the strange and terrible invaders; Porus tried conclusions with them and was defeated in the hard-fought battle beside the Hydaspes. After that he also, as one brave man with another, made friends with the Macedonian king. Both Taxiles and Porus got their reward in an extension of their territories. The first effect of the Macedonian conquest in the Panjab was *to break down the boundaries which divided one little kingdom from another, and create two realms of larger dimensions than India had yet known.* Porus became king of all the country between the Hydaspes and Hyphasis (Beas) — containing, according to one account,[1] 5000 towns not smaller than Cos — and was only so far limited in his sovereignty that his kingdom was counted a province of the Macedonian Empire, and he himself had the standing of a satrap, with the implied obligation of paying tribute.[2] But no Macedonian troops seem to have been stationed in his sphere. Taxiles, who also had his territory enlarged, was more directly subject to Macedonian control. A Macedonian satrap, Philip, remained at his side, and his capital, Taxila, was held by a garrison.[3]

On the lower Indus, below the confluence of the Acesines, the native princes, who had shown themselves untrustworthy, were not left in possession. Here an Irânian nobleman[4] and a Macedonian chief, Pithon the son of Agenor, ruled side by side. To this satrapy certain regions on the west of the Indus which had belonged to the Persian Empire (the Gandava region?) were attached, their population probably being Indian, not Irânian.

Alexander, of course, rooted Greek civilization here as in other parts of the East by a line of new cities along the course of the Indus.

---

[1] Strabo xv. 701.

[2] ἀφῆκεν αὐτὸν ἄρχειν ὧν ἐβασίλευε σατράπην καλούμενον, Plutarch, *Alex.* 60.

[3] Arr. *Anab.* v. 8, 3.

[4] In Arr. *Anab.* vi. 15, 4, Oxyartes is named. But *the* Oxyartes, the father-in-law of Alexander, was satrap of the Paropanisidae, and that he combined that satrapy with the satrapy of the lower Indus, as Niese thinks (i. p. 503), is hard to suppose, since they were not contiguous. There is probably some confusion which we cannot unravel.

We distinguish thus three Indian provinces: (1) that of the upper Indus to its junction with the Acesines, governed by Taxiles and Philip; (2) that of the lower Indus, governed by Oxyartes (?) and Pithon; and (3) that of the country beyond the Hydaspes, governed by Porus.

The troops settled by Alexander in India seem, in part at any rate, to have been, not Macedonians, but Greek mercenaries; and just as in Bactria a national Greek movement against the Macedonians took place, so in India, soon after Alexander left it, there was a conspiracy of the Greek captains against the Macedonian Philip, which culminated in his assassination. But the conspirators were killed and the insurrection suppressed by the Macedonian guards.[1] Soon afterwards Pithon had taken the place of Philip, and the province of the lower Indus had been added to the realm of Porus, which thus reached the sea. This is the situation at Alexander's death (323).

The rivalries which then convulsed the Empire reached to India. Eudamus, who had held command of a Thracian contingent[2] in the province of the upper Indus, now came to the front. Like the satraps of Further Irân, he embraced the royalist cause in 317, whilst Pithon the son of Agenor is found as an adherent of Antigonus. Eudamus seems to have formed the design of creating a yet larger Indian realm by uniting all the provinces under his own hand. Pithon had probably fled to join Antigonus, and Porus was entangled in the snares of Eudamus and murdered.[3] Eudamus was now supreme in the Panjab, master of a force of the elephants which were held to be the strength of the Indian armies. But in 317 he left India to join the united satraps with Eumenes, and he never returned. He was put to death by Antigonus.[4]

But the fever with which India, from its contact with the disturbed area of western Asia, had been infected still worked. The idea of the great kingdom was in the air. It had been in part realized. The old order had been confounded and the old landmarks trampled down. It was the sort of chaos which gives the strong man his opportunity. And the strong man

[1] Arr. *Anab.* vi. 27, 2.
[2] Curtius x. 1, 21.
[3] Diod. xix. 14, 8.
[4] *Ibid.* 44, 1.

appeared in a native Indian, Chandragupta,[1] who had not read the signs of the times in vain.

The origin of a great personality gathers quickly about it in India a rank growth of legend. The real Chandragupta has ceased to be distinguishable at all in the myths as they are set down in later Indian books. In our classical sources the process is only in its earlier stages; the stories were such as were told to Greek travellers a generation or two after the great man's time. Chandragupta, according to their account, was of a low caste,[2] the prototype of Sivaji the Mahratta. As a boy he had seen Alexander, the invincible splendid man from the West.[3] Later on, when he became a great king, Chandragupta worshipped Alexander among his gods.[4] Like Sivaji and many others who have risen to power in India, Chandragupta began his rise as a captain of marauders. He had offended the king of the district where he lived, Nanda or Nandrus,[5] and had taken to the jungle. A lion, it is recorded in the legend as given by Justin, had come upon him when sleeping outworn, and licked him without doing him any hurt. He flung himself into the chaos which prevailed in the Panjab after the death of Eudamus in 316.[6] If a great king was to arise in India, he might be a native as well as a Macedonian. Chandragupta presented himself as a national leader. Successes surrounded him with a superstitious halo. It was believed that the elephant he rode was a wild one which had knelt of its own accord to receive him upon its back. The Macedonian dominion in the land was broken. But its work in doing away with the little principalities stood. The Panjab was one great kingdom. A new power had arisen in India also out of the ruins of Alexander's Empire.[7]

---

[1] In Greek, Σανδρόκοττος or Ἀνδρόκοττος.   [2] Just. xv. 4.
[3] Plutarch, *Alex.* 62.   [4] *Ibid. De seipsum citra inv. laud.* 10.
[5] Nanda in Indian sources; Nandrus probably in Just. xv. 4, 16.
[6] Mr. V. A. Smith, in his useful book on *Asoka* (Rulers of India Series, 1901), in putting the conquest of the Panjab by Chandragupta "in the cold season following the death of Alexander at Babylon in the summer of B.C. 323," seems to have overlooked the Partition of Triparadisus and the career of Eudamus altogether.
[7] Niese thinks that the principality of Taxiles, west of the Hydaspes, was not subject to Chandragupta, and that the Sophytes, whose coins are found near Peshawar, was its ruler.

But Chandragupta's possession of the Indian provinces was, of course, challenged when Seleucus, between 312 and 302, established his authority in the East. Once more a great Macedonian army pushed victoriously into the Panjab. But it was at the moment when the situation in the West was coming to a crisis, and Seleucus was needed to throw his weight into the scale against Antigonus. He had no time to ground his dominion in India. So he agreed with Chandragupta quickly. The new Indian king was left in possession, and he on his part promised alliance, if not allegiance. A marriage cemented the two houses, and Chandragupta furnished Seleucus with 500 elephants to be used in Asia Minor. Those regions on the west of the Indus, which had been detached by Alexander from the Irânian province to which they had belonged, Seleucus now ceded to the Indian king.[1] Thenceforward the relations of the house of Seleucus and that of Chandragupta seem to have been of the friendliest.[2]

But the tendency towards the formation of a great realm, which the Macedonian conquest had set in motion, was not yet arrived at its completion. Chandragupta passed from the Panjab into that more eastern India watered by the Ganges and its tributaries, and carried all before him. His conquest reached to the Bay of Bengal. From the Indus to the mouth of the Ganges was now a single empire, whose centre and seat of government was fixed by the conqueror at Pataliputra (mod. Patna).

And wherever Chandragupta ruled, there the influence of Alexander could be traced. We have seen that the new Indian realm sprang directly out of Alexander's Empire, and that Chandragupta acknowledged its origin in his worship of the Macedonian king. At the altars which Alexander built beside the Hyphasis when he turned back westward it was long the custom for the kings who ruled on the Ganges to offer periodic sacrifices according to Greek rites.[3] Intercourse between the

---

[1] Mr. V. A. Smith (*Asoka*, p. 66) quotes Strabo as saying that Seleucus ceded "a *large part* of Ariane," but *that* Strabo does not say. In giving Arachosia, the Kabul, and even Gedrosia to the new Indian realm Mr. Vincent, I think, exceeds what is even probable, not to say proved.

[2] App. *Syr.* 55; Strabo xv. 689, 724; Just. xv. 4, 20.

[3] Plutarch, *Alex.* 62.

INDIA

court of Pataliputra and the Greek courts of the West was maintained. Megasthenes resided for a time at Pataliputra as the ambassador of Seleucus to Chandragupta, and left the standard work on India to later generations of classical antiquity.[1] Deïmachus of Plataea went as ambassador to the son and successor of Chandragupta, Bindusâra Amitraghâta,[2] and also put the information which he gathered on record. An ambassador of Ptolemy II to India, Dionysius, is mentioned as a third authority.[3] We may presume that Hindoo envoys were likewise to be seen at the Seleucid and Ptolemaïc courts even before Asoka sent his missionaries.

Intercourse between far separated branches of the human family must have been advanced in an altogether new degree when the whole length of Asia from the mouth of the Ganges to the coasts of the Mediterranean was occupied by two friendly empires! And it must be remembered that a Greek merchantman would not now come into India as into an altogether strange land. In the Panjab also under the Indian king he would find the Greek population settled by Alexander. Greek was perhaps widely diffused as a language of commerce in western India and Afghanistan.[4] Of the movements in the commercial world—what we should now so like to know of the mingling of nationalities at the great centres, the life of the road-side and the *khan*, our authorities tell us nothing. They see nothing outside the courts and camps. But even at the courts we discover a curiosity of Hellene and Indian with regard to each other's worlds. We hear of the strange drugs sent by Chandragupta to Seleucus,[5] and of the letter of Bindusâra to Antiochus asking to be furnished for a price with the sweet rich drink which one of the Greek processes of wine-making produced, with a quantity of dried figs for which Asia Minor then as now was famous, and with a teacher of Greek learning, a "sophist." "The figs and the wine," Antiochus wrote back,

---

[1] *F.H.G.* ii. p. 398; Susemihl, *Gesch. d. griech. Lit.* i. p. 547 f.

[2] For Deïmachus see *F.H.G.* ii. p. 440; Susemihl i. p. 656. Amitraghâta, the surname of Bindusâra, is not, I believe, found in Indian sources, but is inferred to be the original of the name this king bears in Greek sources, Ἀμιτροχάδας.

[3] Plin. vi. § 58.

[4] Gardner, *Greek and Scythic Kings of Bactria and India*, p. liii.

[5] Phylarch. frag. 37 = *F.H.G.* i. p. 344.

"shall be sent, but a sophist is not, according to the custom of the Greeks, an article of sale."[1]

But how far-reaching in its effects the Macedonian intervention in India was destined to be began to be seen when the third king of the new Indian realm, Asoka the son of Bindusâra, embraced Buddhism. The teaching of Gautama Sakyamuni, after having been for some 200 years the doctrine of one of the innumerable Indian sects, was now lifted to a position of world-wide importance. The creation of a single great kingdom in India had made possible the extension of a single religion. To the Macedonian conquest therefore the rise of Buddhism in India and the subsequent conquest by Buddhism of Central and Further Asia was in the first instance due. When we hear so often the cheap wisdom uttered with an air of profundity, which depreciates all "Western" influence upon the East as essentially transitory and evanescent, it is interesting to observe the opinion of one who speaks with authority—that "upon the institutions brought in by Alexander the whole subsequent development of India depends."[2]

King Asoka was ardent to propagate the Doctrine in all the earth. In the Greek cities of the West, as far as Cyrene and Epirus, one might have had glimpses of dark men, with the monkish tonsure and the long yellow robe, who were come to roll onward even here the Wheel of the Kingdom of Righteousness. Perhaps the kings themselves—the wine-sodden Antiochus II, the literary and scientific dilettante Ptolemy Philadelphus, the grave Stoic Antigonus — were summoned by the envoys of Asoka to walk in the Eightfold Path—right belief, right will, right word, right deed, right life, right effort, right thought, right self-withdrawal—and to receive the Four Truths concerning the pain in the world and its taking away. "Open your ears, ye kings, the Redemption from death is found!" The record of the sending out of these missionaries is established by Asoka himself, graven on the rocks of India;[3] it is a pity that we have no western account

---

[1] Hegesander, frag. 43 = *F.H.G.* iv. p. 421.   [2] Niese i. p. 508.

[3] "And this is the chiefest conquest in His Majesty's opinion—the conquest by the Law; this also is that effected by His Majesty both in his own dominions and in all the neighbouring realms as far as six hundred leagues—even to where

of the impression which they made. They must have trodden the same roads which three hundred years later were trodden by the apostles of another Faith and another Redemption.

the Greek king (Yona râja) Antiochus dwells, and beyond that Antiochus to where dwell the four kings severally named Ptolemy, Antigonus, Magas and Alexander" (*i.e.* Alexander II of Epirus) . . . "and likewise here, in the King's dominions, among the Yonas" (*i.e.* the Greeks of the Panjab). Vincent A. Smith, *Asoka*, p. 131; *Corp. Inscr. Indic.* i. p. 86. E. Hardy's *Asoka* (Mainz, 1902) I had not yet seen at the time of going to press.

CHAPTER XV

THE FIRST YEARS OF ANTIOCHUS III (223–216)

WE return from our survey of the East to that point in our narrative when we saw the Seleucid King struck down in Asia Minor whilst engaged in recovering his inheritance from Attalus of Pergamos. By the assassination of Seleucus III the royal army was suddenly deprived of its head in the enemy's country; but a successful retirement across the Taurus was effected by the skill of the general Epigenes. For a while the succession to the vacant throne appeared doubtful. Antiochus, the younger son of Seleucus II Kallinikos, then a youth of about eighteen,[1] was far away in Babylonia,[2] and some time must expire before he could appear in the West. Meanwhile the direction of affairs had been at once assumed upon the King's death by his cousin Achaeus. He had acted vigorously against the party responsible for the murder, and had put Nicanor and Apaturius to death. He was strong, able and popular, and public feeling ran in favour of his assuming the diadem. But Achaeus remained true to his absent cousin, proclaimed him king, and himself undertook a new campaign in Asia Minor to restore the authority of the Seleucid house.[3]

The popular voice of the Macedonians in Syria now called

---

[1] He was fifty in 191, Polyb. xx. 8, 1.

[2] Eus. i. 253; Jerome, *in Dan.* 11, 10.

[3] The view which saw in the child Antiochus of the coins (Babelon, p. lxxiv.) and the Antiochus mentioned without surname in the inscription of Seleucia (*C.I.G.* 4458) an infant son of Seleucus III, proclaimed king for a moment on his father's death, is now generally discredited (Wilcken, Niese). Niese adopts this view in his text, but abandons it in a note (ii. p. 777).

for the presence of the young King,[1] and Antiochus moved west. The first dispositions of the new reign were the delivery to Achaeus of full powers in the trans-Tauric country and a similar delegation of the royal authority beyond the Tigris to Molon, the satrap of Media, and his brother Alexander, the satrap of Persis. Antiochus III, however, was not yet his own master. The real director of the affairs of the kingdom was the prime minister, Hermīas. He had shown himself a minister of the type familiar at despotic courts, greedy of power, intolerant of rivals, and murderous in his rancours. His influence was a menace to all prominent persons in the kingdom. Epigenes, the beloved general, was the especial object of his jealousy. Such a *régime* naturally brought its nemesis in the disaffection of the King's high officers. It was generally expected that Achaeus would renounce his allegiance. Molon and Alexander made haste to secure themselves, as they imagined, by rebellion (221). Their neighbours on the east, Arsaces in Parthia, Diodotus in Bactria, showed an example of successful defiance. Molon also now declared himself a king,[2] and essayed to turn away from the house of Seleucus the hearts of the Greek colonists and native tribes in Nearer Irân.

The weaknesses in the frame of the Empire, which ultimately proved fatal, were already indicated in this crisis— its relinquishment of Asia Minor and Irân foreshown. But as yet it did not seem past hope that a strong hand might renew the broken bonds. Achaeus might still with skilful management be retained. In the East one element in the situation made powerfully for the house of Seleucus—its popularity with the Greek cities. Encompassed by alien peoples, the Greeks in the East looked to Antioch for the protection of Hellenism. It was the great advantage the house of Seleucus possessed, and again and again in the course of these times barbarian conquerors and rebel captains found it a permanent force to be reckoned with. The line of policy by which the crisis at this moment could be met was plainly marked out—to avoid all further entanglements, to conciliate

---

[1] Jerome, *loc. cit.*
[2] Coins with the name of King Molon are found, Babelon, p. lxxxvi., *Catalogue*, p. 60.

Achaeus, and to turn the disposition of the eastern Greeks to account. It only required a firm will to carry it through.

Unfortunately the throne was occupied by a youth and swayed by a corrupt minister. At the council held to consider the rebellion in the East, Epigenes advised an immediate advance on the satraps, and urged the passion of loyalty which the appearance of the King in those regions would arouse. Hermias replied with a fury due in part to his hatred of Epigenes, in part to terror of the war. He roundly accused the general of wishing to deliver the King's person into his enemies' hands. The Council were frightened by this outbreak into acquiescence, and only a force under Xenon and Theodotus (nicknamed "One-and-a-half")[1] was sent against Molon. Hermias, however, was still uneasy lest the King might be induced to go to the eastern provinces, and to prevent it he conceived the plan of reopening the controversy with Egypt as to Cœle-Syria, which would keep the King's hands full, and at the same time would not, in view of the character of the reigning Ptolemy, entail much danger. For about this time (winter 222-221)[2] the Egyptian throne, which had been occupied by three great rulers, passed to the contemptible Ptolemy Philopator. It became the interest of Hermias to present before the King's eyes the danger in the west of the Empire in the liveliest colours. The success which Achaeus had met with in Asia Minor gave him an opportunity. Already the Pergamene power had been broken, and Attalus was being driven within ever narrower limits; already Achaeus was to all intents and purposes master of the trans-Tauric country. It was easy to work upon the King's fears and make him see a great conspiracy threatening the Empire on all sides—a league which embraced the king of Egypt in the West as well as the revolting satraps in the East. Hermias removed all doubts by producing a letter (which he had forged) from Ptolemy to Achaeus, urging him to assume the diadem.

In the marriage of the young King, which now took

---

[1] The meaning of the nickname is doubtful. Schweighäuser suggests that it refers to his being above the ordinary height; Müller (*F.H.G.* iii. p. 167) that it refers to the boats used by pirates, called ἡμιόλια.

[2] Niese ii. p. 360, note 2.

THE FIRST YEARS OF ANTIOCHUS III

place, we may see the Seleucid court actuated by the motive of securing its more than ever precarious hold on Asia Minor. The policy initiated by Antiochus II was still followed. The bride chosen for Antiochus III was Laodice, the daughter of Mithridates II of Pontic Cappadocia. She was, no doubt, his first cousin, her mother being that aunt of his whom Mithridates had espoused. She was escorted from Cappadocia by the admiral Diognetus, and the nuptials were celebrated at Seleucia on the Euphrates Bridge, where the court was at the time residing. As soon as the marriage was over, the court moved to Antioch, and preparations for an attack on Egypt were pushed forward.

The position of Molon meanwhile in the East grew increasingly formidable. In his own satrapy of Media he had a defensible country, guarded by mountain and desert, and, as we saw in the case of Pithon,[1] well adapted for the formation of a great military power. He had taken measures to bind the neighbouring satraps to his cause.[2] The native princes, outside the sphere of Macedonian authority, of whom the greatest was Artabazanes of Lesser Media (Âdharbaijân), were ready to support an antagonist of the Seleucid power.[3] The inherent loyalty of the Greek and Macedonian settlers to the royal house Molon fought by largesses, severity, promises and forged dispatches, tending to show the King in an evil light. The generals sent by the court, Xenon and Theodotus, did not dare to offer battle and sat down behind fortifications. Molon became master of Apolloniatis. Then he even marched on Seleucia. The city being on the western bank of the Tigris, he could not reach it without crossing the river, and this Zeuxis, the satrap of Babylonia, prevented by seizing all the boats. Molon had to be content to take up his winter-quarters[4] (of 221) in

---

[1] See p. 41.

[2] ἠσφαλισμένος δὲ καὶ τὰ κατὰ τὰς παρακειμένας σατραπείας διὰ τῆς τῶν προεστώτων εὐνοίας καὶ δωροδοκίας, Pol. v. 43, 6. This is certainly difficult. The rulers of the two satrapies on the north, Parthia and Atropatene, already set up for independent kings and were above the petty sort of bribery implied in δωροδοκία, the satrap of Persis was Molon's own brother, the satraps of Babylonia and Susiana remained faithful to Antiochus. There remains only Carmania.

[3] Polyb. v. 55, 1.

[4] It is astonishing that the practice of going into winter-quarters, which is

Ctesiphon, the military station opposite the city on the other bank, and there wait his opportunity.

These movements of Molon caused a fresh tension at the court. But Hermias still carried his point. Only a general should be sent against a rebel. Kings should go to war with none but kings.[1] Accordingly, late in the summer of 221,[2] whilst the invasion of Cœle-Syria was set on foot under the leadership of the King in person, Xenœtas, an Achaean adventurer, led a new force eastwards. He was given supreme authority over the provincial commanders to conduct operations at his discretion.

Xenœtas marched to Seleucia, where he found Zeuxis. The governors of Susiana and the "Red Sea" province, Diogenes and Pythiades, who were still loyal, joined him by command. He pitched beside the river on the western bank over against the rebels. The information brought him by deserters, who swam the river, showed how strong the royal cause still was in the East. The rank and file of Molon's regular forces, drawn, no doubt, from the Greek or Macedonian colonies, were, they reported, at heart far more attached to the King than to their leader. Xenœtas had only to cross the river and the mass of Molon's army would come over to his side.

The subsequent events do not allow us to think much of the diligence or watchfulness of either of the opposed commanders. Molon was first so slovenly in his patrolling that Xenœtas was able by night to throw across a body of troops nine miles down stream and take up a strong position among the marshes without opposition. The main camp on the west bank was left in charge of Zeuxis and Pythiades. An attempt of Molon to dislodge Xenœtas failed, owing to his defective topographical information, and his detachments floundered helplessly in the morass. When Xenœtas advanced to give the rebel army an opportunity to desert, Molon abandoned his camp and took the road to Media. The advantage which

intelligible enough in Greece, should have been maintained by a Greek army in the climate of Baghdad.

[1] The royalty assumed by Molon was therefore ignored.
[2] Niese ii. p. 366.

Xenœtas had won by his enemy's negligence it was now his turn to throw away by his own. Considering all danger over, he occupied Molon's camp at Ctesiphon, brought over his cavalry for the pursuit, and suffered his troops to give themselves up to riotous indulgence. Then Molon turned swiftly and took the division of Xenœtas by complete surprise. A great part were massacred in drunken slumbers, others, mad with panic, tried to regain the camp of Zeuxis by swimming the Tigris, and in most cases perished. "An impressive and fantastic spectacle was offered by the scene on the river, not only men swimming, but horses, pack-beasts, shields, dead bodies, stuff of all kinds, carried on the surface." The panic spread to the opposite shore, Zeuxis and the other division incontinently fled, and Molon crossed the river, without meeting any resistance, to occupy the original camp of the royal army.

The retirement of the satrap of Babylonia left Seleucia exposed. Even Diomedon, the governor of the city, had accompanied his flight. The eastern capital of the Empire fell forthwith into the rebel's hands. Babylonia was Molon's, and, passing down the river, he took possession of the "Red Sea" province, whose governor, Pythiades, had probably, like Diomedon, fled with Zeuxis. Diogenes, on the other hand, had hurried back to defend his province, and contrived to throw himself into the citadel of Susa, although Molon was already investing it when he arrived. Molon could not afford to stay long in Susiana; leaving therefore a detachment to prosecute the siege, he returned to complete the conquest of the riverlands north of Babylonia, the provinces of Mesopotamia and Parapotamia.

The news of the disaster reached the King at a moment when he was on other grounds disposed to suspend operations against Ptolemy. He had about the same time that Xenœtas left for the East moved out from Apamea, the military headquarters of the Empire, to accomplish the invasion of Cœle-Syria. The gate of that province towards the north was the narrow and swampy valley, called Marsyas, between the Lebanon and Antilibanus mountains. It was commanded on each side by the fortresses of Gerrha and Brochi, and these were held for Ptolemy by Theodotus the Aetolian. In vain the royal army attempted to break through; the lieutenant of Ptolemy brought the Seleucid King to a foolish stand at the very threshold of that province it was proposed to claim by arms. Under these circumstances the news arrived that the army of Xenœtas had been annihilated.

The quarrel, of course, between Hermias and Epigenes now flamed up afresh. Events were confounding the policy of the prime minister. In spite of his raving denunciations, Epigenes had too strong a case not to carry the Council with him. It was resolved that the King should advance against Molon in person. Hermias had the sense to embrace the inevitable; if, however, he could not hinder the expedition, he was determined his rival should win no laurels in it. But to remove him was doubly difficult, since on the one hand his reputation made the King his friend, and on the other he was an idol of the army. When the forces for the East were mustered at Apamea, an occasion to overcome both these obstacles at one stroke offered. The troublous times under the last kings, combined with the loss of the eastern provinces, had acquainted the Seleucid court with what in later times was to become its standing embarrassment—want of money. The pay of the troops fell into arrear, and they began to use the urgency of the present crisis to press their claims. Hermias now came forward and proposed to the King a bargain with which he had no choice but to close; he undertook to satisfy all the demands of the soldiery on condition that Epigenes did not accompany the expedition. This action represented him at the same time to the army as its champion, and attached it to his interests. Epigenes retired into private life. Only the troops drawn from Cyrrhestice (6000 in number) stood by the fallen hero, and their disaffection was not disposed of till after a pitched battle the following year (220), in which the majority of them perished. Even in his retirement Epigenes was an object of fear to the guilty minister. He compassed his death on the charge of corresponding with Molon, a charge which he supported by causing a forged letter from the rebel to be slipped among Epigenes' papers. The hush of terror prevailed in the *entourage* of the King.

The royal army crossed the Euphrates at the end of 221, and traversed Mesopotamia by the route which led close under the northern hills to Antioch (Nisibis) in Mygdonia. In this city a halt of six weeks was made during the most severe portion of the winter, and with the first approach of spring (220) the advance was continued to the Tigris.[1] From this point two alternative routes presented themselves. Hermias wished to march directly upon Molon in Babylonia, following the course of the river on the western bank.[2] The satrap of Babylonia, who was now with the King, was able, from his special knowledge of the country, to show the inconveniences of this plan. Amongst other things, the southern part of Mesopotamia was desolate steppe, where only the wandering Arabs spread their tents, and it would be impossible for the army to find fresh supplies. Having passed through this, a march of six days, they would come upon the elaborate canal-system by which Babylonia was at once irrigated and defended, and if this were held by the enemy it would effectually bar their way; the only alternative would be retreat through the steppe in the face of the enemy, and probably without provisions. Zeuxis therefore urged that they should cross to the eastern side. There, as soon as they reached Apolloniatis, the country was under regular cultivation, and they would be in the midst of plenty. The hold which the house of Seleucus had upon the hearts of the settlers, who were intimidated only into supporting Molon, would be turned to account. Above all, by threatening to cut off Molon from his base in Media they would compel him either to offer battle or run the great danger which a delay, in view of the doubtful temper of his troops, would bring. Before the reason and authority of these arguments Hermias was constrained to give way. The army crossed the Tigris in three bands and advanced southwards. At Dura they reached the northern limit of Molon's conquests in Parapotamia, and found his troops still besieging the town.

[1] Libba, site unknown, probably near Nineveh.
[2] "Covering themselves with this river and the Lycus (Greater Zâb) and the Caprus (Lesser Zâb)," says Polybius. Since these two latter rivers join the Tigris from the *east*, it is hard to see how they could be a protection to an army on the *western* bank. In any case the attack apprehended by Hermias must have been a flank attack from Media.

These they drove off and proceeded for eight days more, when, crossing the ridge of Oricus, they saw at their feet the rich district of Apolloniatis.

Molon was now finding out how precarious his defences were against the magic of the King's person. He could not trust the populations of the provinces he had lately conquered. He could not trust his own army, not at any rate the Greeks and Macedonians, who constituted the bulk no doubt of his regular troops. He saw himself in danger of having his communications with Media cut. Hastily recrossing the Tigris, he purposed to arrest the progress of the royal army in the rugged defiles of Apolloniatis, and placed his chief reliance on the Kurdish irregulars who served with his army as slingers. In this region, accordingly, the two armies met, and some indecisive skirmishes took place between the scouting parties on either side. But the neighbourhood of the King made it enormously harder for the rebel to prevent his army breaking up in his hands. How to use this instrument without losing it became the problem; Molon did not know what wave of feeling might not rush through his troops if the youthful king of the old and glorious house were seen claiming their allegiance. He determined to strike by night, but when, riding out with a picked body, he saw ten young soldiers make away in a body towards the royal camp, his nerve was shaken, and he returned at dawn, a doomed man. The decisive battle was fought on that day. The royal left, where Hermias and Zeuxis commanded, was driven back by Molon, but on the right Molon's brother Neolaus found himself opposed to the King, and all that Molon feared took place. As soon as the King was seen, the troops went over. Molon saw that the game was up, and, together with the other ringleaders in the rebellion, committed suicide. Neolaus hastened to the province of Persis, where his brother Alexander was waiting the event with the remainder of the family of Molon, his mother and his children, and made haste to consummate the self-destruction of his house. The body of Molon was crucified in the Callonitis on the road over the Zagrus, the most conspicuous spot in Media. It was understood that in the punishment of rebel leaders the house of Seleucus followed the practice of the old Achaemenian kings.

The rebellion had been shipwrecked on the respect which the royal name commanded in the popular heart throughout the Greek east. It now remained to settle the affairs of the reconquered districts. To the soldiery who had followed Molon the King had first addressed a severe reprimand; they then shook hands in honest Macedonian fashion and made up the quarrel,[1] and the troops were led back to Media by officers specially appointed to reorganize the province. Antiochus himself moved to Seleucia, to hold his court in the eastern capital. And now his individual personality began to emerge in distinction from that of his minister. Hermias was for turning the punishment of those who had taken part in the rebellion into a debauch of cruelty. Upon Seleucia, which had after all only yielded to superior force in joining Molon, the prime minister was forward to gratify his frightful appetite. The "Adeiganes" were banished. Others of the principal citizens were put to death, or mutilated, or racked. A fine of 1000 talents was laid upon the city. The bent of the young King was all the other way. Prudence and generosity together urged him in the direction of mildness, and he was able to some extent to restrain the minister's enormities. The fine was reduced to 150 talents. Diogenes, who had distinguished himself by his defence of Susa, was rewarded by being transferred to the governorship of Media, and was succeeded in Susiana by Apollodorus. Pythiades was superseded in the "Red Sea" province by Tychon, the *archigrammateus* of the royal army.

Antiochus considered that the moment of prestige should be used to assert the authority of the house of Seleucus in the neighbouring country, or the work would be left half done. He designed in the first place to attack Artabazanes of Lesser Media, who was now in extreme old age. Again Hermias took fright at eastern expeditions and played the old card of Cœle-Syria. But on news arriving that the Queen had been delivered in Syria of a son, a new prospect of power opened before him in case of the King's decease, and he now advocated the eastern expedition as making that contingency more probable.

[1] Antiochus shows towards the ringleaders the character of a Persian king, towards the soldiers that of a Macedonian.

The King accordingly left Seleucia, and led the army across the Zagrus into the Urumiya basin, where the Irânian dynasty had reigned, since the time of Alexander, undisturbed. On the novel appearance of a royal army in these regions Artabazanes bowed to the occasion, and accepted the terms which Antiochus imposed.

For a complete reconquest of the eastern provinces the time was not yet ripe. It would be hazardous in the extreme for the Seleucid King to plunge into distant lands while the hearth of the Empire was threatened by Achaeus and Ptolemy. But before the King set out homewards an event of importance took place in his immediate circle. The dark hopes which Hermias was nursing were penetrated by the royal physician, Apollophanes, between whom and Antiochus a real affection existed. To broach his suspicions to the King was, however, still dangerous, since it was not known how far the influence of the minister over the young man's mind extended. Apollophanes nevertheless ran the risk, and pointedly adjured the King to remember his brother's fate. To his relief, Antiochus confessed that he himself secretly regarded Hermias with aversion and dread, and prayed Apollophanes to make for him a way of escape. There was no lack of persons in that society ready to bear a hand in the destruction of the hated minister. But even with the King's countenance Apollophanes had to work by stealth. On the pretext that Antiochus was suffering from certain disorders, the physician was able to regulate the admissions to the royal apartments, and the King's chamber became itself the rendezvous of the conspirators. Then it was given out that Antiochus had been ordered to walk abroad at dawn, to take the cool air of morning, and Hermias seized the occasion to come at the King's person. It was a trap; the only others present at that unusual hour were those who were in the plot. The King chose for his early walk a path which led them to a lonely spot outside the camp, where he made an excuse to retire. Immediately the conspirators dispatched Hermias with their swords. The news of the prime minister's fall was received with a transport of joy throughout the kingdom. Wherever the royal army came on its homeward march, the King was met with expressions of satisfaction. At Apamea in Syria, where the family of Hermias was residing, his wife was stoned to death by the women of the place, and his children by the children.

By the time that Antiochus returned to Syria (end of 220) the danger from the West had declared itself in a sufficiently palpable form. Even the comparatively short expedition to Âdharbaijân had emboldened Achaeus to throw off the mask. He designed to recross the Taurus, and counted on the support of Cyrrhestice when he appeared in Syria. Leaving Sardis, the seat of his government in Asia Minor, he took the road to Syria. At Laodicea (in Phrygia) he publicly assumed the diadem and the royal name. But immediately he had to meet the same difficulty which had thwarted Molon, the feeling among the Greco-Macedonian soldiery which forbade them to lift their spears against a Seleucid king. Achaeus was obliged to dissimulate the objective of his march. But as the troops moved ever forward towards the Cilician Gates the suspicion of the truth broke upon them, and in Lycaonia they were on the verge of mutiny. Like Cyrus the Younger in somewhat similar circumstances, Achaeus had to cover his real purpose by pointing against the Pisidians—the untamed mountaineers who were at chronic war with all civilized government in Asia Minor. His foray, which yielded a considerable amount of loot to the troops, had the further advantage of regaining their good-will. But he was forced to abandon the idea of an invasion of Syria at the present moment, and retraced his steps to Lydia.

This was the situation which confronted Antiochus on his return from the East. He saw that Achaeus had committed a blunder in uncovering his hostile designs whilst restrained from carrying them out. Syria need fear no attack from Asia Minor for some time to come. In regard, therefore, to Achaeus, Antiochus confined himself for the present to protests and menaces; he turned to deal with the other party to the league, Ptolemy. Once more Apamea hummed with the preparations for an attack on the Ptolemaic power in Palestine.

Polybius tells us that at the council held to discuss the plan of campaign Apollophanes, the physician, first pointed out that, before embarking on an invasion of Coele-Syria, it was of prime importance to recapture the harbour-city of Seleucia, which since the wars of Seleucus II had been in Egyptian possession. The surprising thing is that the urgency of this step was not immediately plain. One would have thought that a hostile garrison established some 12 miles from Antioch, commanding its communication with the sea, to say nothing of the loss of the strongest city in the kingdom, the place where the founder of the royal line reposed, would have been felt as an intolerable burden. It is almost inexplicable that while this remained, enterprises in other directions should have been contemplated. Apollophanes was himself a citizen of Seleucia, exiled probably under the Ptolemaïc *régime*, and this lent warmth to his arguments. The Council was brought to see the obvious. Whilst Theodotus " One-and-a-half " was sent to occupy the passes towards Cœle-Syria and prepare for the invasion, the King himself moved from Apamea to Seleucia and took up a position in the suburbs of the city. Diognetus, the admiral, was at the same time to operate against the city by sea.

The attempts of Antiochus to buy over the governor Leontius, who controlled the city in the Ptolemaïc interest, failed, but he succeeded in corrupting some of his subordinates. It was agreed that if the Seleucid army could gain possession of the outer city which adjoined the harbour, the gates should be opened. On this side alone was it possible to scale the walls. Accordingly, whilst the other generals, Zeuxis and Hermogenes, attacked the gates on the landward side (the Antioch Gate and the Dioscurium Gate), Ardys forced his way into the outer city, supported by Diognetus, who simultaneously brought his squadron to bear on the docks. The officers within the city, who were bought by Antiochus, now prevailed on Leontius to ask for terms. Antiochus agreed to the condition that the free population (6000 in number) should be spared, and the city was surrendered. Those citizens who had been exiled, no doubt the warmer partizans of the house of Seleucus, were restored to their homes and property; otherwise the citizen-body was left undisturbed. A strong garrison was, of course, installed to hold the harbour and citadel. On the side of Egypt no attempt seems to have been made to avert a blow by which their position was so seriously impaired.

Antiochus now received tidings which put a very new complexion upon affairs in the south. It will be remembered that the Ptolemaïc governor in Cœle-Syria was Theodotus the Aetolian. His singular success in repelling the attack of Antiochus in 221 had, in the altered conditions at the Egyptian court under the miserable government of Ptolemy Philopator, only made him the mark of petty jealousies. He was summoned to Alexandria, and he knew well what that meant. In this strait he turned to the Seleucid King. Antiochus received an intimation that Theodotus was ready to deliver the town of Ptolemaïs (Old Testament Accho; modern Acre), the official residence of the governor of Cœle-Syria, into his hands. Panaetolus, a subordinate of Theodotus, would likewise surrender Tyre. This decided Antiochus to defer dealing with Achaeus still longer and to act in the matter of Egypt at once. He once more threaded the Marsyas valley and sat down before Gerrha and Brochi. But here the intelligence reached him that Egypt was taking measures swiftly to crush Theodotus before he could arrive. Nicolaus, himself too an Aetolian, and a soldier who had seen many wars, had been appointed by the Alexandrian court to secure the province, and Theodotus was now closely besieged in Ptolemaïs. There was no time to be lost. Antiochus left his heavy troops to continue the siege of Brochi, and, taking with him only the light-armed, set out to reach Ptolemaïs by the more rugged road which runs down the Phœnician coast. On the news of his approach Nicolaus retired, but ordered his lieutenants, Lagoras, a Cretan, and Dorymenes, an Aetolian, to occupy the pass by Berytus (mod. Bairût). The King, however, succeeded in dislodging them, and, once master of the pass, could afford to wait in position for the rest of the army. Then he advanced and was soon joined by the partizans of Theodotus. The gates of Tyre and then those of Ptolemaïs were opened to him according to the undertaking, and with the cities he got possession of their naval arsenals and considerable stores. He was able to make over to Diognetus, the admiral, no less than forty vessels, half of which were decked ships of war, of three banks of oars and upwards.

In the flush of these first successes Antiochus contemplated an immediate invasion of Egypt itself. But the accounts he received of the Egyptian muster at Pelusium to secure the frontier made him defer an enterprise which had baffled the companions of Alexander, Perdiccas and Antigonus. It seemed more prudent for the present to complete the conquest of Cœle-Syria, a process which consisted in the reduction of the cities one by one.

It was, however, in reality a false move. Egypt was in a state of utter unpreparedness, and an immediate attack would probably have succeeded. The slow conquest of Cœle-Syria gave the Ptolemaïc court just that respite which it needed. It used it well, hiring the ablest captains of Greece to re-organize its forces, and pressing forward its preparations with feverish activity, whilst by invariably receiving foreign embassies at Memphis and making a show of *laissez-faire* it contrived to hoodwink the world completely as to what was on foot. It engaged the good offices of the Greek states, Rhodes, Cyzicus, Byzantium, and the Aetolian League, to mediate in the quarrel, and the diplomatic running to and fro which ensued all served to gain time.

Winter (219-218) found Antiochus still occupied with the siege of Dora, the chief fortified harbour between Carmel and the Philistines. The city, supported from without by Nicolaus, defied his efforts. During the cold season the hardships of the besiegers would be doubled. An aggressive move on the part of Achaeus was again dreaded. Under these circumstances Antiochus agreed to an armistice of four months and hastened back to Seleucia. Garrisons were left in the various strongholds south of the Lebanon, which he had acquired, and the charge of Seleucid interests in that region committed to the old governor Theodotus.

The winter was used by the Egyptian court to continue its preparations, and the drill sergeant was busy at Alexandria. The Seleucid court, on the other hand, reposed upon the contemptuous estimate generally formed of the reigning Ptolemy. As soon as Antiochus had reached Seleucia the troops had been dismissed for months of idleness in their winter-quarters. The time of truce was wasted in futile negotiations. All the old controversy as to the treaties which preceded and succeeded the battle of Ipsus was gone over again. Then no agreement could be arrived at as to Achaeus; the Egyptian court required that the peace should extend to him also, whilst Antiochus stood out that it was monstrous for Ptolemy to interfere between himself and a rebel subject. Warlike operations were accordingly resumed on either side in the spring (218). Antiochus reassembled his forces to complete the subjugation of Cœle-Syria, whilst a Ptolemaïc army mustered at Gaza under Nicolaus. Ample reinforcements and material of war were sent from Egypt, as well as a fleet under the admiral Perigenes, to co-operate with the land-forces.

It seems curious that on his retirement at the end of the previous year's campaign, Antiochus had not secured the passes between Lebanon and the sea, especially since communication with the numerous garrisons in Palestine could only be maintained by way of the coast.[1] Nicolaus was able to occupy in advance the passage at its narrowest point. At Platanus a precipitous ridge bars almost the whole strip of land, already narrow enough, between the mountain and the sea. This naturally strong position for a defender, Nicolaus strengthened further by artificial works and guarded by a large body of troops. He himself remained in support by the town of Porphyreon. The Ptolemaïc fleet was stationed in the neighbourhood under Perigenes, who assisted zealously in the plans of the general.

Antiochus advanced, and on the way renewed the alliance of his house with the Phœnician republic of Aradus. Then he passed Theū-prosōpon,[2] Botrys, which he took, Berytus, Trieres and Calamus. The two latter towns were fired. From Calamus he sent an advanced party ahead under Nicarchus and Theodotus (the Aetolian or One-and-a-half?) to occupy the passage of the Lycus, and moved himself with the heavy troops more leisurely to the river Damūras (mod. Nahr-ad-Dâmûr), where he awaited the return of Nicarchus. The admiral Diognetus at the same time brought his fleet to

---

[1] The entrance into the country by Brochi and Gerrha was still in Egyptian hands.

[2] This is the precipitous headland of Ra's-ash-Shakka. Theū-prosōpon = Phœnician P'nê-El (Pennel).

anchor beside the army. After their return the King went in person to reconnoitre the position of the enemy at Platanus, and on the following day, leaving the heavy troops behind under Nicarchus, himself led the light-armed to the assault of the ridge. The opposed fleets simultaneously engaged close to shore, so that the land and sea fight presented, Polybius says, a single line. In both, the Ptolemaïc forces had at first the better, but Theodotus succeeded in gaining the top of the ridge inland, where it joined the lower slopes of the Lebanon, and then attacked the enemy from above. This turned the day; the force of Nicolaus, evacuating the pass in confusion, fell back upon Sidon. The Egyptian fleet, although still victorious, drew off and accompanied the retirement of the land-forces. Antiochus had succeeded in breaking open the door of Palestine.

The Seleucid army pursued its march along the Phœnician sea-board. From the walls of Sidon the defeated army saw the invaders' tents spread close by. Antiochus did not stop to besiege Sidon—that would have been an immense undertaking—but passed on southwards. It was probably when Ptolemaïs was reached that he ordered Diognetus, who had hitherto waited on the land-forces, to take the fleet back to Tyre, in order to hold the Ptolemaïc fleet, which still kept the harbour of Sidon, in check. The King himself struck up inland to Philoteria on the Sea of Galilee.[1] It was his plan before going farther to establish a belt of Seleucid power across central Palestine. There was direct communication between the coast at Ptolemaïs and the Greco-Macedonian colonies beyond Jordan. Some of the roads traversed the skirt of the Galilean hills, and were commanded on this side of Jordan by Philoteria and the fortress Atabyrium on the isolated conical hill of Tabor; another road went by way of the rich plain which divides the hills of Galilee from those of southern Palestine, and this was barred on the edge of the Jordan depression by the strong city of Scythopolis (Old Testament, Beth-shan; modern, Baisân).

Philoteria and Scythopolis submitted on conditions to the

[1] This is a Ptolemaïc foundation, called after Philotera, the sister of Ptolemy II; it is probably the city which we know by its later name, Tiberias.

Seleucid King and received his garrisons. Atabyrium had to be reduced. A successful stratagem delivered the town into Antiochus' hands. The fall of Tabor following on the surrender of Philoteria and Scythopolis produced a profound impression in the country. The officers in the Egyptian service began to go over, Ceraeas and Hippolochus among the more notable. The latter was a Thessalian *condottiere*, who brought 400 horse along with him.

Antiochus now crossed the Jordan into a region dominated by a galaxy of Greco-Macedonian cities. Pella, proclaiming its Macedonian origin by its name, Camūs and Gephrūs received the invader, and the prestige which accrued thereby to the arms of Antiochus attached the Arab tribes of the neighbouring country to his cause. Their adherence was a distinct gain, especially in view of the provisioning of the expedition. The partizans of Ptolemy threw themselves into Abila under Nicias, a kinsman of Mennaes, but this city too was compelled to open its gates. The most illustrious of all these cities, Gadara, surrendered on the threat of a siege. To complete the work of the campaign it was necessary for Antiochus to strike out about fifty miles to the south. There in the city of Rabbath-ammon or Philadelphia the defenders of the Egyptian cause had congregated, and were harassing the friendly Arabs by raiding their grounds. So strong was the city that although Antiochus subjected it to a regular siege and battered down the walls in two places, he was unable to take it till one of the prisoners showed the underground conduit which supplied the garrison with water. The reduction of Rabbath-ammon brought the campaign of 218 to a close. Nicarchus was left with an adequate force beyond Jordan; Ceraeas and Hippolochus were detached to protect the adherents of the house of Seleucus from molestation in the country about Samaria; the King himself returned to winter in Ptolemaïs.

It would seem that during the winter the Seleucid conquest of Palestine went forward, as the frontier cities of Gaza and Raphia are found to be in the hands of Antiochus at the opening of the campaign of 217. By the spring of that year the Egyptian court considered its preparations complete. It soon became evident that the decisive encounter was at hand. Ptolemy himself took the field, accompanied by his sister-wife, Arsinoë. The Egyptian army halted for its final marshalling in Pelusium, and then advanced across the desert. Antiochus on his part was equally soon on the move. His final dispositions for the march across the desert were made at Gaza. Ptolemy on the fifth evening after leaving Pelusium encamped about five miles short of Raphia, the first town in Palestine. When morning dawned, the Seleucid army was seen in position only a little more than a mile away, with Raphia in its rear. For some days the hosts remained stationary, face to face. Then Antiochus moved still nearer, so that only about five *stadia* separated the stockades of the two camps. Five more days went by without a movement. It was during these that Ptolemy narrowly escaped assassination at the hand of Theodotus the Aetolian, who stole into the Egyptian camp in the dark, and even broke into the state tent—to discover that Ptolemy slept elsewhere! The Ptolemaïc army began to be pinched by the inconveniences of its position; it had the desert behind it, while Antiochus had cultivated land to draw upon. On the sixth day it deployed in battle formation. A picture is drawn for us in a Jewish writing[1] of the queen Arsinoë proceeding along the Egyptian lines, "with lamentation and tears and her hair loosed," to fire the troops in her cause; that she addressed them is stated by Polybius, but it was probably rather in the bold spirit of a Macdeonian princess.[2]

Antiochus accepted the challenge, and the armies closed. The first phase of the battle was an engagement of the cavalry and light-armed troops on both wings, either phalanx waiting its turn in the centre without movement. The issue of this part of the fight was evenly balanced. On the Seleucid right and Ptolemaïc left, where the two kings commanded in person, the lines of Ptolemy were disordered by the recoil of the African elephants from the Indian ones of Antiochus. Taking advantage of this, the household cavalry and light-armed Greek mercenaries of Antiochus broke the Ptolemaïc left. In the excitement of victory the young King pressed the pursuit

[1] 3 Maccabees i. 4.   [2] Polyb. v. 83, 3.

to a dangerous distance from his phalanx. On the other wing the fortunes had been reversed; there the Seleucid horse and the light-armed contingents of Asiatics—Lydians, Arabs and Medes—had been routed by the squadrons of the Thessalian Echecrates and the infantry composed of Greek mercenaries, Thracians and Gauls.

It was now time for the phalanxes to decide the day. Lowering their *sarissas*, the great masses rolled forward and closed. The fruits of the long preparation of the Egyptian court were now reaped. At the first shock the main part of the Seleucid phalanx broke and fled; only the select corps of 10,000, the flower and choice of all the provinces, endured the tussle for a while, and was then forced to follow the flight of the rest. At the moment when Antiochus on the right was already tasting the joy of victory, more experienced eyes observed that the clouds of dust in the centre of the field were moving towards the Seleucid camp. Antiochus wheeled in desperate haste, but it was too late. The whole army was making in full retreat for Raphia. It was a bitter mortification for the young king. He was persuaded "that as far as his part in the battle went, it had been a victory, but that through the base spirit and cowardice of others the enterprise as a whole had foundered."

The defeated army took refuge for the following night at Raphia. But Antiochus was anxious to put a greater distance between himself and Ptolemy,[1] and next day continued his retreat to Gaza. It was from this town that he sent the request which, with the Greeks, was the formal acknowledgment of defeat—the request for permission to bury his dead. Then he set his face homewards, abandoning the conquests of two campaigns. Ptolemy for his part was not disposed to press the pursuit, and rested completely satisfied with the restoration of the *status quo*, the withdrawal of the Seleucid power behind the Lebanon. He simply made a progress through Palestine, where the communities vied with each other in the effusion with which they returned to allegiance. "Perhaps," the historian comments, "it is the usual way of men to adapt their conduct to the occasion; but in an

[1] According to Jerome, *in Dan.* 11, "Per deserta fugiens paene captus est."

especial degree the people of those parts are born time-servers."[1]

Antiochus had other reasons besides the fear of his retreat being harassed to quicken his steps. He did not know what alarming effects the defeat might have on the popular temper. What if Achaeus, to whom the diadem had once been proffered, should now appear in Syria, with all the credit of his successes in Asia Minor, and call upon the populace, Macedonian and native, to desert a prince who was discredited and lamed? Antiochus was concerned, as soon as he reached Antioch, to agree with his southern adversary quickly. He dispatched an embassy, headed by his nephew Antipater. Fortunately, the Ptolemy who now ruled Egypt cared for little except bestiality and *belles lettres*, and Antiochus found him unexpectedly accommodating. He agreed to a year's truce, and Sosibius, the *vizir* of Egypt, was sent to the Syrian court to conclude it. The truce seems to have led almost at once to a definite treaty of peace.[2] Seleucia at any rate Antiochus had won back from Egypt. But in Coele-Syria, after all his efforts, he was obliged to see the old state of things restored.[3]

All his energies were now devoted to the crushing of Achaeus. The winter of 217-216 he spent in renewing his military organization, and preparing on a grand scale for the advance across the Taurus with the coming of spring.

[1] Polyb. v. 86, 9.   [2] Cf. *ibid*. xv. 25, 13.   [3] See Appendix S.

[See an article by Mr. Mahaffy on "The Army of Ptolemy IV at Raphia" in *Hermathena*, No. 24, 1898, pp. 140-152.]

APPENDICES

APPENDIX A (p. 31)

THE question of the native place of Seleucus is compassed with uncertainties. Stephen of Byzantium under Ὠρωπός has πόλις Μακεδονίας, ἐξ ἧς Σέλευκος ὁ Νικάτωρ; and he goes on to say that there was another Oropus in Syria, founded by Seleucus and called after his home. As no Oropus in Macedonia is elsewhere mentioned, the critics readily understand *Europus*, a name found both in Macedonia and in Syria. This is a very nearly certain conjecture; not quite certain perhaps, in view of our imperfect knowledge of the towns both in Macedonia and Syria. It is to be noticed that in Appian also (*Syr.* 57) Oropus is given among the cities founded by Seleucus in Asia with names borrowed from Greece and Macedonia. If in both passages Europus be accepted as a right correction, we are confronted with a fresh dilemma, for in Macedonia we hear of *two* cities called Europus, one on the Axius and one in the district Almopia. Even if we could say which one of these was meant, we should not be much wiser, since the site of both is equally unknown. Lastly, according to Malalas, p. 203, Seleucus was a native of Pella.

At his death in 281 he was, according to Appian (*Syr.* 63), seventy-three; according to Justin xvii. 1, 10, he was seventy-seven. His birth would therefore fall between 358 and 354, and he would be between 31 and 35 at Alexander's death. Alexander was born in 356.

The name of the father of Seleucus was Antiochus. "Antiocho, claro inter Philippi duces viro" (Just. xv. 4, 3) was the account given of him in later times, when his descendants had risen very high in the world, and may possibly be true.

The name Seleucus is one of the *Macedonian*, as distinct from Greek, names found among the Macedonian nobility. It is not, I believe, found among the Greeks till after Alexander. Is it a dialectical variation of the Greek Ζάλευκος, which I suppose means "Very white"?

That Seleucus left Macedonia with Alexander in 333 we gather from Diod. xix. 81, 5; App. *Syr.* 56.

In Arr. *Anab.* v. 13, 4, Seleucus appears as commander of the βασιλικοὶ ὑπασπισταί. We can discern too little of the organization of Alexander's army by the broken lights thrown upon it in our texts to say what this corps was. It was not the *agema*, since the *agema* is expressly distinguished from it in this passage. Nor did it include all the ὑπασπίσται outside the *agema*. J. G. Droysen (i. p. 169, note 3) and H. Droysen (*Alexander des Grossen Heerwesen*, Freiburg, 1885) suppose that the βασιλικοὶ ὑπασπίσται are identical with the βασιλικοὶ παῖδες. To this D. G. Hogarth, *Journal of Philology*, xvii. (1888), p. 18, objects that the παῖδες were "evidently mere boys." But if the παῖδες in the army of Eumenes (Diod. xix. 28, 3) correspond to the βασιλικοὶ παῖδες of the King's army, they fought as regular soldiers.

In the same chapter of Arrian (*Anab.* v. 13) Seleucus is described as τῶν ἑταίρων. We must understand ἑταίρων in the *narrower* sense of the term (Hogarth, *Journal of Philology*, xvii. p. 18).

APPENDIX B (p. 34)

I have discussed in *The Classical Review*, xiv. (1900), p. 396, the character of the command received by Seleucus in 323. From the passages there cited it appears that Seleucus succeeded Perdiccas in the *chiliarchy*, which had been held by Hephaestion at the time of his death, and by Perdiccas in the interval before the death of Alexander. The command was that of the "Companion" cavalry, *i.e.* the cavalry composed of the Macedonian nobility, or at any rate the command of the principal corps in that body. It was thus the proudest position in the army, "summus castrorum tribunatus" (Just. xiii. 4, 17). The chiliarch was closely attached to the Regent as second in command (Diod. xviii. 48, 4).

To the passages cited in the note just mentioned should be added Dexippus, frag. 1, *F.H.G.* iii. p. 667, where the abstract of Photius gives the same statement as his abstract of Arrian—that Perdiccas was given the chiliarchy of Hephaestion by the chiefs in 323. This is hard to reconcile with the statements which represent Perdiccas as having held it *before* the death of Alexander, and Seleucus as having succeeded to it by the partition made in Babylon. Either we must suppose in both abstracts of Photius the confusion which I suggested in my note, or we must suppose that for a little while after the death of Alexander, Perdiccas continued (with the sanction of the chiefs) to hold the chiliarchy till it was transferred to Seleucus.

APPENDIX C (p. 71)

An inscription published by G. Mendel (*Bull. corr. hell.* xxiv. 1900, p. 380), and commented on by Bruno Keil (*Revue de Philol.* xxvi. 1902, p. 257 f.), is of capital importance in this connexion. It consists of two epitaphs on a Bithynian captain who fell in battle. They run as follows :—

I. "A grave of full length encompasses my bones, and yet, O stranger, I quailed not before the brunt of the foemen" (*i.e.* as B. Keil explains it, those who fell in battle usually came home only as "two

APPENDICES

handfuls of white dust, shut in an urn of brass"), "but being one who fought on foot I abode in the forefront of the horse when we strove in the Plain of Corus (Κούρου ... ἐμ πεδίῳ). And before that I died for great glory's sake, I had first smitten a Thracian armed and a man of the Mysians. Wherefore let praise be given to the swift son of Bioëris, Menas the Bithynian, excellent among the captains."

II. "Tears for the tombs of cowards, of them that take their death from sickness ingloriously! I went down with great honour to the grave, fighting beside the stream of Phrygius for my country and my noble parents, after that I had first slain many of the enemy. Wherefore let men speak well of me, the Bithynian Menas, the son of Bioëris, that have passed into the light of praise."

I confess that I should like further evidence that the battle referred to is the battle between Lysimachus and Seleucus, and I have a suspicion the inscription is of later date (the wars between Bithynia and Pergamos). It proves, at any rate, that the Plain of Corus was not in Hellespontine Phrygia, but in Lydia, beside the Phrygius. That was the river beside which the battle of Magnesia was fought, and it would be a striking coincidence if the battle by which Seleucus won Asia Minor and the battle by which his house finally lost it ninety years later were fought upon the same field!

APPENDIX D (p. 98)

The whole question of the partition after Ipsus is extremely obscure. Our authority is Appian, *Syr.* 55, and Appian seems there to write with more than usual carelessness, tumbling together the acquisitions of Seleucus before Ipsus, and his acquisitions after Ipsus without distinction. He says, indeed, that Seleucus acquired "inland Phrygia" (Φρυγίας τῆς ἀνὰ τὸ μεσόγειον, *i.e.* probably, as Niese takes it, Greater Phrygia in distinction from the Hellespontine) by the partition, but if Seleucus at some later time occupied Phrygia (after the rupture with Lysimachus), Appian would be quite likely in his loose way to bring it in here. As Appian is our only authority one would not cavil at his statement were it not that in 287 we find the armies of Lysimachus pursuing Demetrius *as far as the passes of the Taurus* and barricading the passes in his rear (Plutarch, *Dem.* 47), a proceeding not indeed impossible, but improbable if the country north of the Taurus belonged at that time to Seleucus. On the other hand, the story seems to regard Cataonia (*ibid.* 48) as being within his sphere, although the reference is far from conclusive on that point.

APPENDIX E (p. 133)

Who this queen was is a matter of doubt, since she is called the *sister* of Antiochus (Michel, No. 525, l. 22). If she is Stratonice, the expression has to be understood as a court metaphor, and was indeed usual at the Ptolemaïc court (*e.g. C.I.G.* 4694, Berenice, the wife of Ptolemy III, is called ἡ ἀδελφὴ καὶ γυνὴ αὐτοῦ, although not really his sister). The objection to this is that there is no instance at the Seleucid court of a queen not the King's sister being called ἀδελφή. The other hypothesis is that the queen in question was the other wife of Antiochus, the mother of Laodice, and that she *may have been* his sister or half-sister (so Boeckh, *C.I.G.* No. 4694; Dittenberger, ed. i. No. 156). But we now know that Stratonice was still living as queen in 265 or thereabouts (Michel, No. 486), and the Seleucid kings never appear with two legitimate wives simultaneously. It appears to me, therefore, best to understand Stratonice in the queen-sister here. The objection as to no other instance of the use occurring at the Seleucid court is not a strong one in view of the infinitesimal fraction of Seleucid documents which we possess; and the court etiquette, so far as it can be traced, of the Seleucid and Ptolemaïc courts is so closely parallel (Strack, *Rhein. Mus.* lv. 1900, p. 174) that we may believe parallelisms which we can no longer trace existed.

APPENDIX F (p. 135)

How this war between Antiochus and Antigonus synchronizes with other events is impossible to make out with certainty. If we follow the phraseology of Photius' abridgment of Memnon strictly, we have to get in between the death of Seleucus (latter part of 281) and the rupture with Antigonus the following events: (1) the "many wars," by which Antiochus recovers his father's kingdom (the suppression of the Syrian revolt and other simultaneous disturbances); (2) the administration of Patrocles in Asia Minor, with the disaster to Hermogenes; (3) the accession of Nicomedes, his negotiations with Heraclea, terminating in an alliance; (4) the beginning of the war between Antiochus and Nicomedes, with the naval operations near the Bosphorus. All this would seem to require at least two years. Unfortunately, we do not know how far the phraseology of Photius can be pressed, and by the place which the war with Antigonus occupies in Trogus (*Prol.* xxiv.) it would seem to have begun within the first year of Antiochus' reign, being narrated *before* the Illyrian war of Ptolemy Keraunos (end of 281 or beginning of 280). But here again we do not know how far the order of events in the *Prologues* can be pressed. Its place in Trogus seems to me to make at any rate rather against Niese's theory that its *occasion* was the death of Ptolemy Keraunos, and the consequent claims of Antigonus to Macedonia. Also Niese's argument that it was over in 279, because troops of Antigonus and Antiochus fought together at Thermopylae, seems to me questionable.

APPENDIX G (p. 151)

This is nowhere expressly said, but seems suggested by the evidence. We have apparently four of these viceroys of Asia Minor: (1) Patrocles: πέμπει στρατηγὸν Πατροκλέα σὺν ἐκστρατεύματι εἰς τὴν ἐπὶ τάδε τοῦ Ταύρου, Memnon 15 (*F.H.G.* iii. p. 534); (2) Alexander, the King's uncle, who "holds Sardis" (Eus. i. 251), is described (Michel, No. 457) as καταλελειμμένος ὑπὸ τοῦ βασιλέως, and represents the Seleucid power in dealing with a city of Caria (Michel, *ibid.*) and with Smyrna (Michel, No. 19, l. 101); (3) Achaeus, the King's cousin (Polyb. v. 57, 4 and 8; 77, 1), who is not expressly called governor of Lydia, but who has his seat of government in the Lydian capital; (4) Zeuxis, who is called satrap of Lydia, Polyb. xxi. 16, 4, and who is found to exercise authority in Caria (Polyb. xvi. 24, 6; *Sitzungsberichte der Akad. zu Berlin*, 1894, p. 915-917) and in Phrygia (Joseph. xii. § 148 f.).

APPENDIX H (p. 153)

We hear of the *hyparchy* of Eriza (ἡ περὶ Ἔριζαν ὑπαρχία) in the *Hinterland* of Lycia, between the modern Kara-euyuk-bazar and Khorzum, *Bull. corr. hell.* xv. (1891), p. 556. A *hyparch* is spoken of as a subordinate of a satrap by Nicolas of Damascus (frag. 9, *F.H.G.* 111, p. 358), but he is "*hyparch of the whole satrapy,*" ἀλλ' ἐάν γε Βαβυλῶνος σατραπεύσω, σὲ ὕπαρχον καταστήσω τῆς ὅλης σατραπείας.

It has been plausibly suggested (Köhler, *Sitzungsb. der Akad. zu Berlin*, 1884, p. 451; cf. Haussoullier, *Revue de Philol.* xxv. 1901, p. 23) that upon the confusion in popular speech of the terms *satrap* and *hyparchos*, *satrapy* and *hyparchy* rests the statement of Appian (*Syr.* 62) that the Empire of Seleucus Nicator embraced *seventy-four satrapies.* (*Appian does not say that this division was in any sense an innovation of Seleucus*, as every one seems to take it; Appian only mentions the seventy-four satrapies to show how large the Empire was.) We have already seen that the satrap was often called *hyparchos*.

Haussoullier suggests that the four satrapies, into which, according to Strabo xvi. 750, the Syrian Seleucis was divided, were in reality not *satrapies*, but *hyparchies*. He admits, however, that under the later Seleucids at any rate there is evidence for the term satrapy in this instance (*C.I.Lat.* iii. part i. No. 184).

There seems to be a *certain* instance, on the other hand, of the term satrapy being wrongly applied by a historian to a smaller subdivision in Diod. xix. 98, where we read of the *satrapy of Idumaea*. In ch. 95, 2, the expression used is the *eparchy* of Idumaea. Now that *eparchy* is a name for the subdivisions of the satrapy, *i.e.* synonymous with *hyparchy*, we can see by Diod. xix. 44, 4: τοὺς δὲ στρατιώτας ἐπιδιεῖλεν εἰς ἅπασαν τὴν σατραπείαν, καὶ μάλιστα εἰς τὴν ἐπαρχίαν τὴν προσαγορευομένην Ῥάγας.

APPENDIX I (p. 157)

Babelon, p. xxxvii. affirms that Seleucus Nicator minted at Side, and Niese (ii. p. 85, note 4) quotes him with approval, adding this as evidence that Side was subject to Seleucus. It appears to me that a scientific basis in the use of such numismatic evidence is still to seek.

Babelon (p. clxxvi.) makes some useful remarks on the extreme ease with which fancy can play with the monograms on coins and pass off the result as something of scientific value. It may be perhaps questioned whether Babelon has even carried his scepticism far enough. It is extremely suspicious that the result of his own deductions is, by his own admission, to give as the royal minting-places a series of comparatively insignificant towns, whilst the important cities do not appear (p. xxxviii.).

[Mr. Macdonald confirms my distrust of Babelon's results in this matter.]

Appendix J (p. 161)

It is perhaps well to point out that till recently, authorities, misled by the term "ancestors" (Curtius, *Monatsber. der Berlin. Akad.*), 1875, p. 554; Dittenberger, ed. i. No. 166), gave this decree to Antiochus *the Second*. On this supposition was built the theory that Seleucus or Antiochus I enslaved, and Antiochus II liberated, Erythrae, for the wording seemed to imply that the description αὐτόνομος καὶ ἀφορολόγητος was appropriate to the time of Alexander and Antigonus only, not to that of the "ancestors." Curtius, who advanced this theory, omitted to observe that the word συνδιατηρήσομεν implies that the autonomy was not being restored, but *maintained uninterrupted*. But it is true that the language of Antiochus admits that under his house the city had been compelled to pay; the autonomy had been respected, but the *immunity* he now restores.

Appendix K (p. 188)

πρότερόν τε καθ' ὃν καιρὸν ὁ βασιλεὺς Σέλευκος ὑπερέβαλεν εἰς τὴν Σελευκίδα, Smyrnaean Inscription, l. 1, 2. Haussoullier (*Revue de Philol.* xxv. 1901, p. 129 f.) challenges the ordinary interpretation of this inscription, which makes *two* expeditions of Seleucus across the Taurus. According to him the attack of Magnesia on Smyrna comes at the very beginning of the reign. During the progress of Ptolemy Euergetes, Seleucus remains in Asia Minor. Then, after showing his gratitude to Smyrna and bringing Magnesia to terms, he crosses (in 244) the Taurus for the first time. It is true that we cannot certainly deduce from the phrases used two expeditions across the Taurus; on the other hand, the inscription seems to me to state clearly (l. 1, 2) that the troubles of Smyrna from hostile attack *began* with the King's departure. At the time the decree is inscribed the King is absent in Syria (l. 14). If, therefore, there is only one passage of the Taurus in question, he must have been away all the time; he must have bestowed his favours on Smyrna from a distance, and his forces must have quelled Magnesia in his absence. It seems to me more likely that the old interpretation which saw two expeditions is the true one. There must have been a great deal of marching to and fro in those troubled days. And the two expeditions, although not proved absolutely by the phraseology, seem to make it more natural.

APPENDIX L (p. 193)

Adiutorem et suppetias Alexandria (leg. Alexandrum) enim habebat, qui Sardianorum urbem tenebat, Eus. i. p. 251. It has been pointed out that the satrap of Lydia, whose capital, of course, was Sardis, seems to have been viceroy, in the King's absence, of the whole trans-Tauric country (p. 151). If Alexander was the full brother of Laodice, he was a son of Antiochus I. Achaeus, who afterwards sits as viceroy in Sardis, is a cousin of the King (Antiochus III). This Alexander is probably the person in the Smyrnaean Inscription, l. 101, who writes to Smyrna or Magnesia about the grants of land to the military colonists. I believe him to be also the Alexander of the Bargylian Inscription (Michel, No. 457). But, if so, this inscription is probably later than the time of Antiochus I, since it seems unnatural to suppose two terms of office for Alexander, twenty years apart. There is nothing, so far as I can discover, to date the inscription to the reign of Antiochus I. The mention of the games celebrated by the people in honour of "King Antiochus Soter" make rather against, than for, the supposition that he is the King of the rest of the inscription. For the King has been spoken of from the beginning of the inscription (as we now have it) anonymously, and the sudden introduction of a name with full titles appears rather to indicate a new person. The argument from the capture of the Carian coast by Ptolemy I under Antiochus I seems weak when we remember that Antiochus II regained much that had been lost, and that anyway individual cities probably changed hands over and over again in the vicissitudes of the long struggle.

APPENDIX M (p. 194)

It is nowhere said whether this marriage preceded or followed the battle of Ancyra. Reinach and Niese (ii. p. 158) assume that it was subsequent, and that by it Seleucus bought over Mithridates from the party of Antiochus. It seems to me more likely that it belongs to the earlier part of the reign of Seleucus, since (1) it is mentioned by Eusebius in his account of the reign of Antiochus II, although this by itself would not prove much; (2) the marriage of Stratonice, the other sister, with Ariarathes, seems to belong to the reign of Antiochus II (Reinach, *Trois royaumes*, p. 17); and presuming the sisters to be about of an age, the marriage of one is not likely to have been separated by a great interval from that of the other; and (3) Laodice, the daughter of Mithridates by his Seleucid queen, as her name attests, is old enough before 229-228, the date of Antiochus' final defeat, to be delivered over to him by her father, presumably in order to become his wife (see p. 201). If the marriage of Mithridates and the Seleucid princess took place after the battle of Ancyra, this Laodice must have been of a very tender age indeed when she was given up to Antiochus, and one would have also to suppose gratuitously a fresh change of side on the part of Mithridates.

APPENDIX N (p. 201)

I follow Niese (ii. p. 154) provisionally in putting the death of Laodice during the war between Seleucus and Antiochus, which succeeded the truce between Seleucus and Ptolemy, but with misgivings. The text of Appian plainly implies that Laodice was killed by Ptolemy at the beginning of his invasion of Seleucid Asia, *i.e.* soon after 246. But Laodice was certainly alive in Ephesus when the Ptolemaïc officer wrote his dispatch (see p. 185), and, according to Plutarch, she supported Antiochus in his revolt against Seleucus. If, therefore, we believe the assumption of an independent authority by Antiochus to *follow* the peace with Egypt, and this is the more modern view as against the older view of Niebuhr and Droysen, we must in some way correct the statement of Appian. We may do this by supposing either (1) that Laodice really was killed by the Ptolemaïc forces *at some later date*, or (2) that Appian carelessly exaggerates the vengeance taken by Ptolemy for Berenice's murder, which really did consist in dealing a great blow to Laodice's power, so as to include the actual *killing* of Laodice. The latter alternative seems to me as possible as the former. In fact it is not easy to understand how the Ptolemaïc forces should have got possession of Laodice when once she had withdrawn into the interior from Ephesus. If we maintain Appian's statement as it stands as well as Plutarch's, we must revert to the view that the revolt of Antiochus, *i.e.* the setting up a separate government by Laodice in the name of the boy Antiochus, occurred in the early stages of the war between Seleucus and Ptolemy.

APPENDIX O (p. 233)

Niese (ii. p. 125) cites a coin (Babelon, *Catal.* No. 17) to prove that Seleucus struck money at Sidon. But the evidence does not seem very certain. All that Babelon affirms is that the coin is "certainly of Syrian make." The ground for supposing that it was struck at Sidon is that it bears a monogram which appears to be the same as a monogram found on some coins of Alexander attributed by Müller to Sidon, Babelon, *Rois de Syrie*, p. xxxvii.

I may remark here that there is, as far as I can see, no ground to suppose that the authority of the house of Seleucus reached Phœnicia south of the Eleutherus or Syria south of Lebanon before the time of Antiochus III. Cœle-Syria was, no doubt, *claimed* by Seleucus after Ipsus, but when he found Ptolemy in possession there, he allowed the matter to drop. The statement of Sulpicius Severus (*Hist. Sac.* ii. 17, 4) that the Jews paid tribute to Seleucus is worthless. Babelon assigns a number of the coins of the earlier Seleucids to Cœle-Syrian mints, but Mr. Macdonald tells me that he considers the grounds for doing so quite inadequate, and that there is *no entirely reliable numismatic evidence* to show an authority of the earlier Seleucids in the region in question.

Appendix P (p. 251)

Elam, as we saw, was the old Semitic name for the country which, under Alexander and his successors, was called Susiana. The Greek names Elymaïs, Elymaei, are generally thought to reproduce the Semitic Elam. But their use offers difficulties. In the first place the Elymaei are *distinguished from* the Susians, and when we go on to ask where the Elymaei are located we meet with strange contradictions. Polybius, who is the first to mention them, places them *in the north of Media* (v. 44, 9). Strabo makes the Elymaei one of the fighting peoples of the hills of Lûristân who, together with the Cossaei, raid the peoples of the plain, the Babylonians and Susians (xi. 522, 524; xv. 732; xvi. 739, 744). Gabiene, Massabatice, and Corbiane are ἐπαρχίαι of Elymaïs. In Pliny, Elymaïs lies on the coast *south of Susiana*, from which it is divided by the river Eulaeus. Massabatice (called Messabatene) is north of Susiana (vi. § 134 f.) This position of Elymaïs comes close to Ptol. vi. 3, 3, where the Elymaei are described as holding τῆς Σουσιανῆς τὰ ἐπὶ θαλάσσῃ. But in vi. 2, 6, we have quite another statement which brings us back to that of Polybius; Elymaïs is there in the north of Media. Of course it is easy to frame hypotheses to account for this confusion. There may have been a hill people whose name, by an accident, sounded like that of the Elamites. Or the Elymaei and the Susians may have been really parts of the same people—the old Semitic name being sometimes applied to that branch which held its independence among the hills, sometimes to the dwellers by the coast. The Elymaei of northern Media again may be different from the Elymaei of the hills above Babylonia, or an offshoot of the same stock. In the East of to-day we know that Kurds and Turcomans are found in scattered communities in widely diverse regions.

Appendix Q (p. 271)

There seem to have been more than one city called Alexandria or Alexandropolis in the region of Drangiana and Arachosia. The determination of their sites, and their identification with modern cities, is a very perplexed question. Droysen discusses it at large (ii. p. 674 f.). His provisional conclusion identifies Alexandria of the Arachosians with Ghazni, Alexandropolis in Sacastene with Kal'at-i-Ghilzai, and Alexandria in Sacastene with Kandahar. But this is not generally accepted; the common opinion, endorsed by Kaerst in his recent book (*Gesch. des hellenist. Zeitalt.* 1901), identifies Alexandria of the Arachosians with Kandahar. Discussion seems unsatisfactory when our data are so uncertain, and any result must be merely provisional till the country has been further explored.

APPENDIX R (p. 273)

Droysen (ii. p. 686 f.) infers three different cities; Kaerst (*Gesch. d. hellenist. Zeitalt.* i. p. 371) thinks one more probable. Tomaschek (*Berich. d. Akad. d. Wissensch. zu Wien.* 1890, vol. cxxi. Abh. viii. p. 19) makes Alexandria ἐν Ὤροις coincide with the modern Sônmiâni at the mouth of the Puraly. This identification gives rise to further difficulties, since (1) if the Arbis is the Puraly, as is commonly supposed, the site will not square with the accounts of Alexander's march, and (2) if the Arbis is not the Puraly, the town founded by Nearchus must be different from Alexandria. The map of Kiepert places Rambacia 50 miles inland and nearly 100 from the mouth of the Arbis.

APPENDIX S (p. 320)

It would seem from the narrative of Polybius that Antiochus abandoned Cœle-Syria completely. And it is almost unthinkable that the victorious Ptolemy, however supine, should have agreed to less. It must, however, be admitted that there are two pieces of evidence which leave us puzzled: (1) Achaeus in 215 hopes to raise *Phœnicia and Cœle-Syria* on his behalf (Polyb. viii. 19, 11); (2) there exists a coin of Ptolemaïs with the legend Ἀντιοχέων τῶν ἐν Πτολεμαΐδι and the date, year 99, *i.e.* 214-213 B.C., Babelon, *Rois de Syrie*, lxxxvi., *Catal.* No. 456. Babelon says: "La lecture de la date est certaine."

[Mr. G. F. Hill now points out to me that Rouvier, in the *Revue Biblique* of July 1899, contests Babelon's dating of this coin, and puts it as late as *the reign of the Emperor Claudius.*]

CPSIA information can be obtained at www.ICGtesting.com
Printed in the USA
BVOW09s1348270714

360508BV00017B/137/P